Apologies to the lady who passed by me on the street, those people at the café, the people at the store where I buy my lottery tickets, and both the employee and the customer at the bank. Thank you very much for your help.

Kazunari Kakei

Back during the summer when I was drawing these stories, I collapsed on the roadside. The doctor told me I fainted from fatigue. I basically felt like the stereotypical manga creator that you read about in manga who doesn't get out enough.

NORA: The Last Chronicle of Devildom is Kazunari Kakei's first manga series. It debuted in the April 2004 issue of *Monthly Shonen Jump* and eventually spawned a second series, *SUREBREC: NORA the 2nd*, which premiered in *Monthly Shonen Jump*'s March 2007 issue.

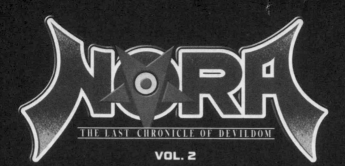

NORA
THE LAST CHRONICLE OF DEVILDOM

VOL. 2

STORY AND ART BY
KAZUNARI KAKEI

English Adaptation/Park Cooper and Barb Lien-Cooper
Translation/Nori Minami
Touch-up Art & Lettering/Wayne Truman
Design/Sam Elzway
Editor/Carol Fox

Editor in Chief, Books/Alvin Lu
Editor in Chief, Magazines/Marc Weidenbaum
VP, Publishing Licensing/Rika Inouye
VP, Sales & Product Marketing/Gonzalo Ferreyra
VP, Creative/Linda Espinosa
Publisher/Hyoe Narita

Printed in the U.S.A.

Published by VIZ Media, LLC
P.O. Box 77010
San Francisco, CA 94107

10 9 8 7 6 5 4 3 2 1
First printing, December 2008

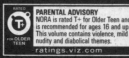

SHONEN JUMP ADVANCED
Manga Edition

NORA
THE LAST CHRONICLE OF DEVILDOM

Volume 2: The Rage Ignites

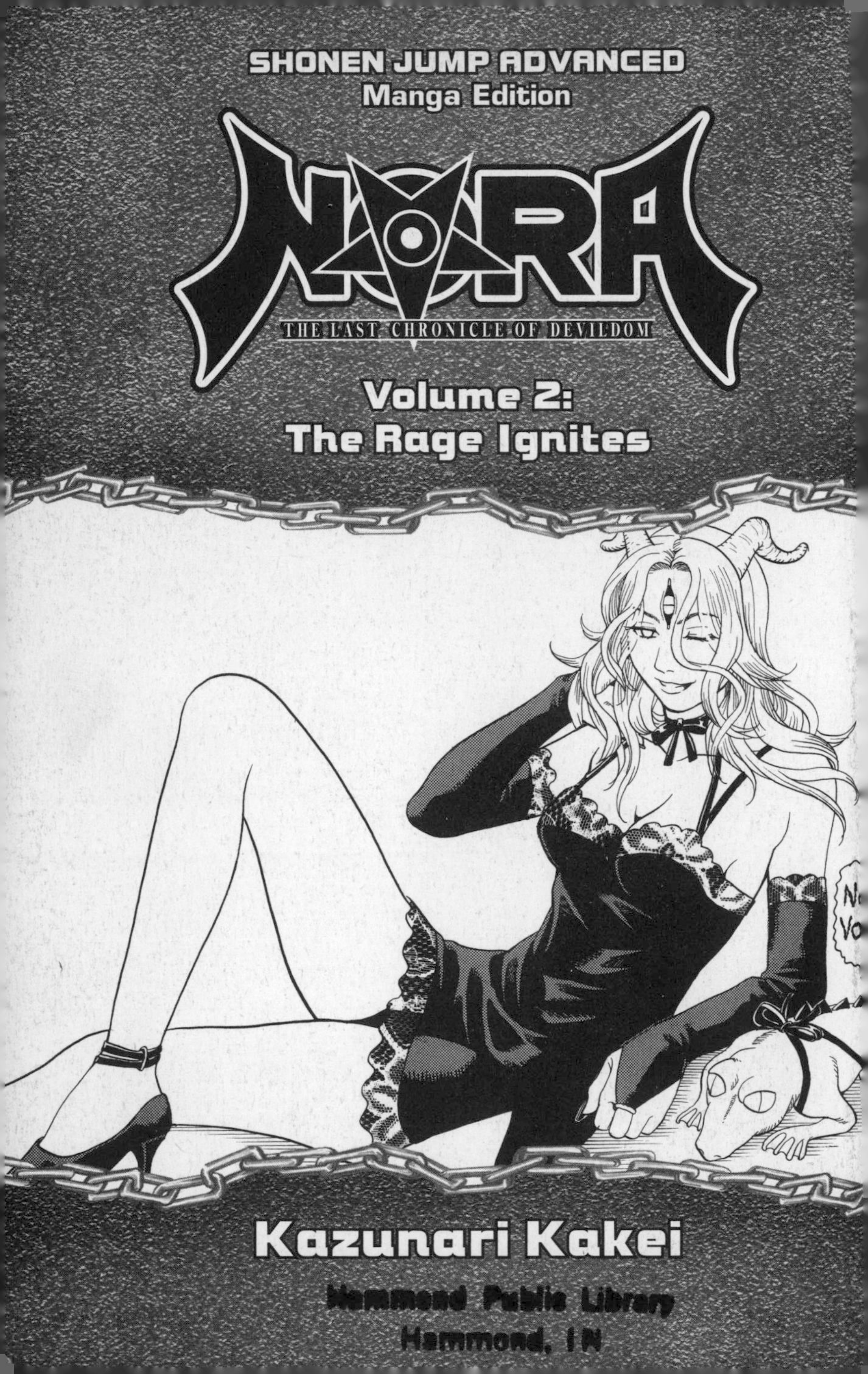

Kazunari Kakei

CHARACTERS

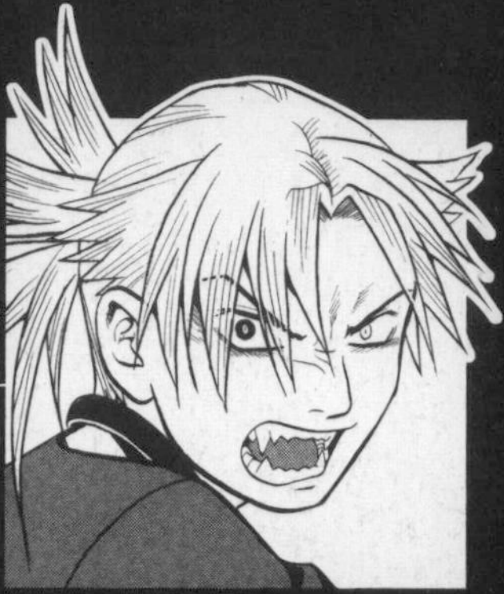

NORA

A TROUBLEMAKING, MANGY DEVIL DOG FROM THE DEMON WORLD. NORA IS AS SHORT-TEMPERED AS HE IS SIMPLE-MINDED. ALSO KNOWN AS THE "VICIOUS DOG OF DISASTER," HE IS THE LEGENDARY HOUND OF HECK HIMSELF: CERBERUS. WHILE NOT THE SMARTEST DOG IN THE POUND, HIS RAW POWER IS SAID TO SURPASS EVEN THAT OF THE DARK LIEGE.

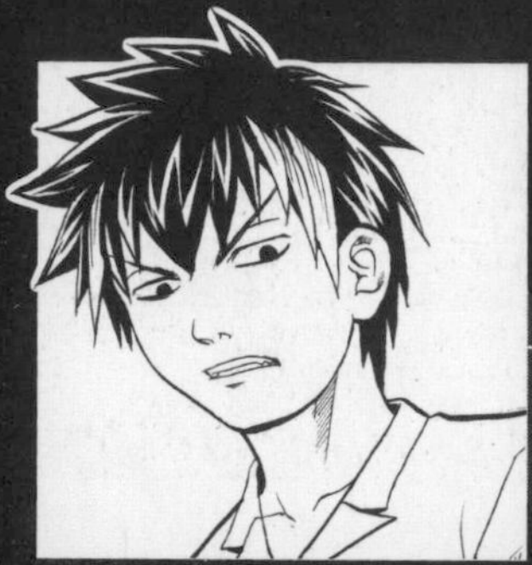

KAZUMA

KAZUMA MAGARI IS SMART, GOOD AT SPORTS, AND THE PRESIDENT OF HIS SCHOOL'S STUDENT COUNCIL. HE IS ALSO THE MASTER OF NORA, THE STRAY DOG OF HELL. ALTHOUGH CALM AND COMPOSED ON THE OUTSIDE, KAZUMA IS A BIT OF A FIEND WHEN ANGERED. AS A RESULT, HIS FELLOW STUDENTS FEAR HIM. IN SHORT, HE'S A SELF-RIGHTEOUS HUMAN WHO IS, IN HIS OWN WAY, MORE DEVILISH THAN AN ACTUAL DEMON.

TENRYO ACADEMY MIDDLE SCHOOL STUDENT COUNCIL

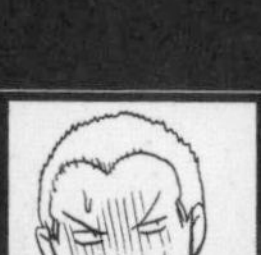

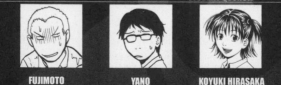

FUJIMOTO

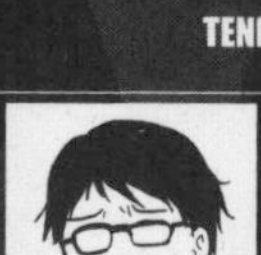

YANO

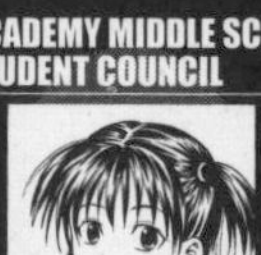

KOYUKI HIRASAKA

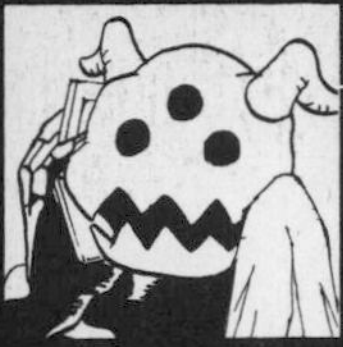

THE DARK LIEGE

SHE'S THE DEMON WORLD'S BIG BOSS, AS WELL AS THE ONE RESPONSIBLE FOR SENDING NORA OFF TO THE HUMAN WORLD AFTER NOT KNOWING WHAT ELSE TO DO WITH THIS DISOBEDIENT DEVIL PUP. WHEN WEARING HER GLAMOUR (NOT SHOWN), SHE'S A REAL HOTTIE. ALTHOUGH BUSY BEING EVIL, THE DARK LIEGE NEVER NEGLECTS HER DAILY BEAUTY REGIMEN!

KNELL

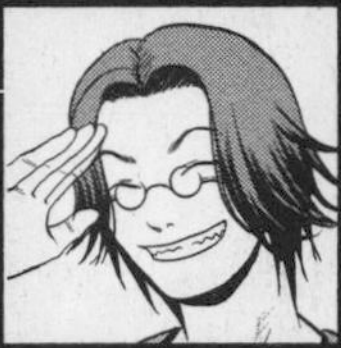

A FLIRTY YOUNG MAN WHO LOVES THE LADIES. WHEN NOT BUSY BEING A PERV, HE'S ALSO ADEPT AT DEFLECTING DEMON ATTACKS. IGUNISU MAGIA (FIRE-TYPE MAGIC TO ALL YOU LAYPEOPLE) HAS NO EFFECT ON HIM, FOR INSTANCE. HE'S ALSO A MEMBER OF THE RESISTANCE, WHICH OPPOSES THE DARK LIEGE'S RULE.

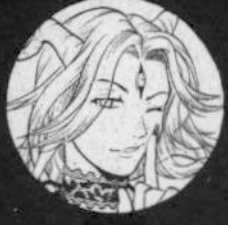

LISTEN TO TEACHER! THE DARK LIEGE EXPLAINS IT ALL ♥

HELLO DARLINGS! DARK LIEGE HERE! MISS ME? ♥

GOLLY, MY NORA'S BEEN A BAD PUPPY. HERE I AM WITH A WHOLE RESISTANCE TO DEAL WITH, NOT TO MENTION THESE PESKY OUTLAW DEMONS, AND NORA ACTUALLY HAD THE NERVE TO SASS ME! FINALLY, I DECIDED ENOUGH WAS TOO MUCH!

BECAUSE I'M AS CLEVER AS I AM BUSTY, I SENT MY STRAY DOG TO THE HUMAN WORLD. HE WON'T BE LONELY—I GAVE HIM A MASTER, AFTER ALL. I TOLD NORA IT WAS NOW HIS JOB TO TAKE CARE OF THE OUTLAW DEMONS THAT HAD TRESPASSED INTO THE HUMAN WORLD. IT WAS LIKE KILLING TWO BIRDS WITH ONE STONE. AREN'T I A GENIUS? ♥

I CHOSE THAT DEVIOUS SCHOOLBOY KAZUMA MAGARI TO BE IN CHARGE OF NORA'S "OBEDIENCE TRAINING!" I'M SO SMART!

ACTUALLY, I FORCED NORA INTO A MASTER AND SERVANT CONTRACT WITH KAZUMA. NORA IS NOW A "FAMILIAR SPIRIT" TO HIM. IN OTHER WORDS, MY PUPPY CAN NO LONGER USE MAGIC OR RELEASE HIS SEAL SPELL SO HE CAN BECOME A DEMON DOG AGAIN WITHOUT HIS NEW MASTER'S APPROVAL. NEITHER OF THEM WAS ENTHUSIATIC ABOUT THIS DEAL AT FIRST, BUT IT SEEMS LIKE THEY'RE JOINING FORCES AGAINST THE OUTLAW DEMONS ANYWAY. THEY'RE SO DEPENDABLE! ♥

BUT THEN, WHILE I WAS OUT GETTING A BEAUTY TREATMENT, THEY RAN ACROSS KNELL, A DEMON FROM THE RESISTANCE. MOREOVER, BECAUSE HE GAVE OUT TOO MANY "APPROVALS," KAZUMA GOT HIMSELF HURT, THE SILLY BILLY!

BOYS CAN BE SO MUCH TROUBLE! I'M SO WORRIED THAT I MAY JUST HAVE TO CANCEL MY NEXT BEAUTY TREATMENT. TRAGIQUE!

NORA

THE LAST CHRONICLE OF DEVILDOM

CONTENTS

Volume 2:
The Rage Ignites

7.99

9

Teen

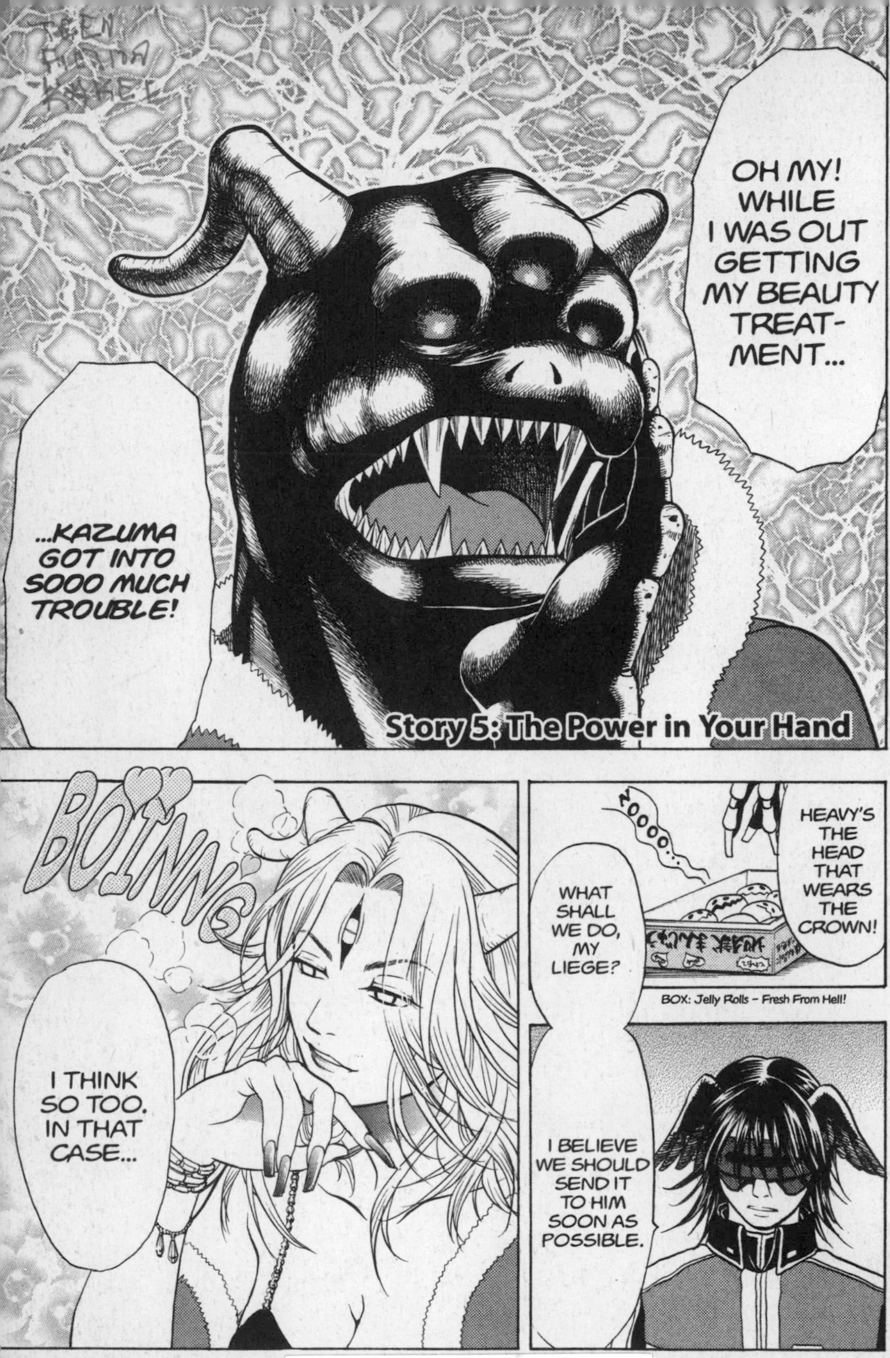
OH MY! WHILE I WAS OUT GETTING MY BEAUTY TREAT-MENT...
...KAZUMA GOT INTO SOOO MUCH TROUBLE!
Story 5: The Power in Your Hand
HEAVY'S THE HEAD THAT WEARS THE CROWN!
ZOOOO...
WHAT SHALL WE DO, MY LIEGE?
BOX: Jelly Rolls – Fresh From Hell!
I BELIEVE WE SHOULD SEND IT TO HIM SOON AS POSSIBLE.
BOINNG
I THINK SO TOO. IN THAT CASE...

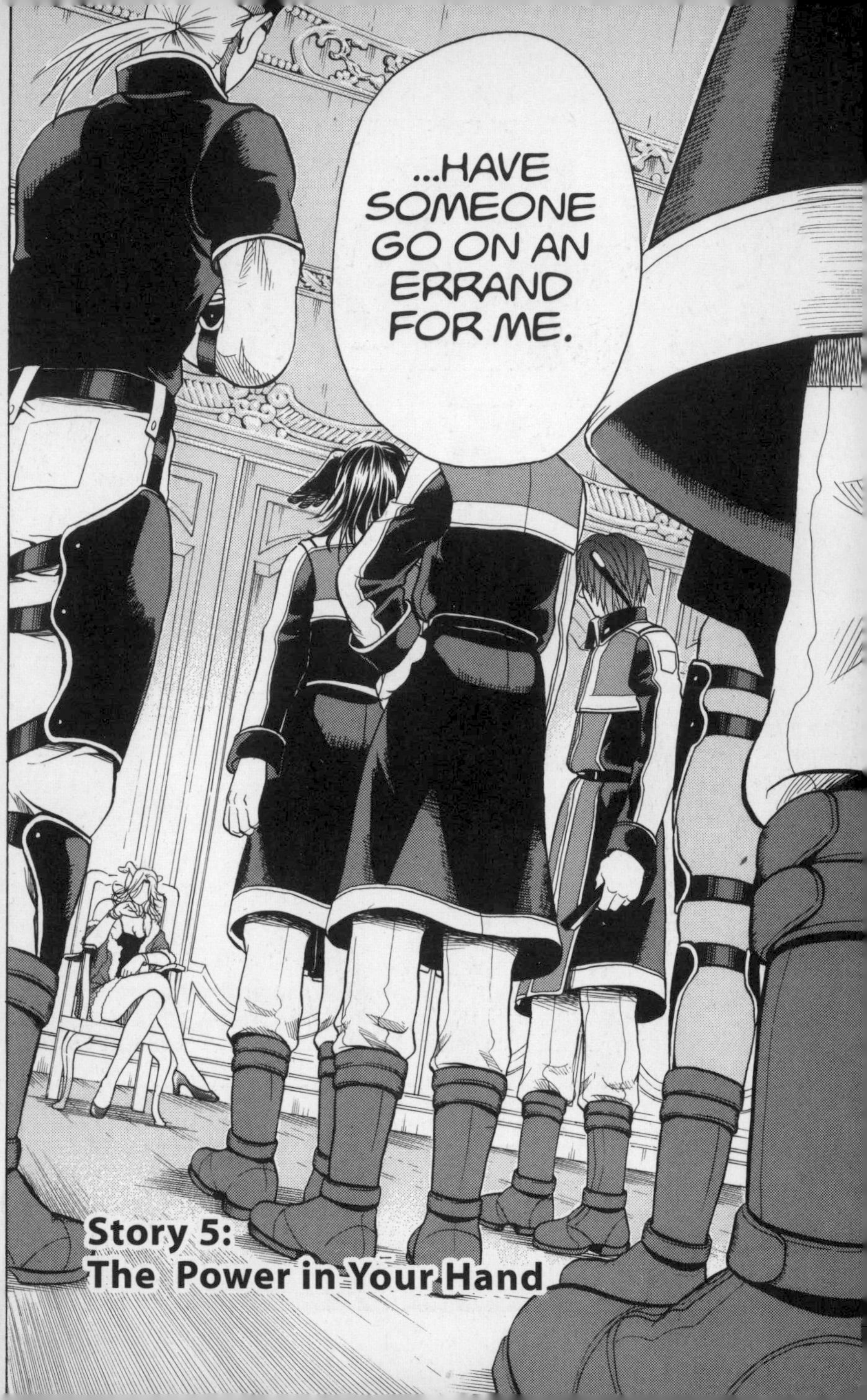
...HAVE SOMEONE GO ON AN ERRAND FOR ME.

Story 5: The Power in Your Hand

READ THIS WAY

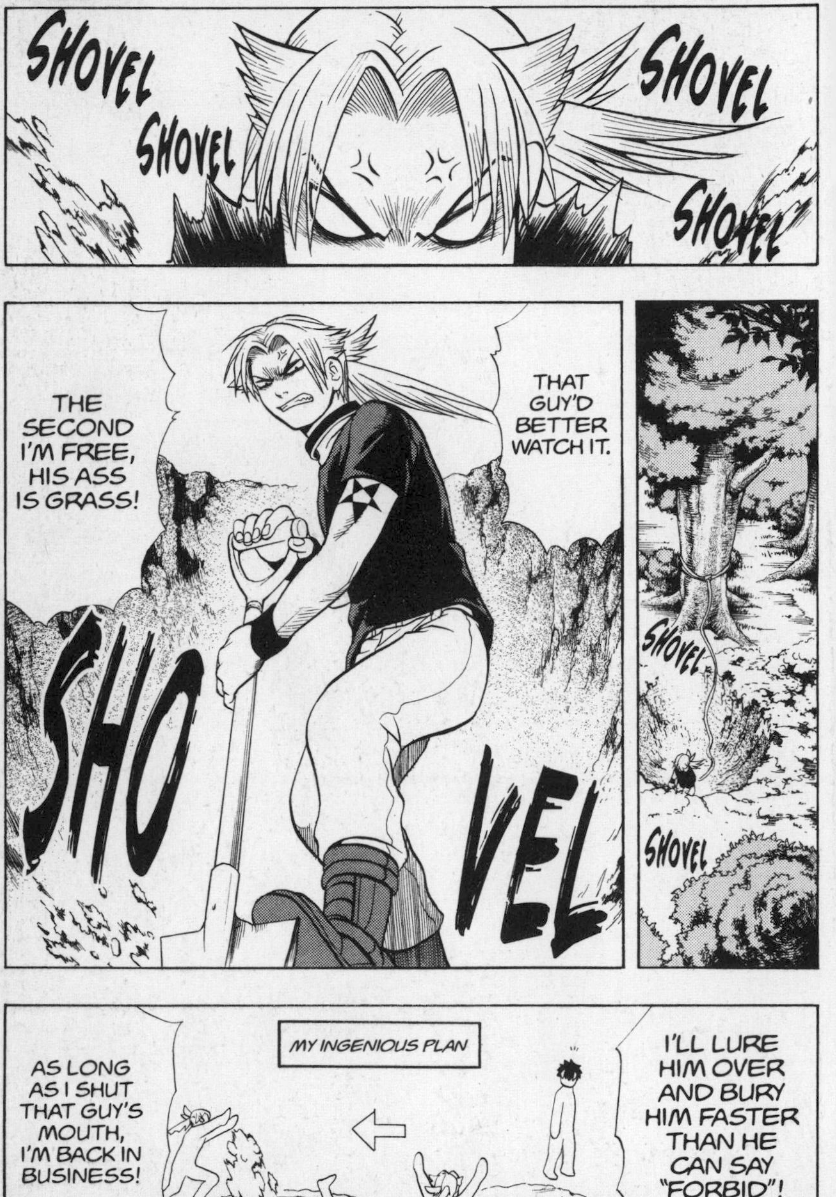
SHOVEL
SHOVEL
SHOVEL
SHOVEL
SHOVEL
SHOVEL
THAT GUY'D BETTER WATCH IT.
THE SECOND I'M FREE, HIS ASS IS GRASS!
SHOVEL
MY INGENIOUS PLAN
I'LL LURE HIM OVER AND BURY HIM FASTER THAN HE CAN SAY "FORBID"!
AS LONG AS I SHUT THAT GUY'S MOUTH, I'M BACK IN BUSINESS!

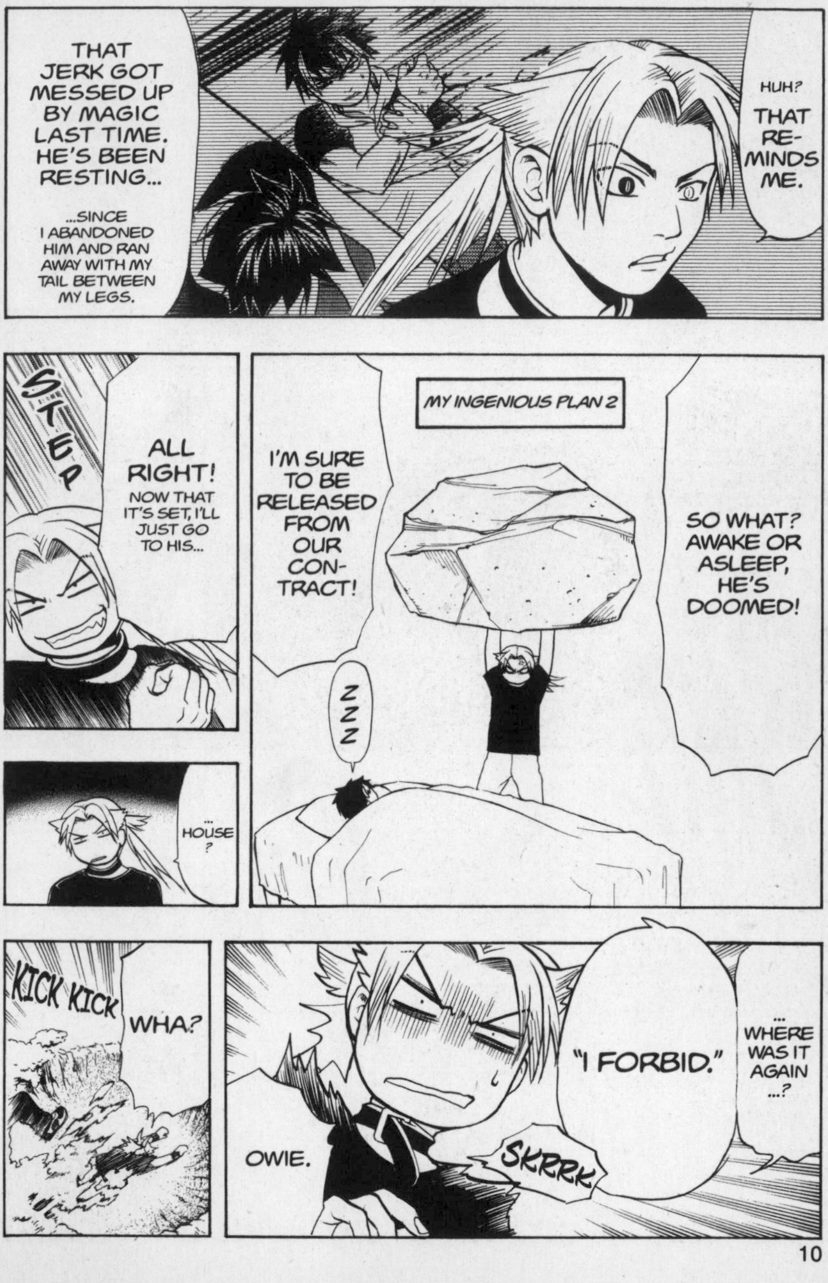
HUH?
THAT RE-MINDS ME.
THAT JERK GOT MESSED UP BY MAGIC LAST TIME. HE'S BEEN RESTING...
...SINCE I ABANDONED HIM AND RAN AWAY WITH MY TAIL BETWEEN MY LEGS.
MY INGENIOUS PLAN 2
SO WHAT? AWAKE OR ASLEEP, HE'S DOOMED!
I'M SURE TO BE RELEASED FROM OUR CON-TRACT!
ZZZ
STEP
ALL RIGHT!
NOW THAT IT'S SET, I'LL JUST GO TO HIS...
...HOUSE?
...WHERE WAS IT AGAIN...?
"I FORBID."
SKRRK
OWIE.
KICK KICK
WHA?

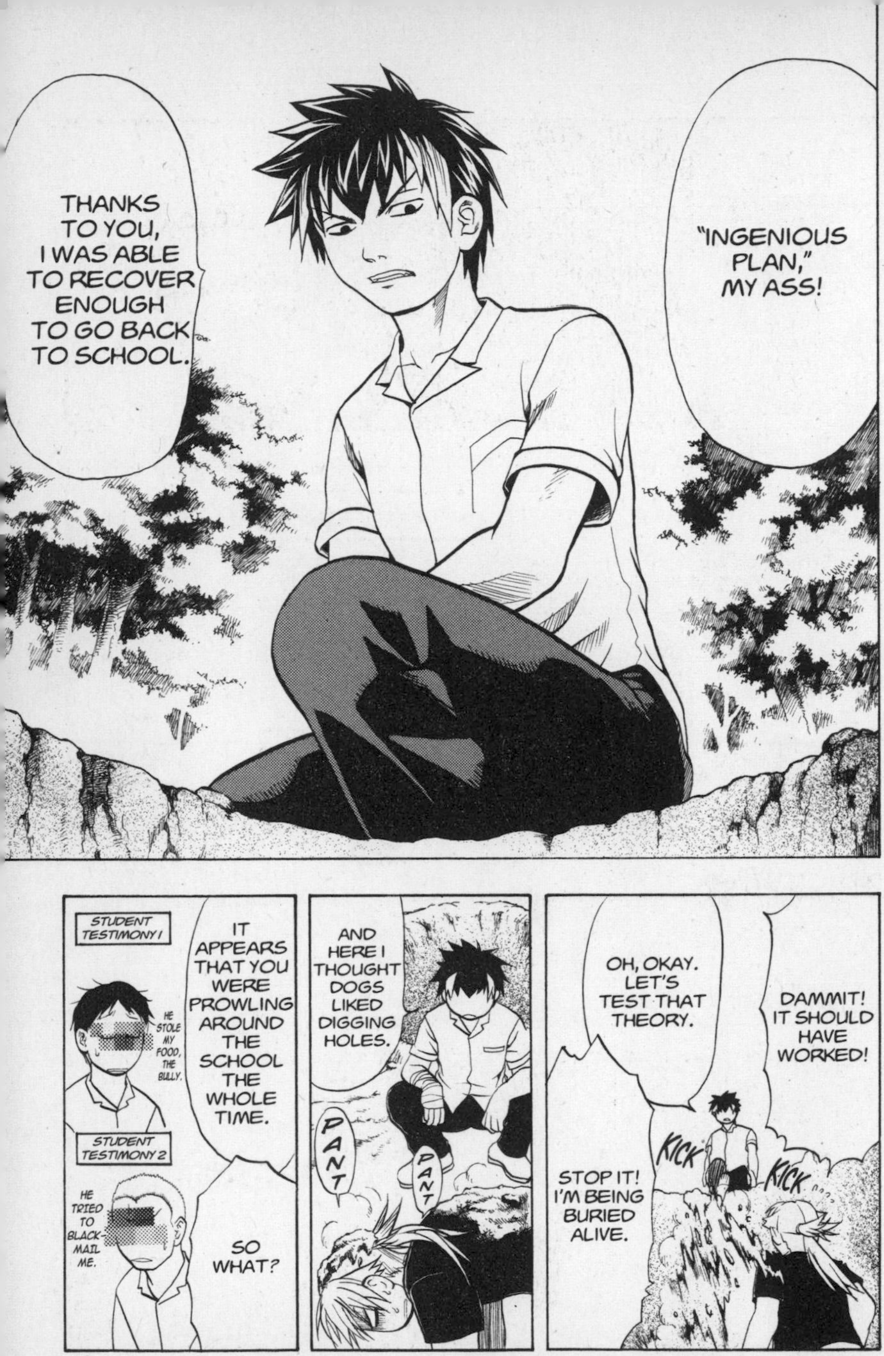
"INGENIOUS PLAN," MY ASS!
THANKS TO YOU, I WAS ABLE TO RECOVER ENOUGH TO GO BACK TO SCHOOL.
DAMMIT! IT SHOULD HAVE WORKED!
OH, OKAY. LET'S TEST THAT THEORY.
KICK
KICK
STOP IT! I'M BEING BURIED ALIVE.
AND HERE I THOUGHT DOGS LIKED DIGGING HOLES.
PANT
PANT
IT APPEARS THAT YOU WERE PROWLING AROUND THE SCHOOL THE WHOLE TIME.
STUDENT TESTIMONY 1
HE STOLE MY FOOD, THE BULLY.
STUDENT TESTIMONY 2
HE TRIED TO BLACK-MAIL ME.
SO WHAT?

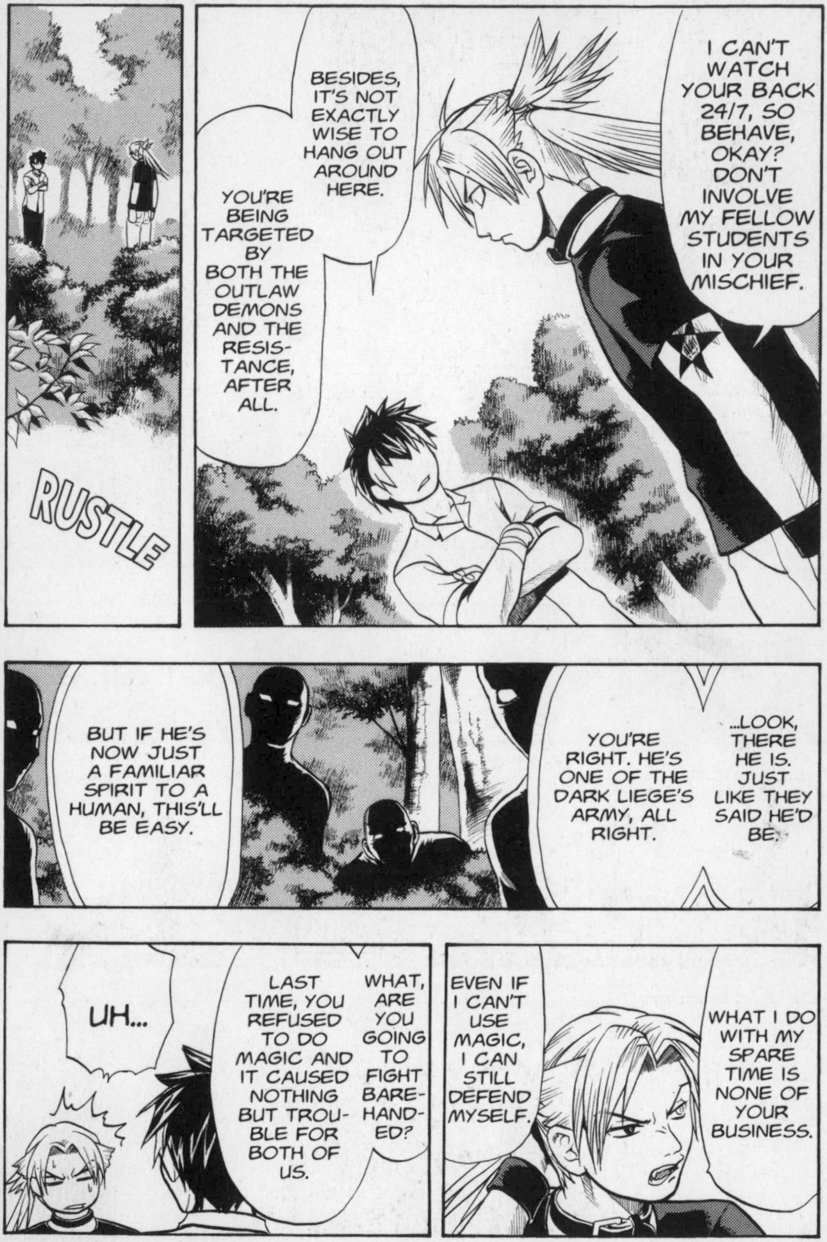
I CAN'T WATCH YOUR BACK 24/7, SO BEHAVE, OKAY? DON'T INVOLVE MY FELLOW STUDENTS IN YOUR MISCHIEF.
BESIDES, IT'S NOT EXACTLY WISE TO HANG OUT AROUND HERE.
YOU'RE BEING TARGETED BY BOTH THE OUTLAW DEMONS AND THE RESIS-TANCE, AFTER ALL.
RUSTLE
...LOOK, THERE HE IS. JUST LIKE THEY SAID HE'D BE.
YOU'RE RIGHT. HE'S ONE OF THE DARK LIEGE'S ARMY, ALL RIGHT.
BUT IF HE'S NOW JUST A FAMILIAR SPIRIT TO A HUMAN, THIS'LL BE EASY.
WHAT I DO WITH MY SPARE TIME IS NONE OF YOUR BUSINESS.
EVEN IF I CAN'T USE MAGIC, I CAN STILL DEFEND MYSELF.
WHAT, ARE YOU GOING TO FIGHT BARE-HAND-ED?
LAST TIME, YOU REFUSED TO DO MAGIC AND IT CAUSED NOTHING BUT TROU-BLE FOR BOTH OF US.
UH...

READ THIS WAY

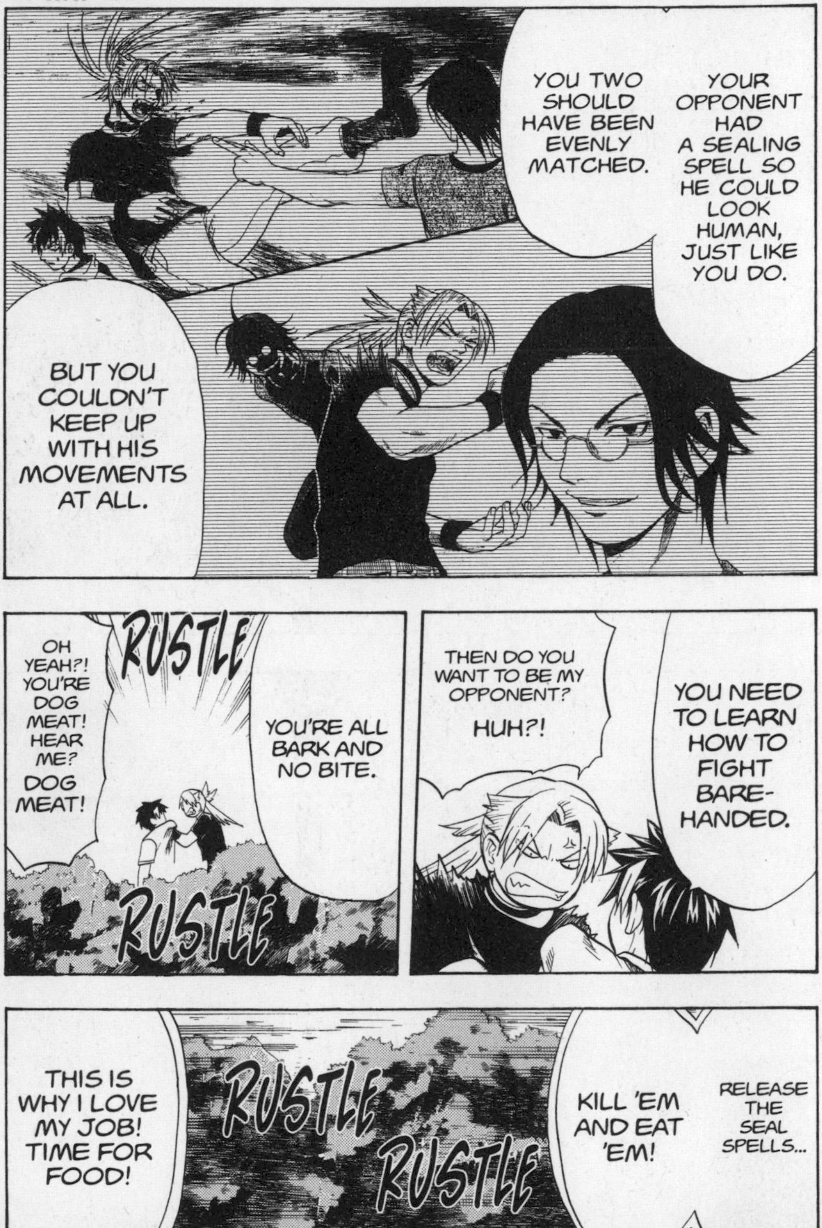
YOUR OPPONENT HAD A SEALING SPELL SO HE COULD LOOK HUMAN, JUST LIKE YOU DO.
YOU TWO SHOULD HAVE BEEN EVENLY MATCHED.
BUT YOU COULDN'T KEEP UP WITH HIS MOVEMENTS AT ALL.
YOU NEED TO LEARN HOW TO FIGHT BARE-HANDED.
THEN DO YOU WANT TO BE MY OPPONENT?
HUH?!
YOU'RE ALL BARK AND NO BITE.
RUSTLE
OH YEAH?! YOU'RE DOG MEAT! HEAR ME? DOG MEAT!
RUSTLE
RELEASE THE SEAL SPELLS...
KILL 'EM AND EAT 'EM!
RUSTLE
RUSTLE
THIS IS WHY I LOVE MY JOB! TIME FOR FOOD!

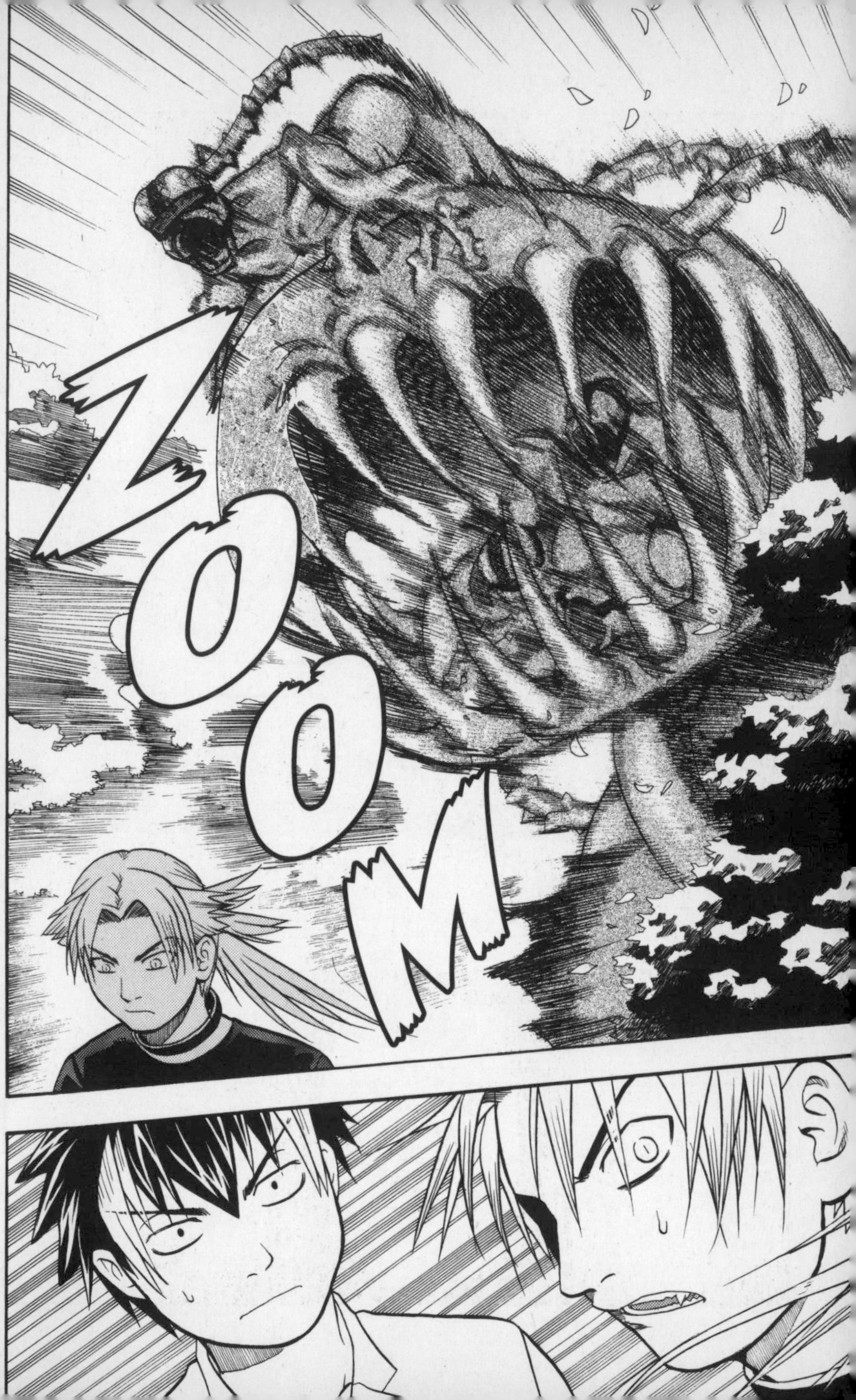
ZOOM

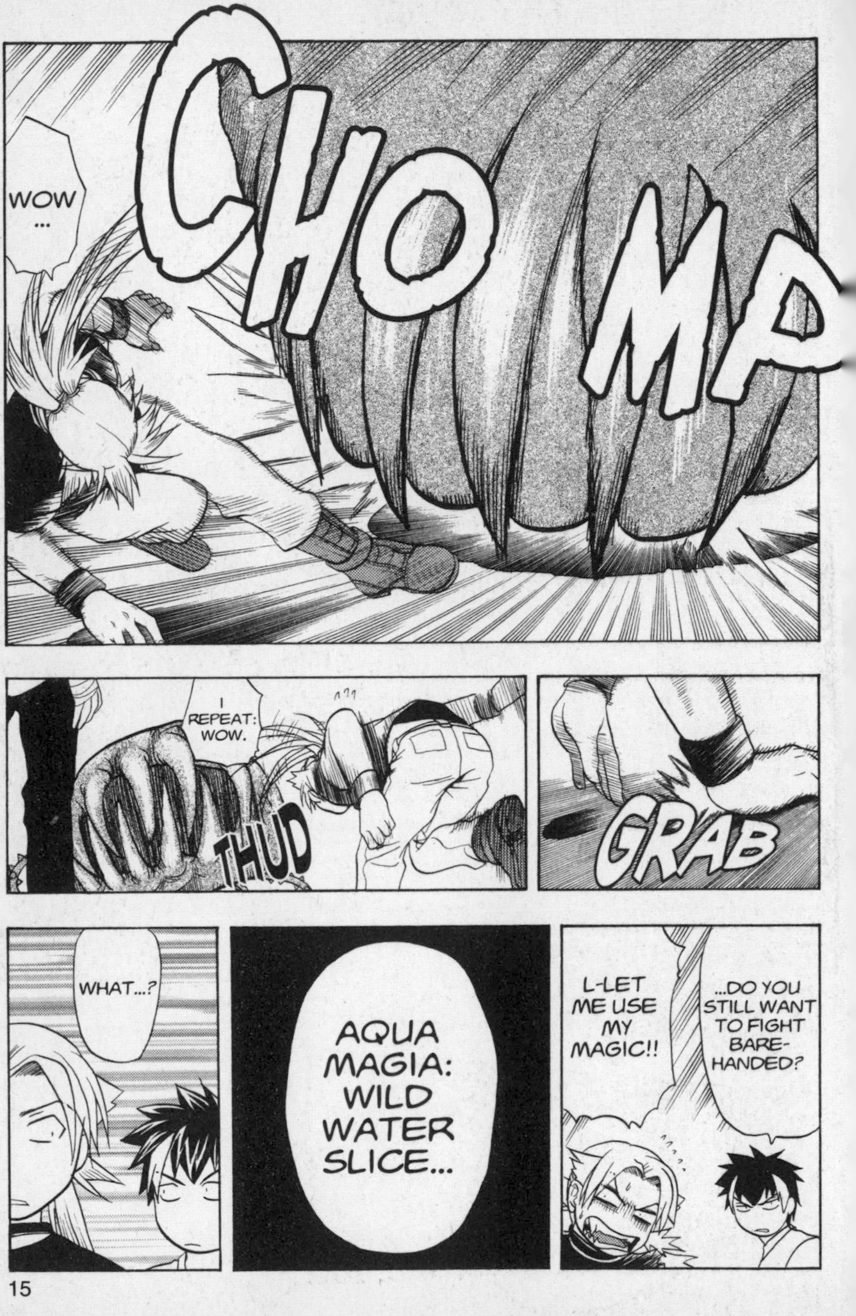
CHOMP
WOW ...
GRAB
I REPEAT: WOW.
THUD
...DO YOU STILL WANT TO FIGHT BARE-HANDED?
L-LET ME USE MY MAGIC!!
AQUA MAGIA: WILD WATER SLICE...
WHAT...?

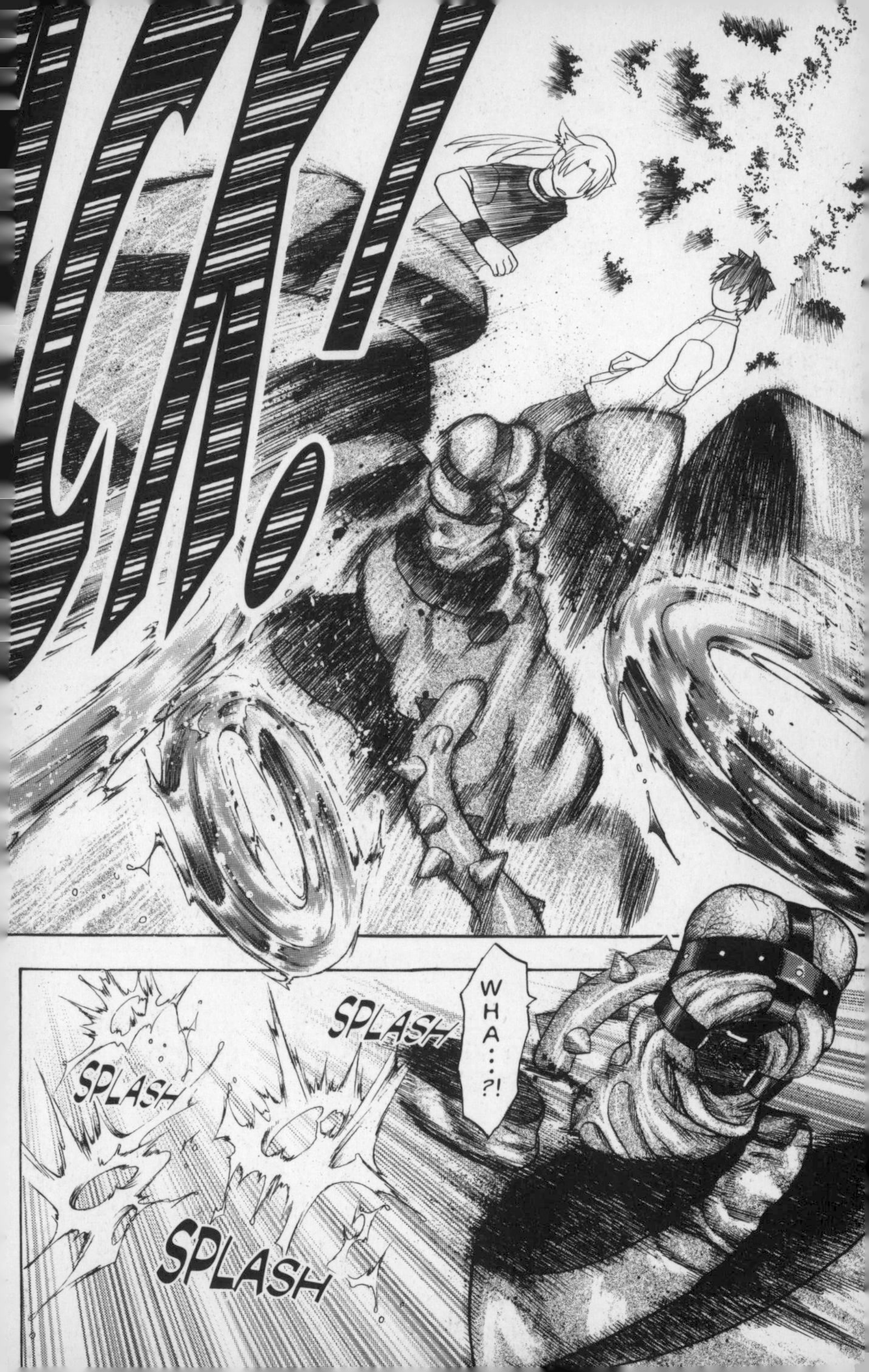
WHA...?!
SPLASH
SPLASH
SPLASH

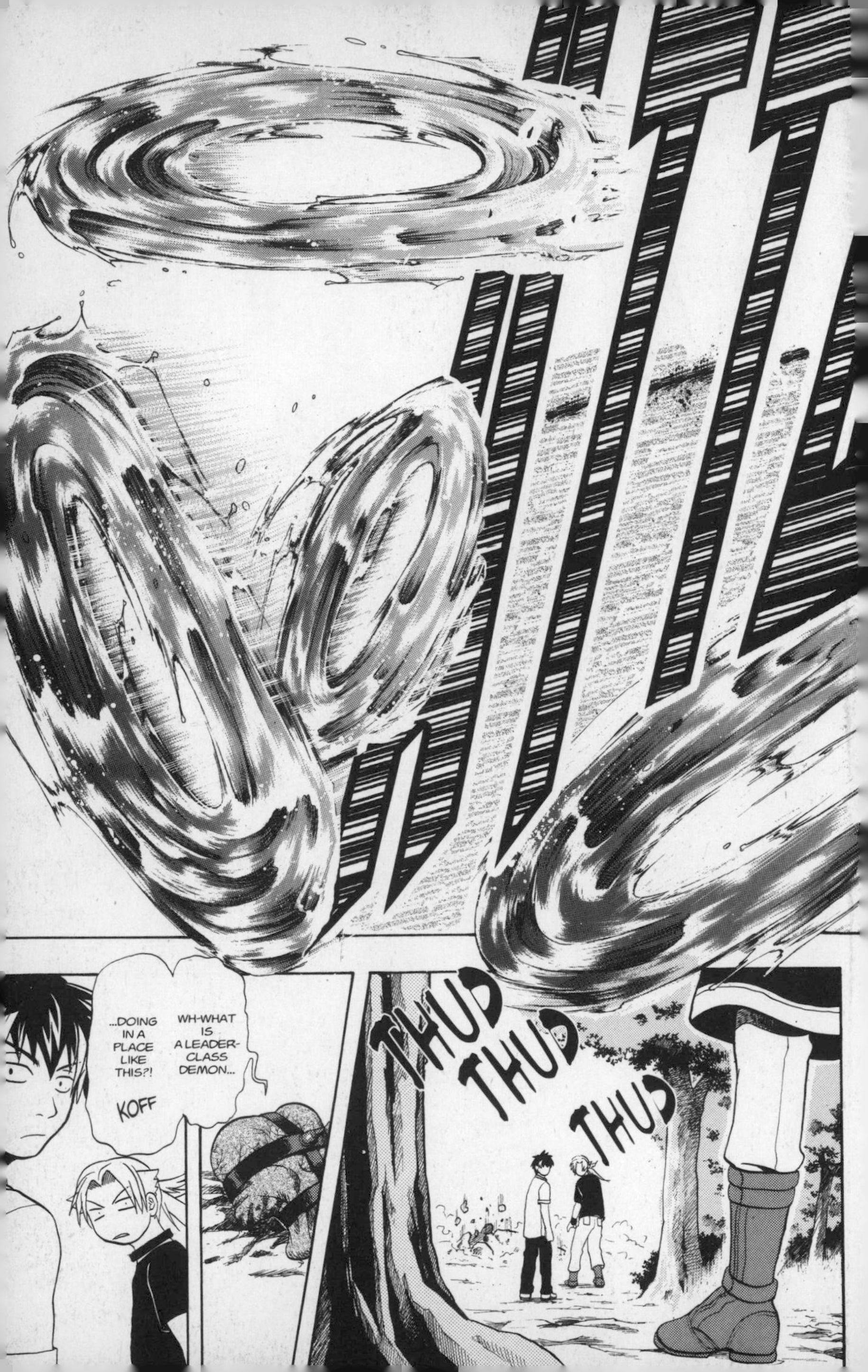
THUD
THUD
THUD
WH-WHAT IS A LEADER-CLASS DEMON... ...DOING IN A PLACE LIKE THIS?!
KOFF

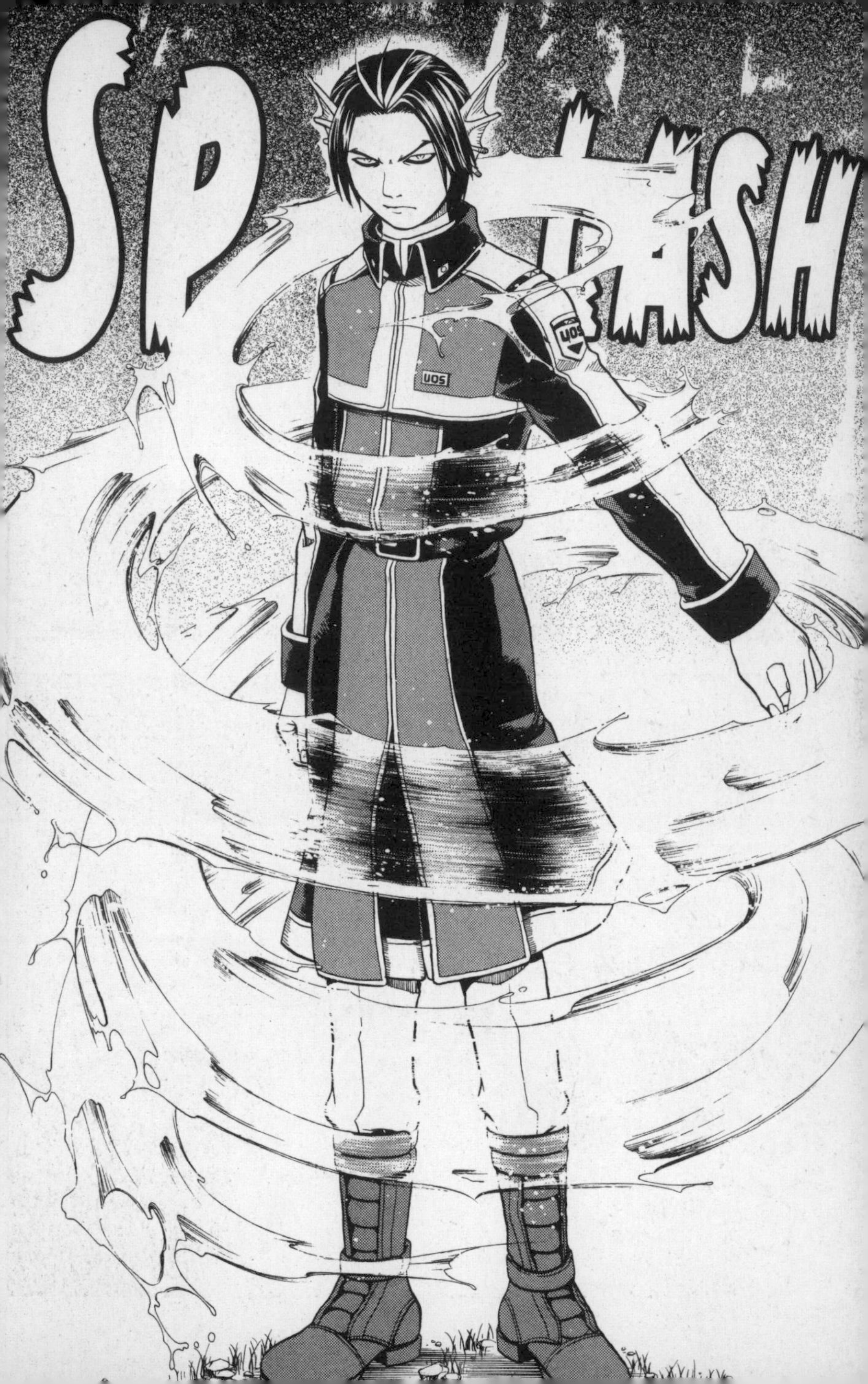
SPLASH
UOS
UOS

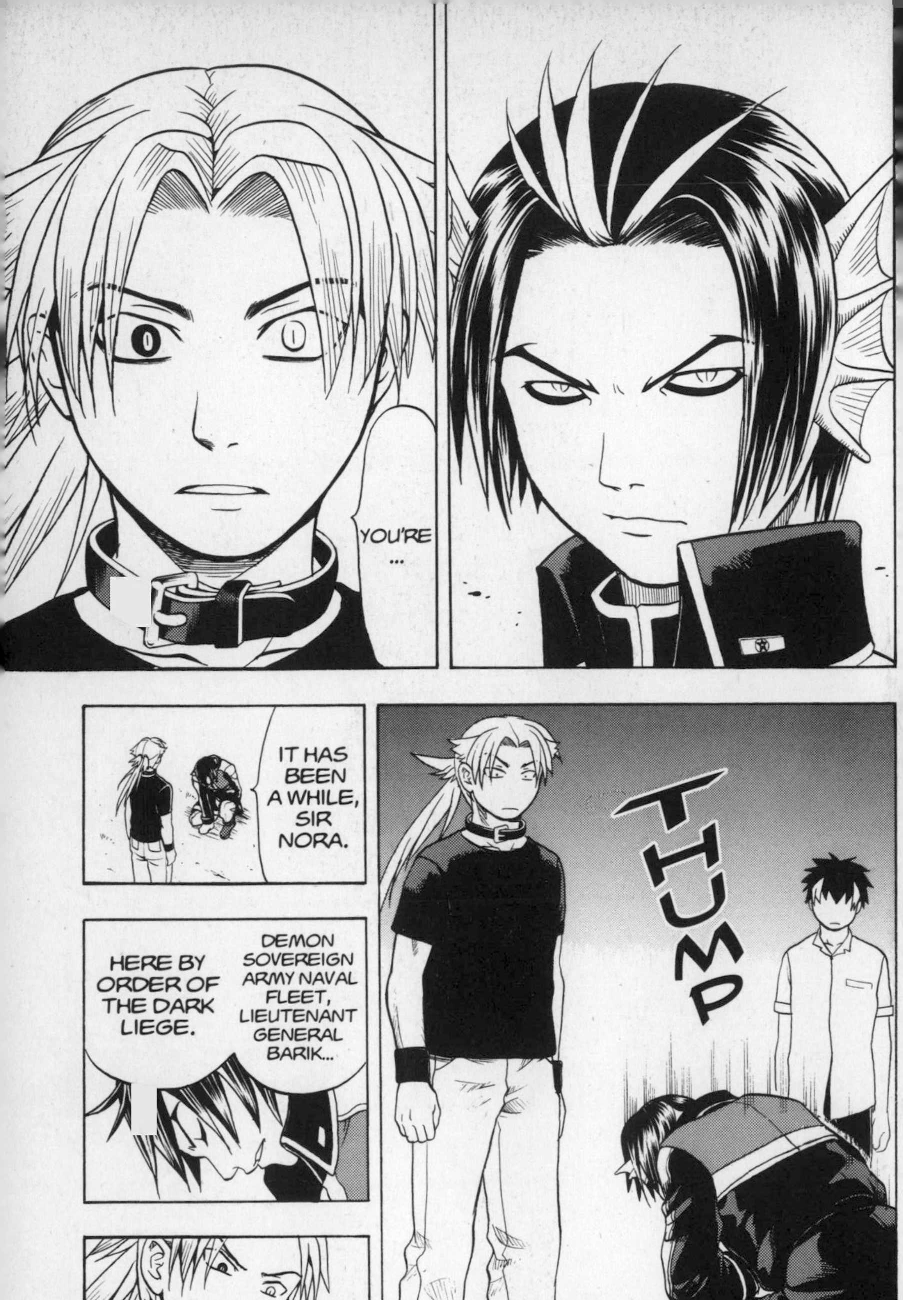
YOU'RE ...
THUMP
IT HAS BEEN A WHILE, SIR NORA.
DEMON SOVEREIGN ARMY NAVAL FLEET, LIEUTENANT GENERAL BARIK...
HERE BY ORDER OF THE DARK LIEGE.

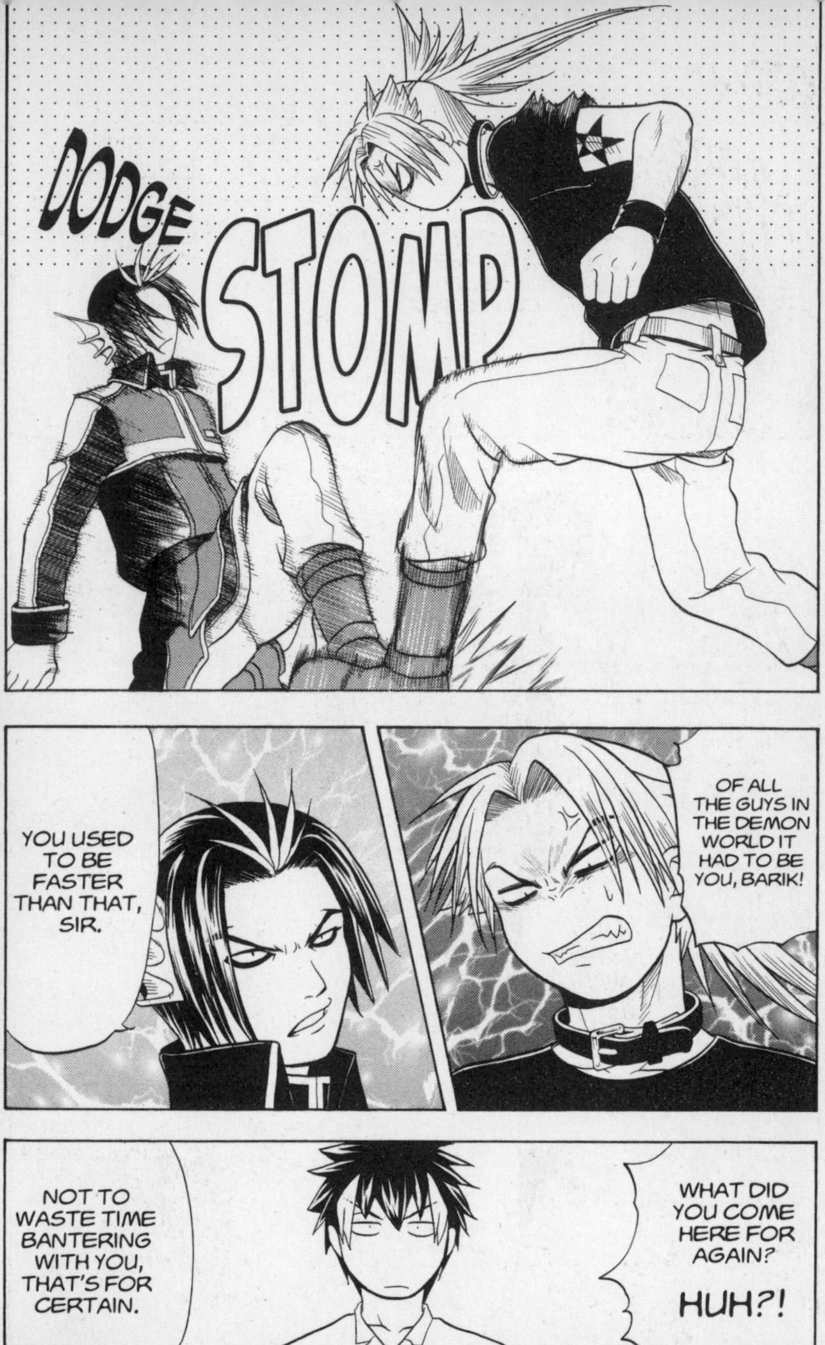
DODGE
STOMP
OF ALL THE GUYS IN THE DEMON WORLD IT HAD TO BE YOU, BARIK!
YOU USED TO BE FASTER THAN THAT, SIR.
WHAT DID YOU COME HERE FOR AGAIN?
HUH?!
NOT TO WASTE TIME BANTERING WITH YOU, THAT'S FOR CERTAIN.

READ THIS WAY

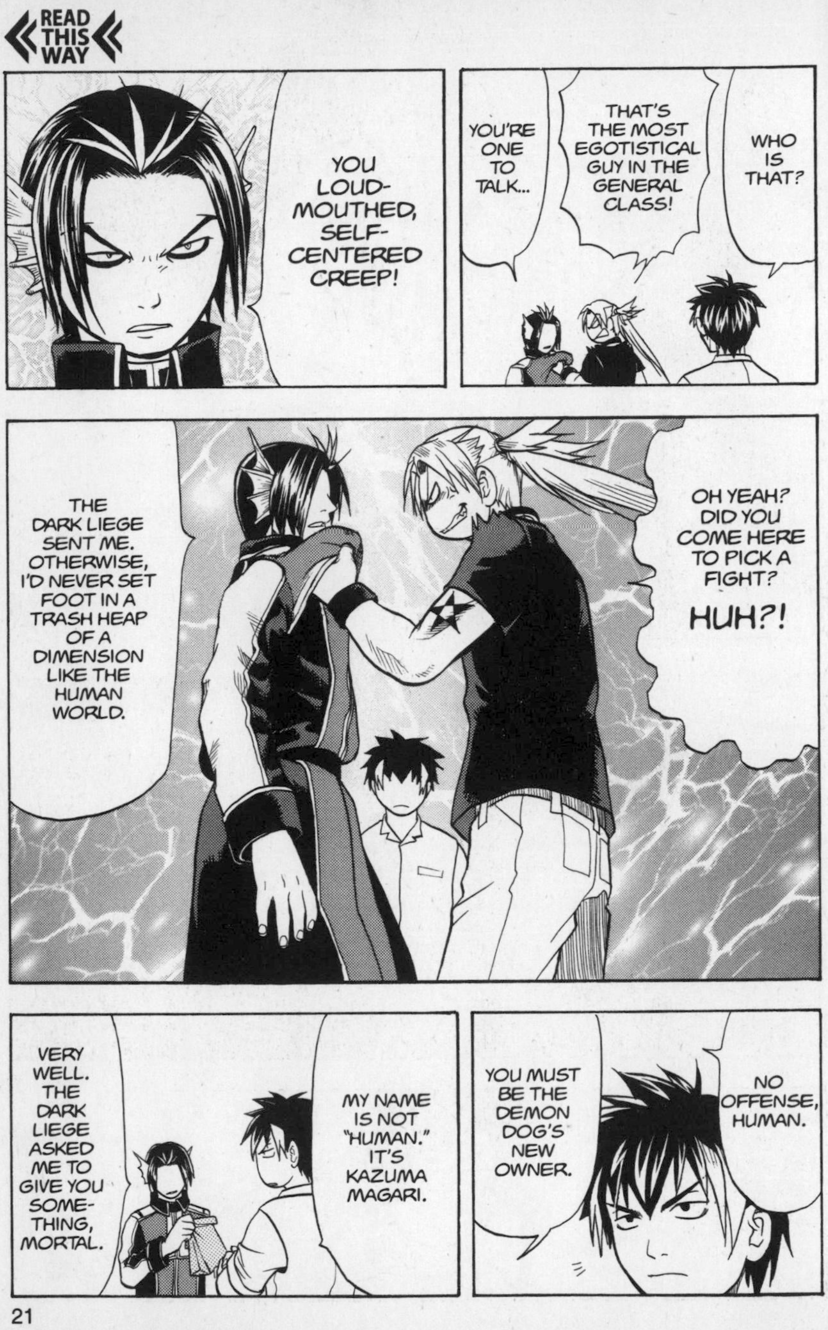

WHO IS THAT?
THAT'S THE MOST EGOTISTICAL GUY IN THE GENERAL CLASS!
YOU'RE ONE TO TALK...
YOU LOUD-MOUTHED, SELF-CENTERED CREEP!
OH YEAH? DID YOU COME HERE TO PICK A FIGHT?
HUH?!
THE DARK LIEGE SENT ME. OTHERWISE, I'D NEVER SET FOOT IN A TRASH HEAP OF A DIMENSION LIKE THE HUMAN WORLD.
NO OFFENSE, HUMAN.
YOU MUST BE THE DEMON DOG'S NEW OWNER.
MY NAME IS NOT "HUMAN." IT'S KAZUMA MAGARI.
VERY WELL. THE DARK LIEGE ASKED ME TO GIVE YOU SOME-THING, MORTAL.

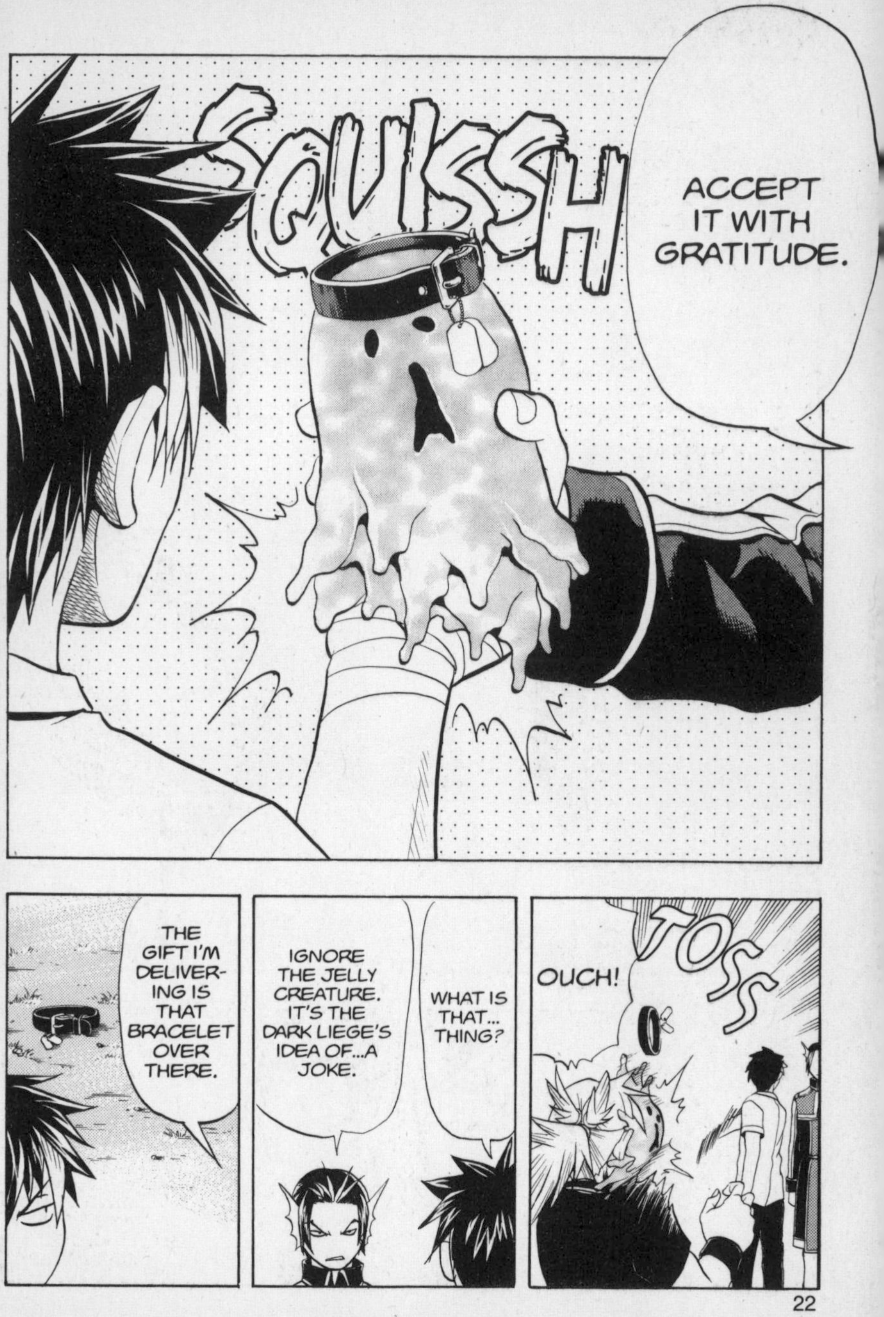
SQUISH
ACCEPT IT WITH GRATITUDE.
TOSS
OUCH!
WHAT IS THAT... THING?
IGNORE THE JELLY CREATURE. IT'S THE DARK LIEGE'S IDEA OF...A JOKE.
THE GIFT I'M DELIVER-ING IS THAT BRACELET OVER THERE.

READ THIS WAY

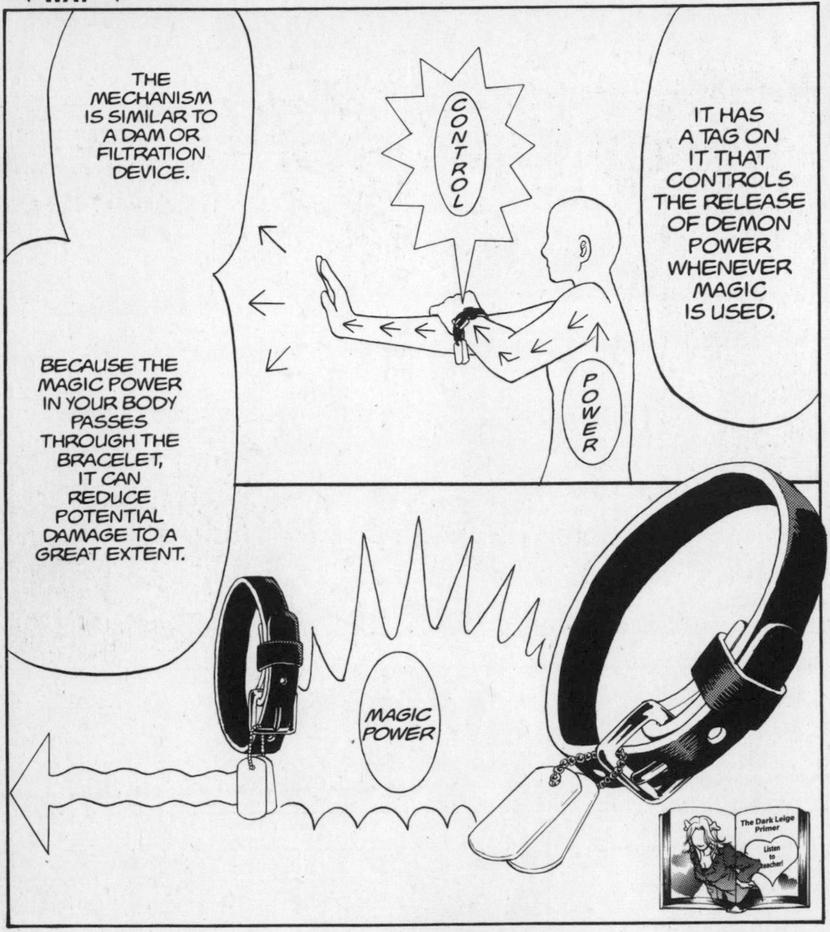
IT HAS A TAG ON IT THAT CONTROLS THE RELEASE OF DEMON POWER WHENEVER MAGIC IS USED.
CONTROL
POWER
THE MECHANISM IS SIMILAR TO A DAM OR FILTRATION DEVICE.
BECAUSE THE MAGIC POWER IN YOUR BODY PASSES THROUGH THE BRACELET, IT CAN REDUCE POTENTIAL DAMAGE TO A GREAT EXTENT.
MAGIC POWER
The Dark Leige Primer
Listen to teacher!

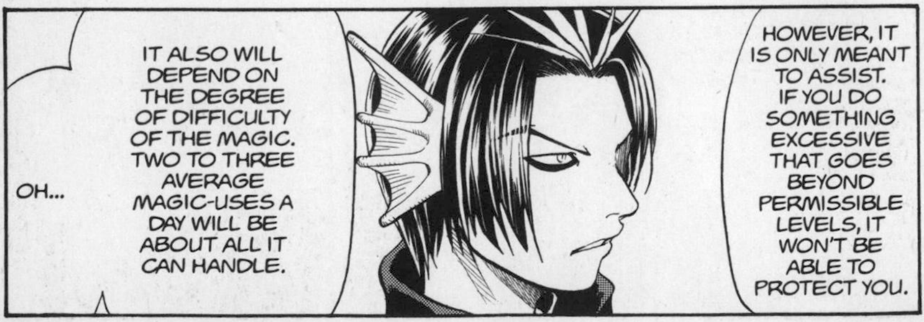
HOWEVER, IT IS ONLY MEANT TO ASSIST. IF YOU DO SOMETHING EXCESSIVE THAT GOES BEYOND PERMISSIBLE LEVELS, IT WON'T BE ABLE TO PROTECT YOU.
IT ALSO WILL DEPEND ON THE DEGREE OF DIFFICULTY OF THE MAGIC. TWO TO THREE AVERAGE MAGIC-USES A DAY WILL BE ABOUT ALL IT CAN HANDLE.
OH...

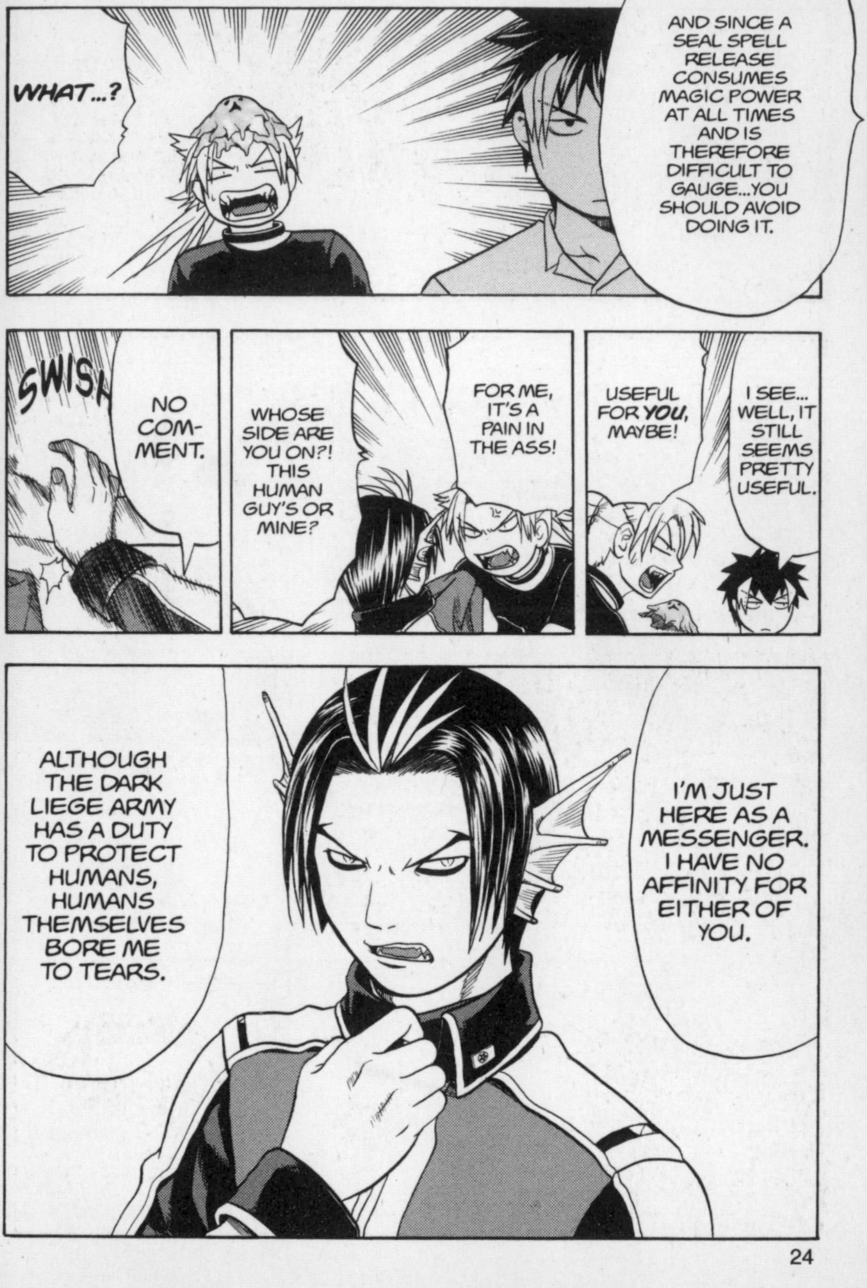
AND SINCE A SEAL SPELL RELEASE CONSUMES MAGIC POWER AT ALL TIMES AND IS THEREFORE DIFFICULT TO GAUGE...YOU SHOULD AVOID DOING IT.
WHAT...?
I SEE... WELL, IT STILL SEEMS PRETTY USEFUL.
USEFUL FOR ***YOU***, MAYBE!
FOR ME, IT'S A PAIN IN THE ASS!
WHOSE SIDE ARE YOU ON?! THIS HUMAN GUY'S OR MINE?
NO COM-MENT.
SWISH
I'M JUST HERE AS A MESSENGER. I HAVE NO AFFINITY FOR EITHER OF YOU.
ALTHOUGH THE DARK LIEGE ARMY HAS A DUTY TO PROTECT HUMANS, HUMANS THEMSELVES BORE ME TO TEARS.

READ THIS WAY

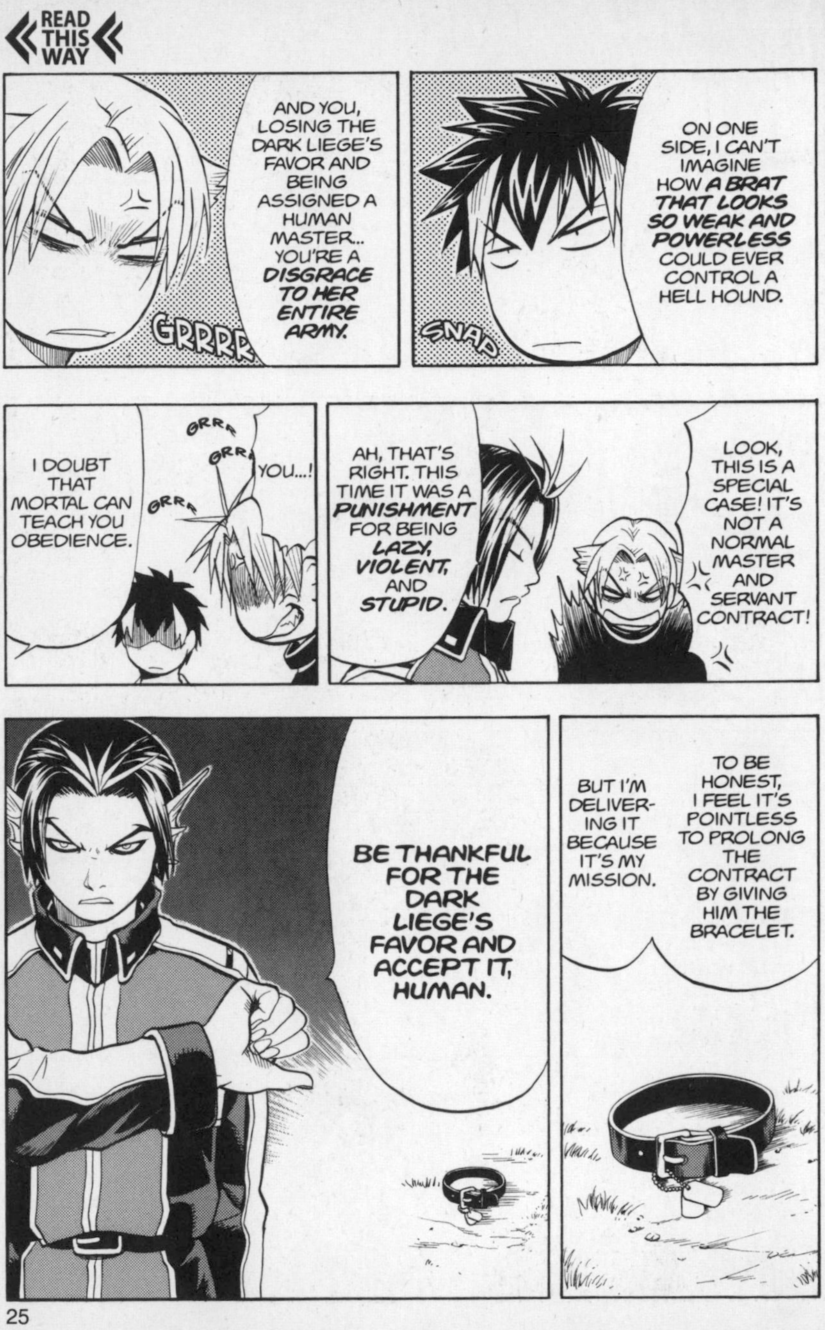
ON ONE SIDE, I CAN'T IMAGINE HOW ***A BRAT THAT LOOKS SO WEAK AND POWERLESS*** COULD EVER CONTROL A HELL HOUND.
SNAP
AND YOU, LOSING THE DARK LIEGE'S FAVOR AND BEING ASSIGNED A HUMAN MASTER... YOU'RE A ***DISGRACE TO HER ENTIRE ARMY.***
GRRRR
LOOK, THIS IS A SPECIAL CASE! IT'S NOT A NORMAL MASTER AND SERVANT CONTRACT!
AH, THAT'S RIGHT. THIS TIME IT WAS A ***PUNISHMENT*** FOR BEING ***LAZY, VIOLENT,*** AND ***STUPID.***
GRRR
GRRR
YOU...!
GRRR
I DOUBT THAT MORTAL CAN TEACH YOU OBEDIENCE.
TO BE HONEST, I FEEL IT'S POINTLESS TO PROLONG THE CONTRACT BY GIVING HIM THE BRACELET.
BUT I'M DELIVERING IT BECAUSE IT'S MY MISSION.
BE THANKFUL FOR THE DARK LIEGE'S FAVOR AND ACCEPT IT, HUMAN.

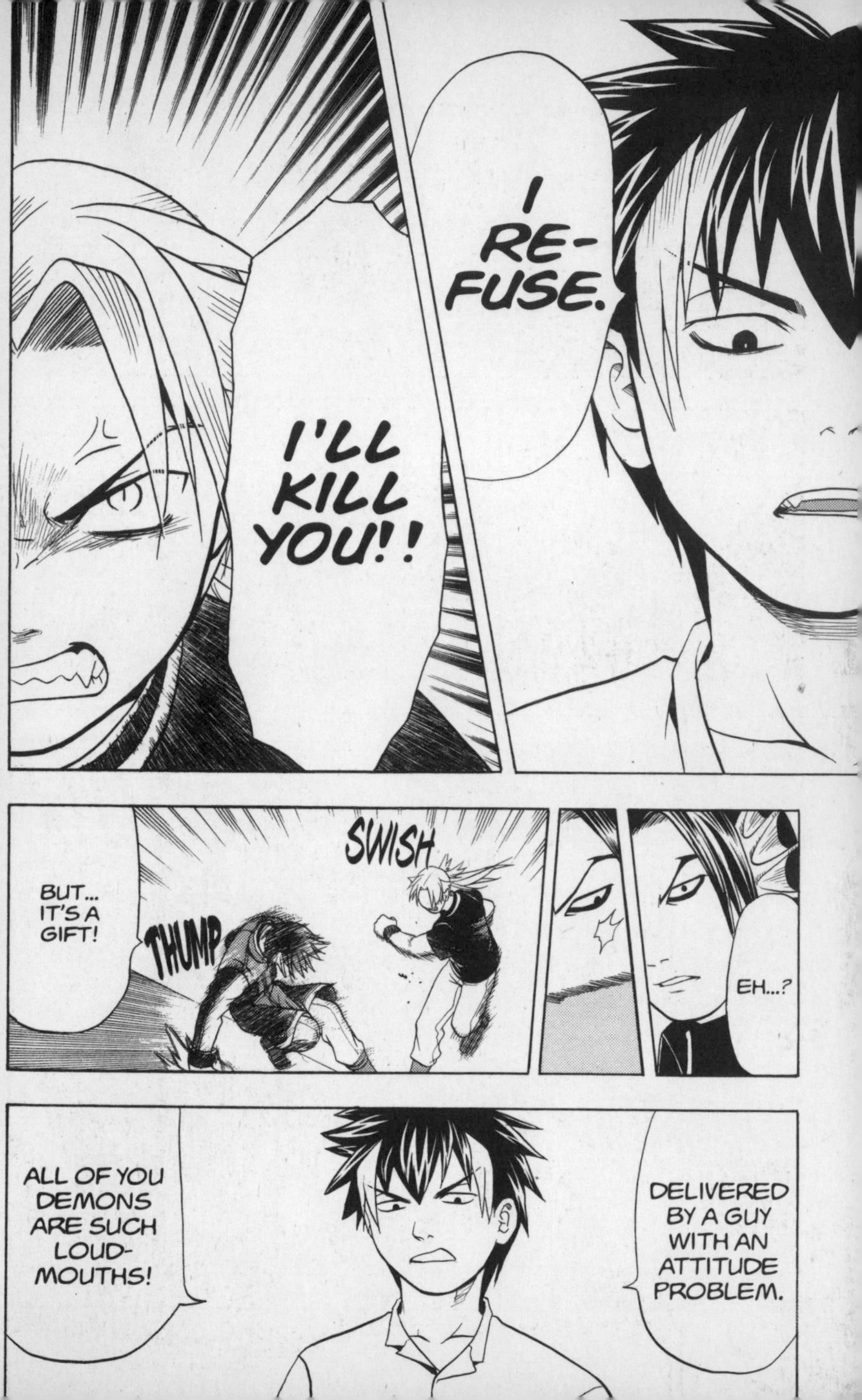
I REFUSE.
I'LL KILL YOU!!
EH...?
SWISH
BUT... IT'S A GIFT!
THUMP
DELIVERED BY A GUY WITH AN ATTITUDE PROBLEM.
ALL OF YOU DEMONS ARE SUCH LOUDMOUTHS!

READ THIS WAY

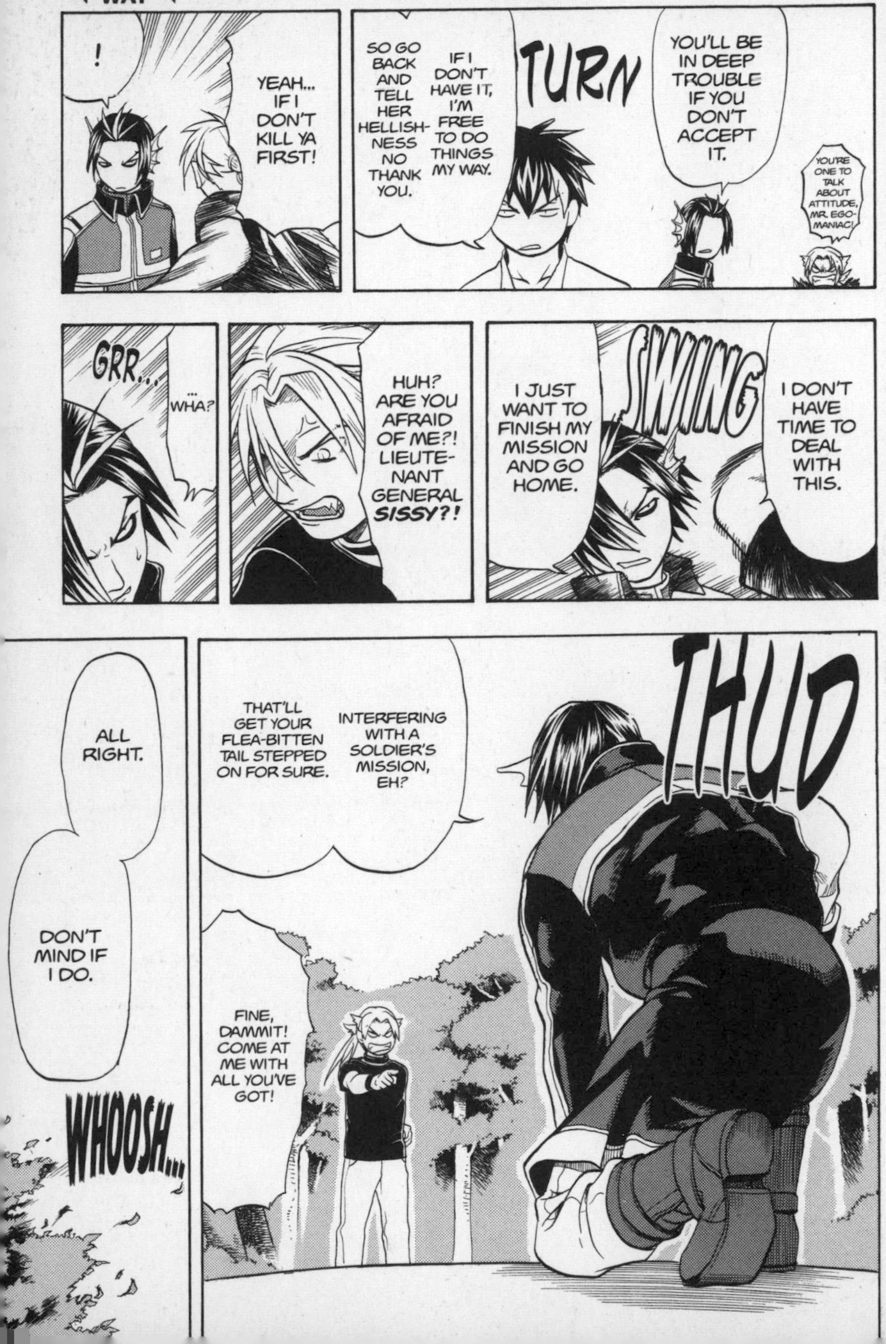
YOU'LL BE IN DEEP TROUBLE IF YOU DON'T ACCEPT IT.
YOU'RE ONE TO TALK ABOUT ATTITUDE, MR. EGO-MANIAC!
TURN
IF I DON'T HAVE IT, I'M FREE TO DO THINGS MY WAY.
SO GO BACK AND TELL HER HELLISHNESS NO THANK YOU.
YEAH... IF I DON'T KILL YA FIRST!
!
I DON'T HAVE TIME TO DEAL WITH THIS.
SWING
I JUST WANT TO FINISH MY MISSION AND GO HOME.
HUH? ARE YOU AFRAID OF ME?! LIEUTENANT GENERAL *SISSY*?!
... WHA?
GRR...
THUD
INTERFERING WITH A SOLDIER'S MISSION, EH?
THAT'LL GET YOUR FLEA-BITTEN TAIL STEPPED ON FOR SURE.
FINE, DAMMIT! COME AT ME WITH ALL YOU'VE GOT!
ALL RIGHT.
DON'T MIND IF I DO.
WHOOSH...

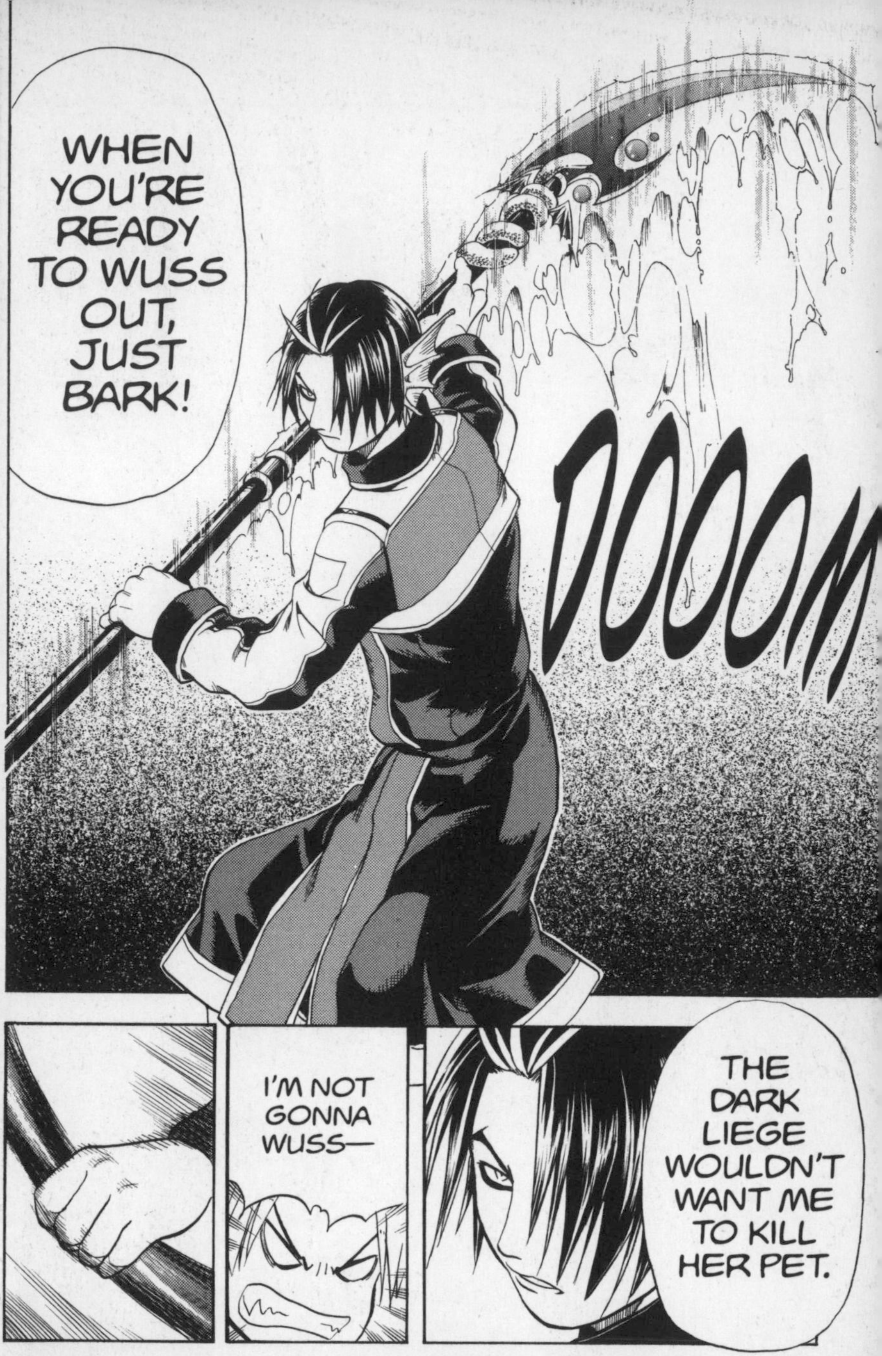
WHEN YOU'RE READY TO WUSS OUT, JUST BARK!
DOOOM
THE DARK LIEGE WOULDN'T WANT ME TO KILL HER PET.
I'M NOT GONNA WUSS—

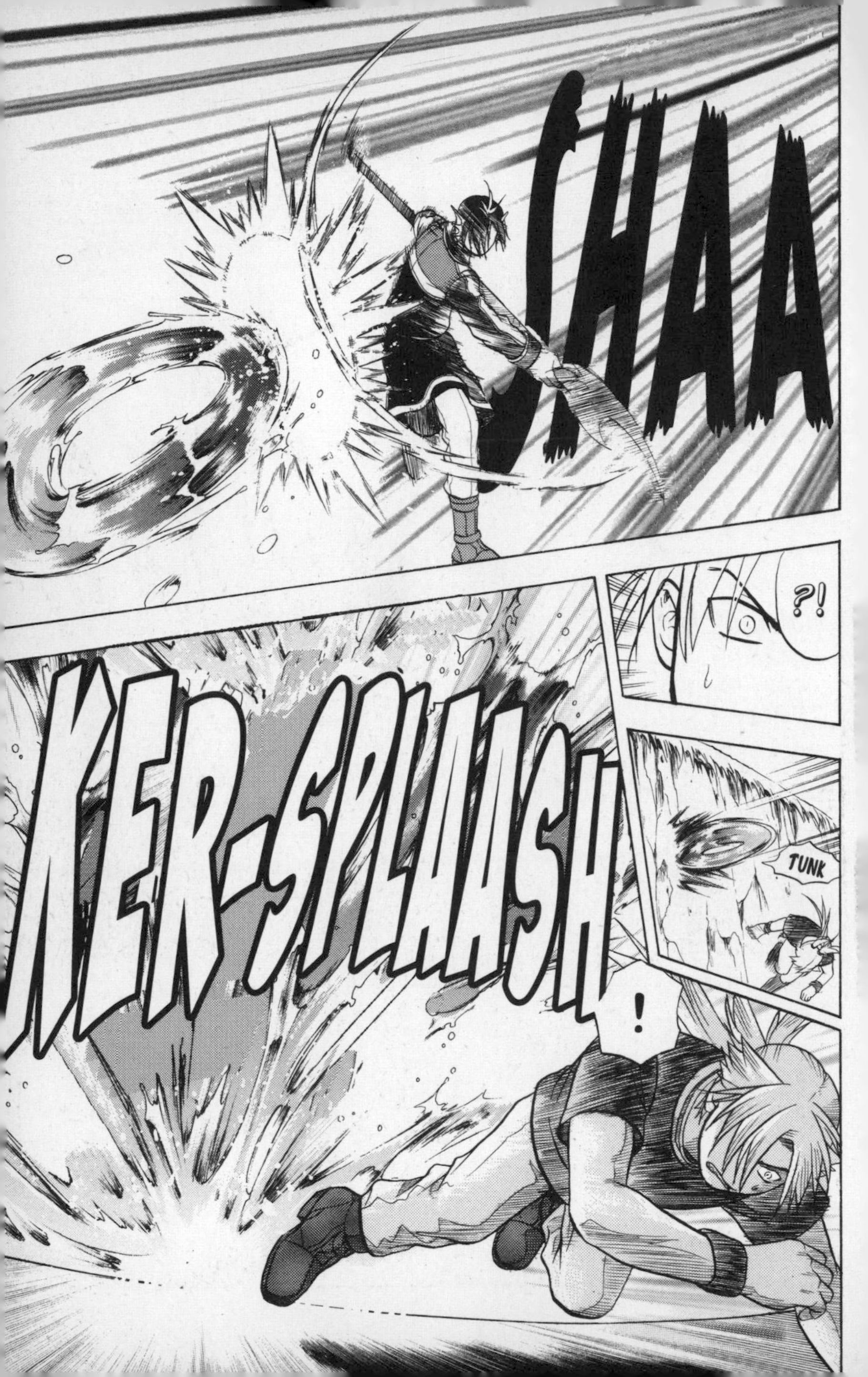
SHAA
KER-SPLAASH
?!
TUNK
!

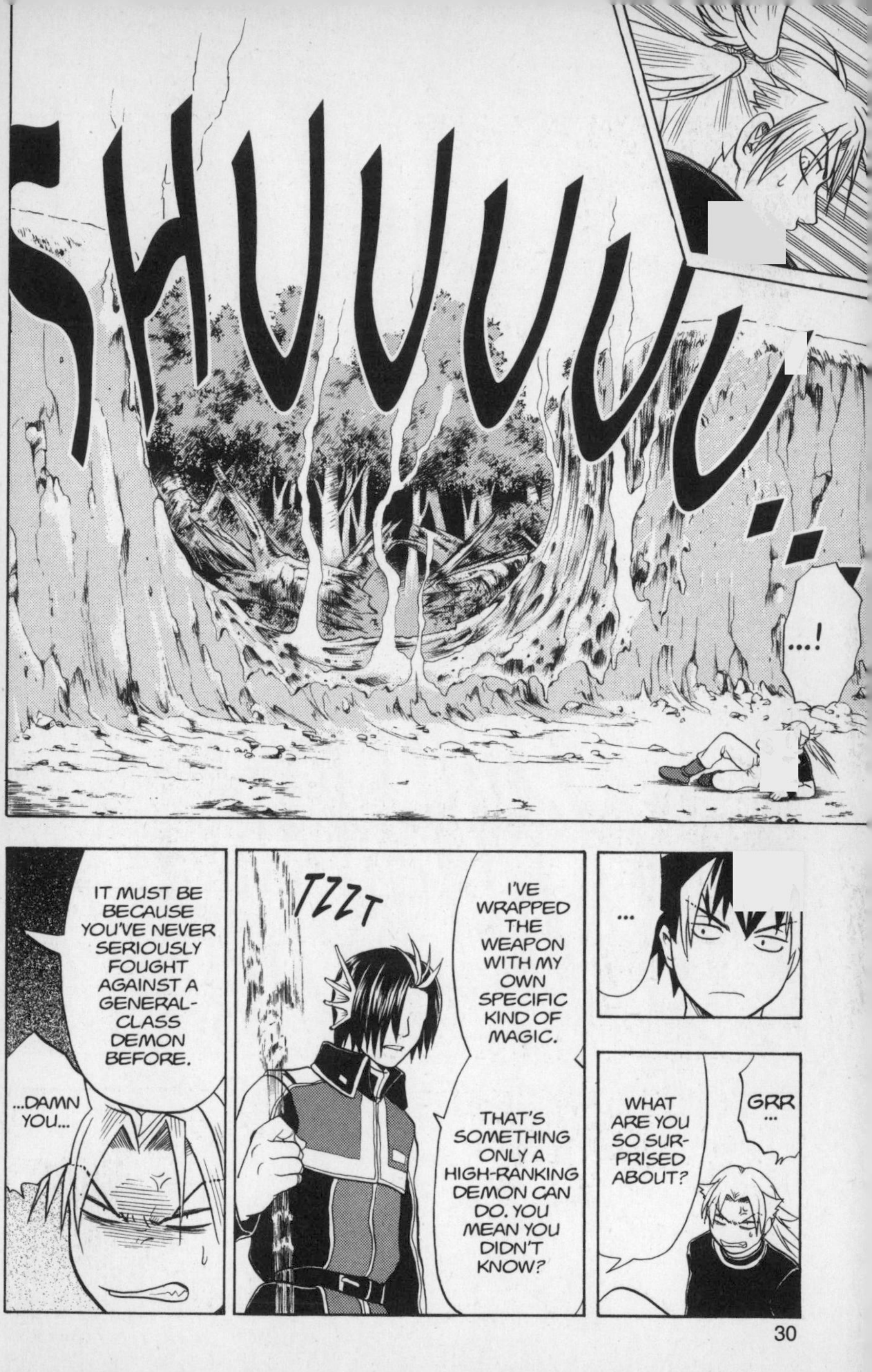
SHUUUU...
...!
...
GRR...
WHAT ARE YOU SO SUR-PRISED ABOUT?
TZZT
I'VE WRAPPED THE WEAPON WITH MY OWN SPECIFIC KIND OF MAGIC.
THAT'S SOMETHING ONLY A HIGH-RANKING DEMON CAN DO. YOU MEAN YOU DIDN'T KNOW?
IT MUST BE BECAUSE YOU'VE NEVER SERIOUSLY FOUGHT AGAINST A GENERAL-CLASS DEMON BEFORE.
...DAMN YOU...

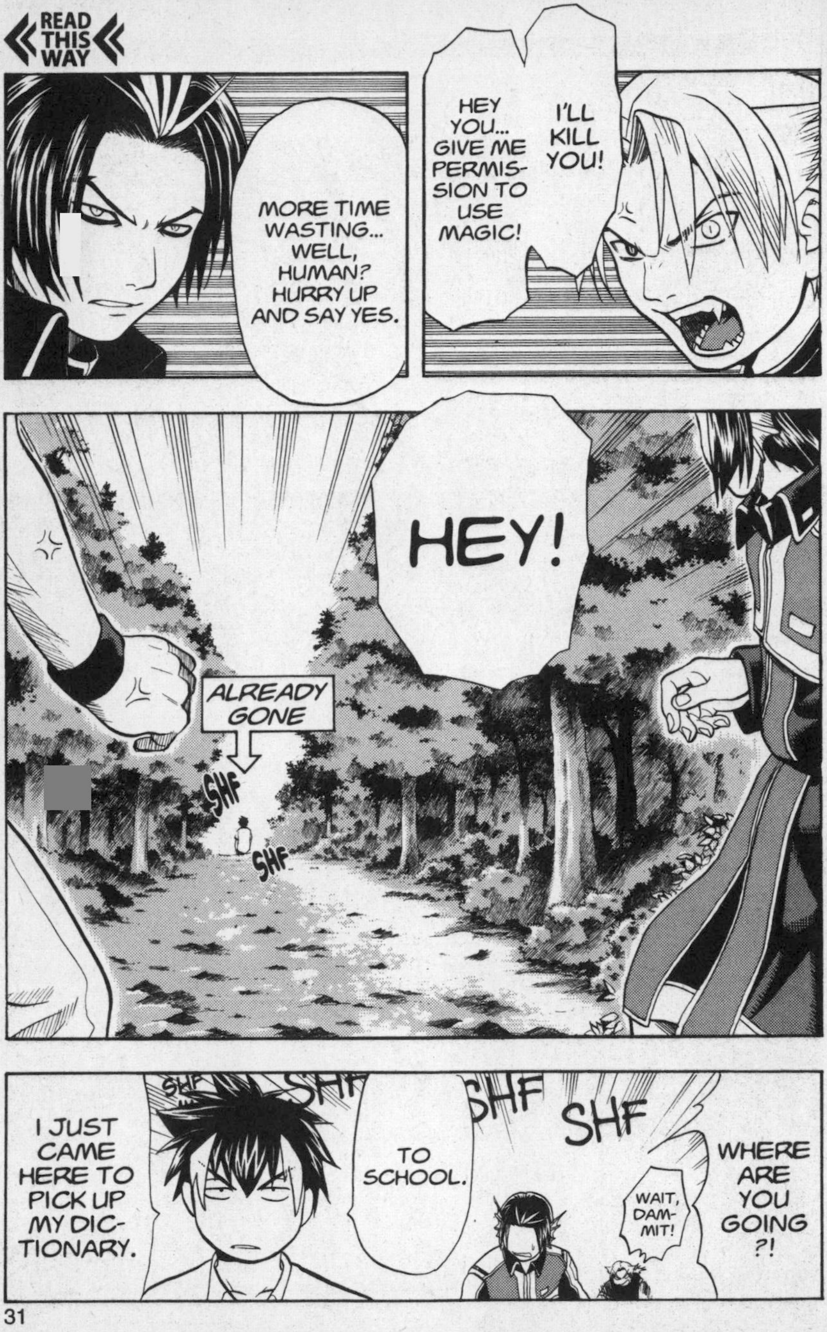
READ THIS WAY
I'LL KILL YOU!
HEY YOU... GIVE ME PERMISSION TO USE MAGIC!
MORE TIME WASTING... WELL, HUMAN? HURRY UP AND SAY YES.
HEY!
ALREADY GONE
SHF
SHF
WHERE ARE YOU GOING?!
WAIT, DAMMIT!
SHF
SHF
SHF
SHF
TO SCHOOL.
I JUST CAME HERE TO PICK UP MY DICTIONARY.

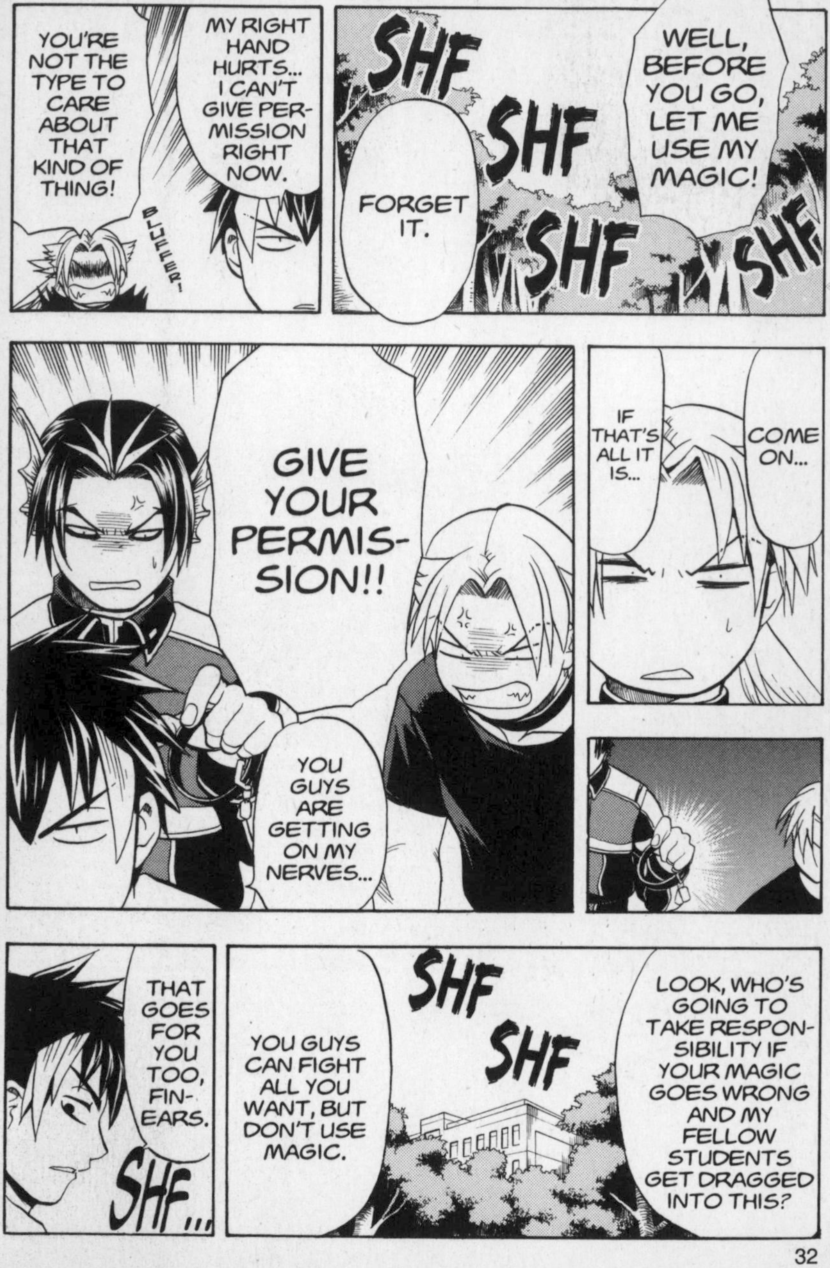
SHF
WELL, BEFORE YOU GO, LET ME USE MY MAGIC!
SHF
FORGET IT.
SHF
SHF
MY RIGHT HAND HURTS... I CAN'T GIVE PERMISSION RIGHT NOW.
YOU'RE NOT THE TYPE TO CARE ABOUT THAT KIND OF THING!
BLUFFER!
COME ON...
IF THAT'S ALL IT IS...
GIVE YOUR PERMISSION!!
YOU GUYS ARE GETTING ON MY NERVES...
LOOK, WHO'S GOING TO TAKE RESPONSIBILITY IF YOUR MAGIC GOES WRONG AND MY FELLOW STUDENTS GET DRAGGED INTO THIS?
SHF
SHF
YOU GUYS CAN FIGHT ALL YOU WANT, BUT DON'T USE MAGIC.
THAT GOES FOR YOU TOO, FIN-EARS.
SHF...

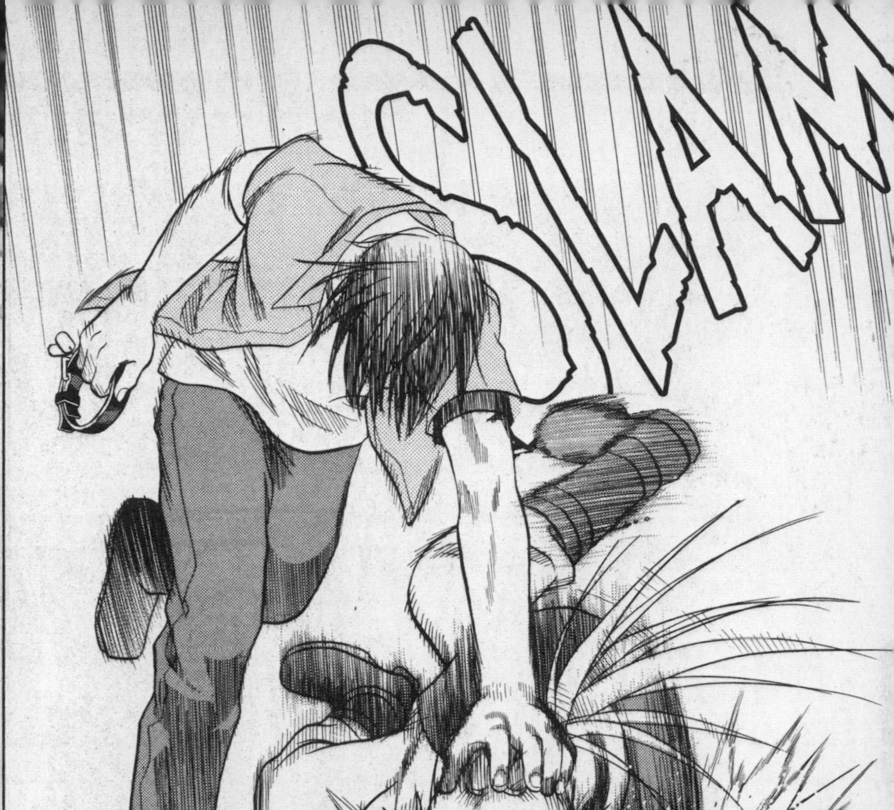
SLAM

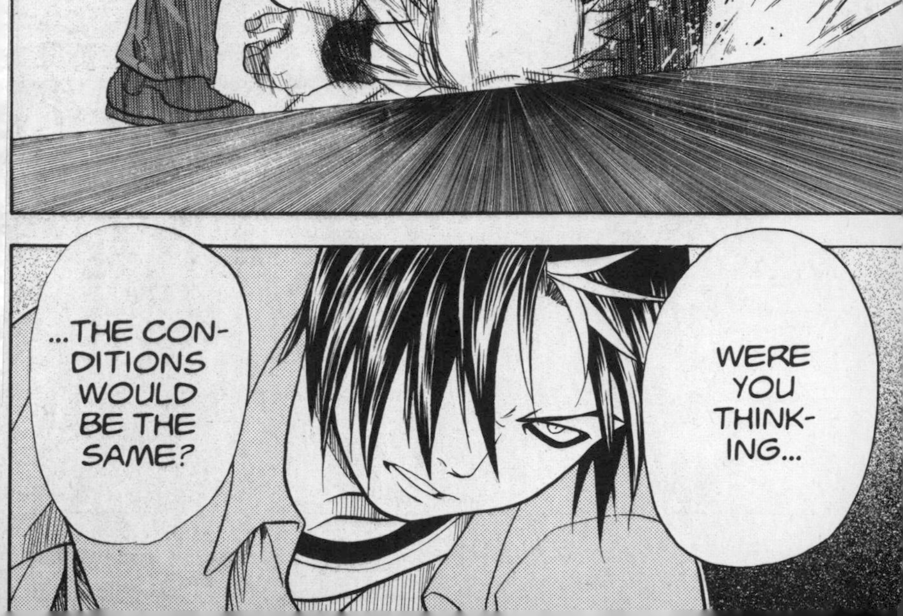
WERE YOU THINK-ING...
...THE CON-DITIONS WOULD BE THE SAME?

READ THIS WAY

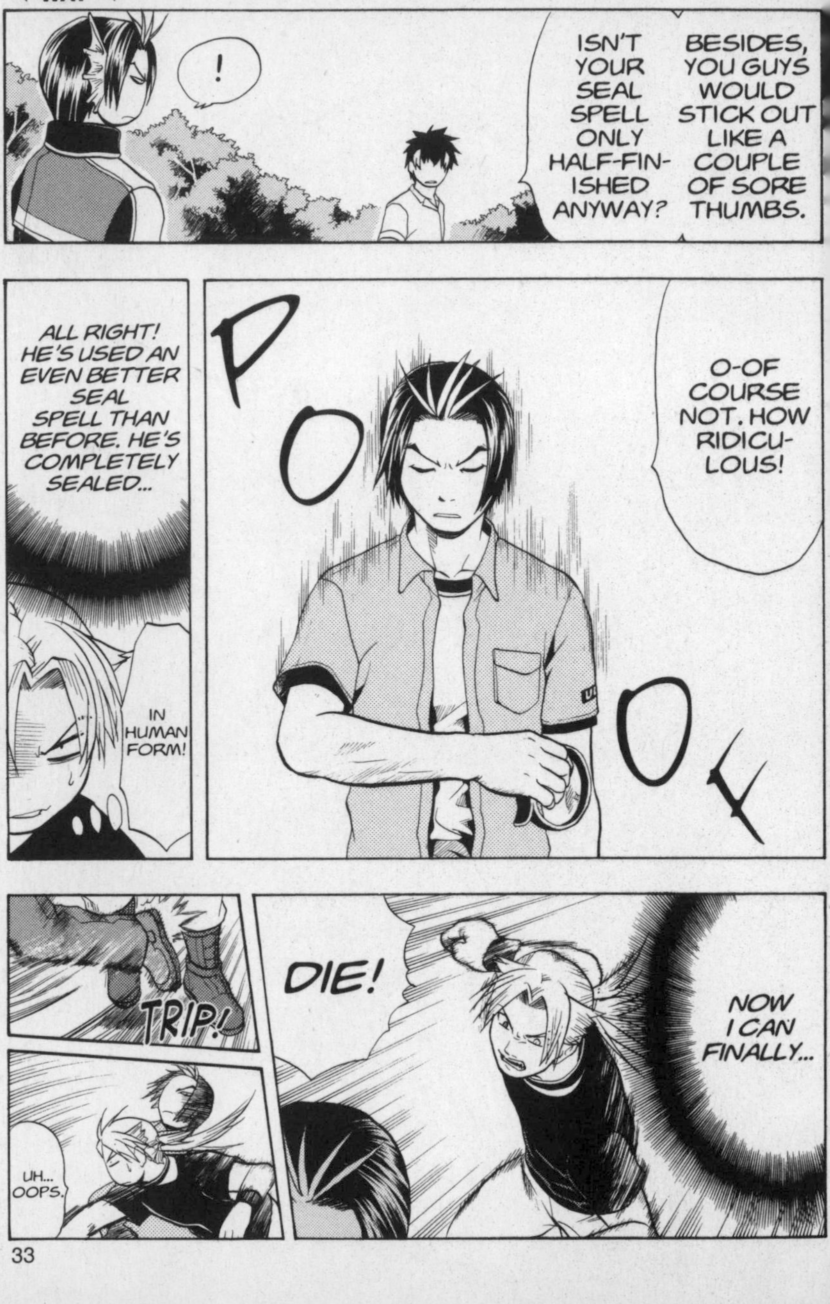
BESIDES, YOU GUYS WOULD STICK OUT LIKE A COUPLE OF SORE THUMBS.
ISN'T YOUR SEAL SPELL ONLY HALF-FIN-ISHED ANYWAY?
!
O-OF COURSE NOT. HOW RIDICU-LOUS!
POOF
ALL RIGHT! HE'S USED AN EVEN BETTER SEAL SPELL THAN BEFORE. HE'S COMPLETELY SEALED...
IN HUMAN FORM!
NOW I CAN FINALLY...
DIE!
TRIP!
UH... OOPS.

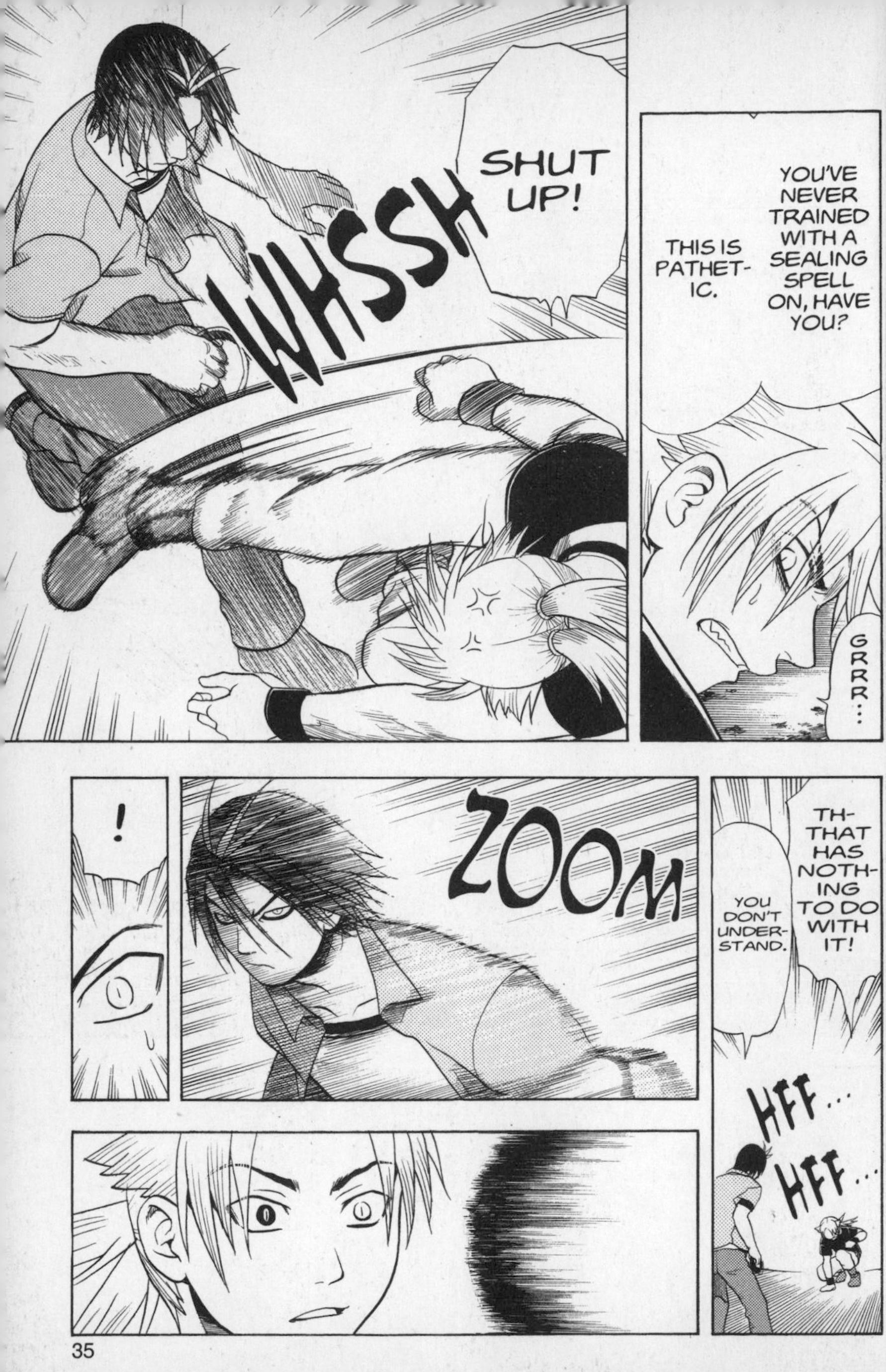
YOU'VE NEVER TRAINED WITH A SEALING SPELL ON, HAVE YOU?
THIS IS PATHETIC.
GRRR...
SHUT UP!
WHSSH
TH-THAT HAS NOTHING TO DO WITH IT!
YOU DON'T UNDERSTAND.
HFF... HFF...
ZOOM
!

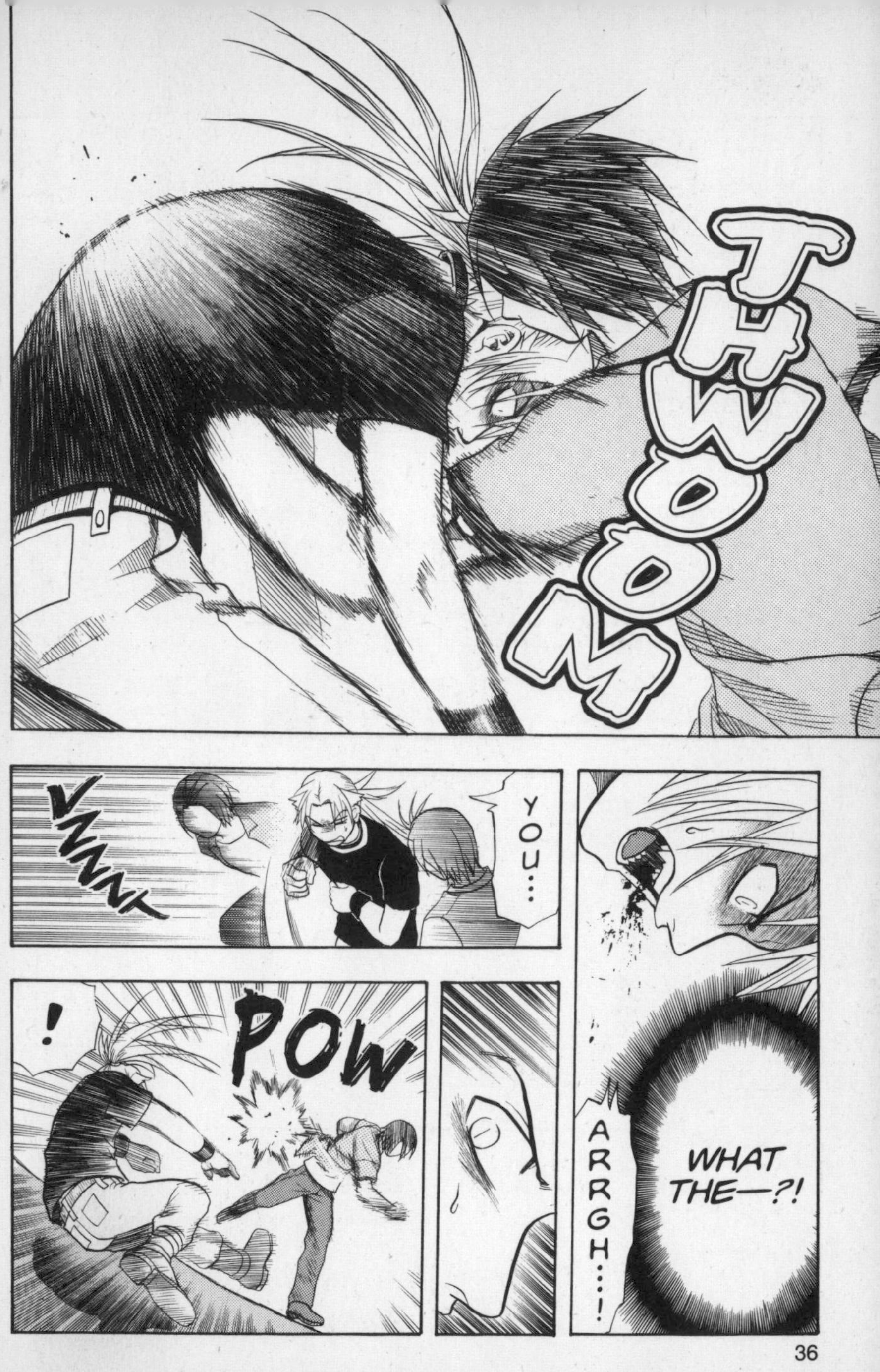
THWOOM
ARRGH...!
WHAT THE—?!
YOU...
!
POW

READ THIS WAY

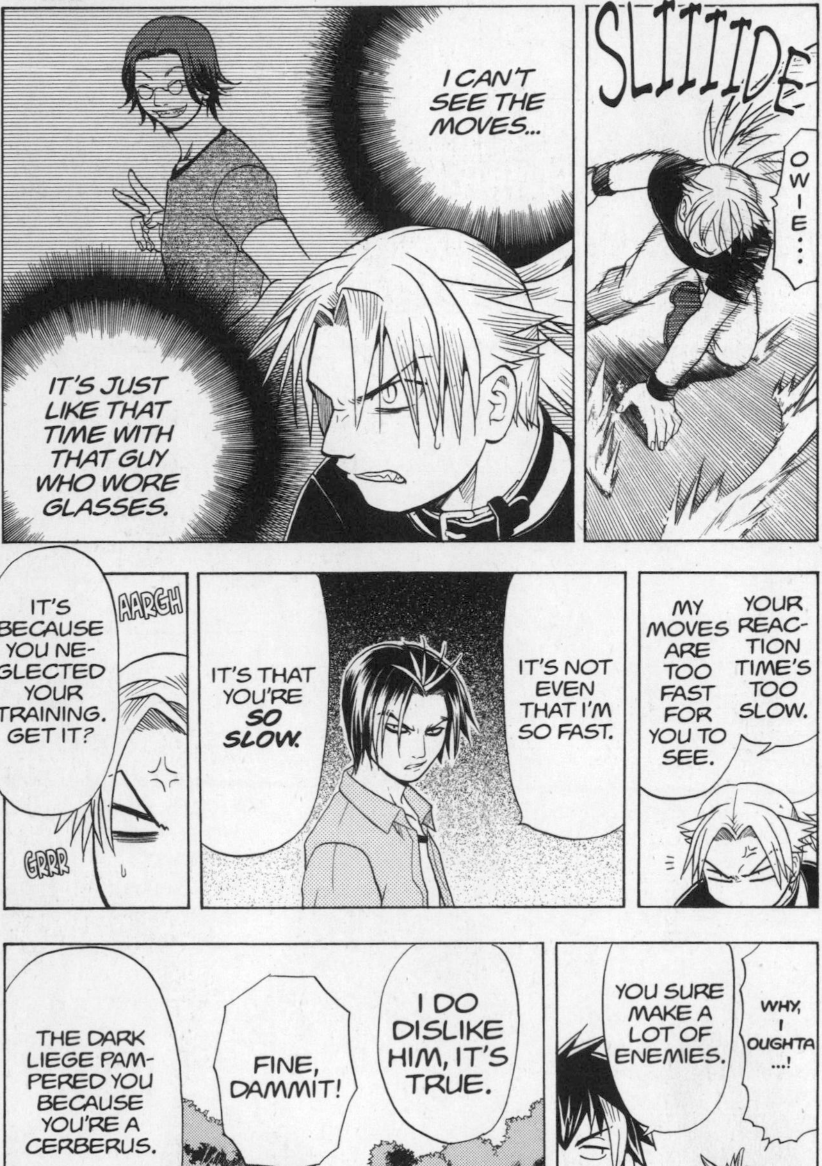
SLIIIDE
OWIE...
I CAN'T SEE THE MOVES...
IT'S JUST LIKE THAT TIME WITH THAT GUY WHO WORE GLASSES.
YOUR REACTION TIME'S TOO SLOW.
MY MOVES ARE TOO FAST FOR YOU TO SEE.
IT'S NOT EVEN THAT I'M SO FAST.
IT'S THAT YOU'RE **SO SLOW.**
AARGH
IT'S BECAUSE YOU NEGLECTED YOUR TRAINING. GET IT?
GRRR
YOU SURE MAKE A LOT OF ENEMIES.
WHY, I OUGHTA...!
I DO DISLIKE HIM, IT'S TRUE.
FINE, DAMMIT!
THE DARK LIEGE PAMPERED YOU BECAUSE YOU'RE A CERBERUS.

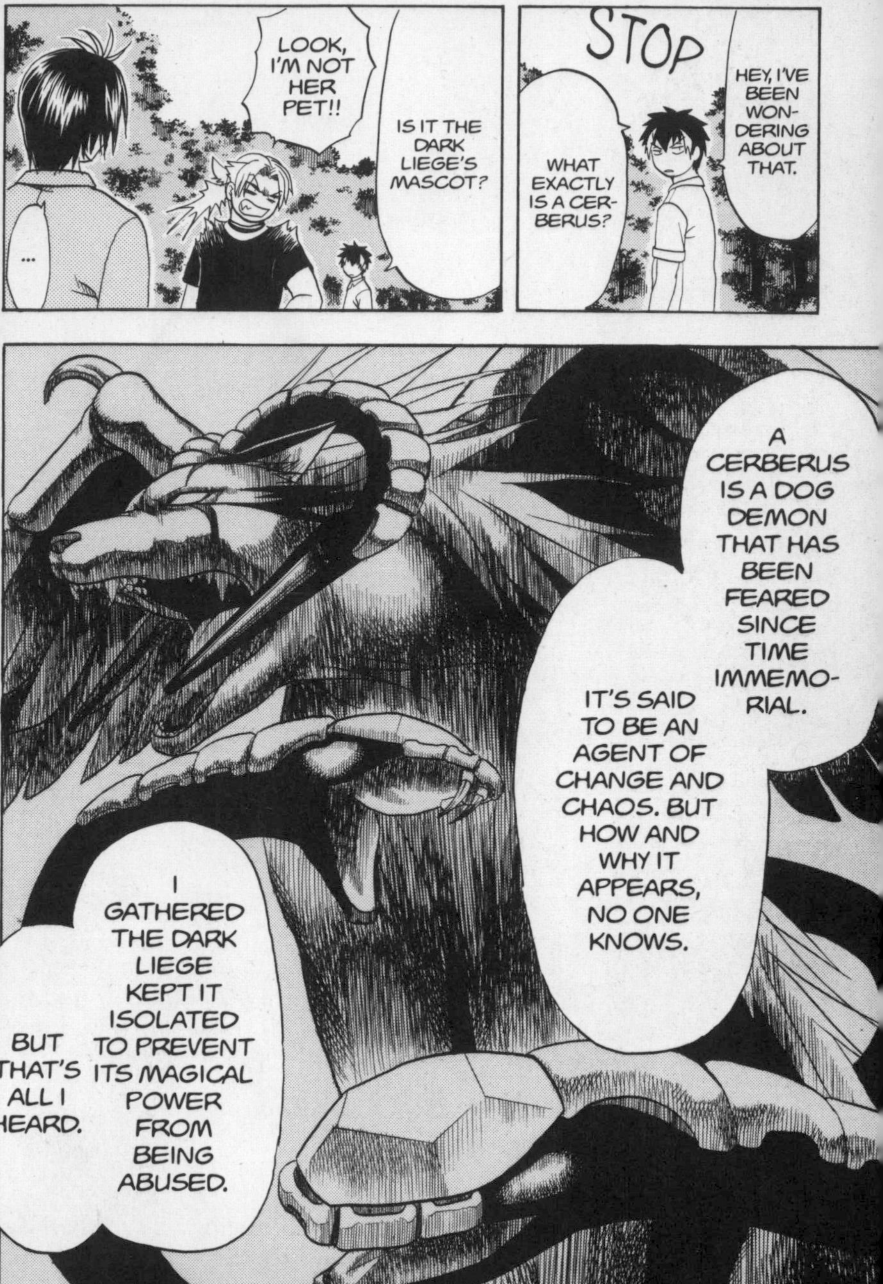
STOP
HEY, I'VE BEEN WON-DERING ABOUT THAT.
WHAT EXACTLY IS A CER-BERUS?
IS IT THE DARK LIEGE'S MASCOT?
LOOK, I'M NOT HER PET!!
...
A CERBERUS IS A DOG DEMON THAT HAS BEEN FEARED SINCE TIME IMMEMO-RIAL.
IT'S SAID TO BE AN AGENT OF CHANGE AND CHAOS. BUT HOW AND WHY IT APPEARS, NO ONE KNOWS.
I GATHERED THE DARK LIEGE KEPT IT ISOLATED TO PREVENT ITS MAGICAL POWER FROM BEING ABUSED.
BUT THAT'S ALL I HEARD.

READ THIS WAY

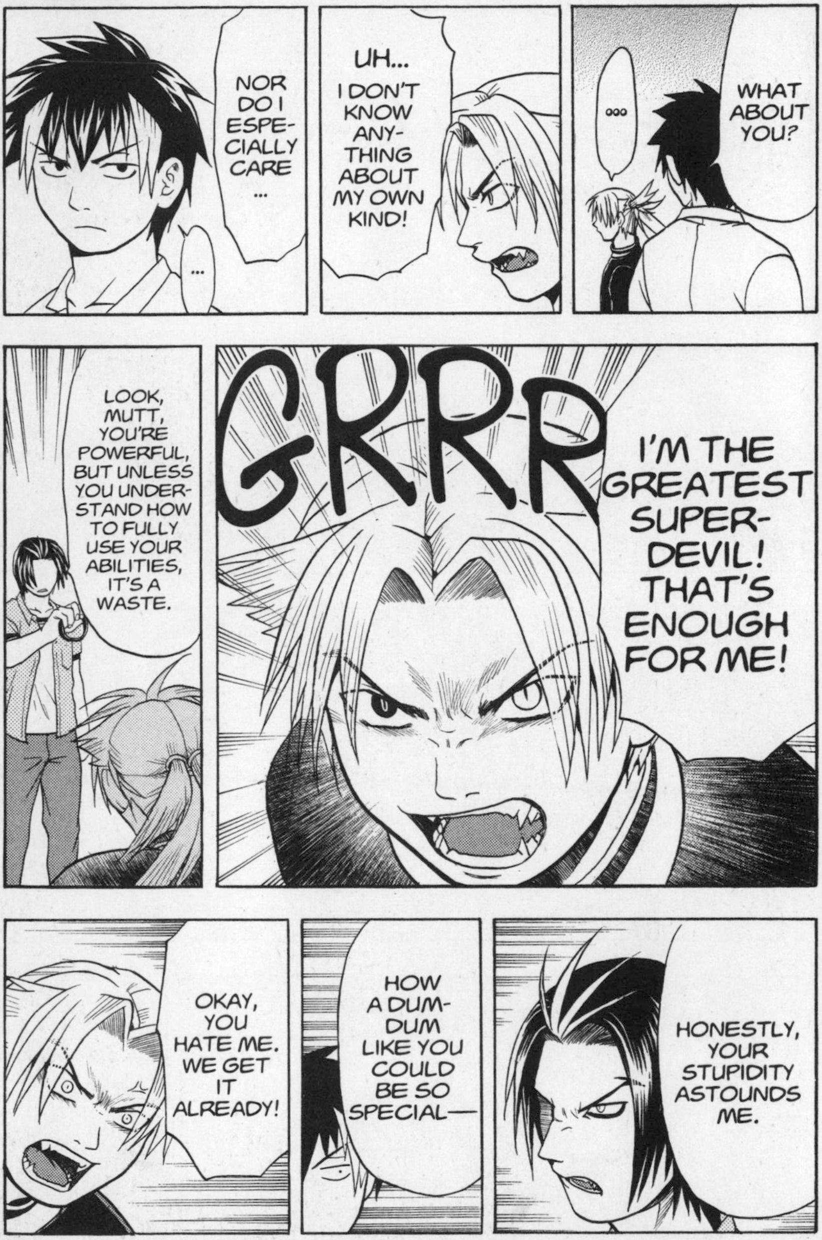
WHAT ABOUT YOU?
...
UH... I DON'T KNOW ANYTHING ABOUT MY OWN KIND!
NOR DO I ESPECIALLY CARE...
...
GRRR
I'M THE GREATEST SUPER-DEVIL! THAT'S ENOUGH FOR ME!
LOOK, MUTT, YOU'RE POWERFUL, BUT UNLESS YOU UNDERSTAND HOW TO FULLY USE YOUR ABILITIES, IT'S A WASTE.
HONESTLY, YOUR STUPIDITY ASTOUNDS ME.
HOW A DUM-DUM LIKE YOU COULD BE SO SPECIAL—
OKAY, YOU HATE ME. WE GET IT ALREADY!

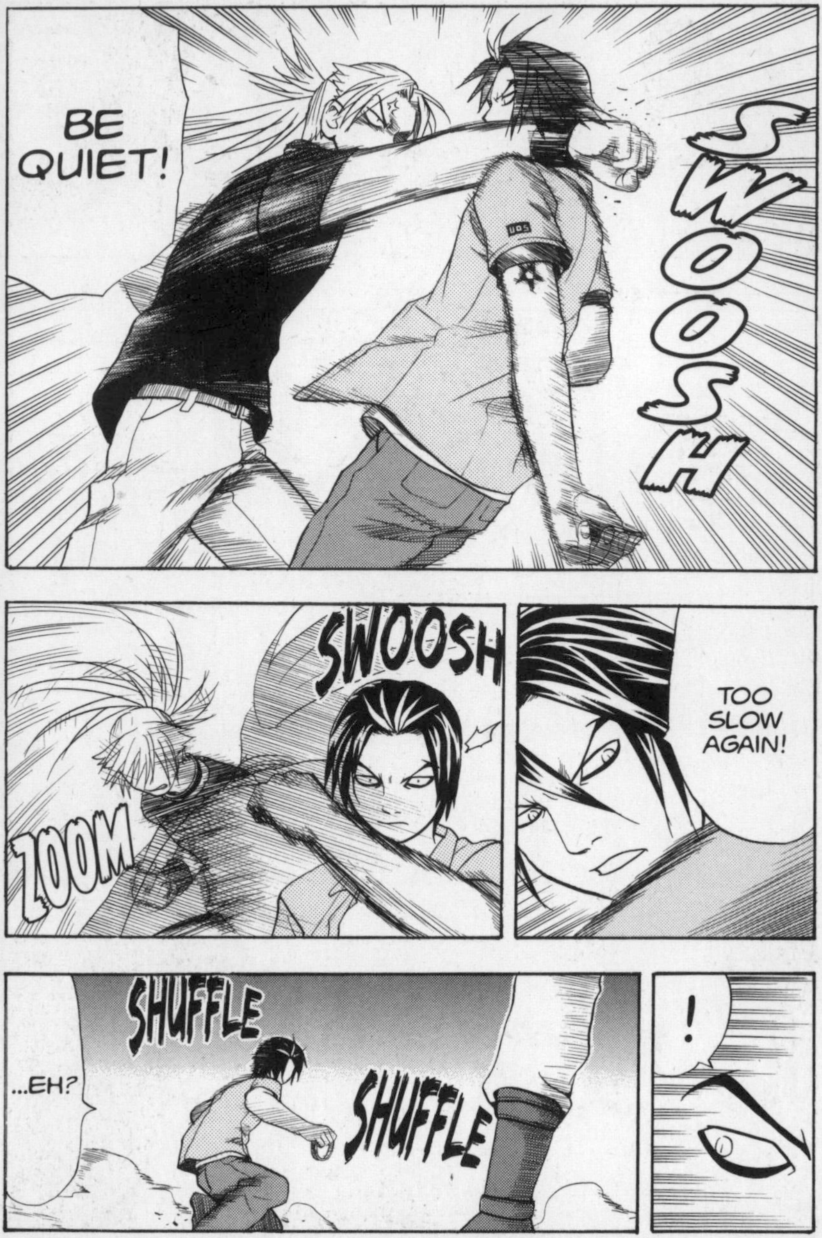
SWOOSH
BE QUIET!
TOO SLOW AGAIN!
SWOOSH
ZOOM
!
SHUFFLE
SHUFFLE
...EH?

READ THIS WAY

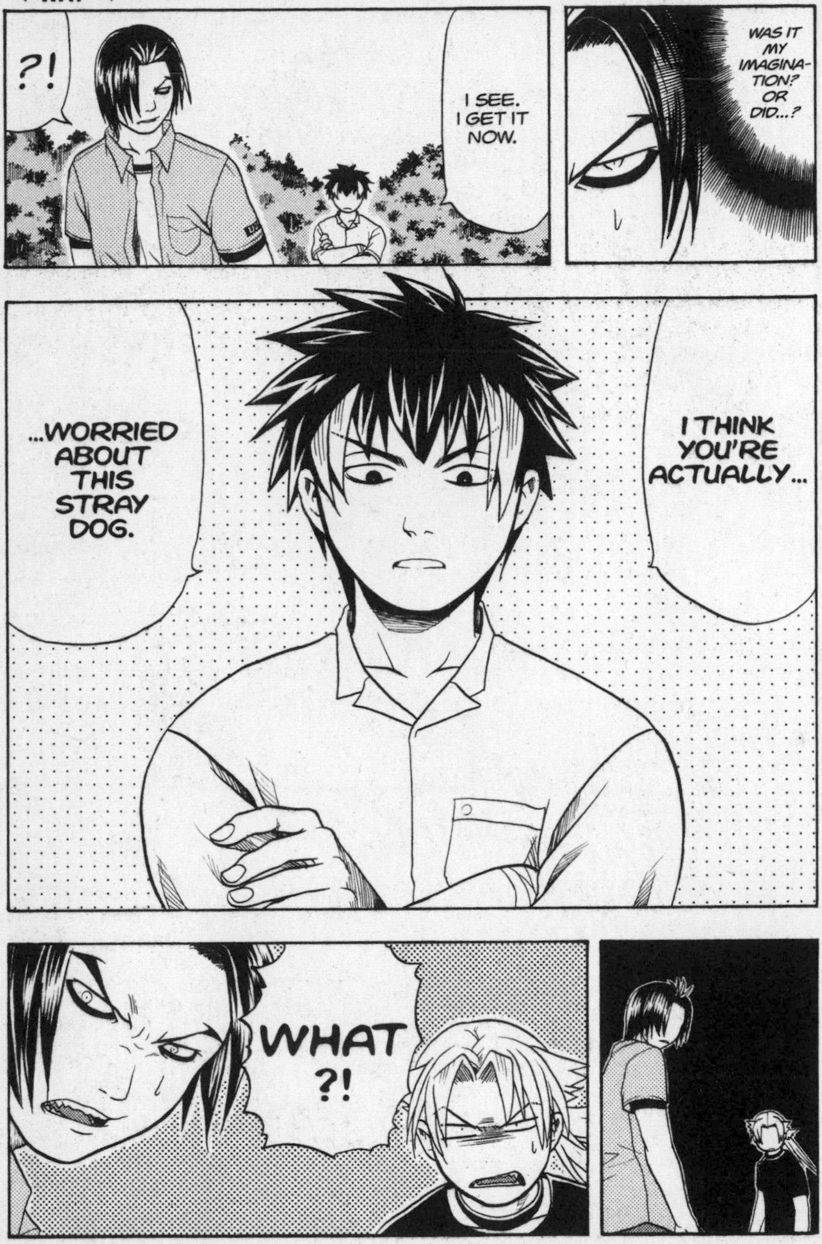
WAS IT MY IMAGINATION? OR DID...?
I SEE. I GET IT NOW.
?!
I THINK YOU'RE ACTUALLY...
...WORRIED ABOUT THIS STRAY DOG.
WHAT ?!

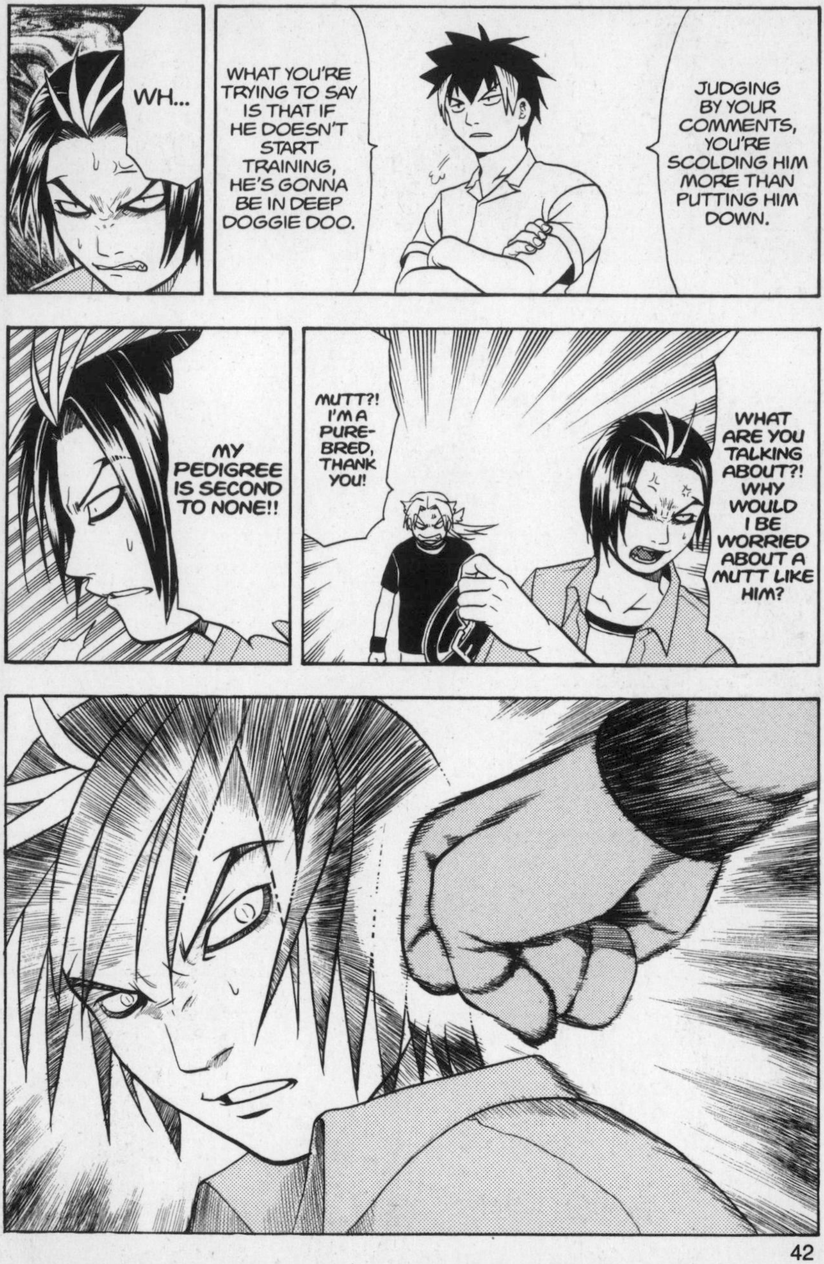
JUDGING BY YOUR COMMENTS, YOU'RE SCOLDING HIM MORE THAN PUTTING HIM DOWN.
WHAT YOU'RE TRYING TO SAY IS THAT IF HE DOESN'T START TRAINING, HE'S GONNA BE IN DEEP DOGGIE DOO.
WH...
WHAT ARE YOU TALKING ABOUT?! WHY WOULD I BE WORRIED ABOUT A MUTT LIKE HIM?
MUTT?! I'M A PUREBRED, THANK YOU!
MY PEDIGREE IS SECOND TO NONE!!

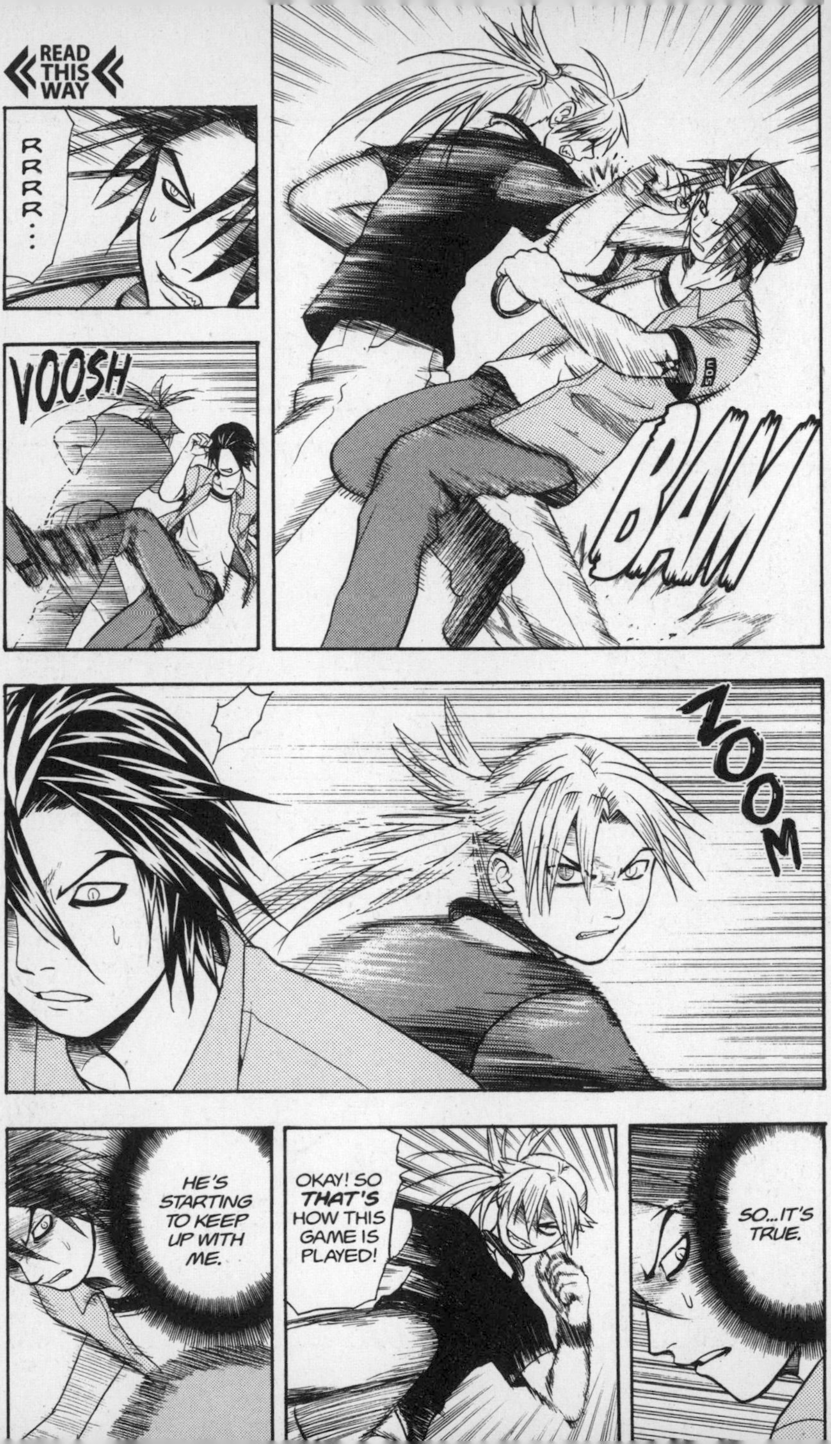
READ THIS WAY
BAM
RRRR...
VOOSH
ZOOM
SO...IT'S TRUE.
OKAY! SO THAT'S HOW THIS GAME IS PLAYED!
HE'S STARTING TO KEEP UP WITH ME.

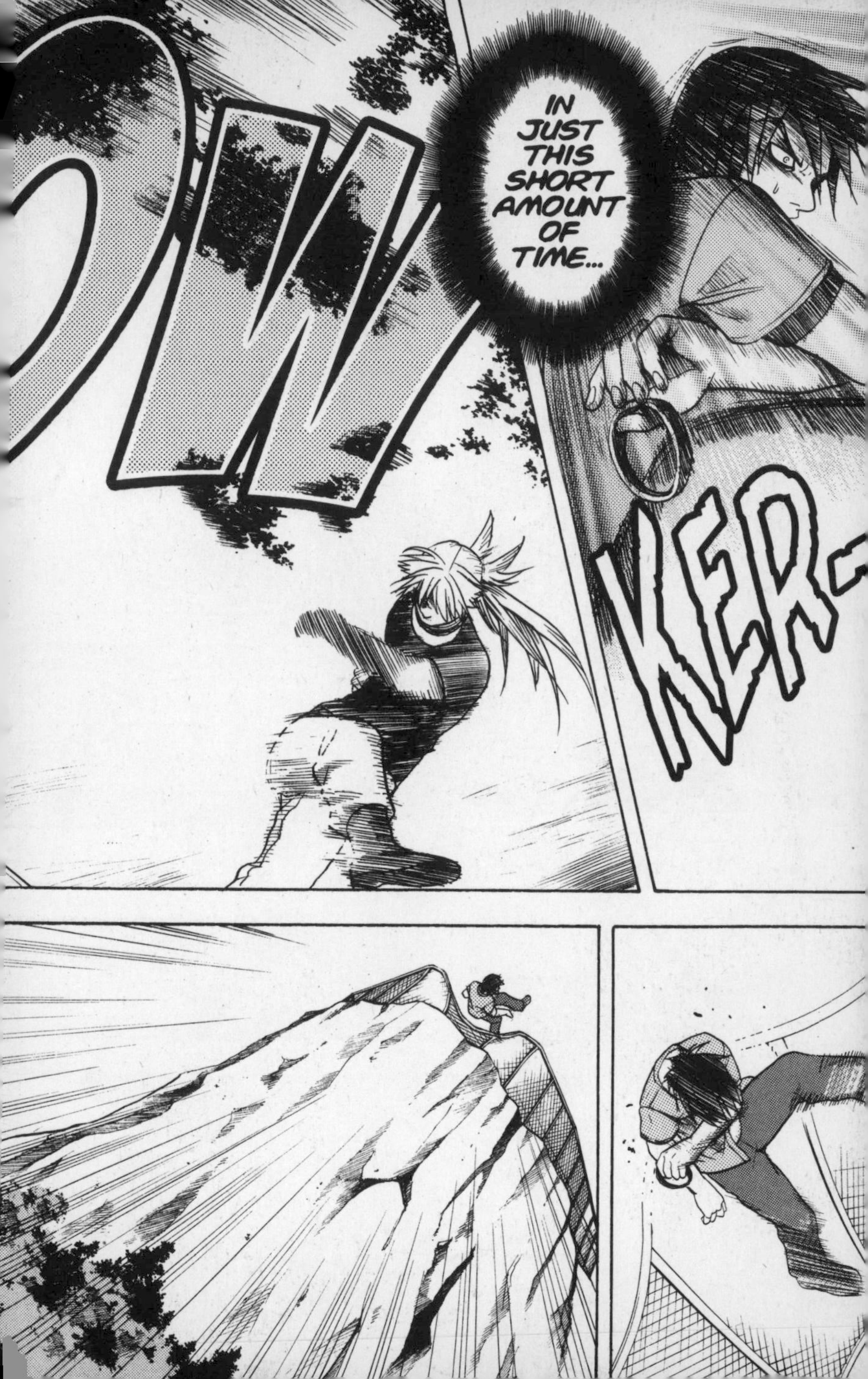
IN JUST THIS SHORT AMOUNT OF TIME...
KER-
OW

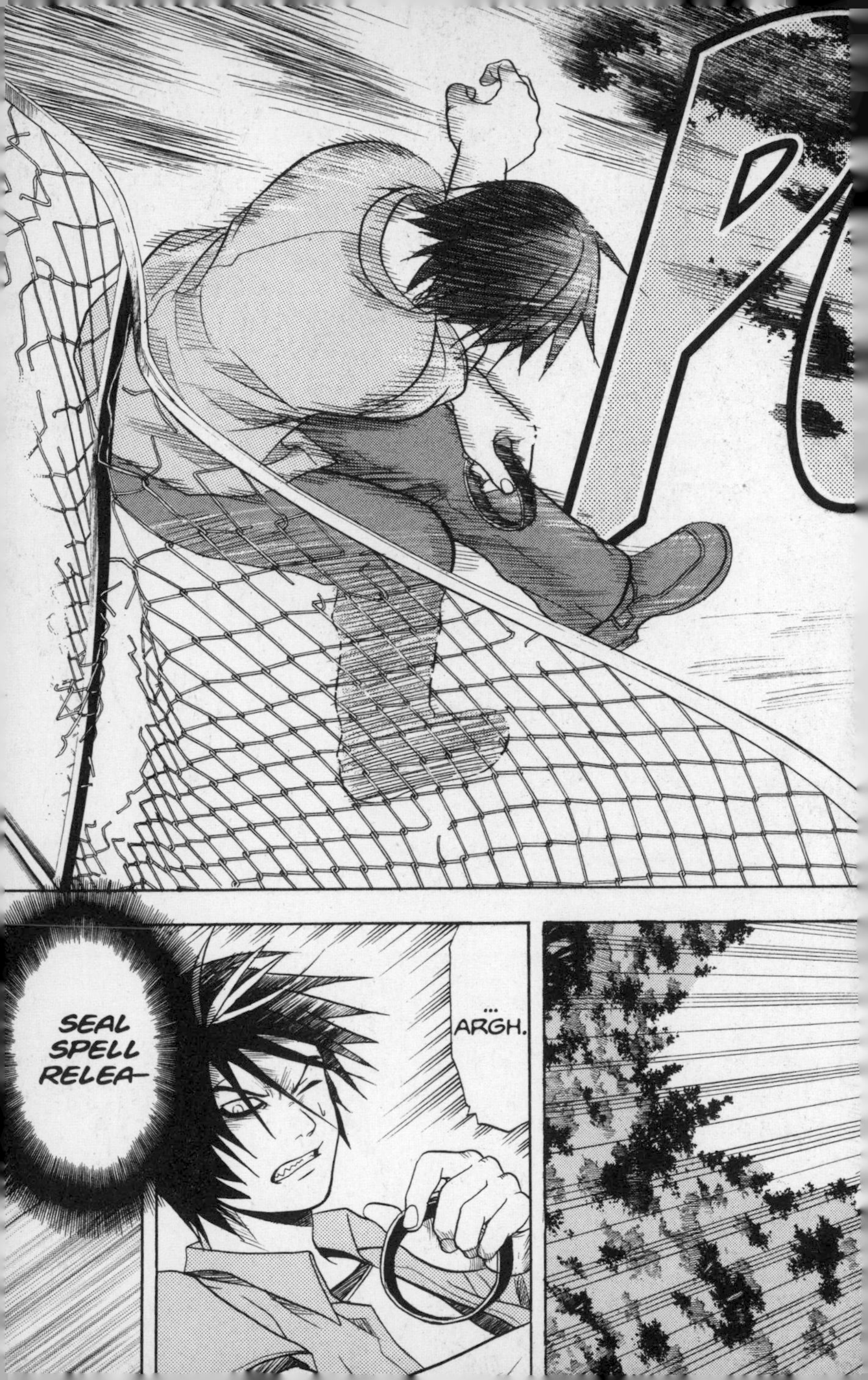
SEAL SPELL RELEA—
...ARGH.

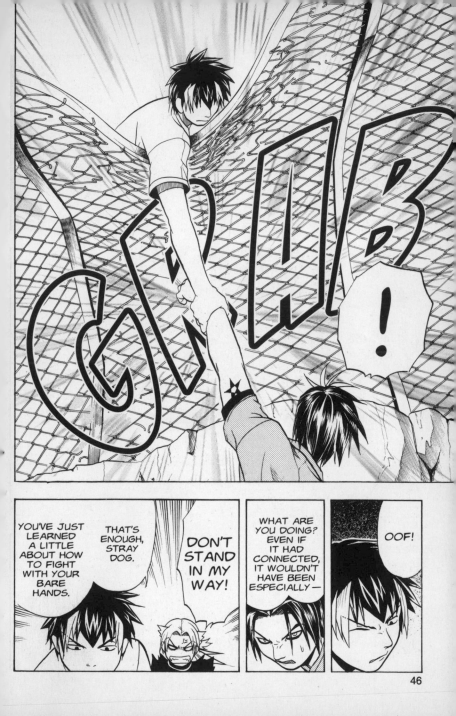

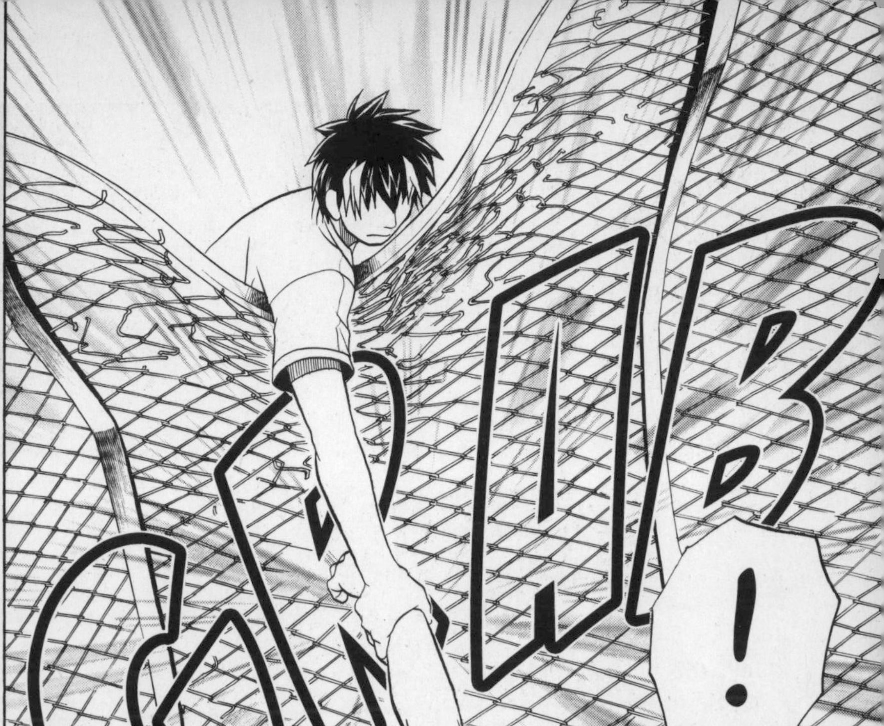
GRAB
!
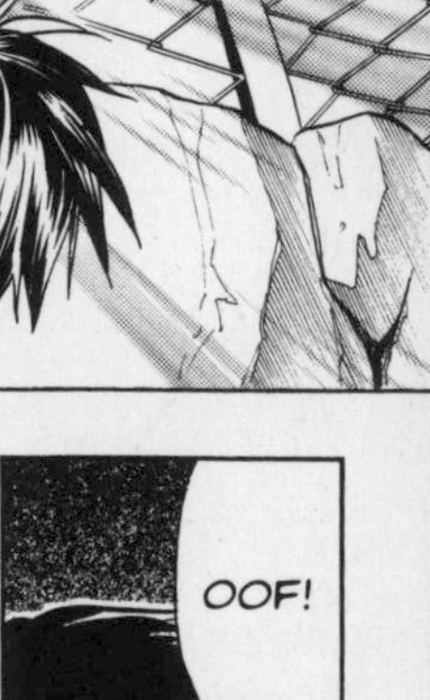
OOF!
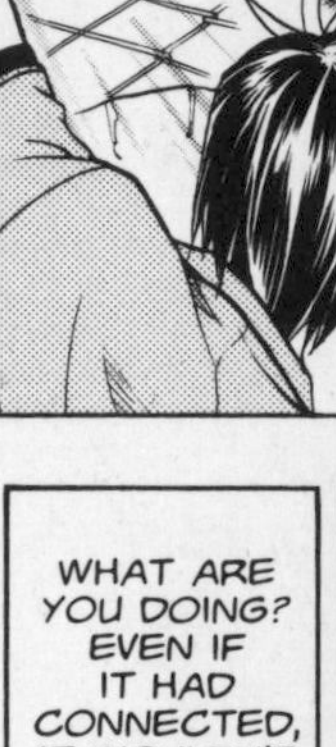
WHAT ARE YOU DOING? EVEN IF IT HAD CONNECTED, IT WOULDN'T HAVE BEEN ESPECIALLY—
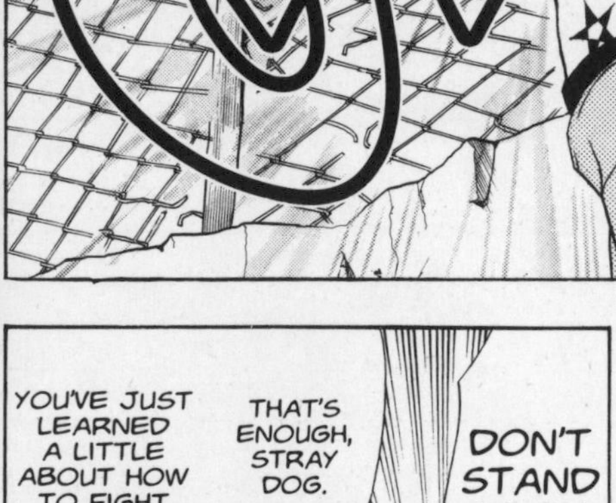
THAT'S ENOUGH, STRAY DOG.
YOU'VE JUST LEARNED A LITTLE ABOUT HOW TO FIGHT WITH YOUR BARE HANDS.
DON'T STAND IN MY WAY!

READ THIS WAY

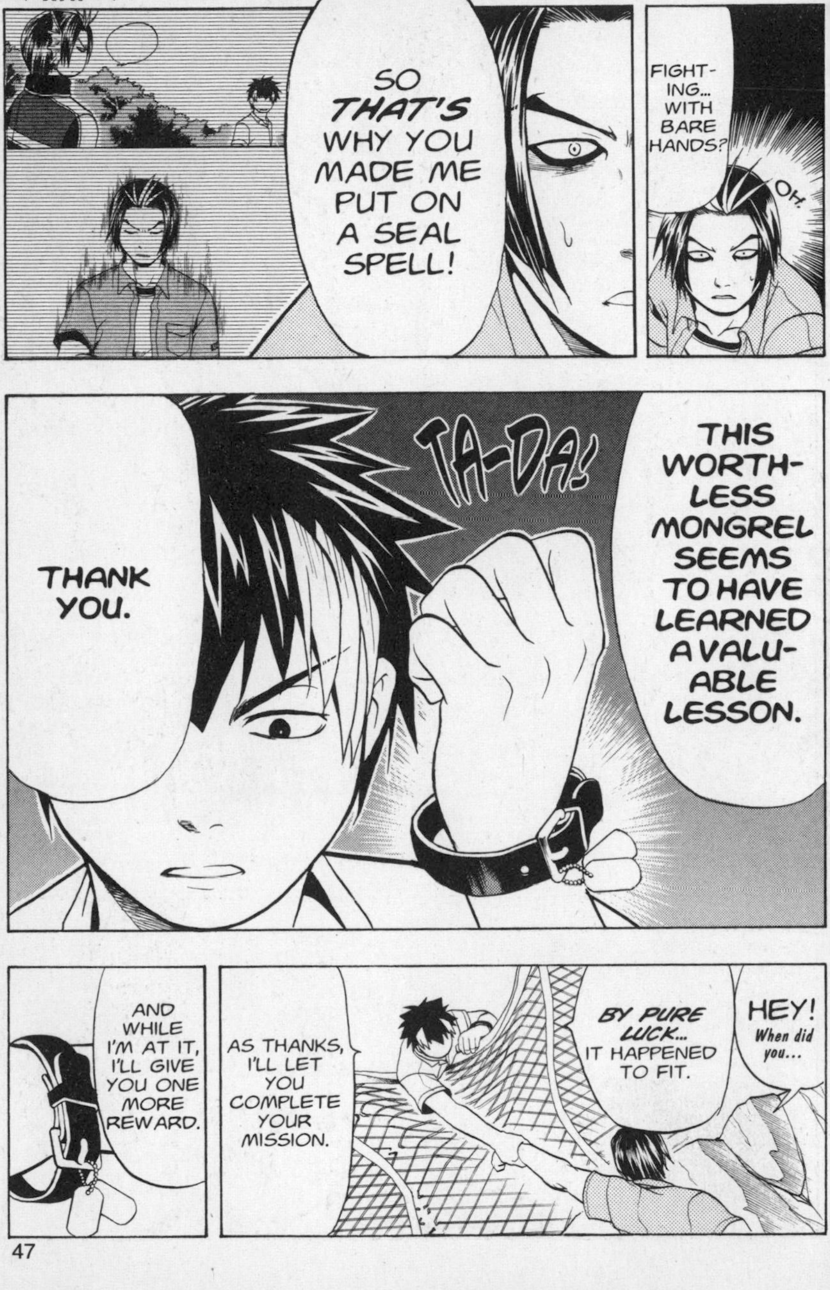

FIGHT-ING... WITH BARE HANDS?
OH.
SO *THAT'S* WHY YOU MADE ME PUT ON A SEAL SPELL!
THIS WORTH-LESS MONGREL SEEMS TO HAVE LEARNED A VALU-ABLE LESSON.
TA-DA!
THANK YOU.
HEY! When did you...
BY PURE LUCK... IT HAPPENED TO FIT.
AS THANKS, I'LL LET YOU COMPLETE YOUR MISSION.
AND WHILE I'M AT IT, I'LL GIVE YOU ONE MORE REWARD.

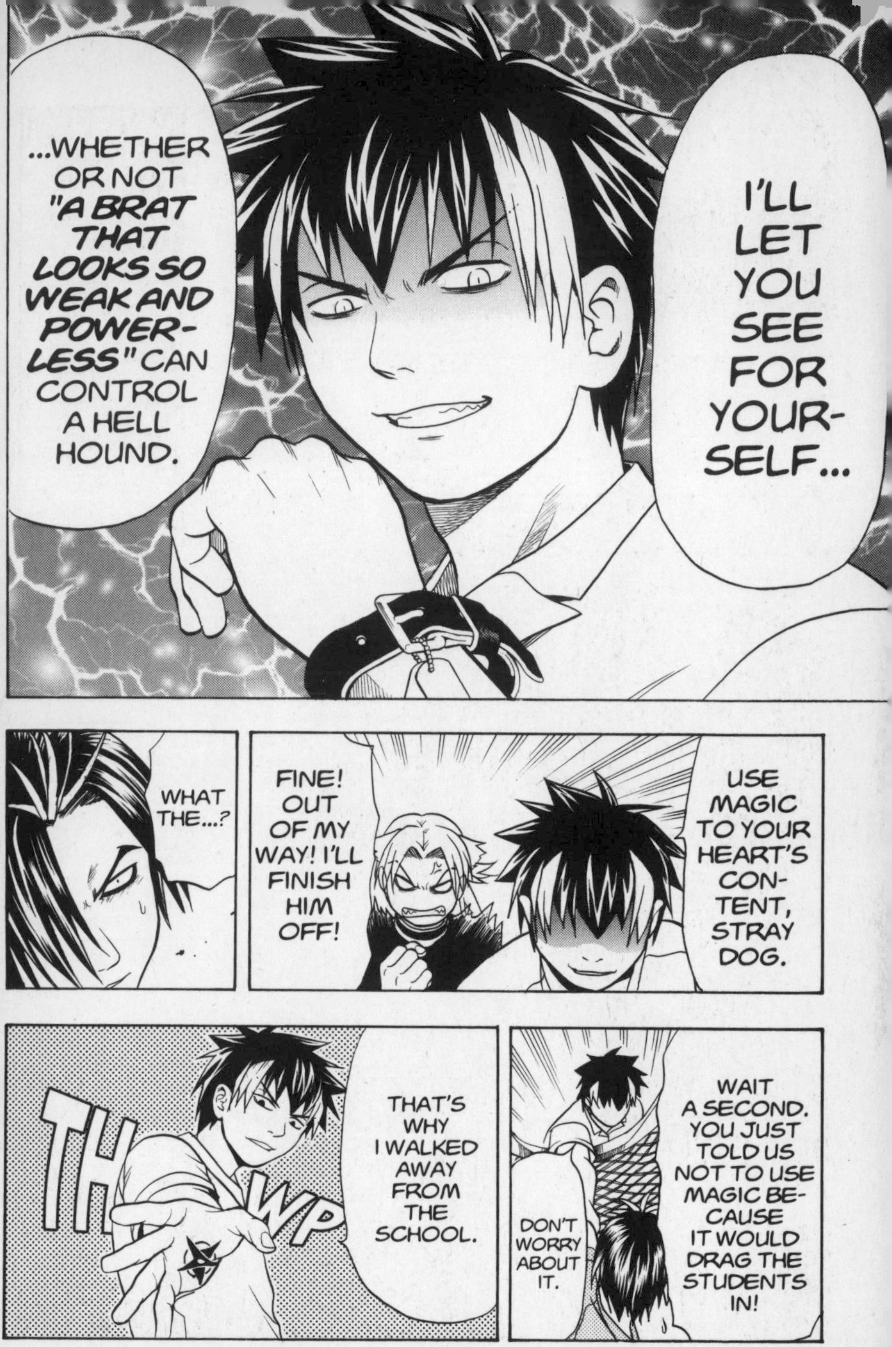
I'LL LET YOU SEE FOR YOURSELF...
...WHETHER OR NOT "A BRAT THAT LOOKS SO WEAK AND POWERLESS" CAN CONTROL A HELL HOUND.
USE MAGIC TO YOUR HEART'S CONTENT, STRAY DOG.
FINE! OUT OF MY WAY! I'LL FINISH HIM OFF!
WHAT THE...?
WAIT A SECOND. YOU JUST TOLD US NOT TO USE MAGIC BECAUSE IT WOULD DRAG THE STUDENTS IN!
DON'T WORRY ABOUT IT.
THAT'S WHY I WALKED AWAY FROM THE SCHOOL.
THWP

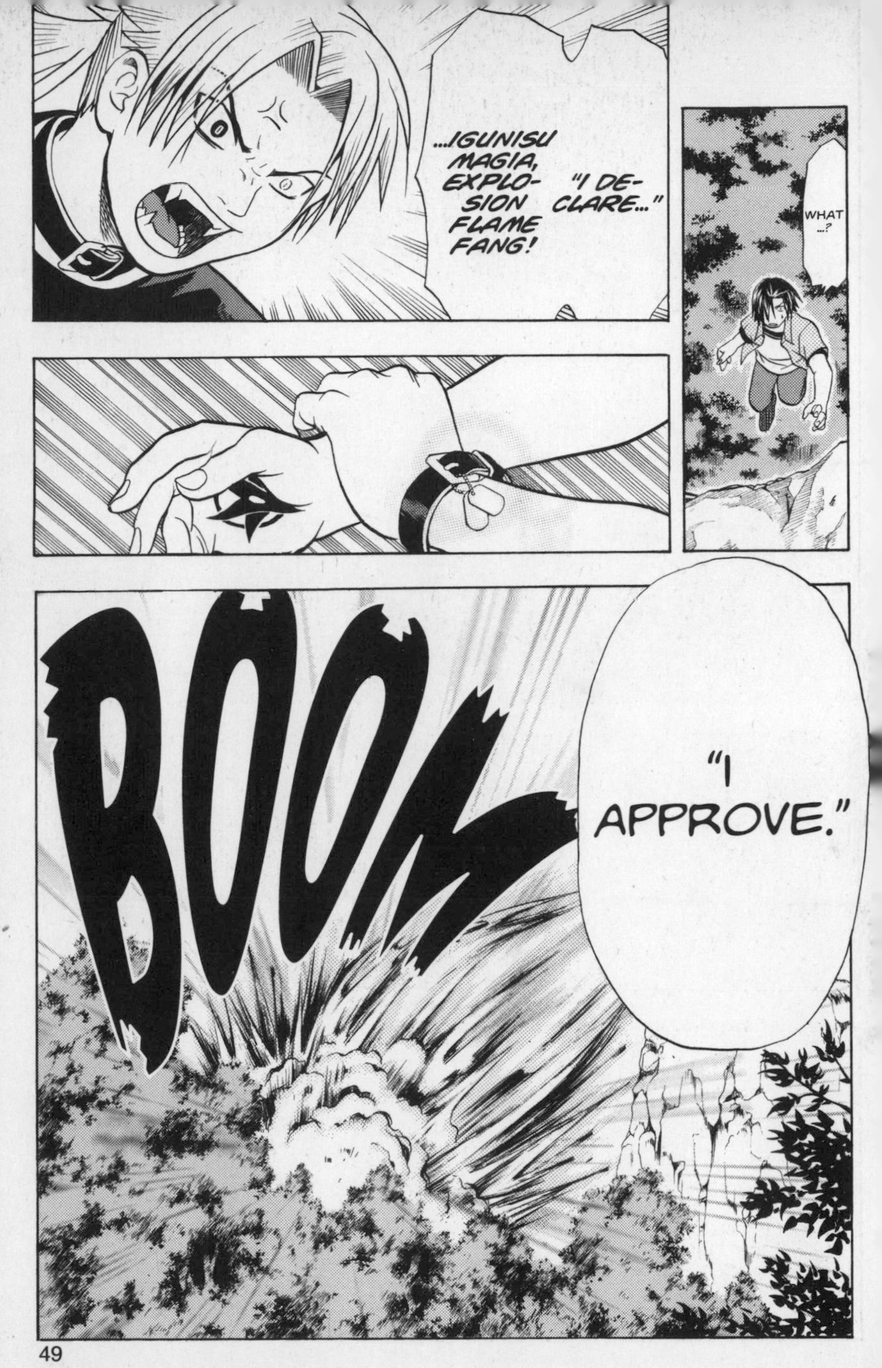
WHAT ...?
"I DE-CLARE..."
...IGUNISU MAGIA, EXPLO-SION FLAME FANG!
"I APPROVE."
BOOM

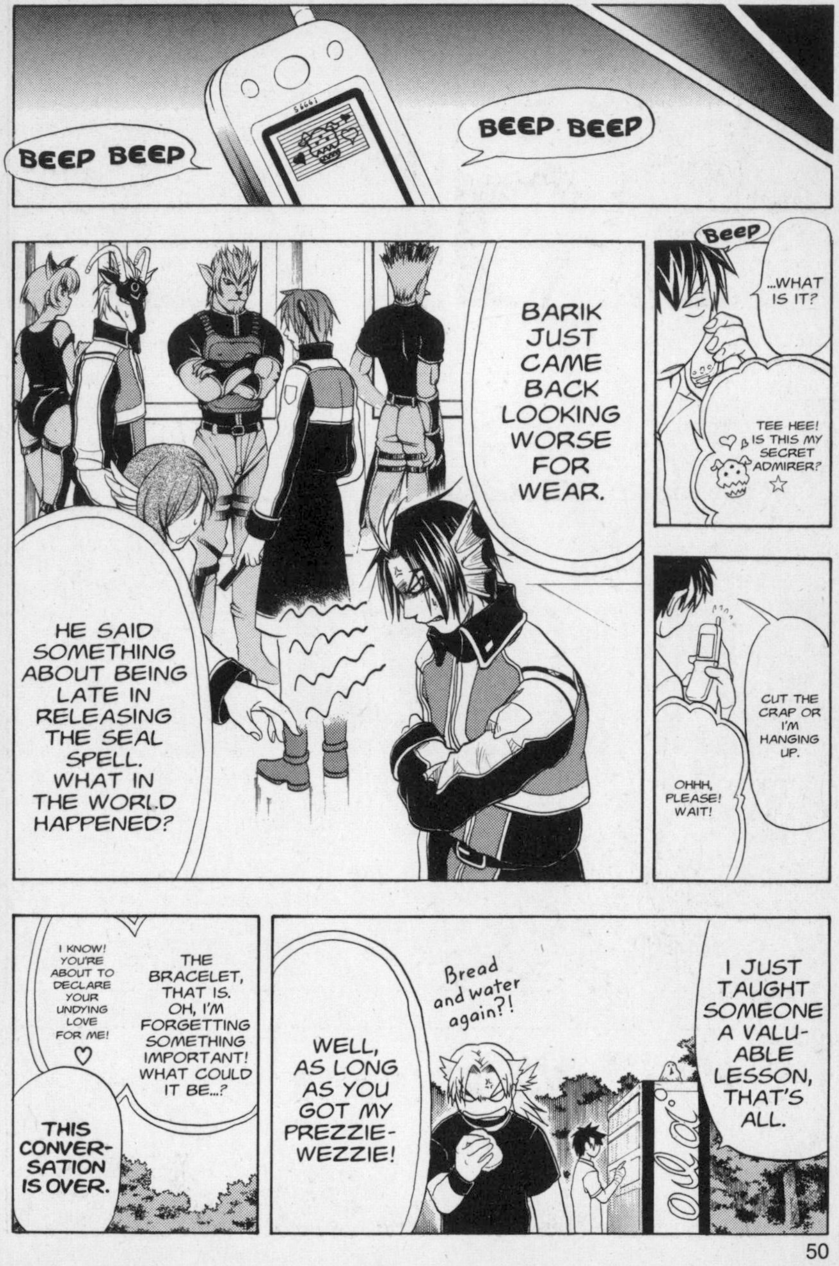
BEEP BEEP
BEEP BEEP
Beep
...WHAT IS IT?
TEE HEE! IS THIS MY SECRET ADMIRER?
CUT THE CRAP OR I'M HANGING UP.
OHHH, PLEASE! WAIT!
BARIK JUST CAME BACK LOOKING WORSE FOR WEAR.
HE SAID SOMETHING ABOUT BEING LATE IN RELEASING THE SEAL SPELL. WHAT IN THE WORLD HAPPENED?
I JUST TAUGHT SOMEONE A VALUABLE LESSON, THAT'S ALL.
Bread and water again?!
WELL, AS LONG AS YOU GOT MY PREZZIE-WEZZIE!
THE BRACELET, THAT IS. OH, I'M FORGETTING SOMETHING IMPORTANT! WHAT COULD IT BE...?
I KNOW! YOU'RE ABOUT TO DECLARE YOUR UNDYING LOVE FOR ME! ♡
THIS CONVERSATION IS OVER.

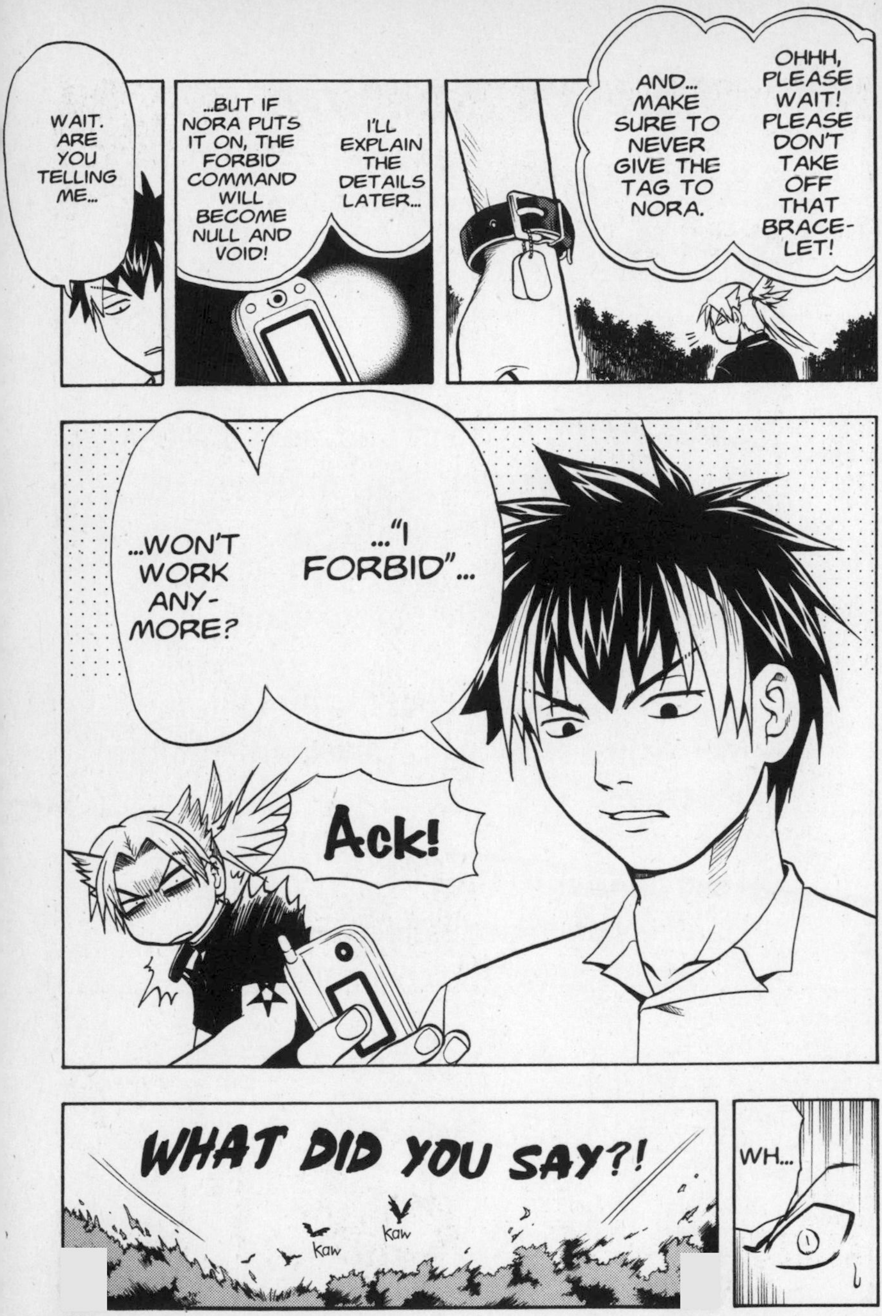
OHHH, PLEASE WAIT! PLEASE DON'T TAKE OFF THAT BRACELET!
AND... MAKE SURE TO NEVER GIVE THE TAG TO NORA.
I'LL EXPLAIN THE DETAILS LATER...
...BUT IF NORA PUTS IT ON, THE FORBID COMMAND WILL BECOME NULL AND VOID!
WAIT. ARE YOU TELLING ME...
..."I FORBID"...
...WON'T WORK ANYMORE?
Ack!
WH...
WHAT DID YOU SAY?!
Kaw
Kaw

Letter Section

Q & A

Q: How old is Nora? –Y from Hokkaido
A: Roughly speaking, I draw him as if he's about 16 years old.

Q: Since Nora was at a pound, does it mean he was abandoned? –S from Tokyo city
A: Ah…that would be telling.

Q: Does Mr. Kakei really eat tuna and octopus raw?
–Pen name: Hanru of Chiba Prefecture
A: Mainly just salmon now. I've had enough of octopi.

Q: I can't find the Dark Liege in Volume 1! Help! –N of Ehime Prefecture
A: Please turn over the cover and look!

We Love Hearing From You!

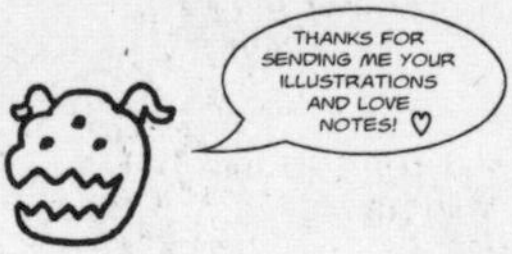
THANKS FOR SENDING ME YOUR ILLUSTRATIONS AND LOVE NOTES! ♡

Write to:
Kazunari Kakei
c/o NORA Editor, VIZ Media
P.O. Box 77010
SAN FRANCISCO, CA
94107

Story 6: The Pride in Your Heart

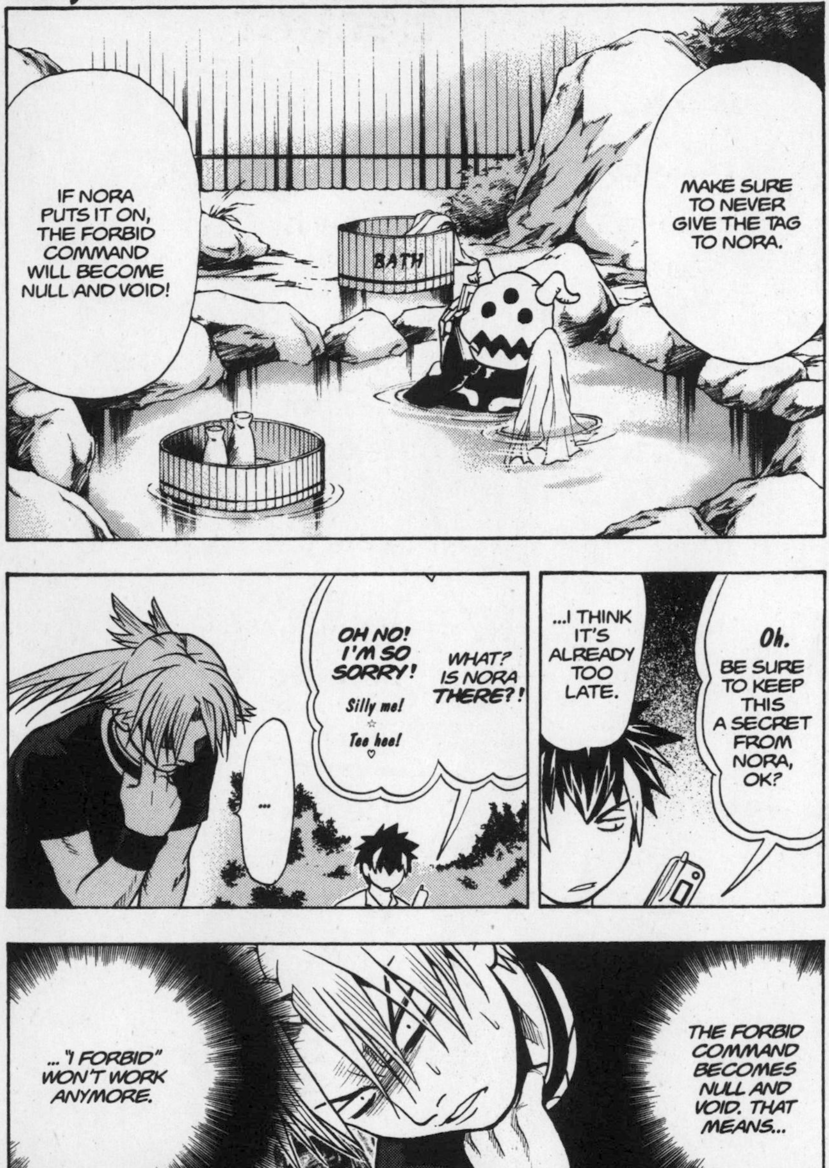
MAKE SURE TO NEVER GIVE THE TAG TO NORA.
BATH
IF NORA PUTS IT ON, THE FORBID COMMAND WILL BECOME NULL AND VOID!
Oh. BE SURE TO KEEP THIS A SECRET FROM NORA, OK?
...I THINK IT'S ALREADY TOO LATE.
WHAT? IS NORA THERE?!
OH NO! I'M SO SORRY! Silly me! ☆ Tee hee! ♡
...
THE FORBID COMMAND BECOMES NULL AND VOID. THAT MEANS...
..."I FORBID" WON'T WORK ANYMORE.

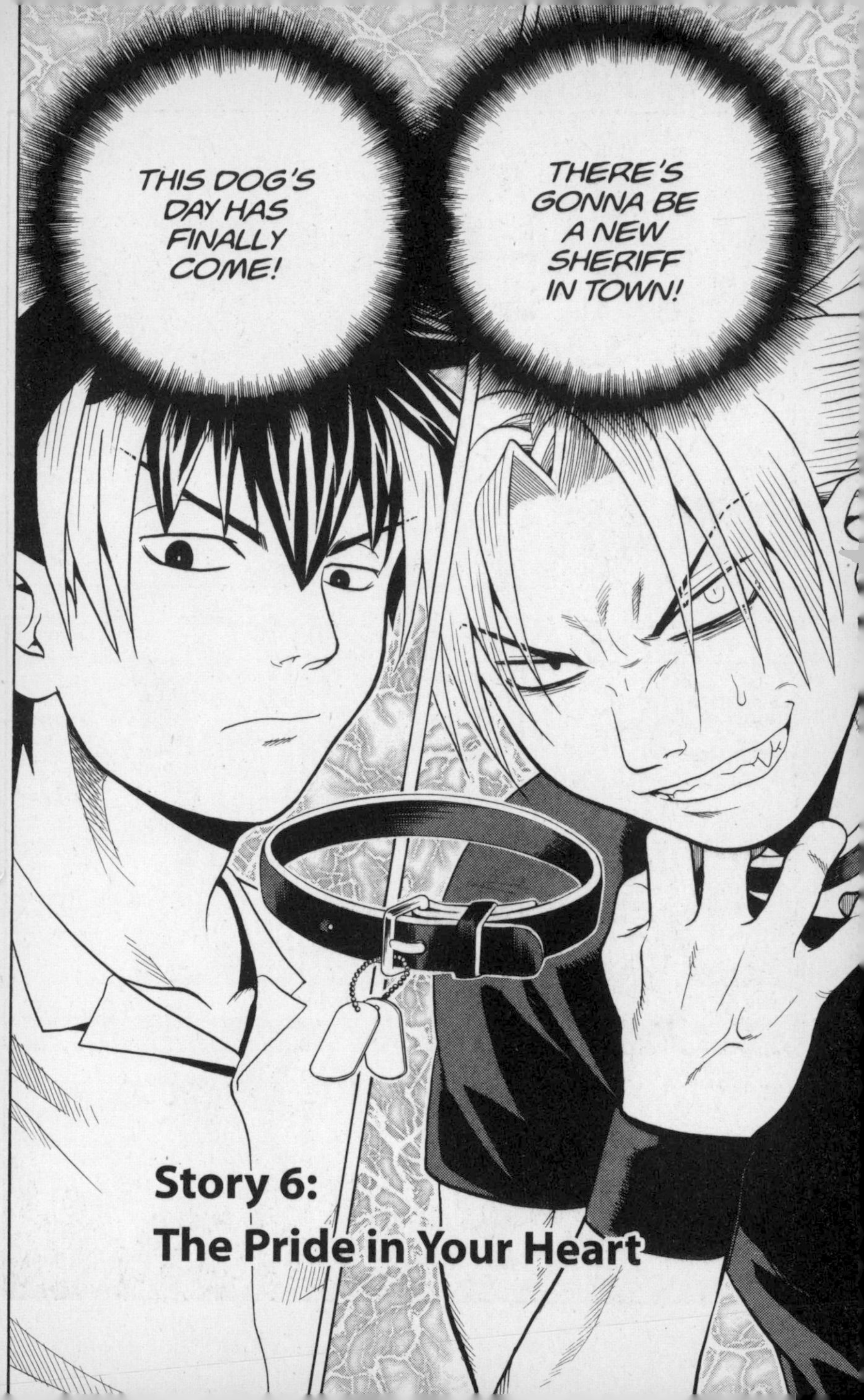
THERE'S GONNA BE A NEW SHERIFF IN TOWN!
THIS DOG'S DAY HAS FINALLY COME!
Story 6:
The Pride in Your Heart

READ THIS WAY

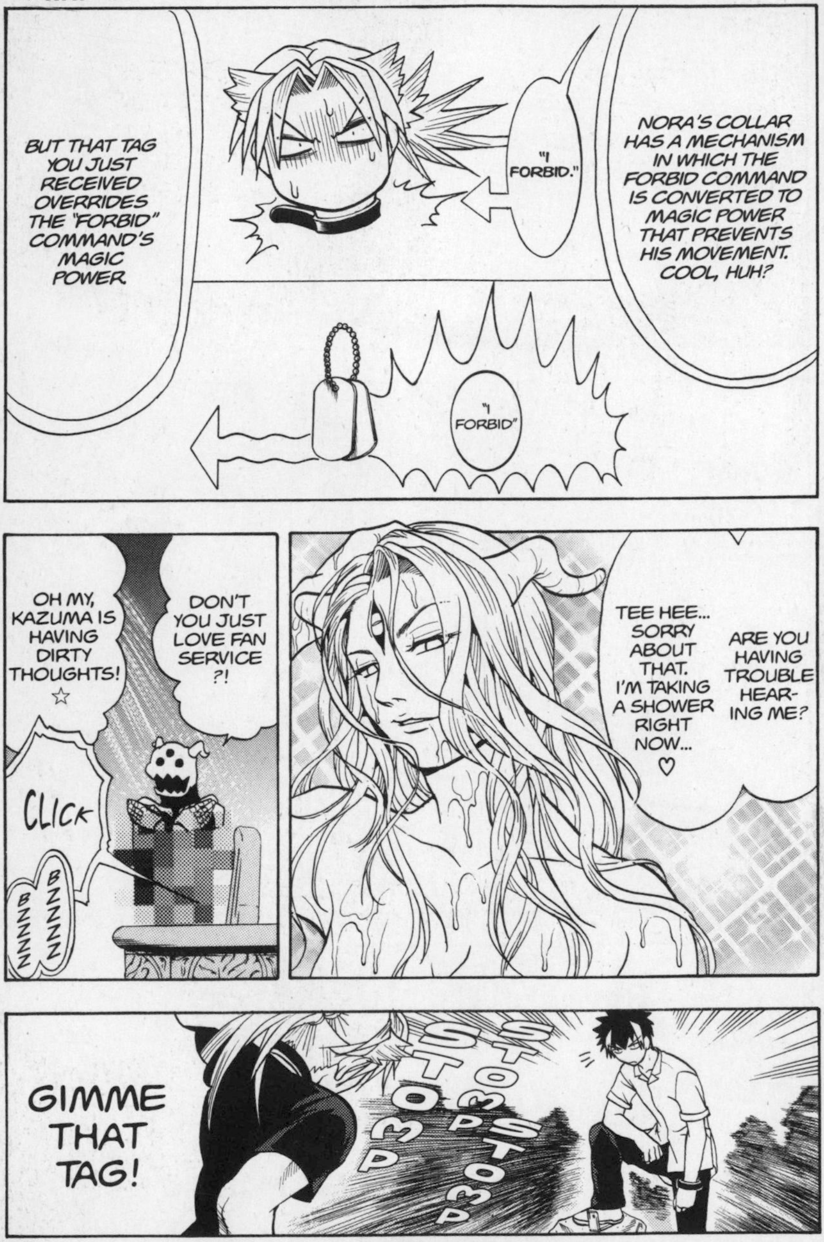
NORA'S COLLAR HAS A MECHANISM IN WHICH THE FORBID COMMAND IS CONVERTED TO MAGIC POWER THAT PREVENTS HIS MOVEMENT. COOL, HUH?
"I FORBID."
BUT THAT TAG YOU JUST RECEIVED OVERRIDES THE "FORBID" COMMAND'S MAGIC POWER.
"I FORBID"
ARE YOU HAVING TROUBLE HEARING ME?
TEE HEE... SORRY ABOUT THAT. I'M TAKING A SHOWER RIGHT NOW... ♡
DON'T YOU JUST LOVE FAN SERVICE?!
OH MY, KAZUMA IS HAVING DIRTY THOUGHTS! ☆
CLICK
BZZZZ
BZZZZ
STOMP STOMP
STOMP STOMP
GIMME THAT TAG!

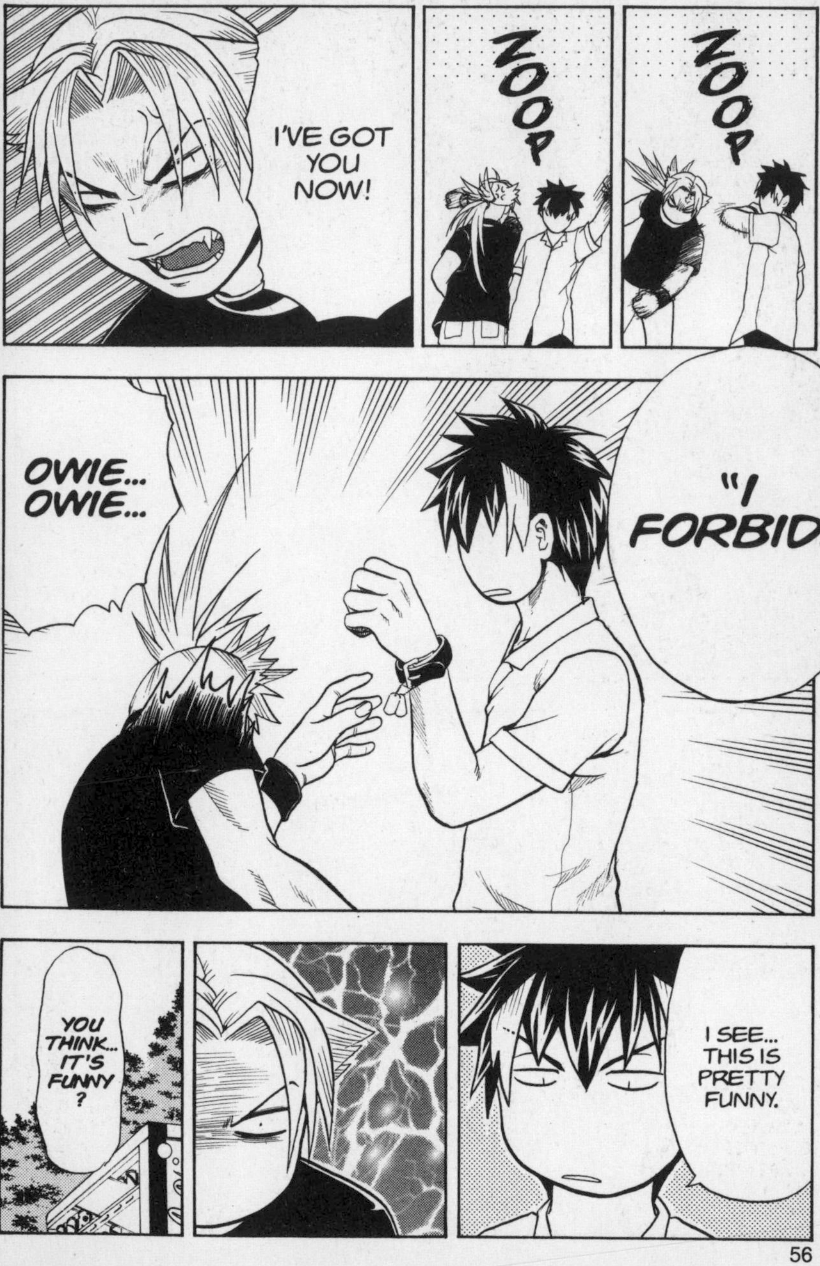
I'VE GOT YOU NOW!
ZOOP
ZOOP
OWIE... OWIE...
"I FORBID."
YOU THINK... IT'S FUNNY?
I SEE... THIS IS PRETTY FUNNY.

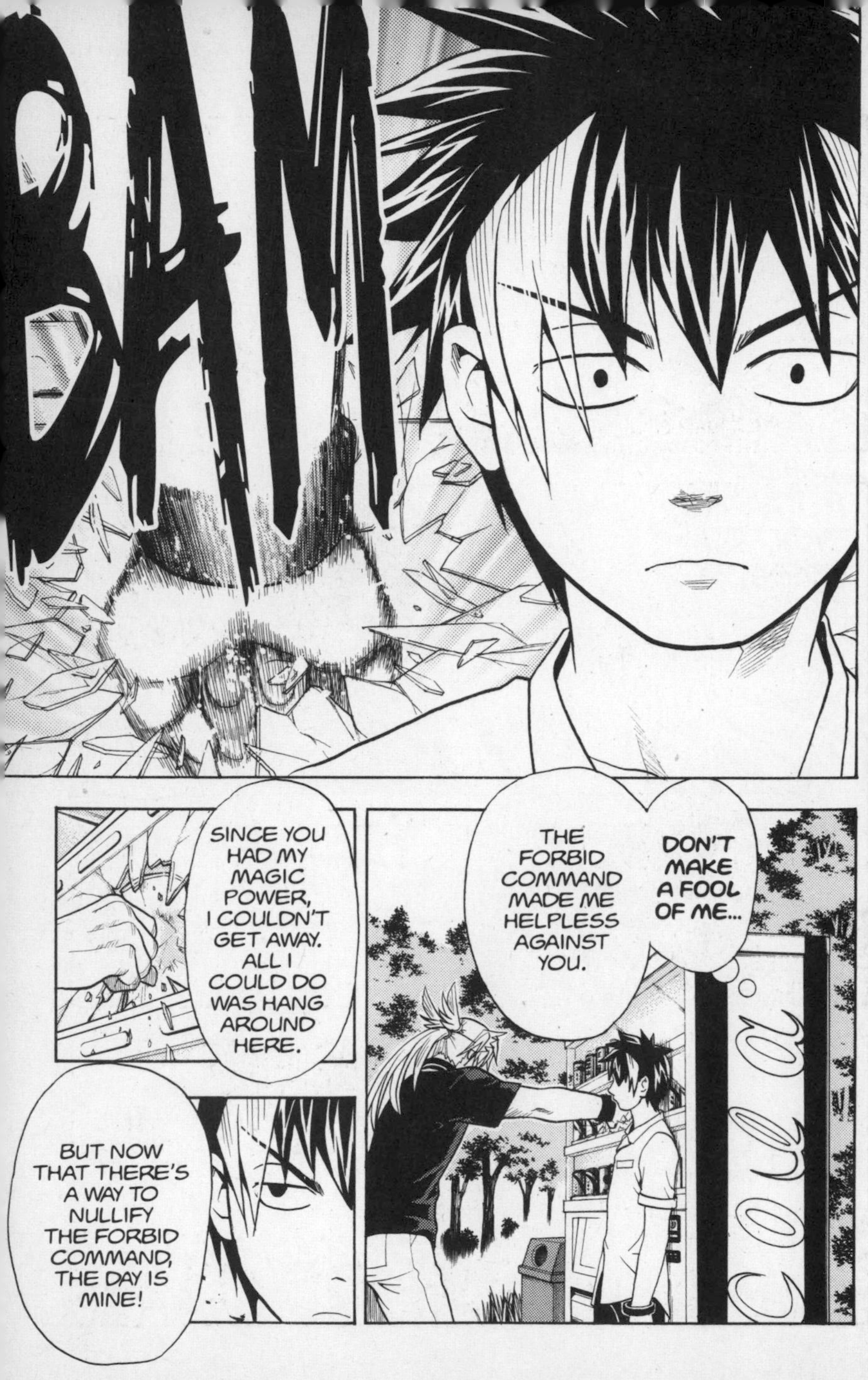
BAM
DON'T MAKE A FOOL OF ME...
THE FORBID COMMAND MADE ME HELPLESS AGAINST YOU.
SINCE YOU HAD MY MAGIC POWER, I COULDN'T GET AWAY. ALL I COULD DO WAS HANG AROUND HERE.
BUT NOW THAT THERE'S A WAY TO NULLIFY THE FORBID COMMAND, THE DAY IS MINE!

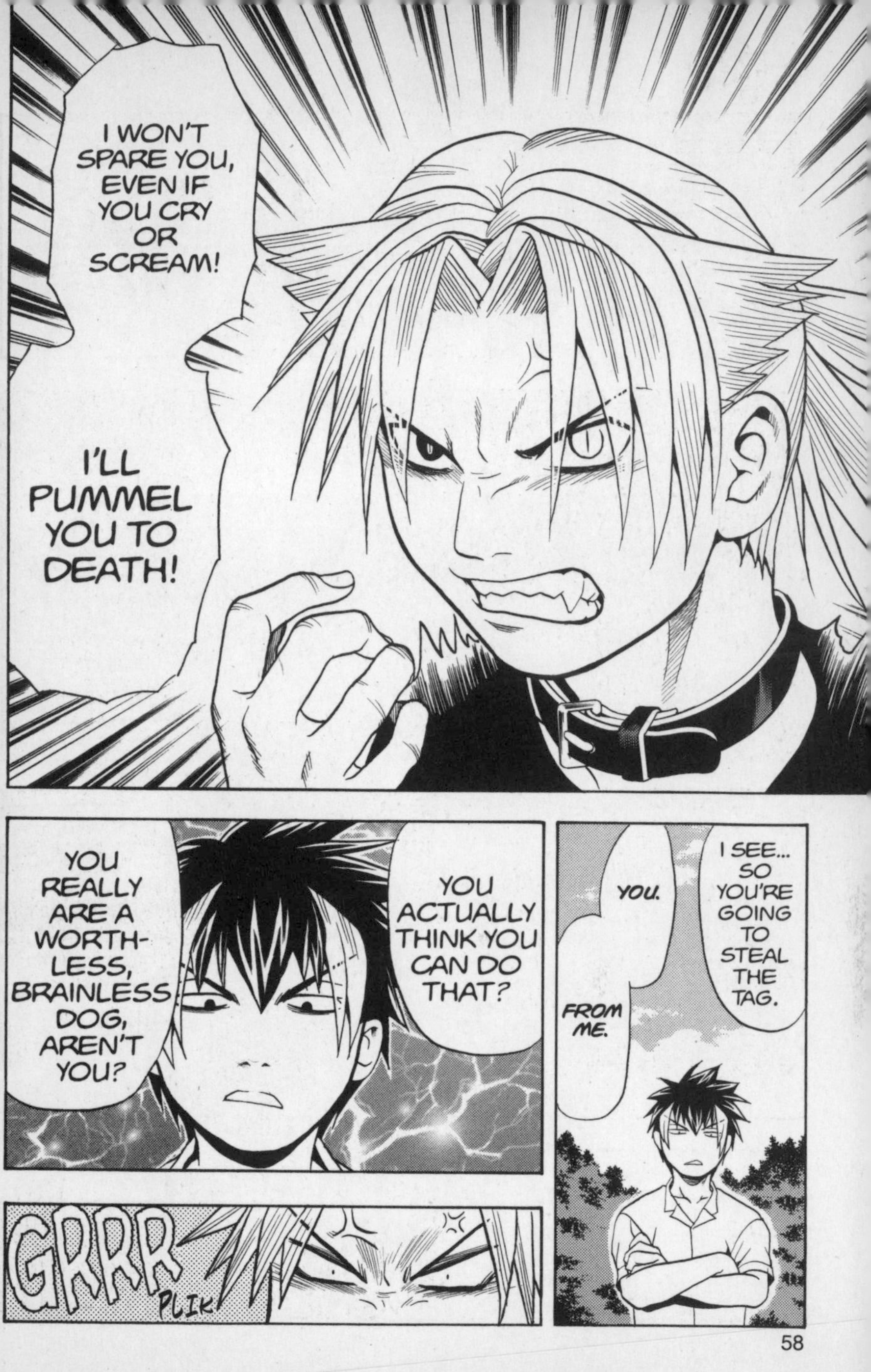
I WON'T SPARE YOU, EVEN IF YOU CRY OR SCREAM!
I'LL PUMMEL YOU TO DEATH!
I SEE... SO YOU'RE GOING TO STEAL THE TAG.
YOU.
FROM ME.
YOU ACTUALLY THINK YOU CAN DO THAT?
YOU REALLY ARE A WORTHLESS, BRAINLESS DOG, AREN'T YOU?
GRRR
PLIK

READ THIS WAY

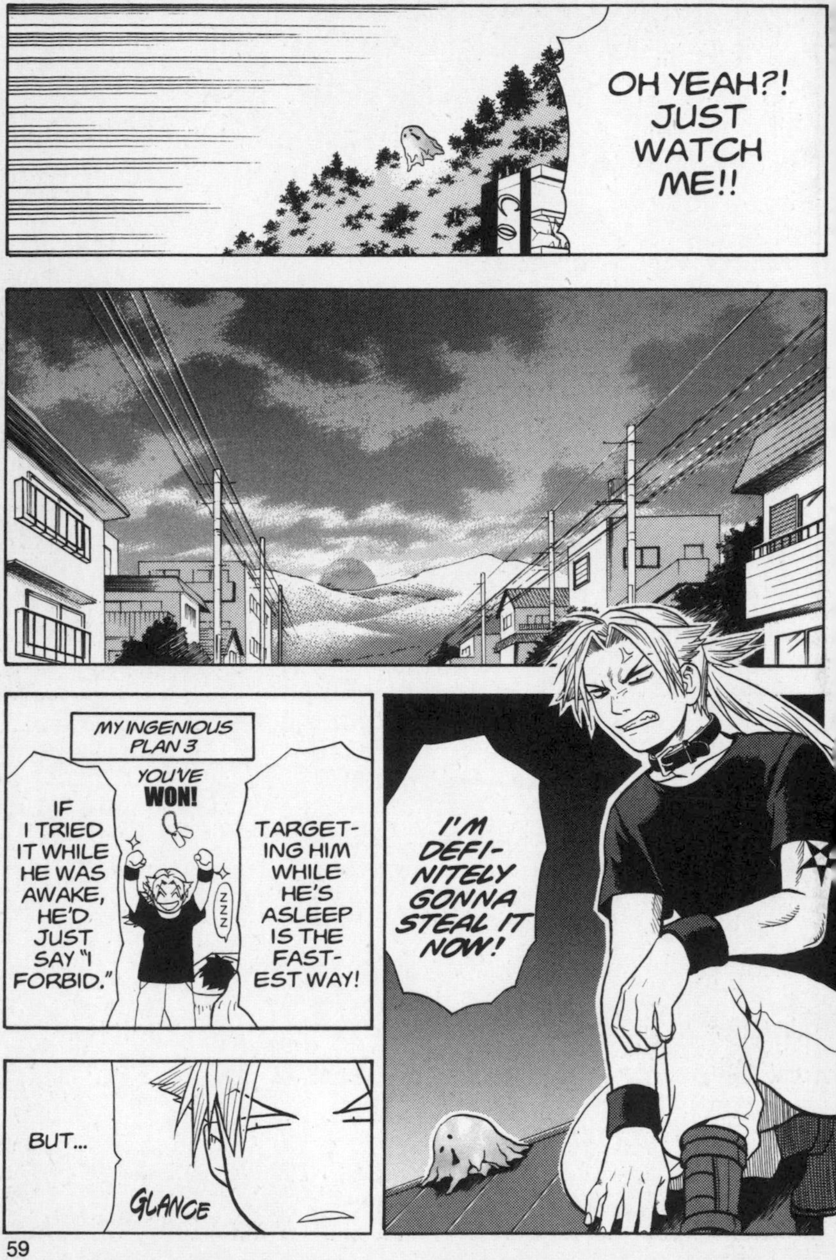
OH YEAH?! JUST WATCH ME!!
I'M DEFINITELY GONNA STEAL IT NOW!
MY INGENIOUS PLAN 3
TARGETING HIM WHILE HE'S ASLEEP IS THE FASTEST WAY!
YOU'VE WON!
ZZZ
IF I TRIED IT WHILE HE WAS AWAKE, HE'D JUST SAY "I FORBID."
BUT...
GLANCE

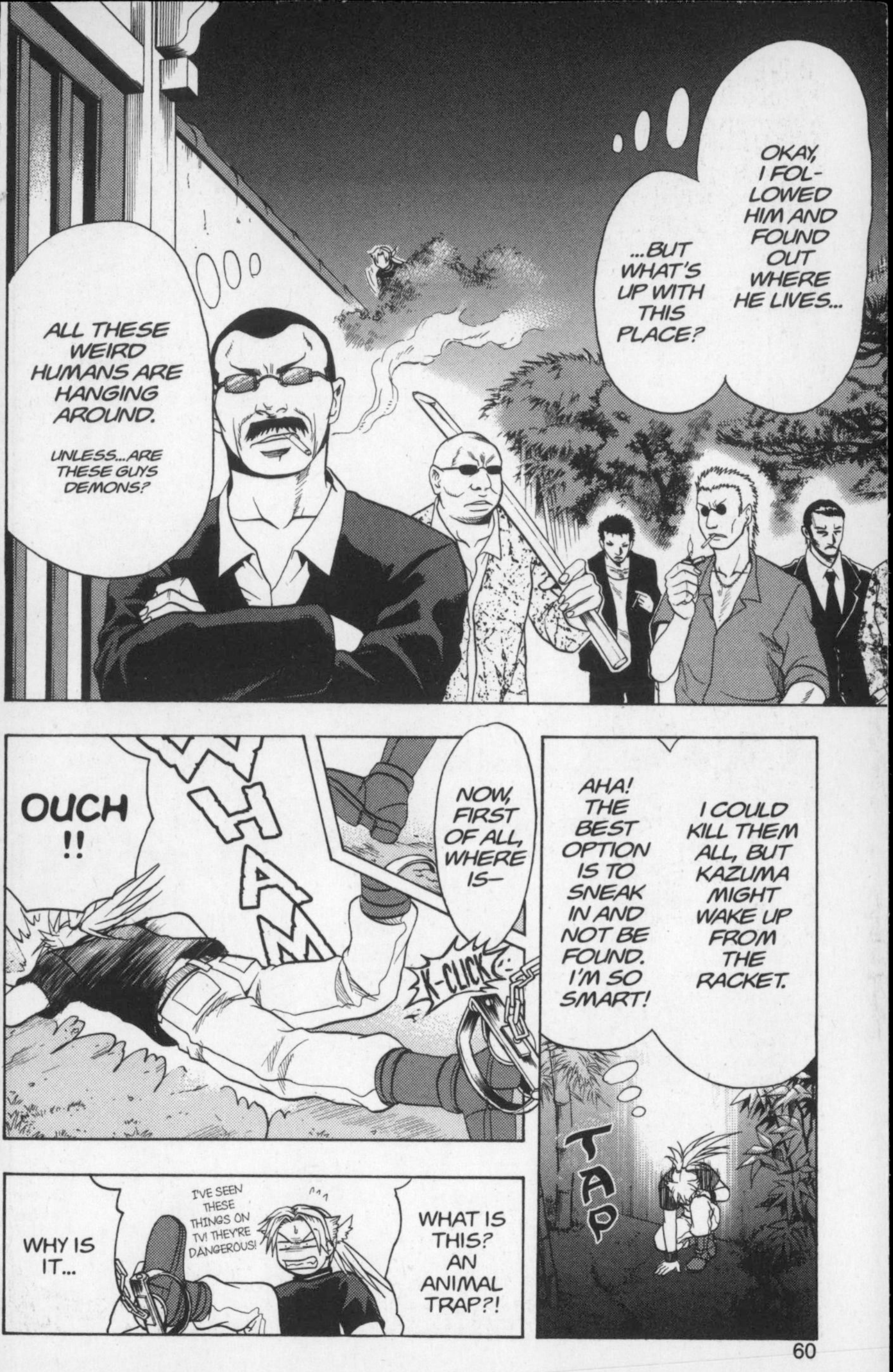
OKAY, I FOL- LOWED HIM AND FOUND OUT WHERE HE LIVES...
...BUT WHAT'S UP WITH THIS PLACE?
ALL THESE WEIRD HUMANS ARE HANGING AROUND.
UNLESS...ARE THESE GUYS DEMONS?
I COULD KILL THEM ALL, BUT KAZUMA MIGHT WAKE UP FROM THE RACKET.
AHA! THE BEST OPTION IS TO SNEAK IN AND NOT BE FOUND. I'M SO SMART!
TAP
TAP
NOW, FIRST OF ALL, WHERE IS—
K-CLICK
WHAM
OUCH !!
WHAT IS THIS? AN ANIMAL TRAP?!
I'VE SEEN THESE THINGS ON TV! THEY'RE DANGEROUS!
WHY IS IT...

READ THIS WAY

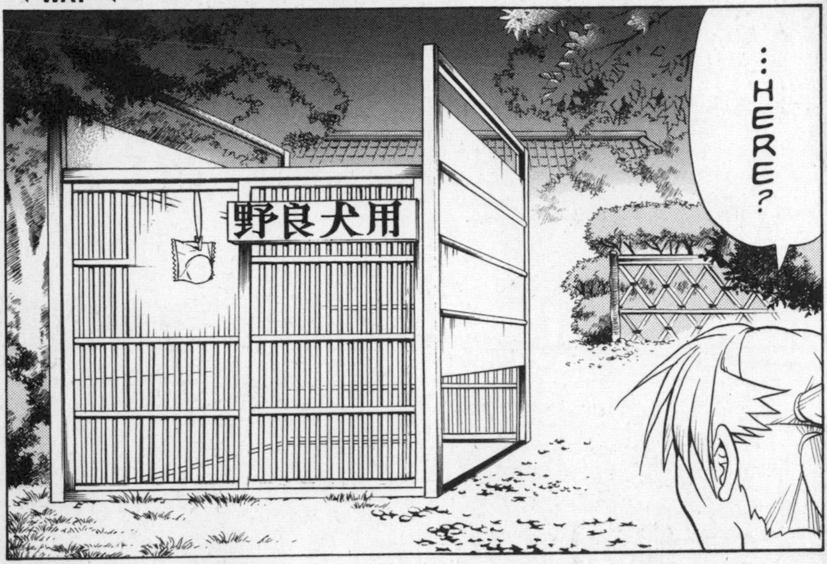
...HERE?
野良犬用

SIGN: STRAY DOG TRAP

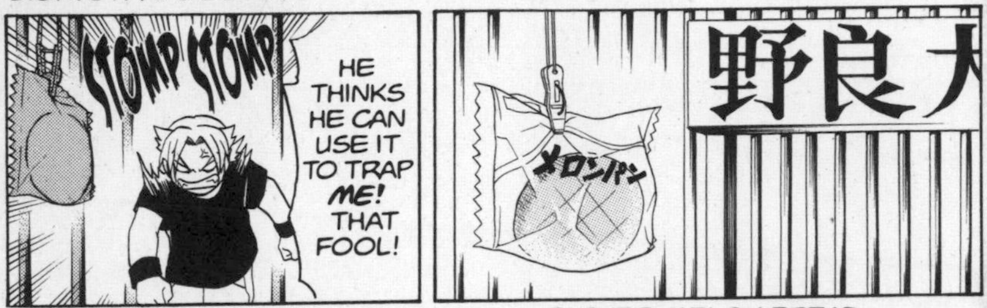
野良犬
メロンパン
HE THINKS HE CAN USE IT TO TRAP *ME!* THAT FOOL!
STOMP STOMP

PACKET: MELON BREAD

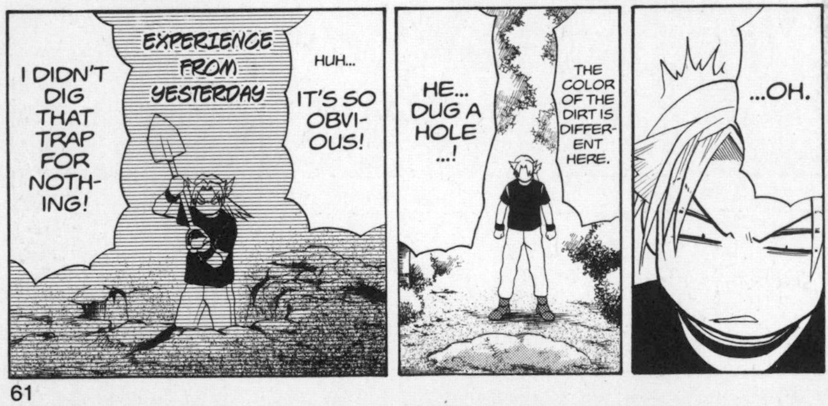
...OH.
THE COLOR OF THE DIRT IS DIFFERENT HERE.
HE... DUG A HOLE ...!
HUH... IT'S SO OBVIOUS!
EXPERIENCE FROM YESTERDAY
I DIDN'T DIG THAT TRAP FOR NOTHING!

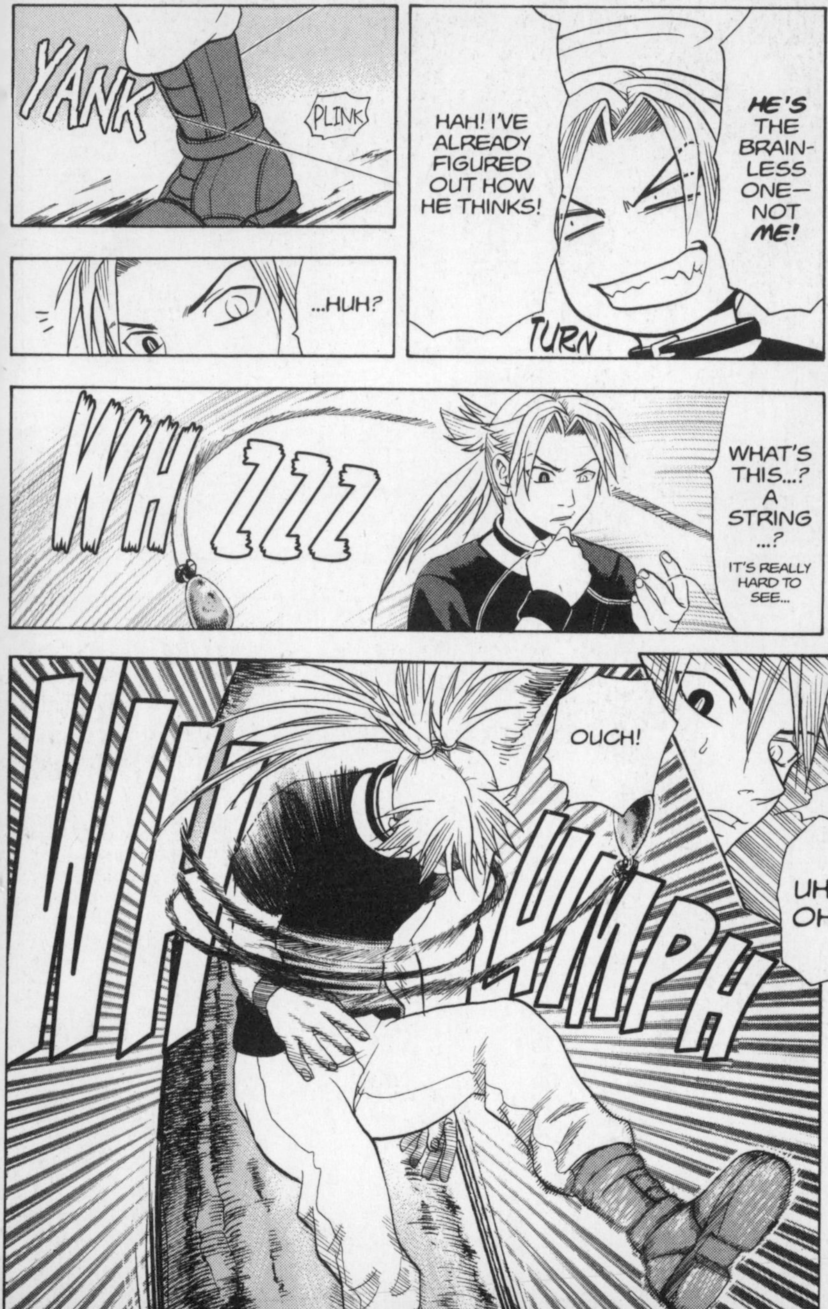
YANK
PLINK
...HUH?
HAH! I'VE ALREADY FIGURED OUT HOW HE THINKS!
HE'S THE BRAIN-LESS ONE— NOT **ME!**
TURN
WHZZZ
WHAT'S THIS...? A STRING ...?
IT'S REALLY HARD TO SEE...
WHUMPH
OUCH!
UH-OH.

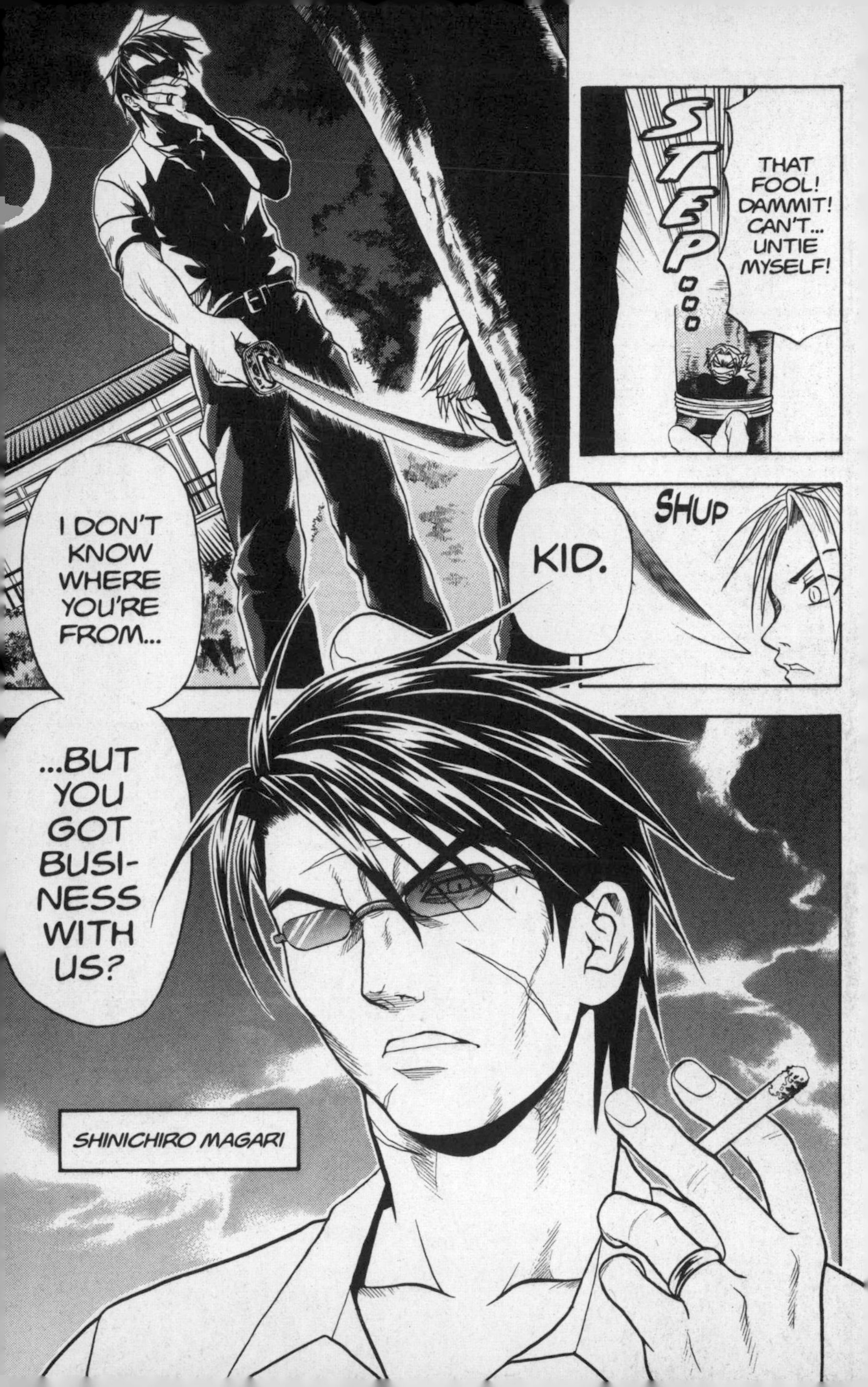
STEP...
THAT FOOL! DAMMIT! CAN'T... UNTIE MYSELF!
SHUP
KID.
I DON'T KNOW WHERE YOU'RE FROM...
...BUT YOU GOT BUSI-NESS WITH US?
SHINICHIRO MAGARI

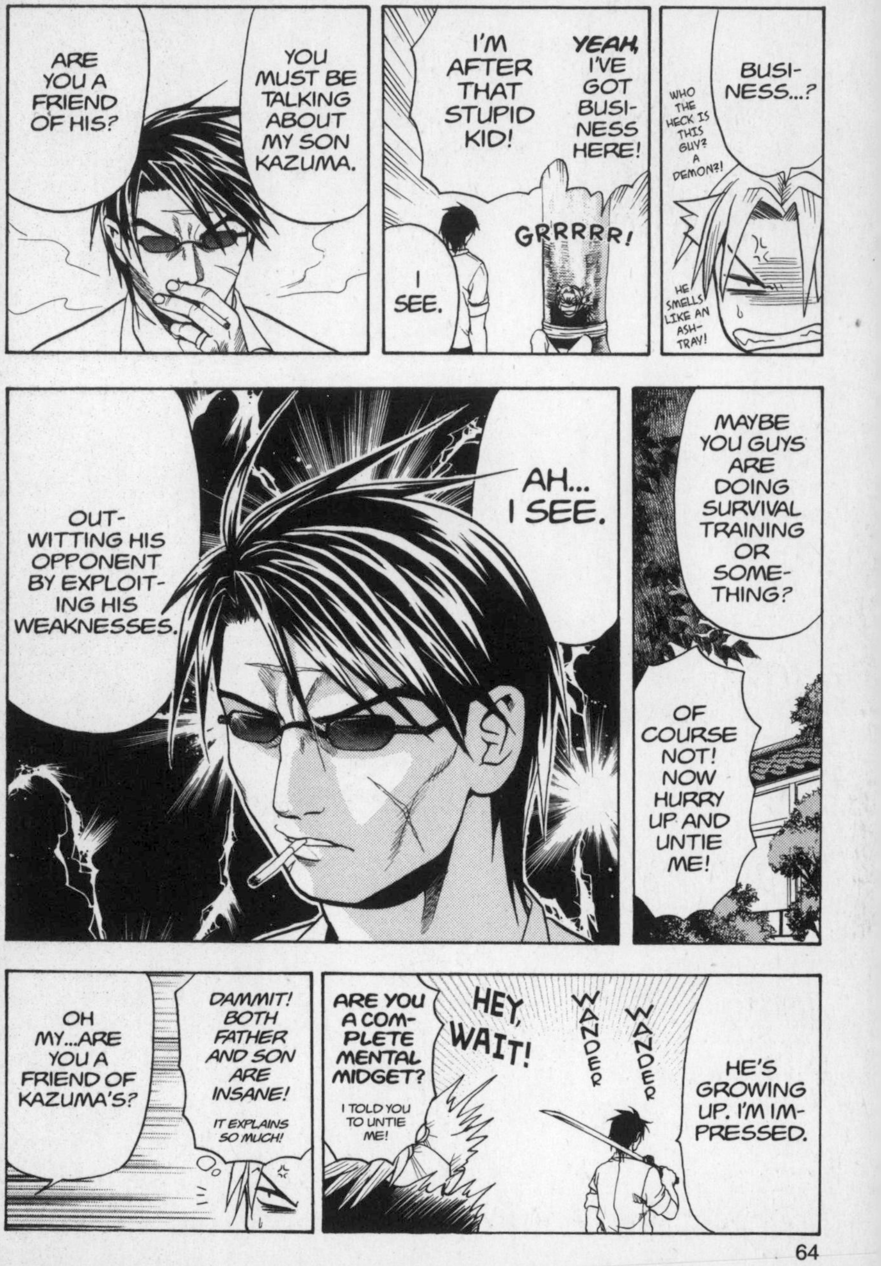
BUSINESS...?
WHO THE HECK IS THIS GUY? A DEMON?!
HE SMELLS LIKE AN ASHTRAY!
YEAH, I'VE GOT BUSINESS HERE!
I'M AFTER THAT STUPID KID!
GRRRRR!
I SEE.
YOU MUST BE TALKING ABOUT MY SON KAZUMA.
ARE YOU A FRIEND OF HIS?
MAYBE YOU GUYS ARE DOING SURVIVAL TRAINING OR SOMETHING?
OF COURSE NOT! NOW HURRY UP AND UNTIE ME!
AH... I SEE.
OUTWITTING HIS OPPONENT BY EXPLOITING HIS WEAKNESSES.
HE'S GROWING UP. I'M IMPRESSED.
WANDER
WANDER
HEY, WAIT!
ARE YOU A COMPLETE MENTAL MIDGET?
I TOLD YOU TO UNTIE ME!
DAMMIT! BOTH FATHER AND SON ARE INSANE!
IT EXPLAINS SO MUCH!
OH MY...ARE YOU A FRIEND OF KAZUMA'S?

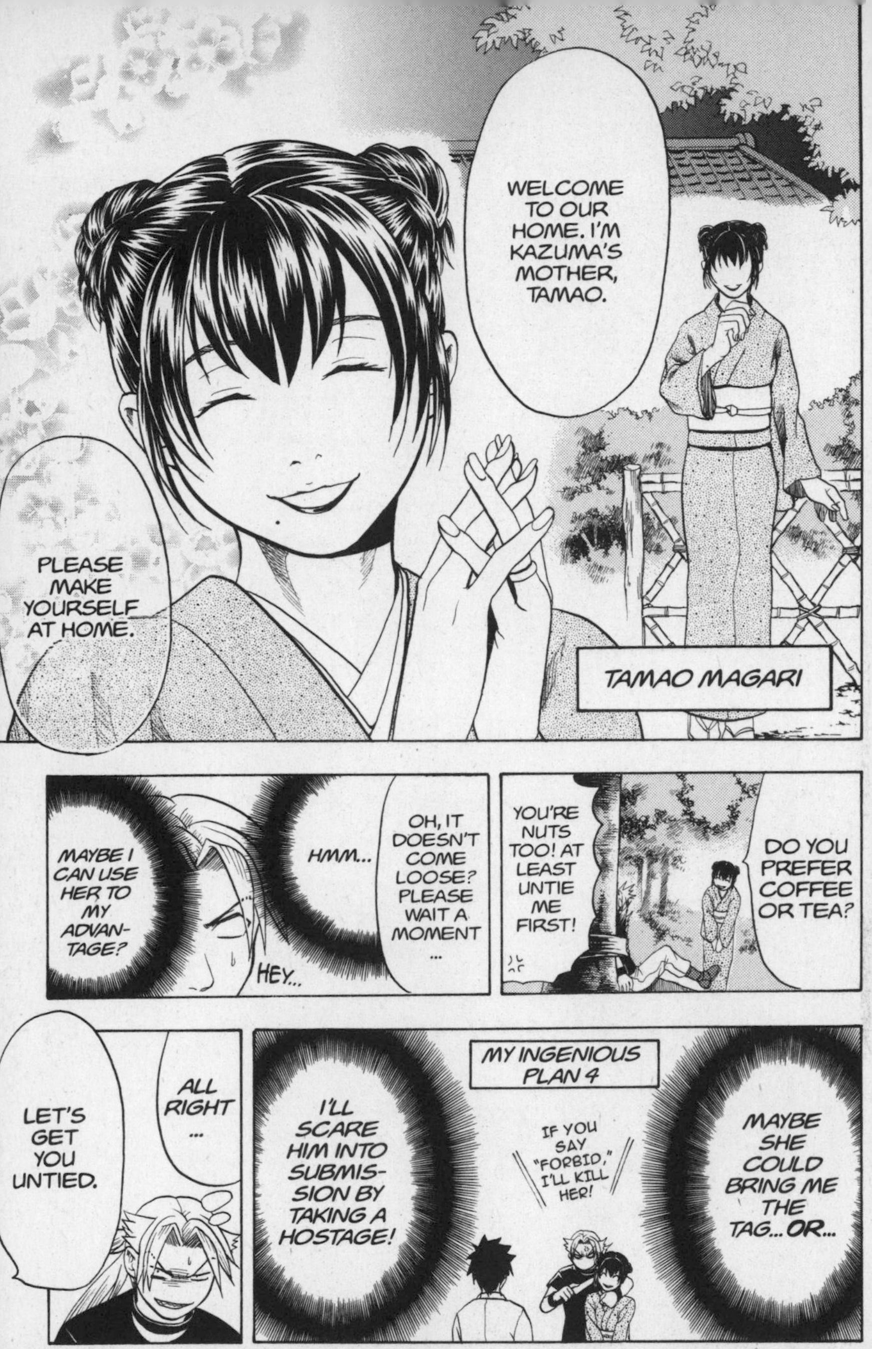
WELCOME TO OUR HOME. I'M KAZUMA'S MOTHER, TAMAO.
PLEASE MAKE YOURSELF AT HOME.
TAMAO MAGARI
DO YOU PREFER COFFEE OR TEA?
YOU'RE NUTS TOO! AT LEAST UNTIE ME FIRST!
OH, IT DOESN'T COME LOOSE? PLEASE WAIT A MOMENT ...
HMM...
HEY...
MAYBE I CAN USE HER TO MY ADVAN-TAGE?
MY INGENIOUS PLAN 4
MAYBE SHE COULD BRING ME THE TAG... OR...
IF YOU SAY "FORBID," I'LL KILL HER!
I'LL SCARE HIM INTO SUBMIS-SION BY TAKING A HOSTAGE!
ALL RIGHT ...
LET'S GET YOU UNTIED.

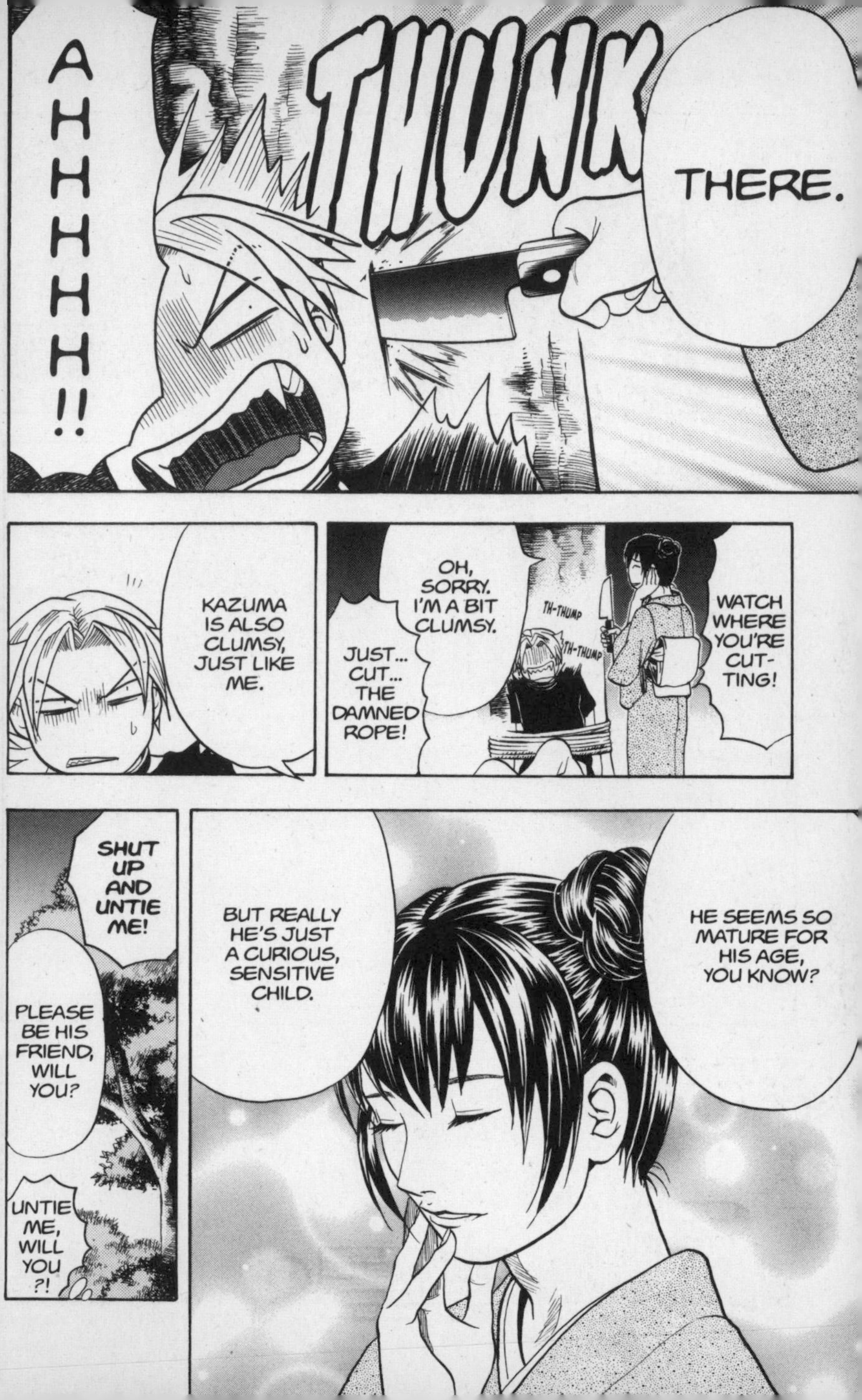
THERE.
THUNK
AHHHHH!!
WATCH WHERE YOU'RE CUT-TING!
TH-THUMP
TH-THUMP
OH, SORRY. I'M A BIT CLUMSY.
JUST... CUT... THE DAMNED ROPE!
KAZUMA IS ALSO CLUMSY, JUST LIKE ME.
HE SEEMS SO MATURE FOR HIS AGE, YOU KNOW?
BUT REALLY HE'S JUST A CURIOUS, SENSITIVE CHILD.
SHUT UP AND UNTIE ME!
PLEASE BE HIS FRIEND, WILL YOU?
UNTIE ME, WILL YOU ?!

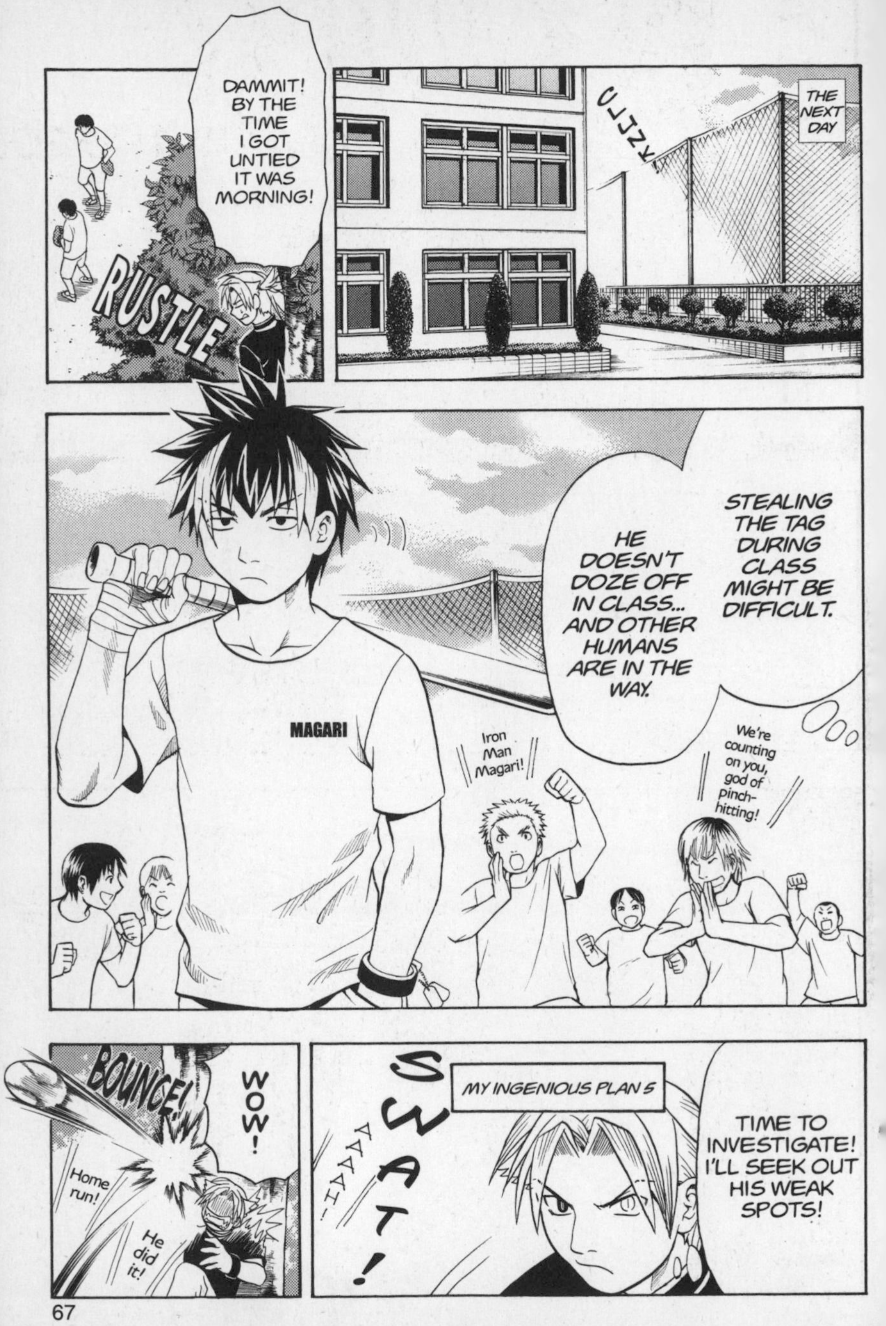
THE NEXT DAY
DAMMIT! BY THE TIME I GOT UNTIED IT WAS MORNING!
RUSTLE
STEALING THE TAG DURING CLASS MIGHT BE DIFFICULT.
HE DOESN'T DOZE OFF IN CLASS... AND OTHER HUMANS ARE IN THE WAY.
MAGARI
We're counting on you, god of pinch-hitting!
Iron Man Magari!
MY INGENIOUS PLAN 5
TIME TO INVESTIGATE! I'LL SEEK OUT HIS WEAK SPOTS!
SWAT!
AAAAH!
BOUNCE!
WOW!
Home run!
He did it!

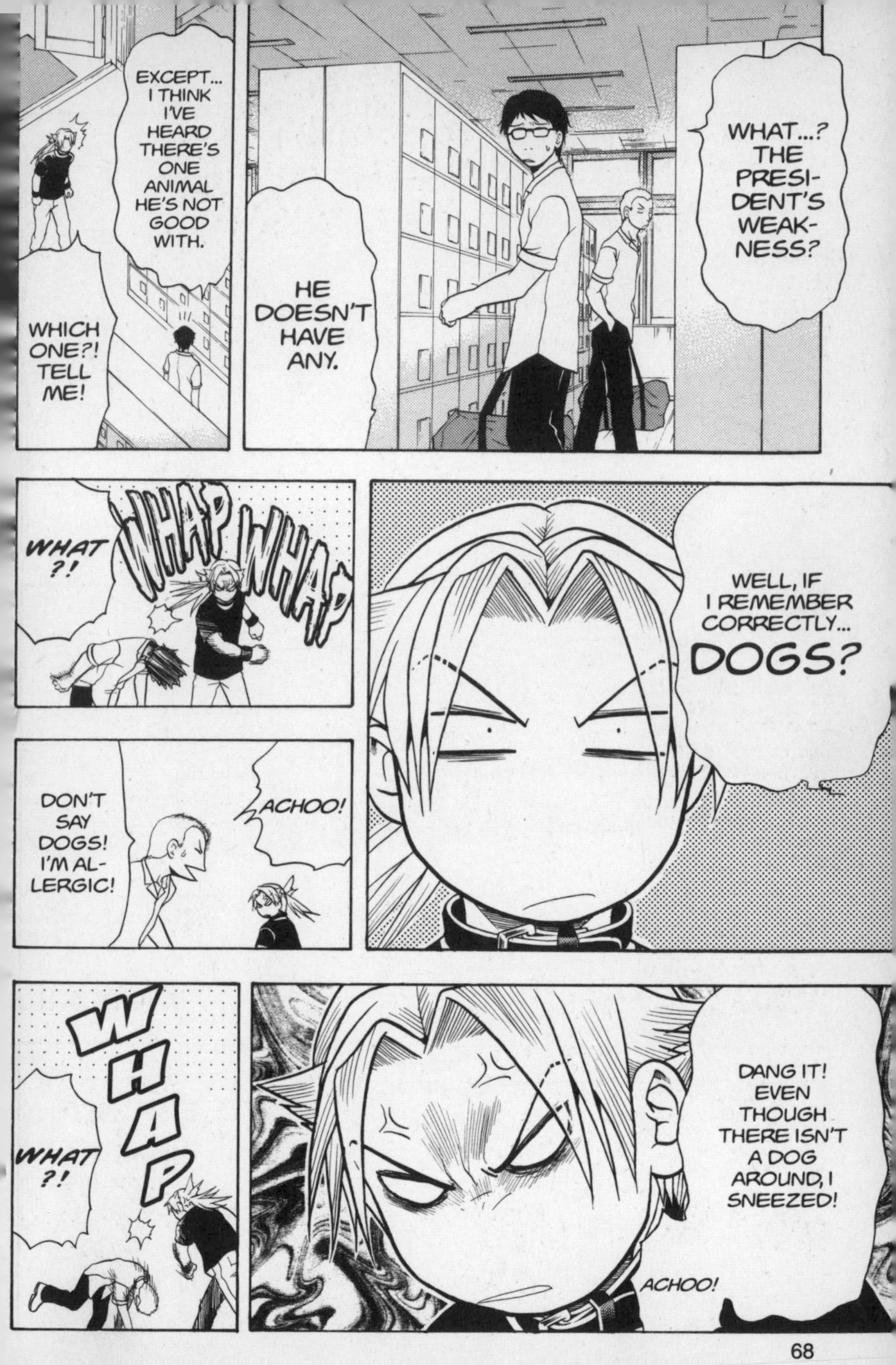
WHAT...? THE PRESIDENT'S WEAKNESS?
HE DOESN'T HAVE ANY.
EXCEPT... I THINK I'VE HEARD THERE'S ONE ANIMAL HE'S NOT GOOD WITH.
WHICH ONE?! TELL ME!
WELL, IF I REMEMBER CORRECTLY... DOGS?
WHAP WHAP
WHAT?!
ACHOO!
DON'T SAY DOGS! I'M ALLERGIC!
DANG IT! EVEN THOUGH THERE ISN'T A DOG AROUND, I SNEEZED!
ACHOO!
WHAP
WHAT?!

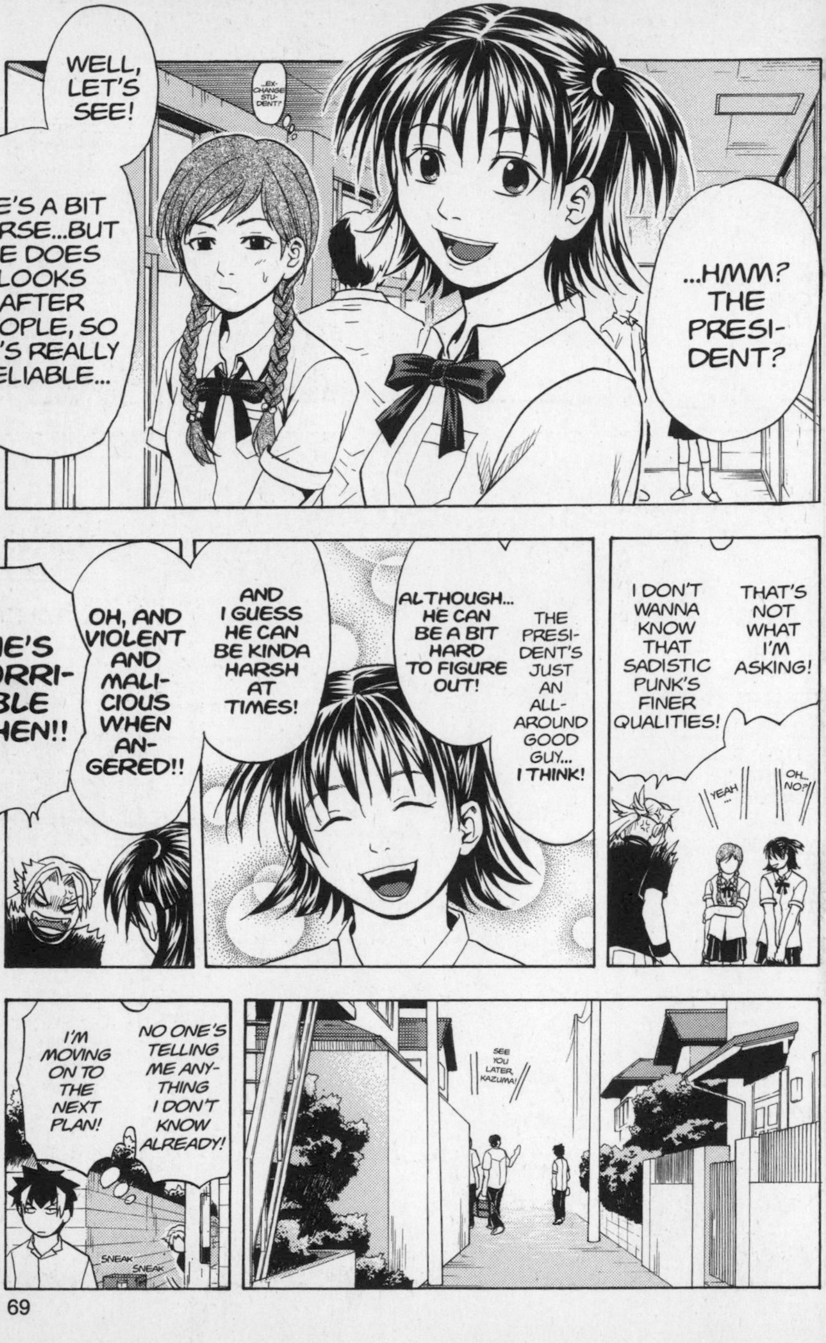
...HMM? THE PRESIDENT?
...EXCHANGE STUDENT?
WELL, LET'S SEE!
HE'S A BIT TERSE...BUT HE DOES LOOKS AFTER PEOPLE, SO HE'S REALLY RELIABLE...
I DON'T WANNA KNOW THAT SADISTIC PUNK'S FINER QUALITIES!
THAT'S NOT WHAT I'M ASKING!
OH... NO?
YEAH...
THE PRESIDENT'S JUST AN ALL-AROUND GOOD GUY... I THINK!
ALTHOUGH... HE CAN BE A BIT HARD TO FIGURE OUT!
AND I GUESS HE CAN BE KINDA HARSH AT TIMES!
OH, AND VIOLENT AND MALICIOUS WHEN ANGERED!!
HE'S HORRIBLE THEN!!
SEE YOU LATER, KAZUMA!
NO ONE'S TELLING ME ANYTHING I DON'T KNOW ALREADY!
I'M MOVING ON TO THE NEXT PLAN!
SNEAK
SNEAK

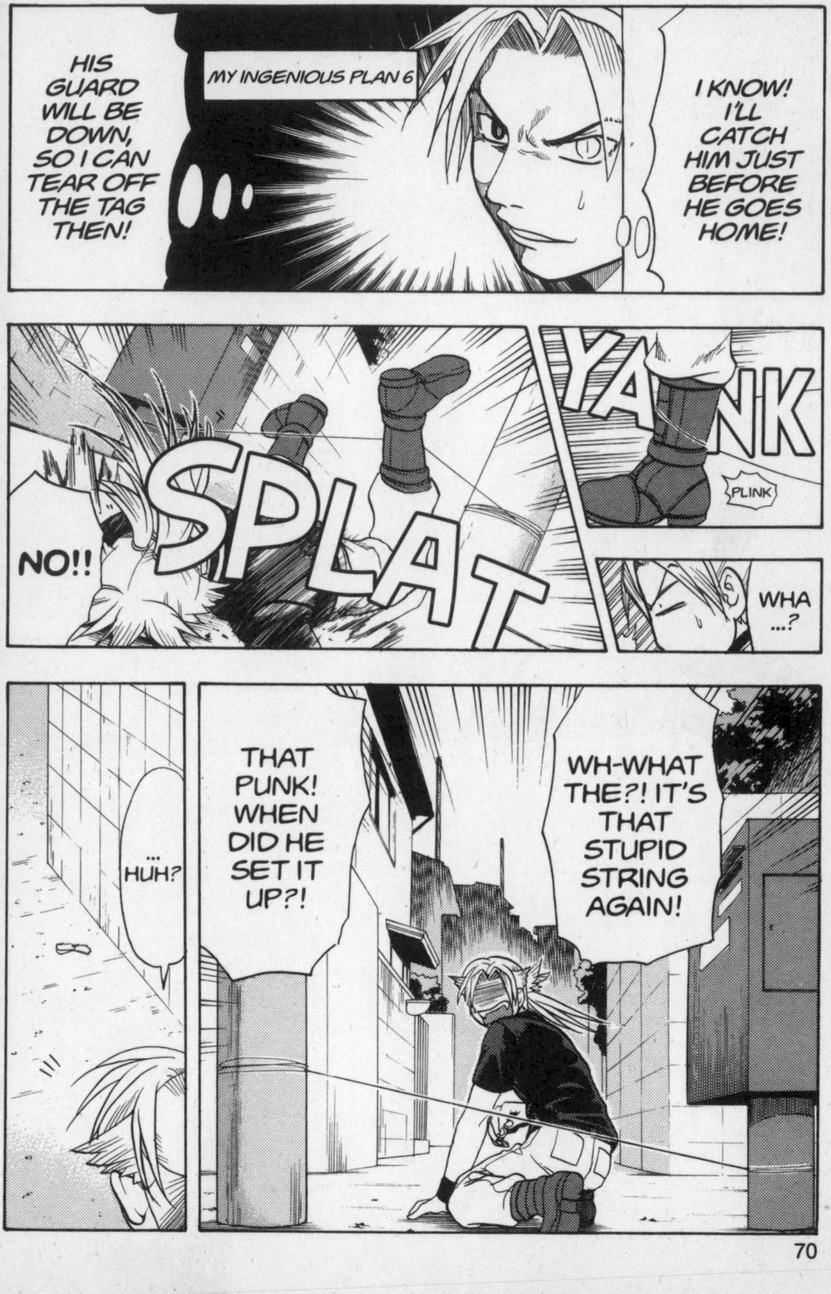
I KNOW! I'LL CATCH HIM JUST BEFORE HE GOES HOME!
MY INGENIOUS PLAN 6
...
HIS GUARD WILL BE DOWN, SO I CAN TEAR OFF THE TAG THEN!
YA NK
PLINK
WHA ...?
SPLAT
NO!!
WH-WHAT THE?! IT'S THAT STUPID STRING AGAIN!
THAT PUNK! WHEN DID HE SET IT UP?!
... HUH?

READ THIS WAY

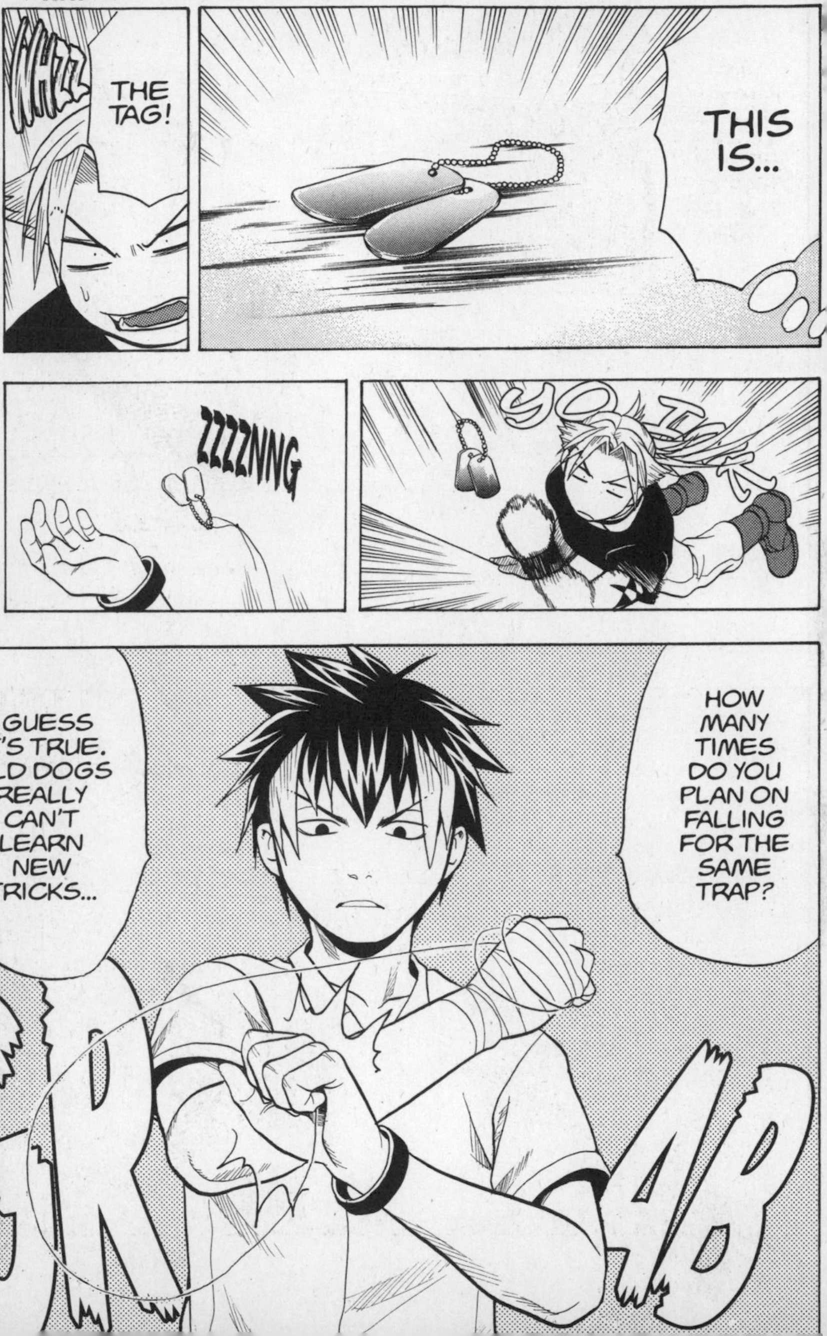
THIS IS...
THE TAG!
WHZZZ
ZZZZNNG
HOW MANY TIMES DO YOU PLAN ON FALLING FOR THE SAME TRAP?
I GUESS IT'S TRUE. OLD DOGS REALLY CAN'T LEARN NEW TRICKS...
GRAB

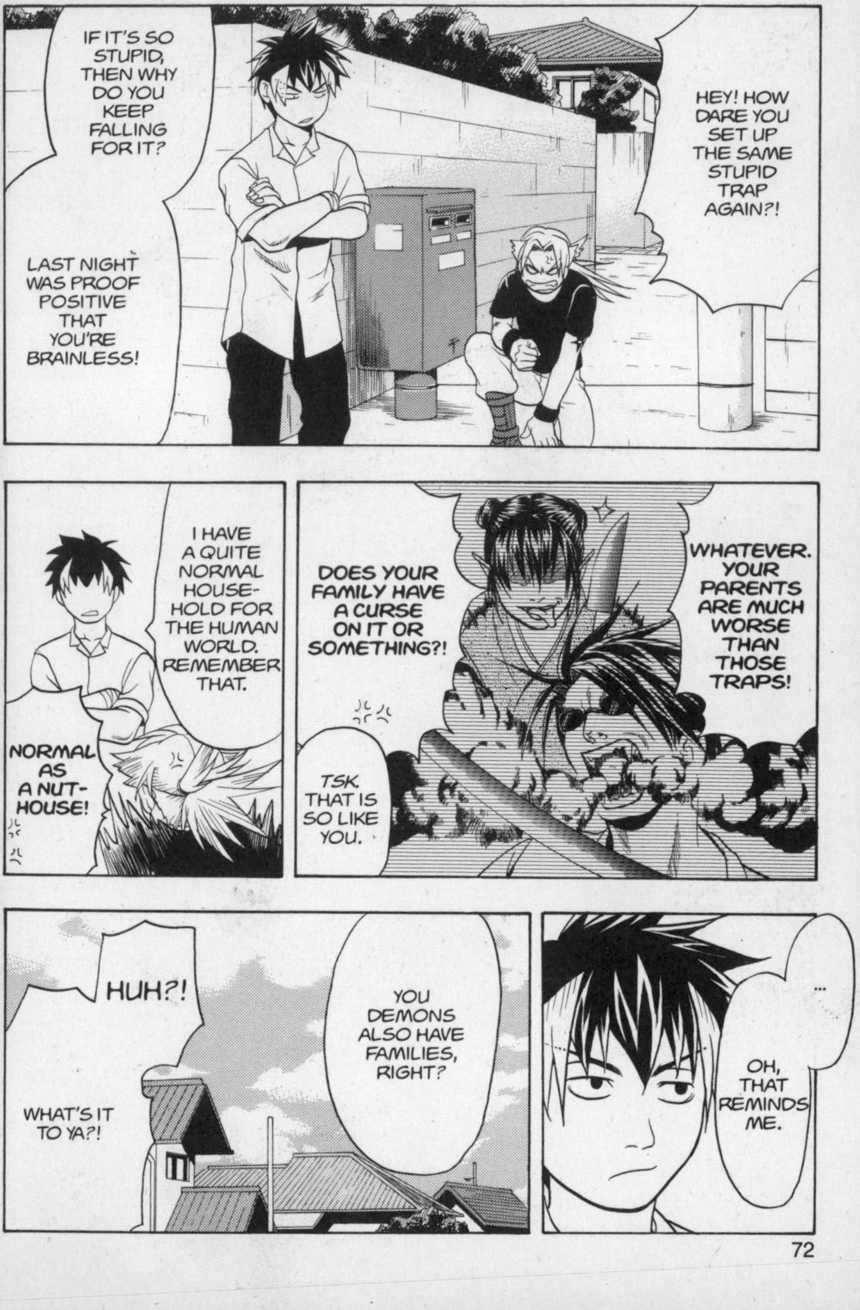
HEY! HOW DARE YOU SET UP THE SAME STUPID TRAP AGAIN?!
IF IT'S SO STUPID, THEN WHY DO YOU KEEP FALLING FOR IT?
LAST NIGHT WAS PROOF POSITIVE THAT YOU'RE BRAINLESS!
WHATEVER. YOUR PARENTS ARE MUCH WORSE THAN THOSE TRAPS!
DOES YOUR FAMILY HAVE A CURSE ON IT OR SOMETHING?!
TSK. THAT IS SO LIKE YOU.
I HAVE A QUITE NORMAL HOUSEHOLD FOR THE HUMAN WORLD. REMEMBER THAT.
NORMAL AS A NUT-HOUSE!
...
OH, THAT REMINDS ME.
YOU DEMONS ALSO HAVE FAMILIES, RIGHT?
HUH?!
WHAT'S IT TO YA?!

READ THIS WAY

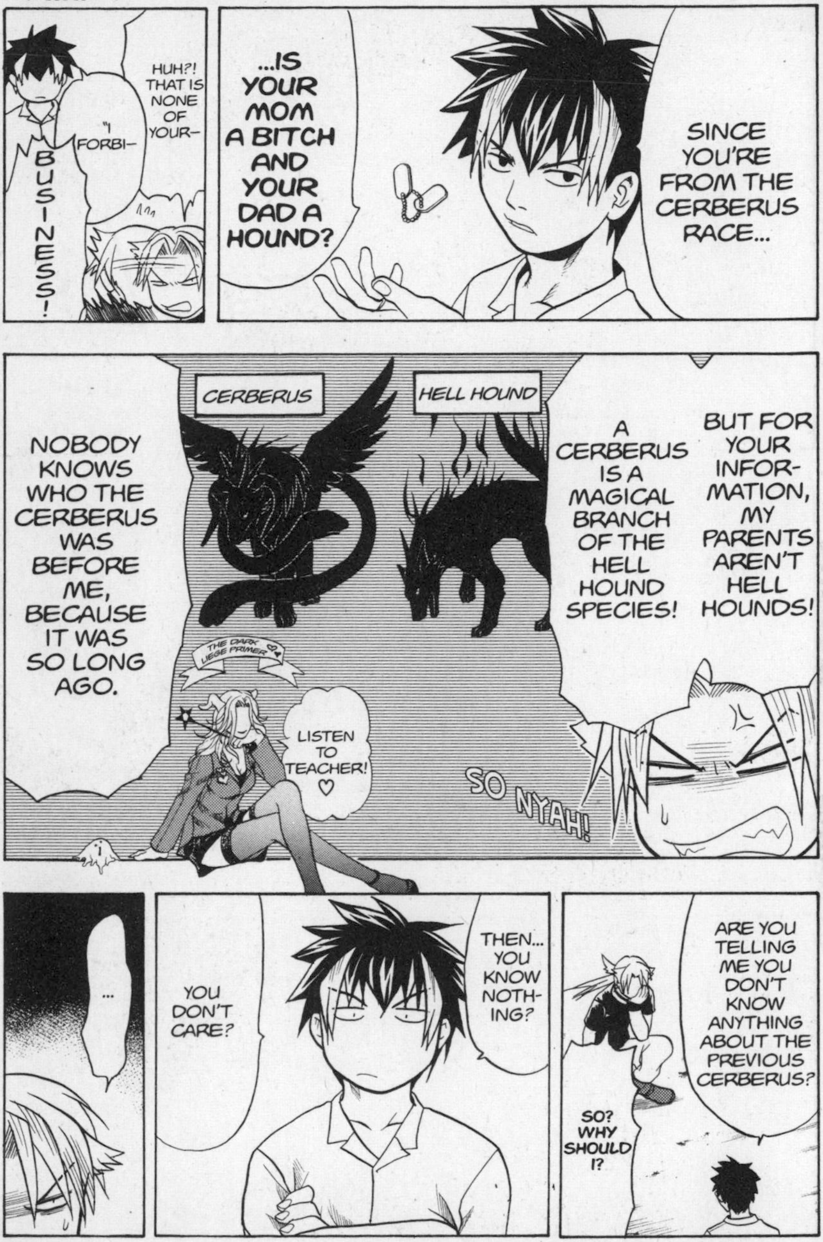

SINCE YOU'RE FROM THE CERBERUS RACE...
...IS YOUR MOM A BITCH AND YOUR DAD A HOUND?
HUH?! THAT IS NONE OF YOUR—
BUSINESS!
"I FORBI—
BUT FOR YOUR INFORMATION, MY PARENTS AREN'T HELL HOUNDS!
A CERBERUS IS A MAGICAL BRANCH OF THE HELL HOUND SPECIES!
HELL HOUND
CERBERUS
SO NYAH!
LISTEN TO TEACHER! ♡
THE DARK LIEGE PRIMER
NOBODY KNOWS WHO THE CERBERUS WAS BEFORE ME, BECAUSE IT WAS SO LONG AGO.
ARE YOU TELLING ME YOU DON'T KNOW ANYTHING ABOUT THE PREVIOUS CERBERUS?
SO? WHY SHOULD I?
THEN... YOU KNOW NOTHING?
YOU DON'T CARE?
...

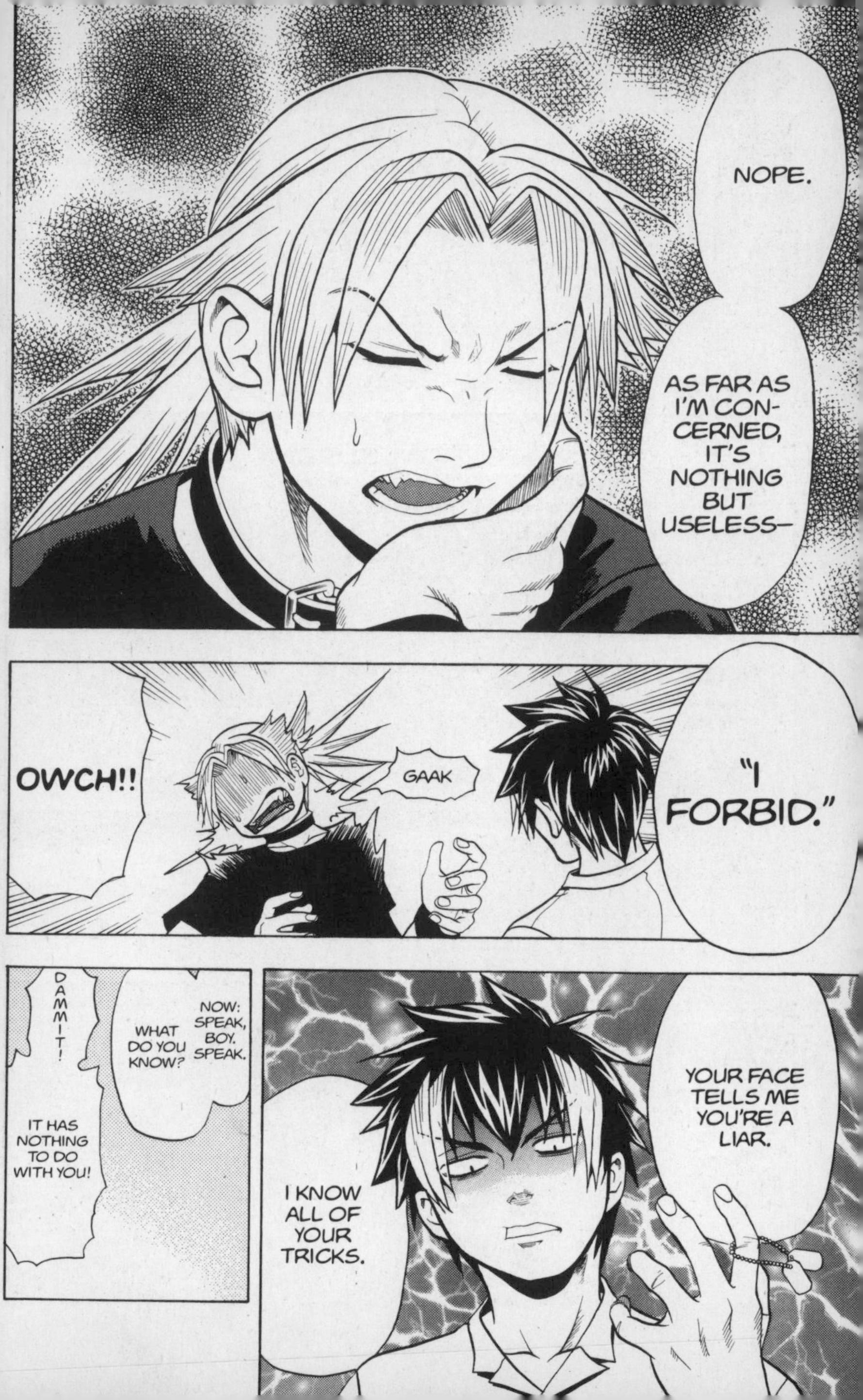
NOPE.
AS FAR AS I'M CONCERNED, IT'S NOTHING BUT USELESS—
"I FORBID."
GAAK
OWCH!!
YOUR FACE TELLS ME YOU'RE A LIAR.
I KNOW ALL OF YOUR TRICKS.
NOW: SPEAK, BOY. SPEAK.
WHAT DO YOU KNOW?
DAMMIT!
IT HAS NOTHING TO DO WITH YOU!

READ THIS WAY

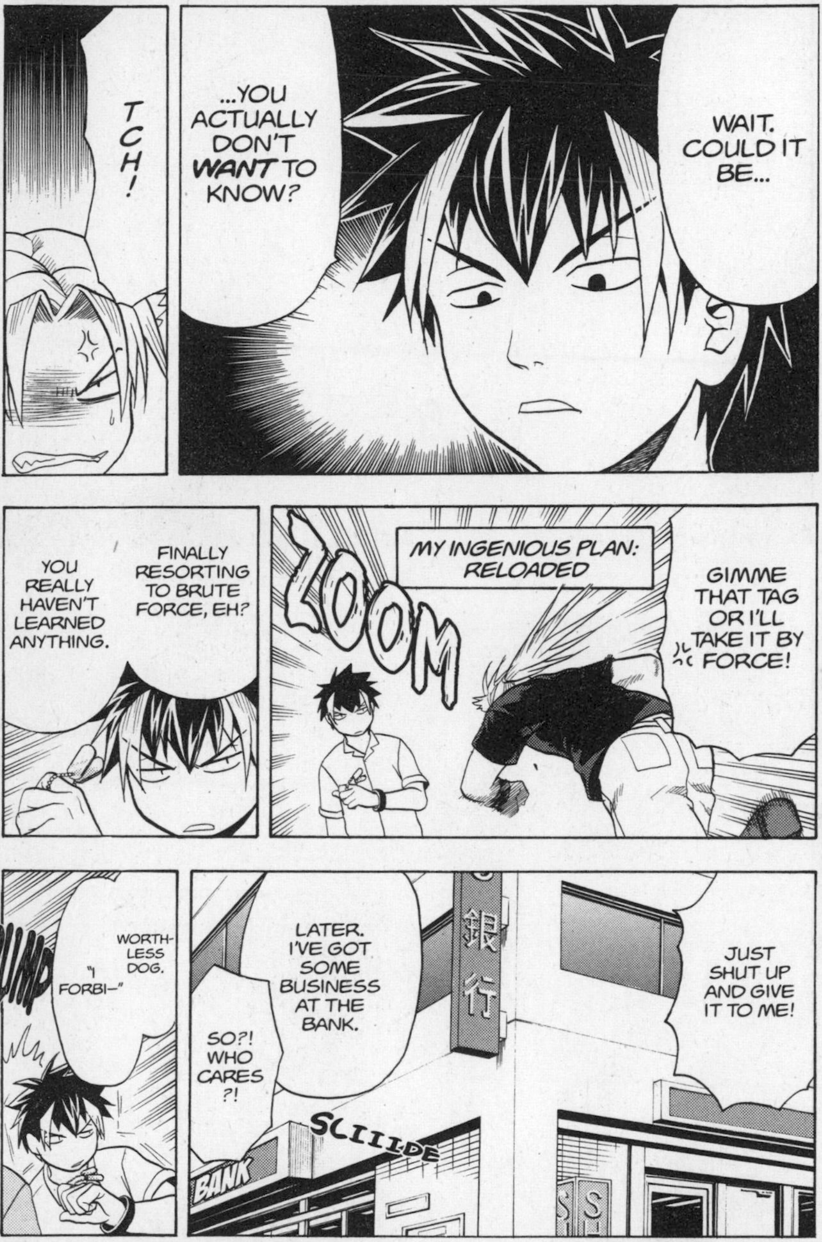
WAIT. COULD IT BE...
...YOU ACTUALLY DON'T WANT TO KNOW?
TCH!
MY INGENIOUS PLAN: RELOADED
GIMME THAT TAG OR I'LL TAKE IT BY FORCE!
ZOOM
FINALLY RESORTING TO BRUTE FORCE, EH?
YOU REALLY HAVEN'T LEARNED ANYTHING.
JUST SHUT UP AND GIVE IT TO ME!
LATER. I'VE GOT SOME BUSINESS AT THE BANK.
SO?! WHO CARES?!
SLIIIDE
BANK
銀行
BUMP
WORTH-LESS DOG.
"I FORBI–"

SIGN: BANK

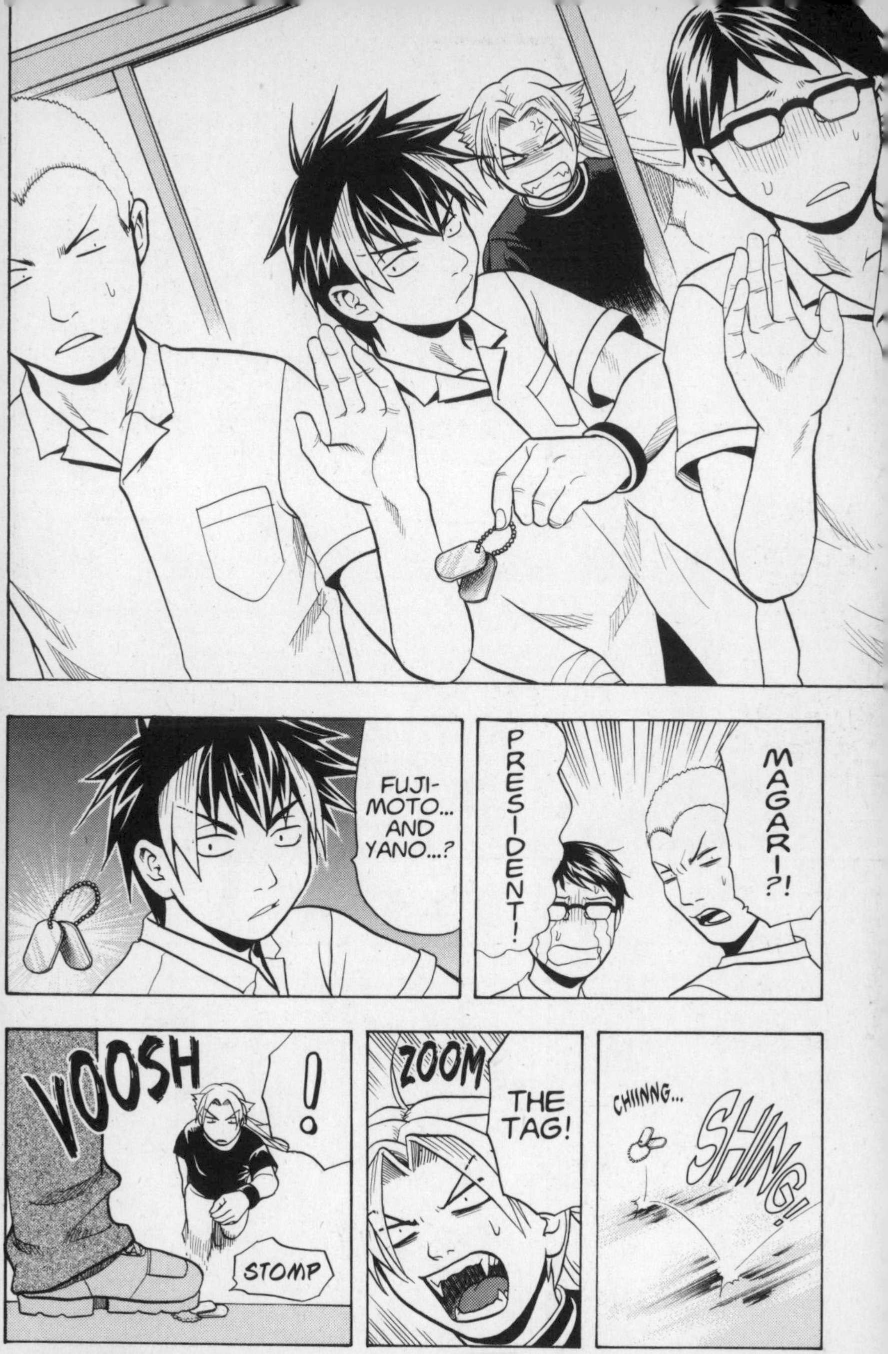
MAGARI-?!
PRESIDENT!
FUJI-MOTO... AND YANO...?
CHIINNG...
SHING!
ZOOM
THE TAG!
VOOSH
!
STOMP

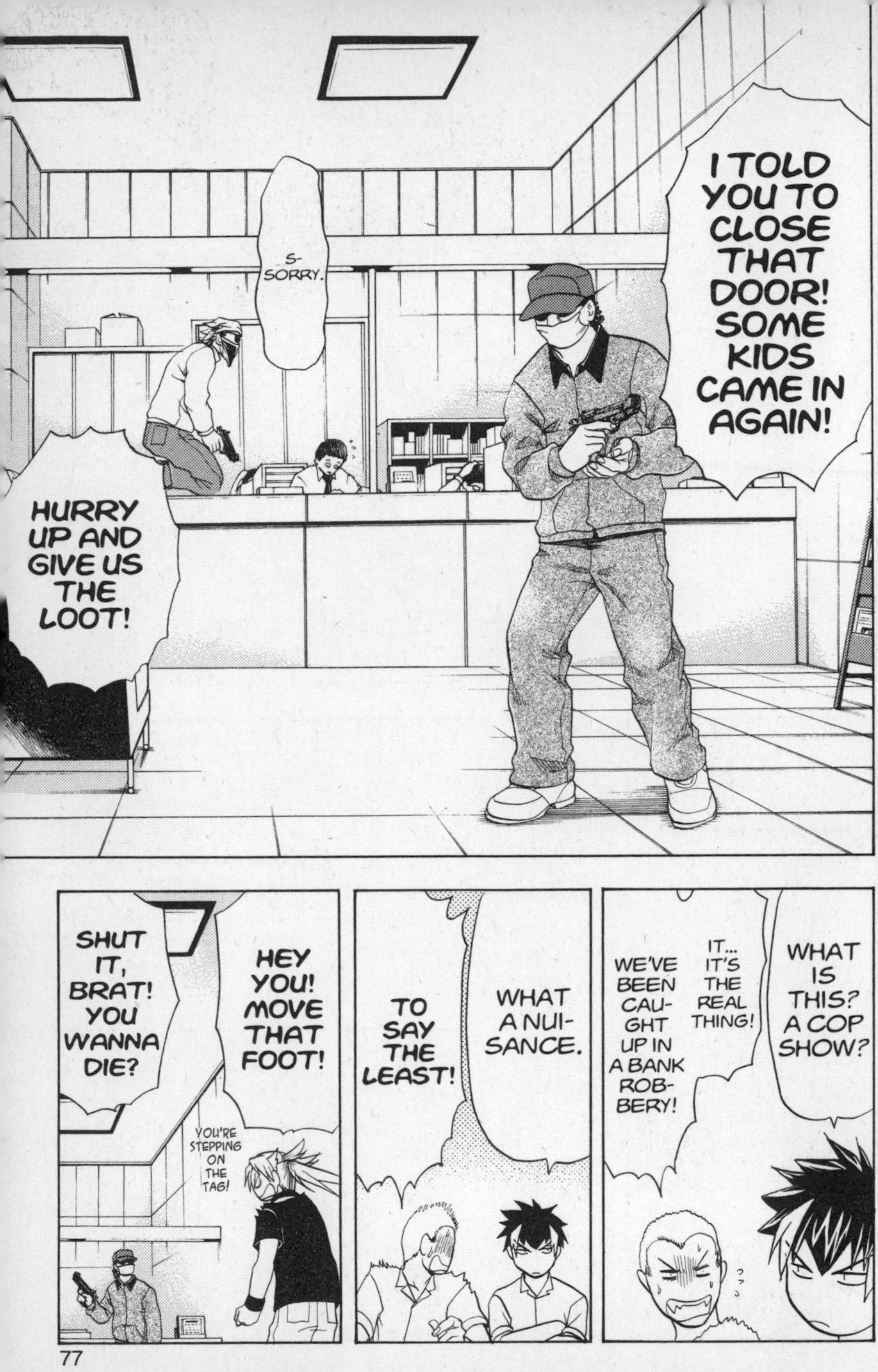
I TOLD YOU TO CLOSE THAT DOOR! SOME KIDS CAME IN AGAIN!
S-SORRY.
HURRY UP AND GIVE US THE LOOT!
WHAT IS THIS? A COP SHOW?
IT... IT'S THE REAL THING!
WE'VE BEEN CAUGHT UP IN A BANK ROBBERY!
WHAT A NUISANCE.
TO SAY THE LEAST!
HEY YOU! MOVE THAT FOOT!
YOU'RE STEPPING ON THE TAG!
SHUT IT, BRAT! YOU WANNA DIE?

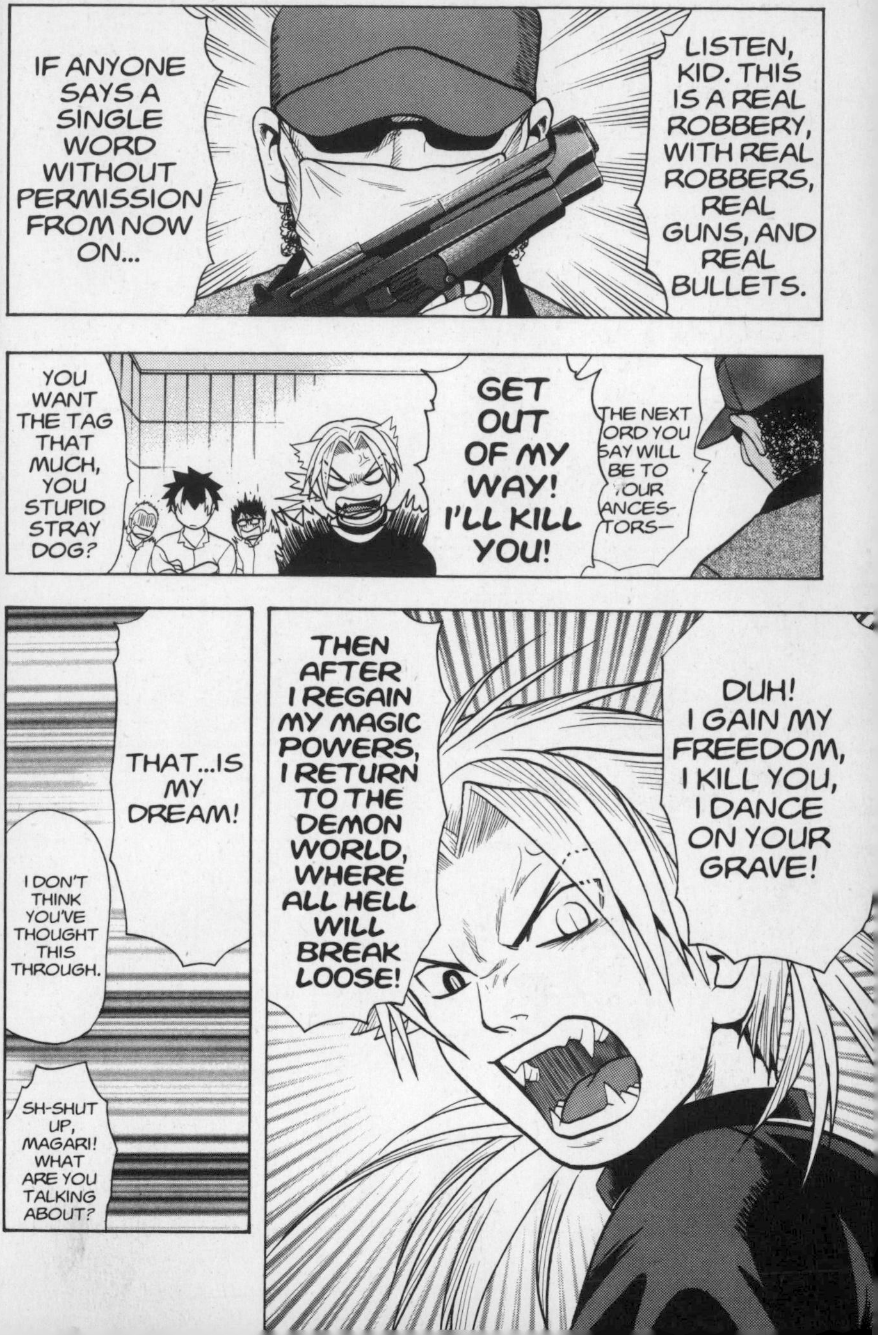
LISTEN, KID. THIS IS A REAL ROBBERY, WITH REAL ROBBERS, REAL GUNS, AND REAL BULLETS.
IF ANYONE SAYS A SINGLE WORD WITHOUT PERMISSION FROM NOW ON...
THE NEXT ORD YOU SAY WILL BE TO OUR ANCES- TORS—
GET OUT OF MY WAY! I'LL KILL YOU!
YOU WANT THE TAG THAT MUCH, YOU STUPID STRAY DOG?
DUH! I GAIN MY FREEDOM, I KILL YOU, I DANCE ON YOUR GRAVE!
THEN AFTER I REGAIN MY MAGIC POWERS, I RETURN TO THE DEMON WORLD, WHERE ALL HELL WILL BREAK LOOSE!
THAT...IS MY DREAM!
I DON'T THINK YOU'VE THOUGHT THIS THROUGH.
SH-SHUT UP, MAGARI! WHAT ARE YOU TALKING ABOUT?

READ THIS WAY

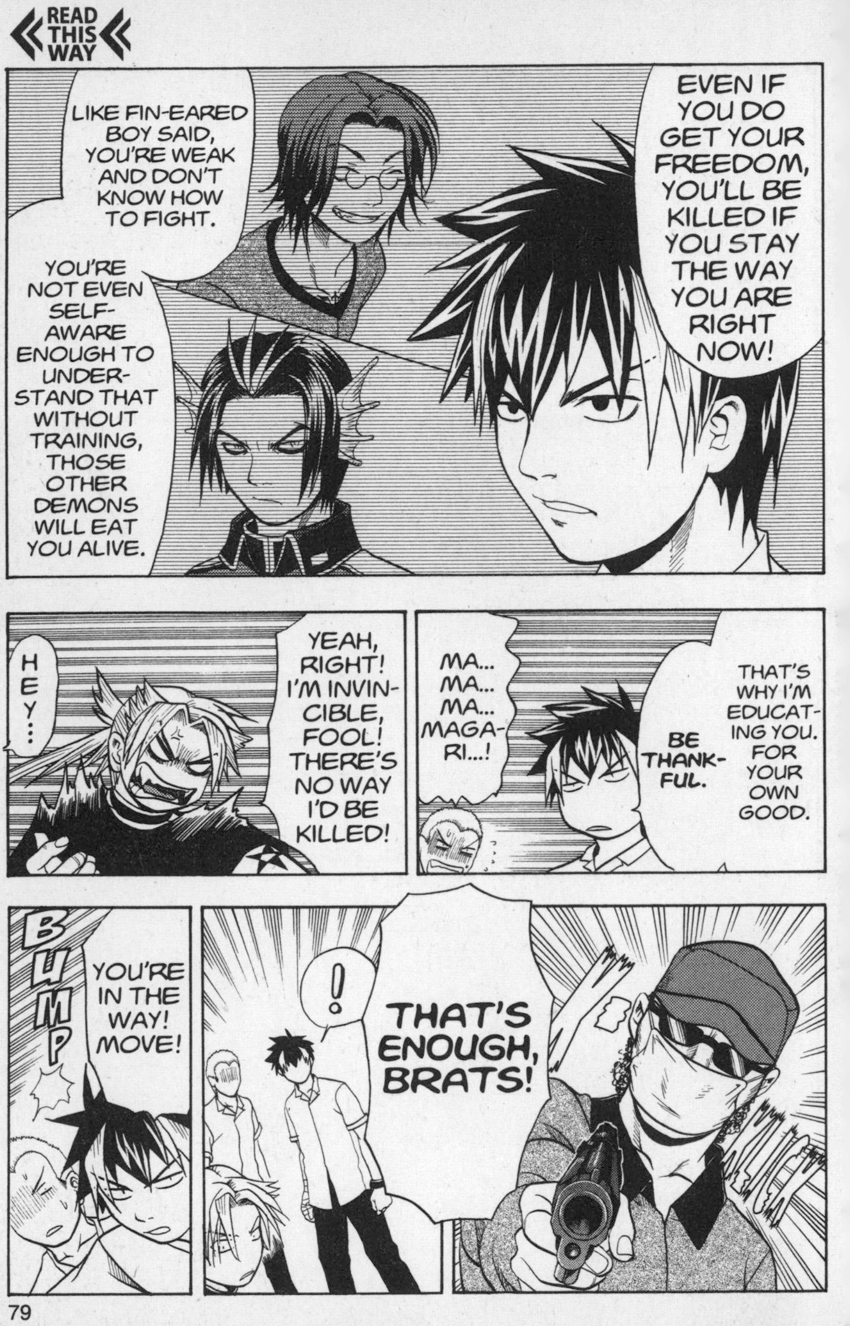
EVEN IF YOU DO GET YOUR FREEDOM, YOU'LL BE KILLED IF YOU STAY THE WAY YOU ARE RIGHT NOW!
LIKE FIN-EARED BOY SAID, YOU'RE WEAK AND DON'T KNOW HOW TO FIGHT.
YOU'RE NOT EVEN SELF-AWARE ENOUGH TO UNDERSTAND THAT WITHOUT TRAINING, THOSE OTHER DEMONS WILL EAT YOU ALIVE.
THAT'S WHY I'M EDUCATING YOU. FOR YOUR OWN GOOD.
BE THANKFUL.
MA... MA... MA... MAGARI...!
YEAH, RIGHT! I'M INVINCIBLE, FOOL! THERE'S NO WAY I'D BE KILLED!
HEY...
!
THAT'S ENOUGH, BRATS!
BUMP
YOU'RE IN THE WAY! MOVE!

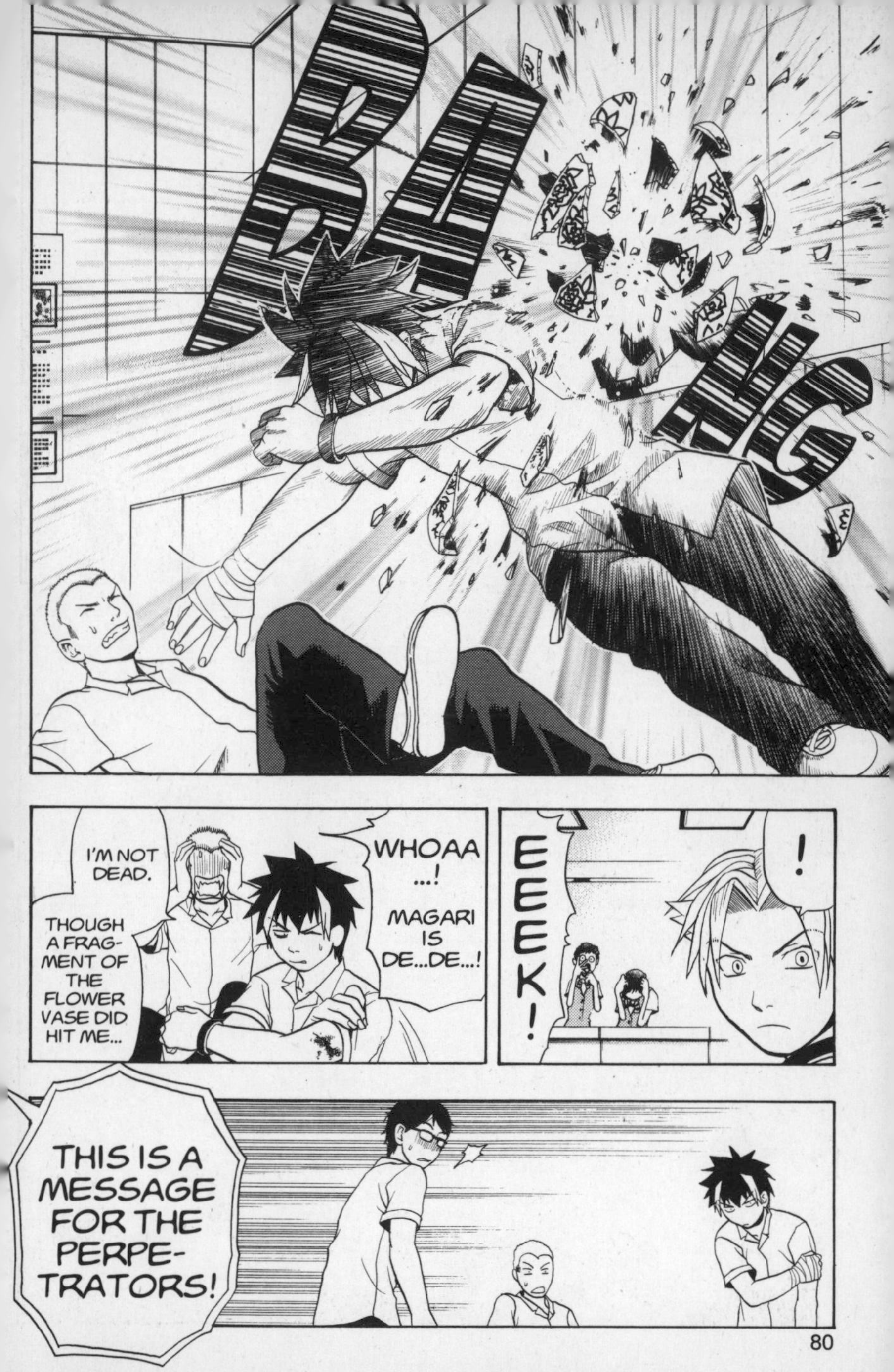
BA
NG
!
EEEEK!
WHOAA ...! MAGARI IS DE...DE...!
I'M NOT DEAD.
THOUGH A FRAGMENT OF THE FLOWER VASE DID HIT ME...
THIS IS A MESSAGE FOR THE PERPETRATORS!

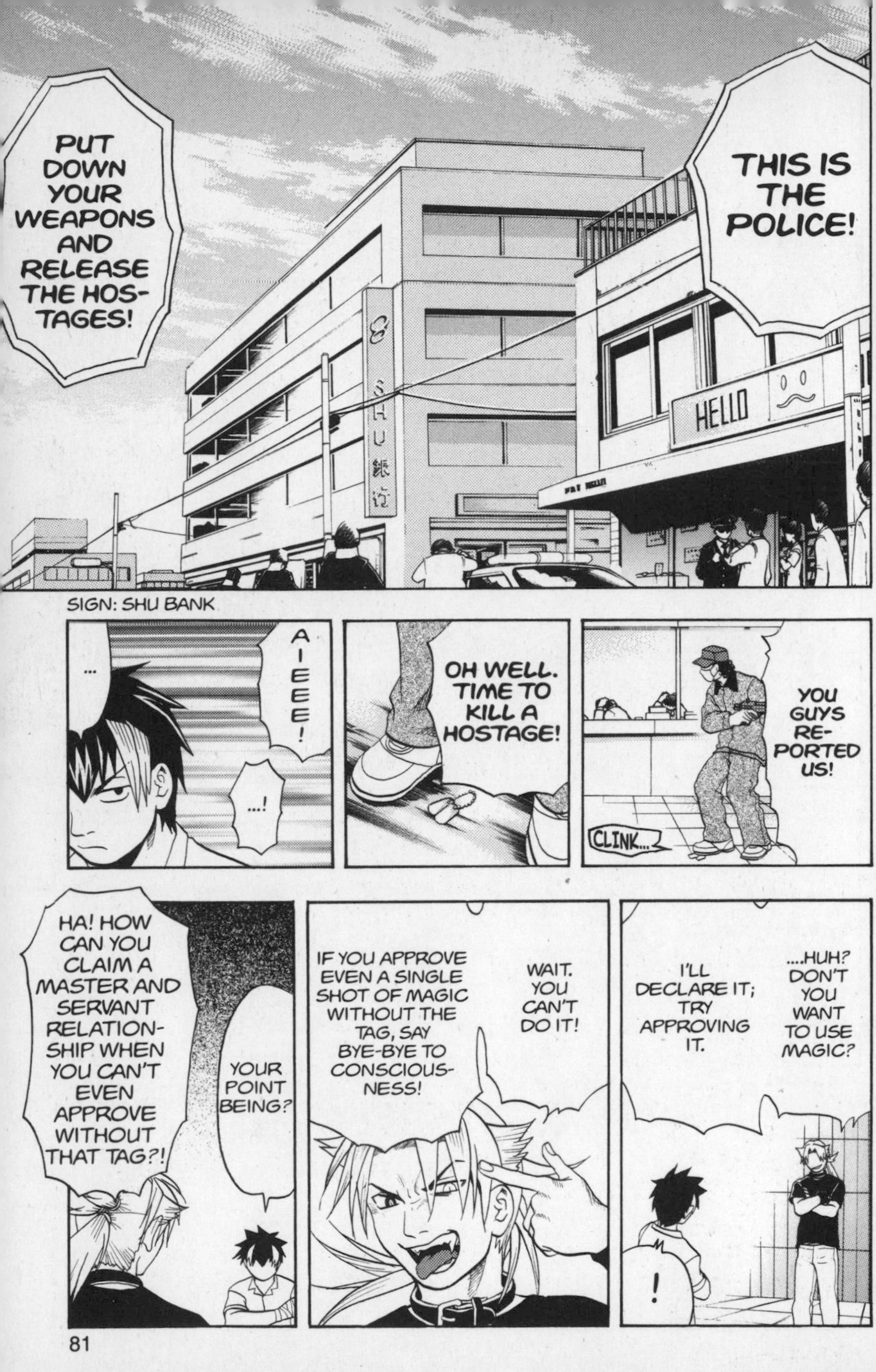
THIS IS THE POLICE!
PUT DOWN YOUR WEAPONS AND RELEASE THE HOSTAGES!
HELLO
SIGN: SHU BANK
YOU GUYS REPORTED US!
CLINK...
OH WELL. TIME TO KILL A HOSTAGE!
AIEEE!
...!
...
...HUH? DON'T YOU WANT TO USE MAGIC?
I'LL DECLARE IT; TRY APPROVING IT.
!
WAIT. YOU CAN'T DO IT!
IF YOU APPROVE EVEN A SINGLE SHOT OF MAGIC WITHOUT THE TAG, SAY BYE-BYE TO CONSCIOUSNESS!
YOUR POINT BEING?
HA! HOW CAN YOU CLAIM A MASTER AND SERVANT RELATIONSHIP WHEN YOU CAN'T EVEN APPROVE WITHOUT THAT TAG?!

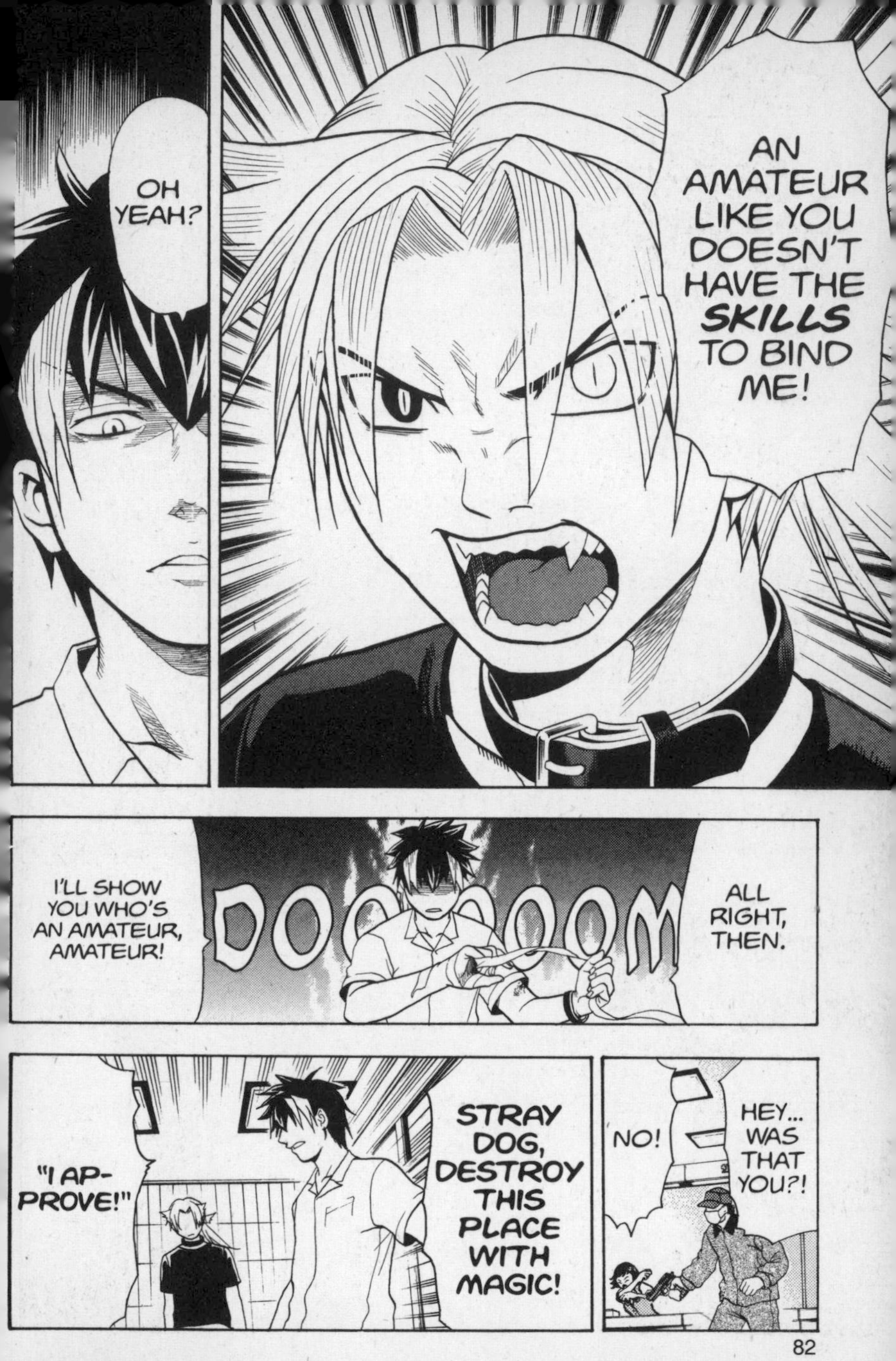
AN AMATEUR LIKE YOU DOESN'T HAVE THE **SKILLS** TO BIND ME!
OH YEAH?
ALL RIGHT, THEN.
DOOOOOM
I'LL SHOW YOU WHO'S AN AMATEUR, AMATEUR!
HEY... WAS THAT YOU?!
NO!
STRAY DOG, DESTROY THIS PLACE WITH MAGIC!
"I AP-PROVE!"

READ THIS WAY

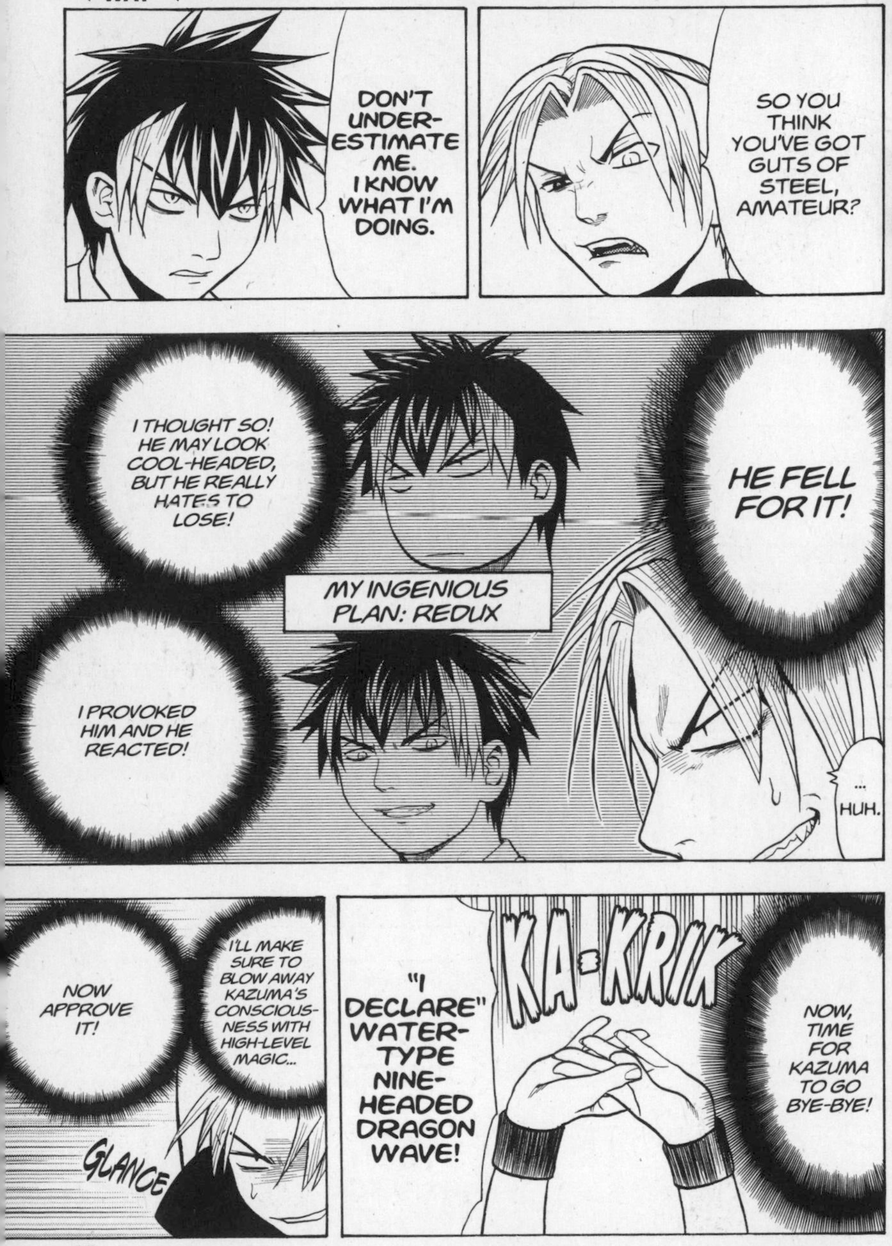
SO YOU THINK YOU'VE GOT GUTS OF STEEL, AMATEUR?
DON'T UNDER-ESTIMATE ME. I KNOW WHAT I'M DOING.
HE FELL FOR IT!
... HUH.
I THOUGHT SO! HE MAY LOOK COOL-HEADED, BUT HE REALLY HATES TO LOSE!
MY INGENIOUS PLAN: REDUX
I PROVOKED HIM AND HE REACTED!
NOW, TIME FOR KAZUMA TO GO BYE-BYE!
KA-KRIK
"I DECLARE" WATER-TYPE NINE-HEADED DRAGON WAVE!
I'LL MAKE SURE TO BLOW AWAY KAZUMA'S CONSCIOUS-NESS WITH HIGH-LEVEL MAGIC...
NOW APPROVE IT!
GLANCE

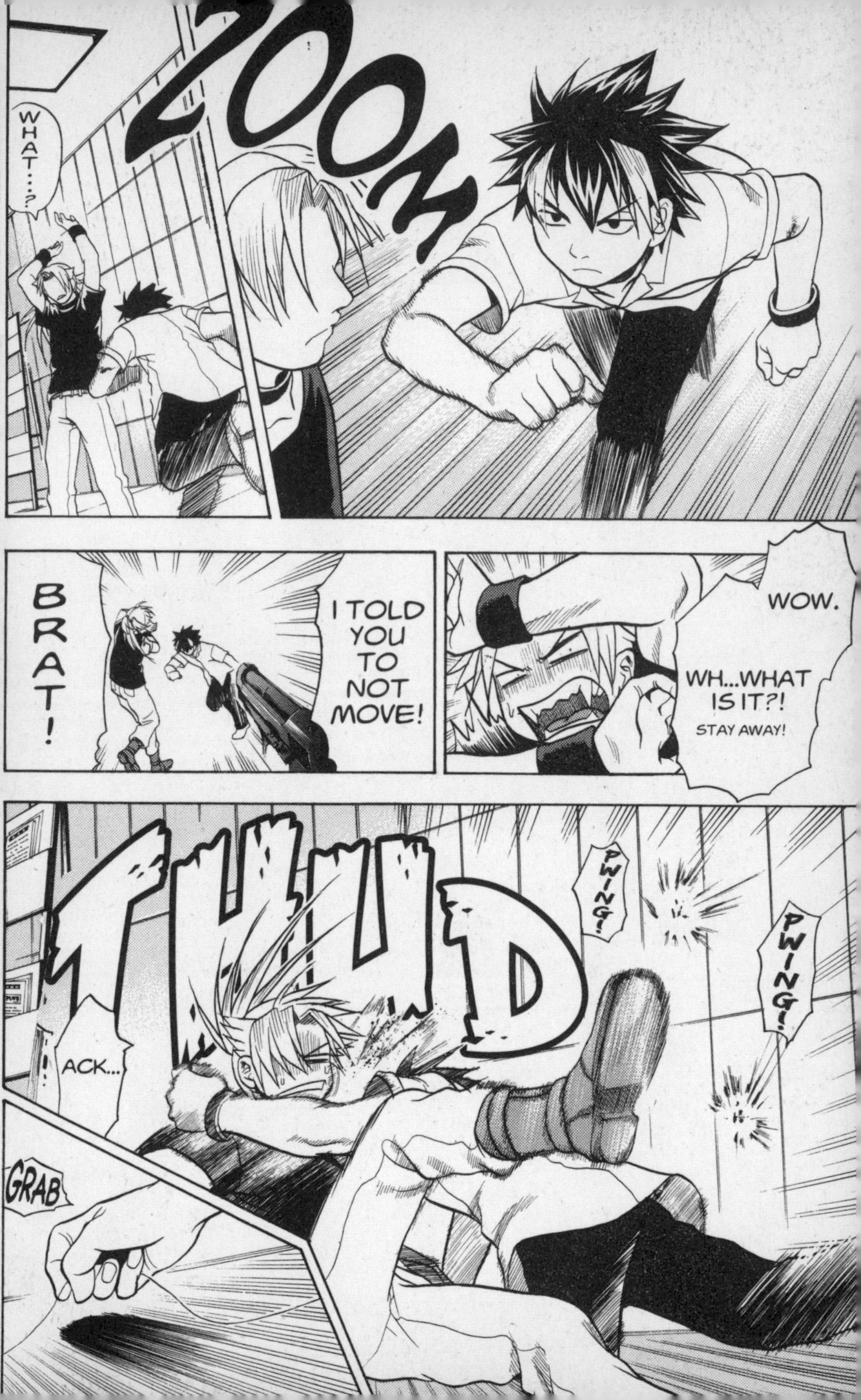
ZOOM
WHAT...?
WOW.
WH...WHAT IS IT?!
STAY AWAY!
I TOLD YOU TO NOT MOVE!
BRAT!
THUD
PWING!
PWING!
ACK...
GRAB

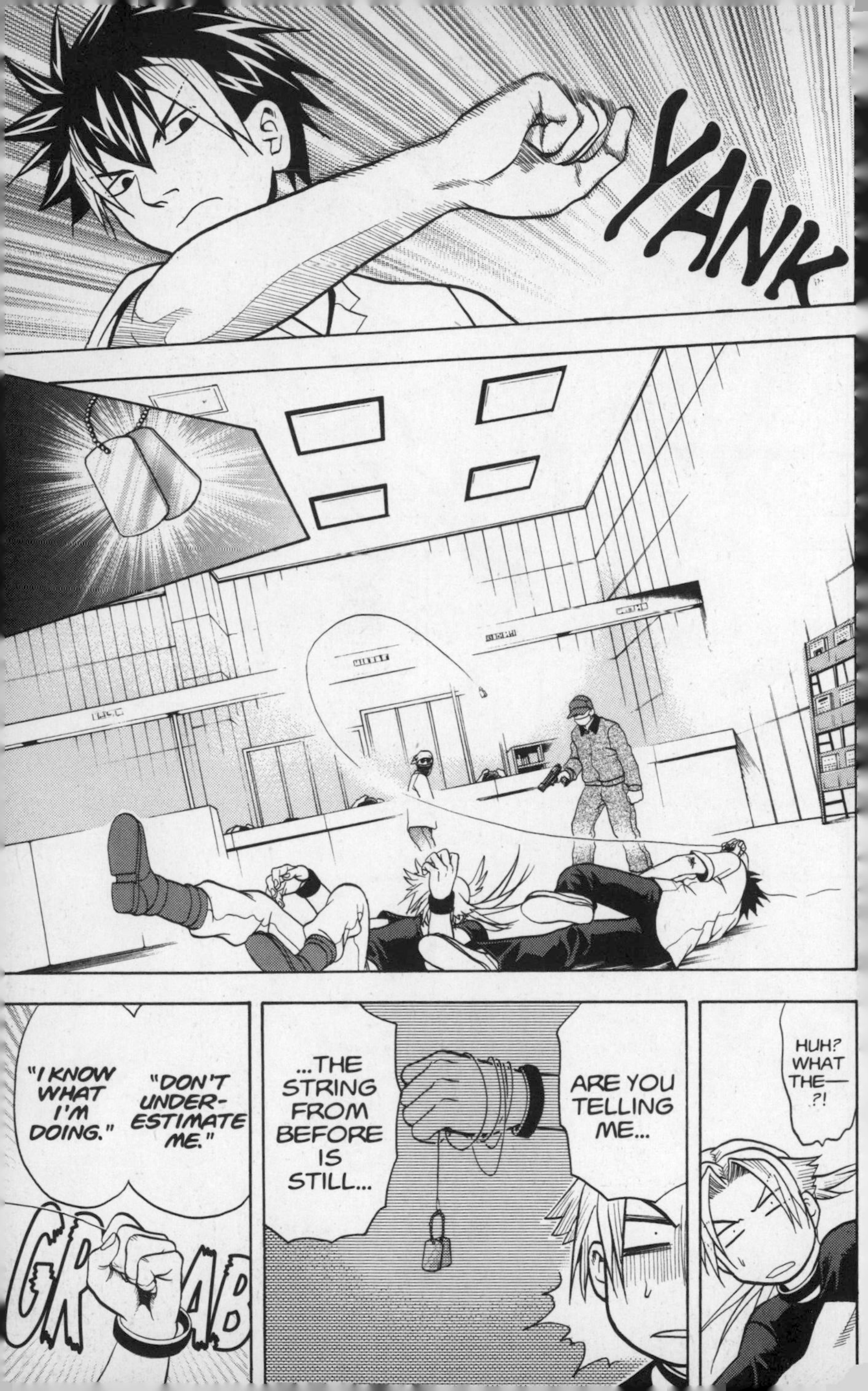
YANK
HUH? WHAT THE—?!
ARE YOU TELLING ME...
...THE STRING FROM BEFORE IS STILL...
"I KNOW WHAT I'M DOING."
"DON'T UNDER-ESTIMATE ME."
GRAB

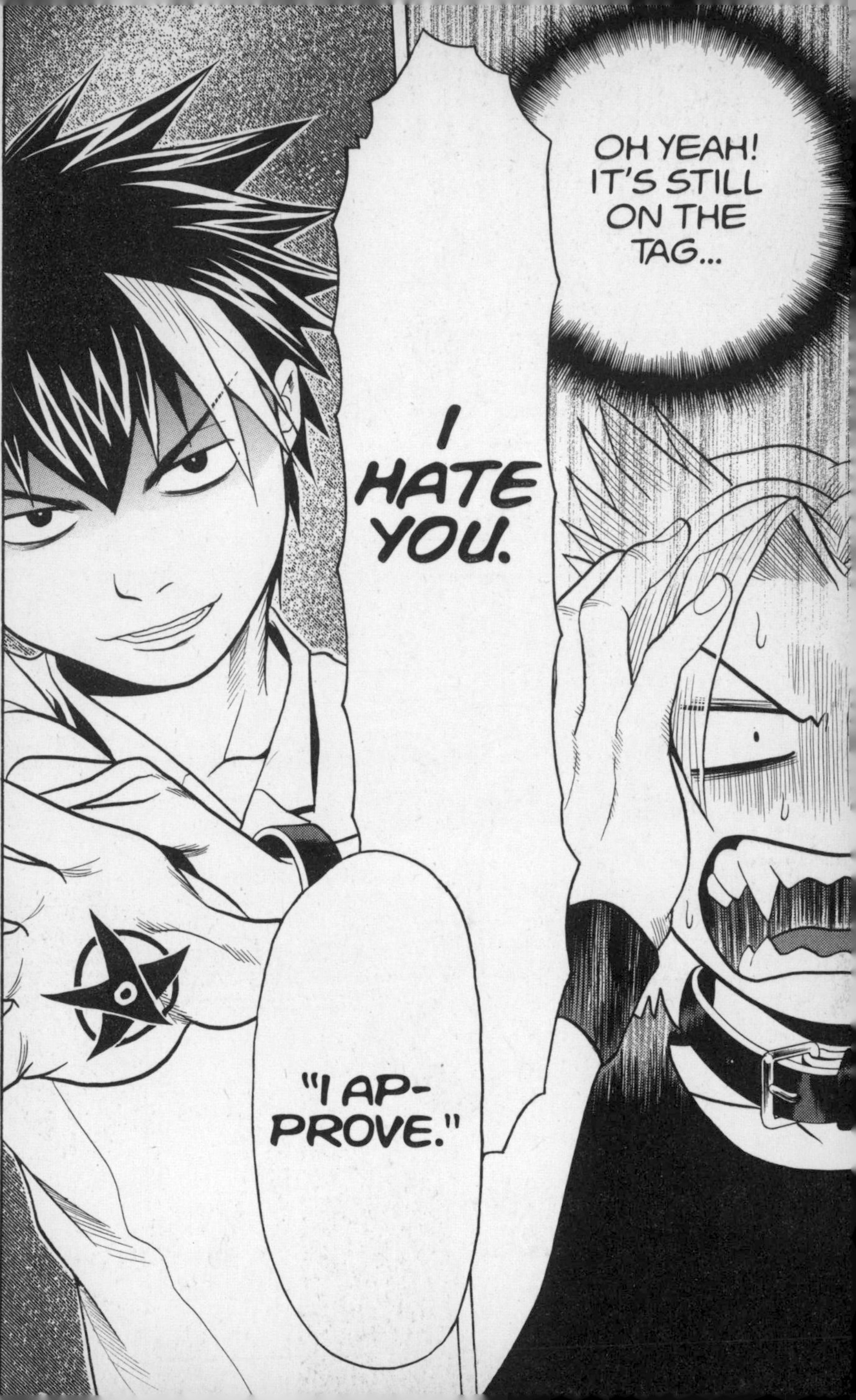
OH YEAH! IT'S STILL ON THE TAG...
I HATE YOU.
"I AP-PROVE."

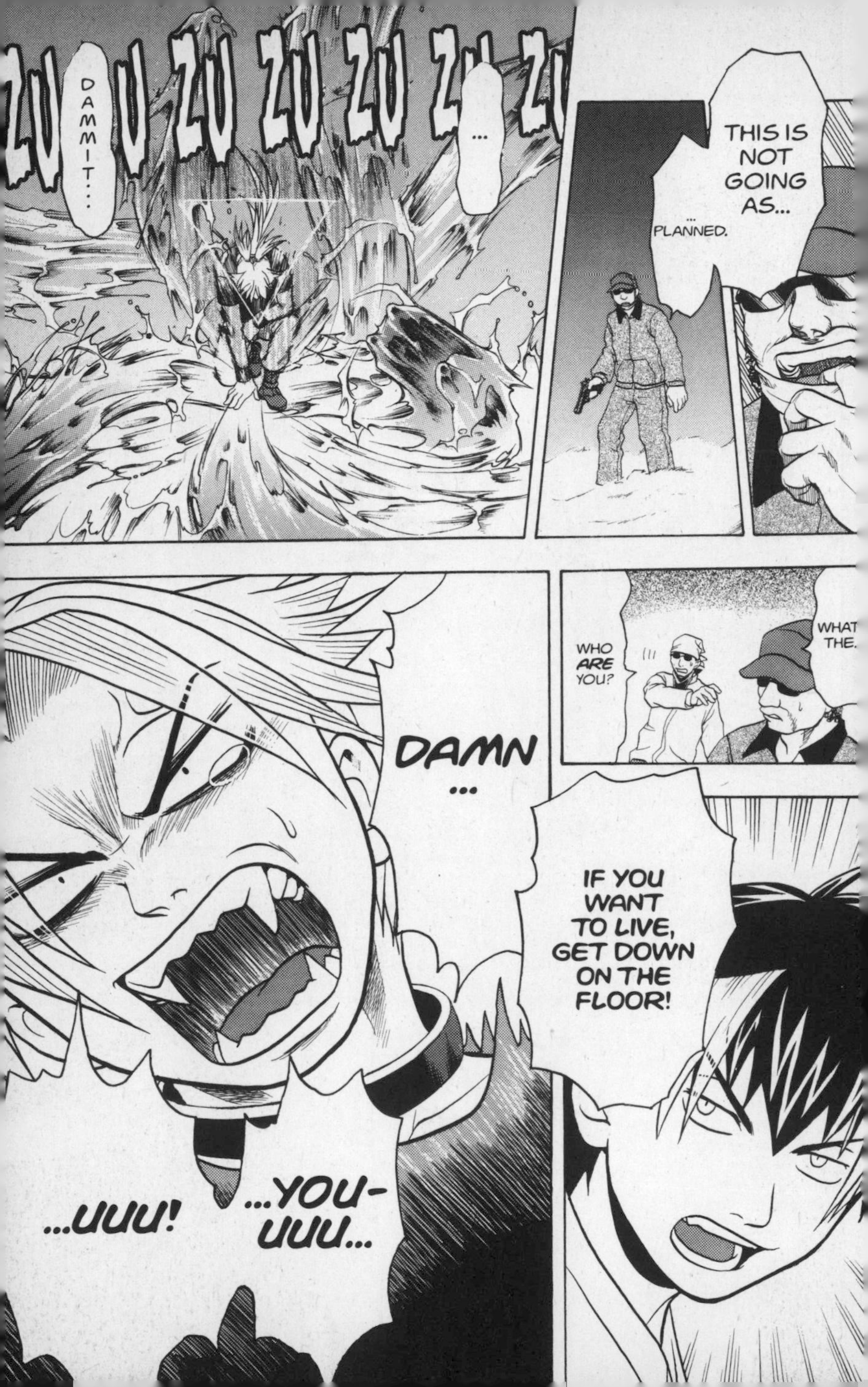
THIS IS NOT GOING AS...
... PLANNED.
ZU ZU ZU ZU ZU ZU ZU ZU
...
DAMMIT...
WHAT THE.
WHO ARE YOU?
IF YOU WANT TO LIVE, GET DOWN ON THE FLOOR!
DAMN ...
...YOU-UUU...
...UUU!

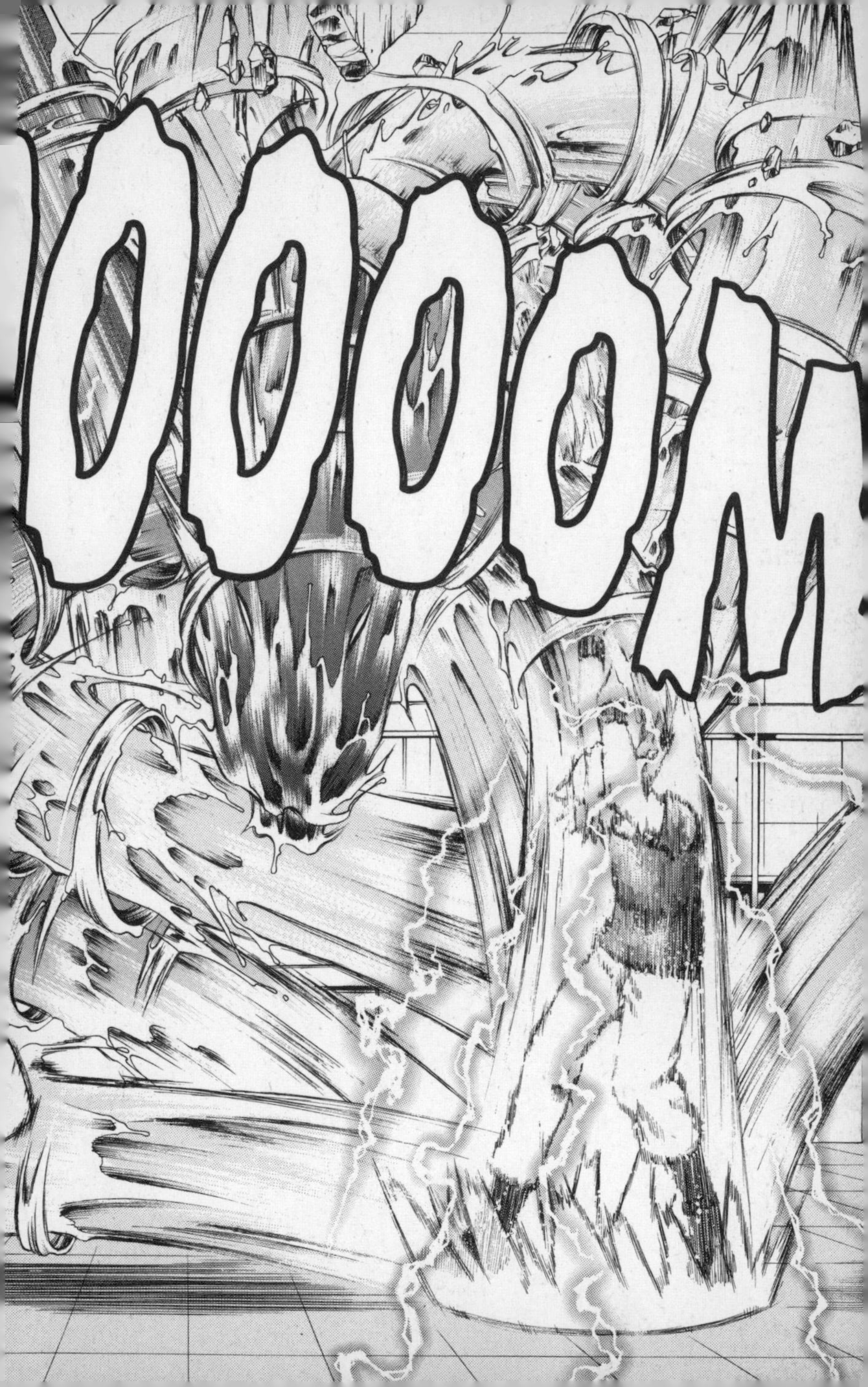
OOOOM

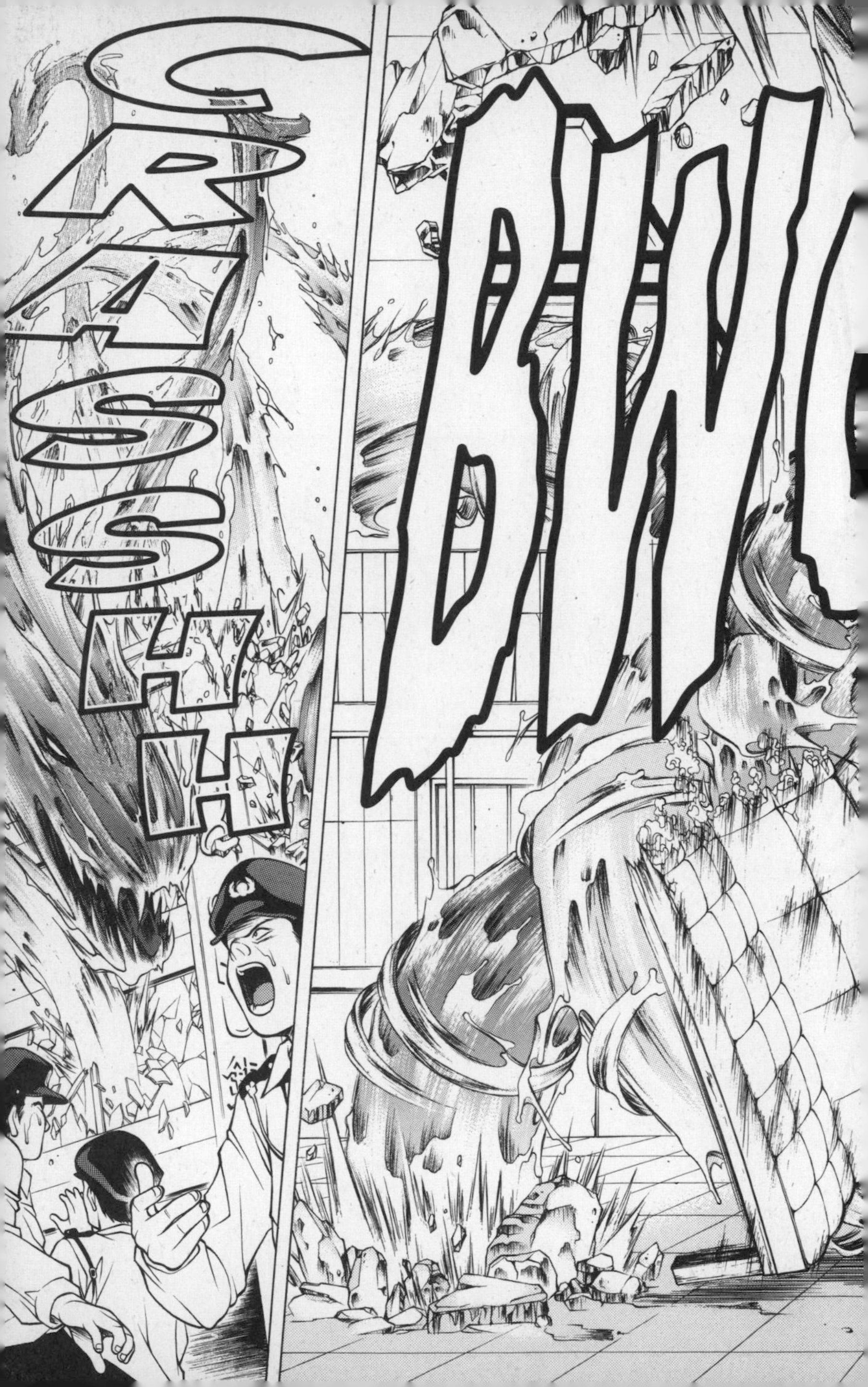
CRASSHH

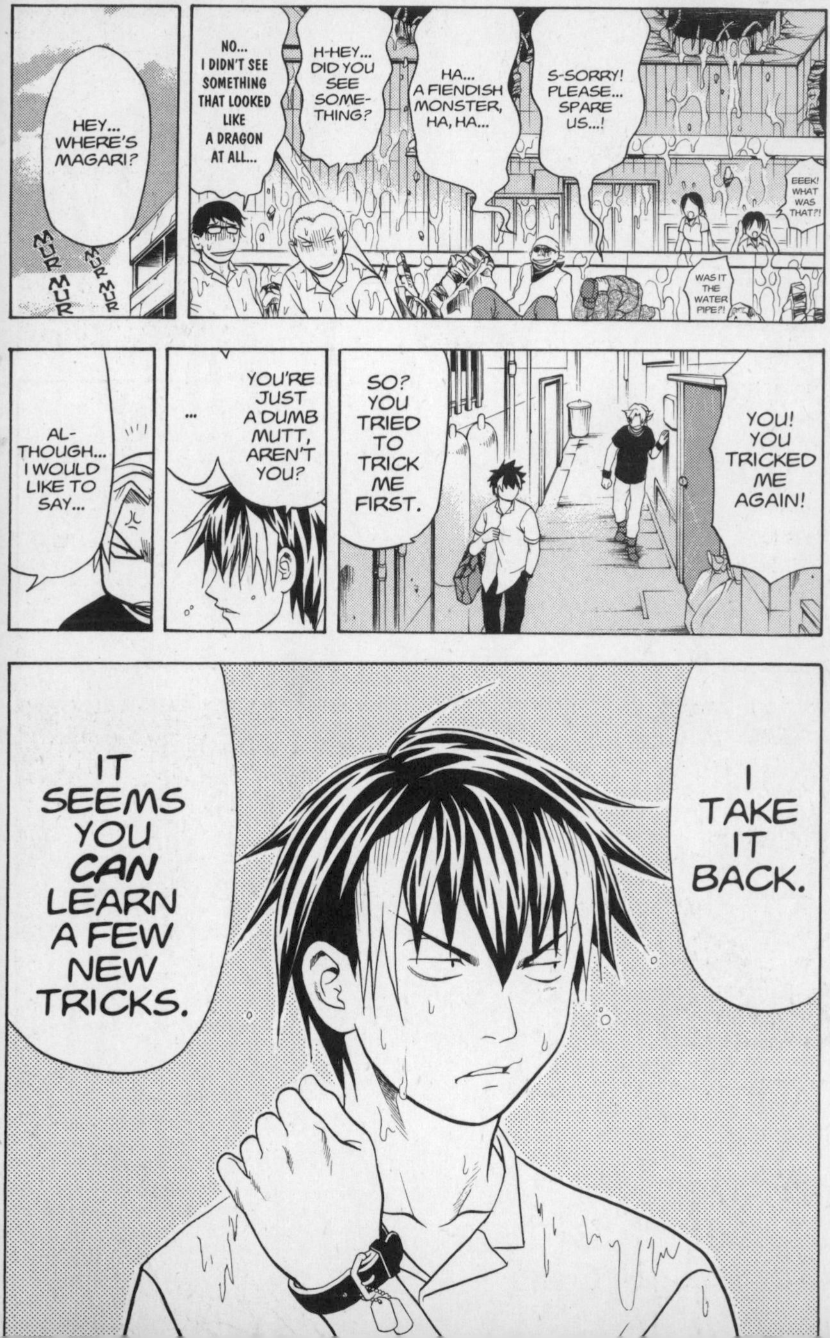
S-SORRY! PLEASE... SPARE US...!
HA... A FIENDISH MONSTER, HA, HA...
H-HEY... DID YOU SEE SOME-THING?
NO... I DIDN'T SEE SOMETHING THAT LOOKED LIKE A DRAGON AT ALL...
EEEK! WHAT WAS THAT?!
WAS IT THE WATER PIPE?!
HEY... WHERE'S MAGARI?
MUR MUR
MUR MUR
YOU! YOU TRICKED ME AGAIN!
SO? YOU TRIED TO TRICK ME FIRST.
YOU'RE JUST A DUMB MUTT, AREN'T YOU?
...
AL-THOUGH... I WOULD LIKE TO SAY...
I TAKE IT BACK.
IT SEEMS YOU *CAN* LEARN A FEW NEW TRICKS.

READ THIS WAY

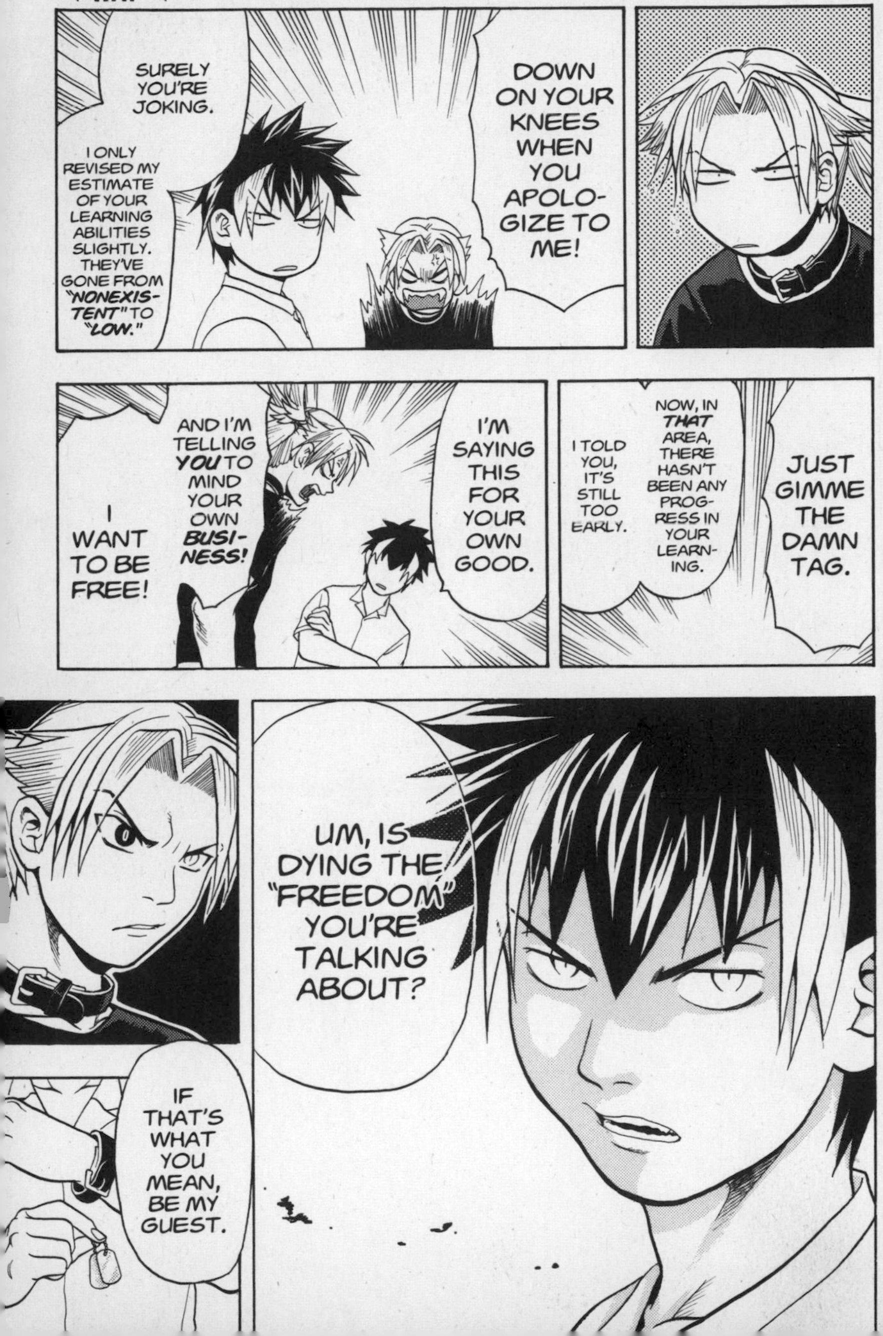
DOWN ON YOUR KNEES WHEN YOU APOLOGIZE TO ME!
SURELY YOU'RE JOKING.
I ONLY REVISED MY ESTIMATE OF YOUR LEARNING ABILITIES SLIGHTLY. THEY'VE GONE FROM "NONEXISTENT" TO "LOW."
JUST GIMME THE DAMN TAG.
NOW, IN THAT AREA, THERE HASN'T BEEN ANY PROGRESS IN YOUR LEARNING.
I TOLD YOU, IT'S STILL TOO EARLY.
I'M SAYING THIS FOR YOUR OWN GOOD.
AND I'M TELLING YOU TO MIND YOUR OWN BUSINESS!
I WANT TO BE FREE!
UM, IS DYING THE "FREEDOM" YOU'RE TALKING ABOUT?
IF THAT'S WHAT YOU MEAN, BE MY GUEST.

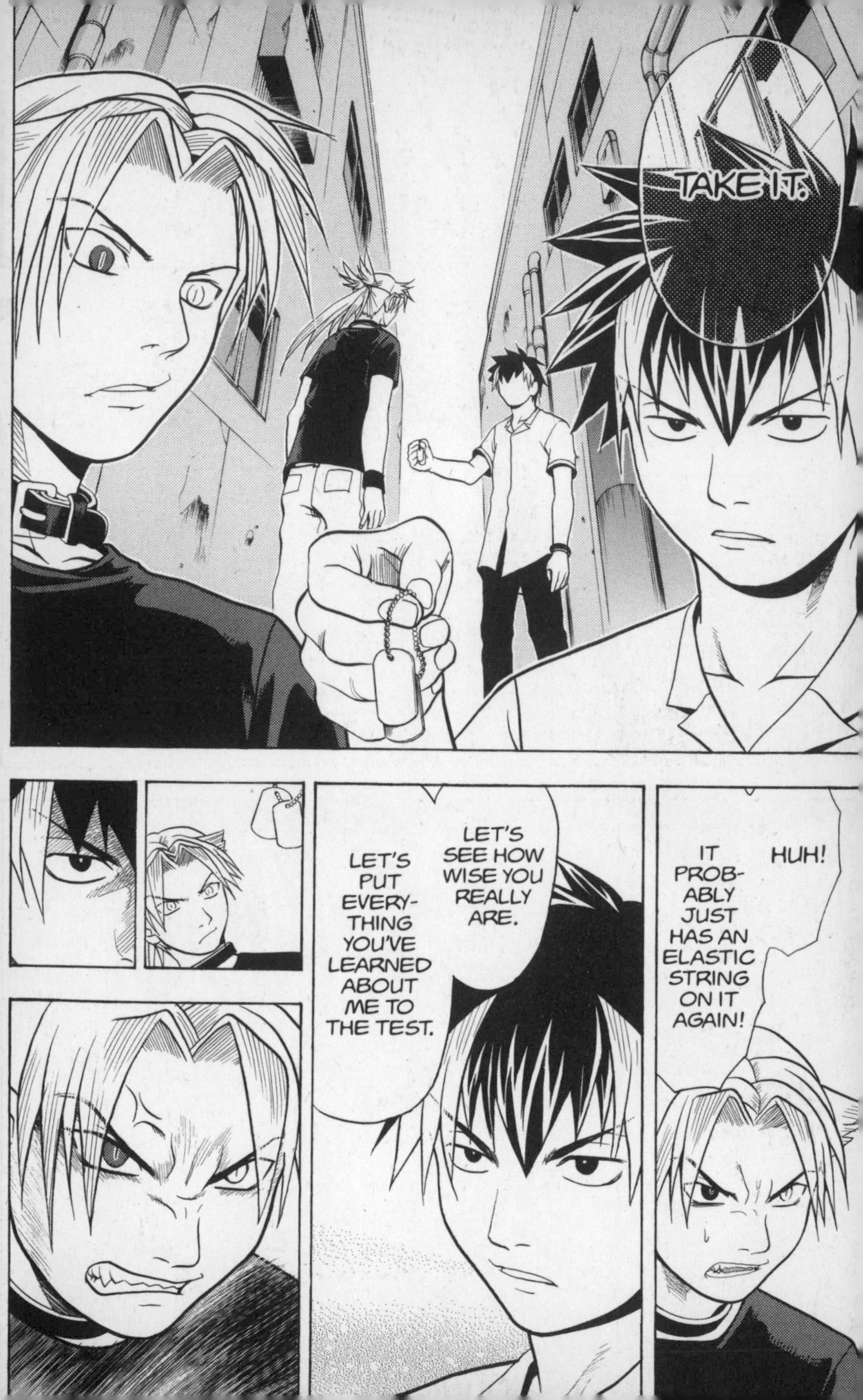
TAKE IT.
HUH!
IT PROBABLY JUST HAS AN ELASTIC STRING ON IT AGAIN!
LET'S SEE HOW WISE YOU REALLY ARE.
LET'S PUT EVERYTHING YOU'VE LEARNED ABOUT ME TO THE TEST.

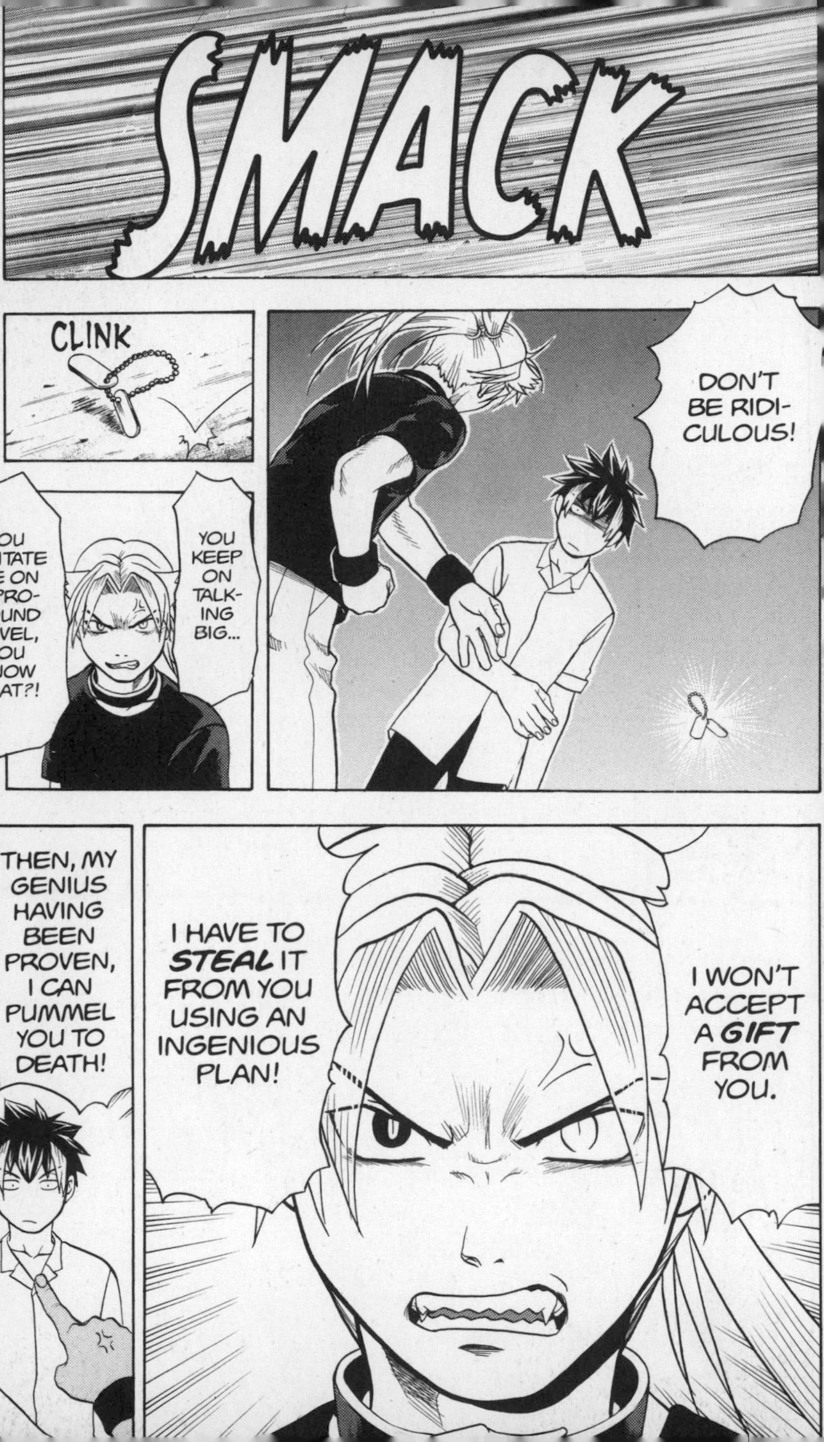
SMACK
DON'T BE RIDICULOUS!
CLINK
YOU KEEP ON TALKING BIG...
YOU IRRITATE ME ON A PROFOUND LEVEL, YOU KNOW THAT?!
I WON'T ACCEPT A GIFT FROM YOU.
I HAVE TO STEAL IT FROM YOU USING AN INGENIOUS PLAN!
THEN, MY GENIUS HAVING BEEN PROVEN, I CAN PUMMEL YOU TO DEATH!

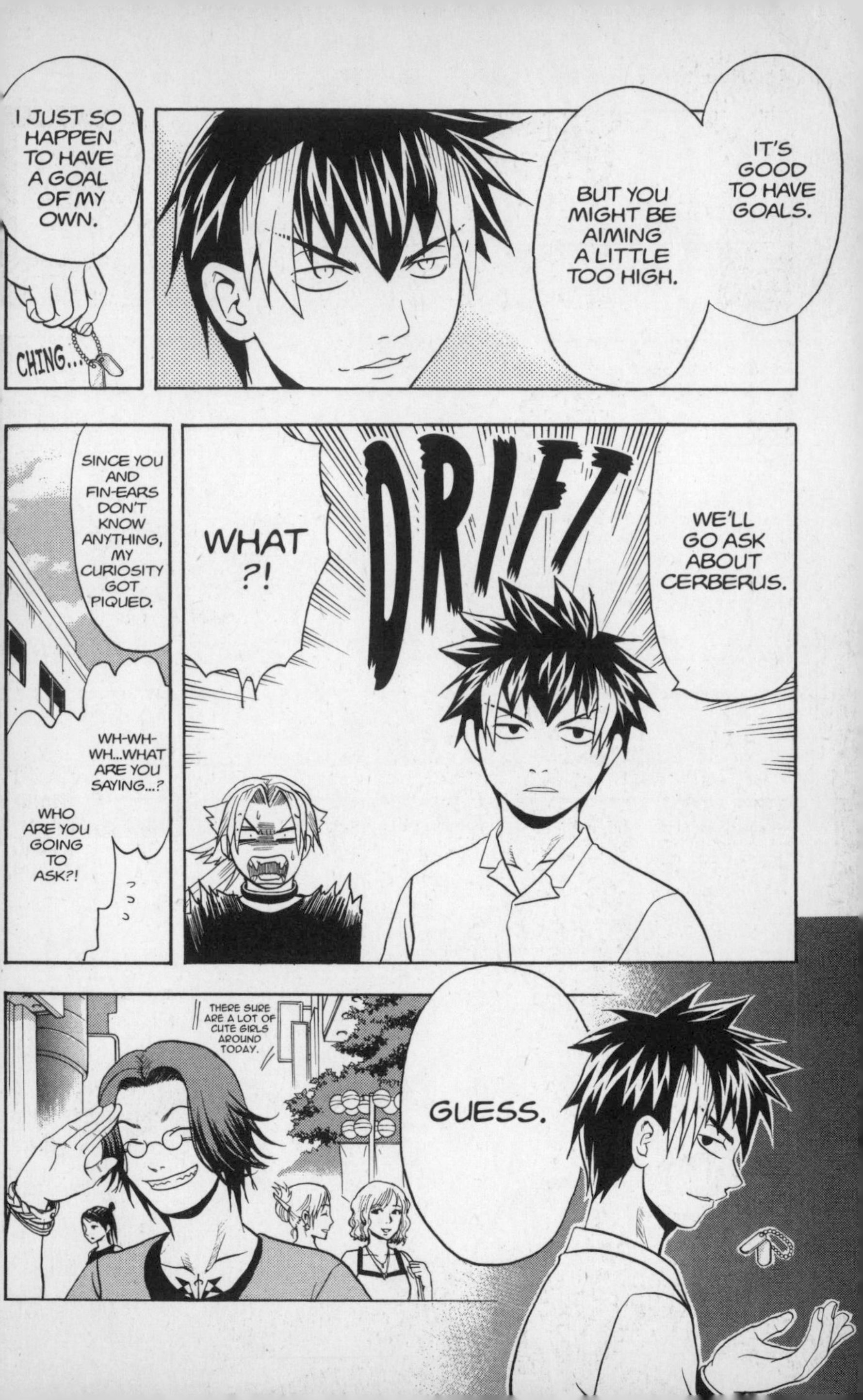
IT'S GOOD TO HAVE GOALS.
BUT YOU MIGHT BE AIMING A LITTLE TOO HIGH.
I JUST SO HAPPEN TO HAVE A GOAL OF MY OWN.
CHING...
WE'LL GO ASK ABOUT CERBERUS.
DRIFT
WHAT ?!
SINCE YOU AND FIN-EARS DON'T KNOW ANYTHING, MY CURIOSITY GOT PIQUED.
WH-WH-WH...WHAT ARE YOU SAYING...?
WHO ARE YOU GOING TO ASK?!
GUESS.
THERE SURE ARE A LOT OF CUTE GIRLS AROUND TODAY.

READ THIS WAY

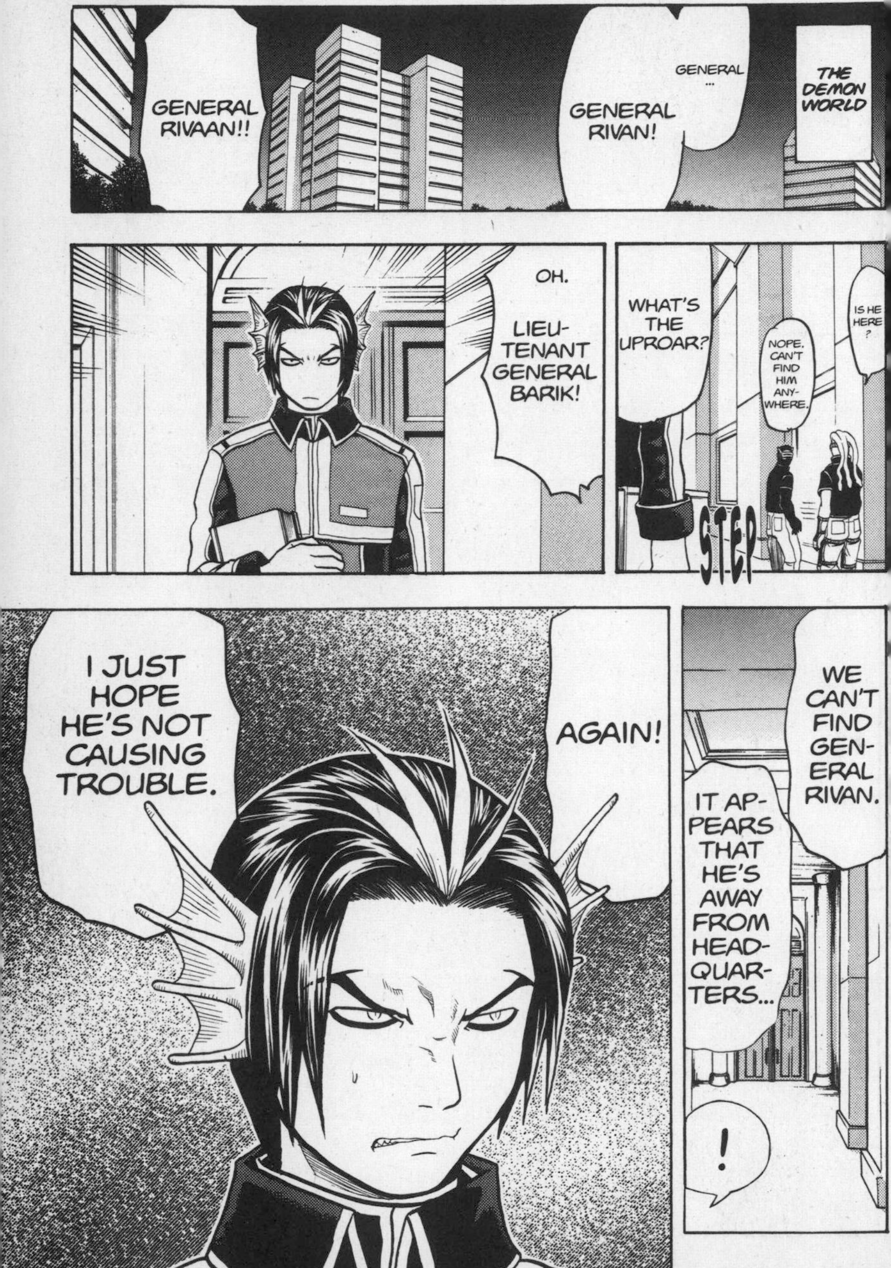
THE DEMON WORLD
GENERAL ...
GENERAL RIVAN!
GENERAL RIVAAN!!
IS HE HERE?
NOPE. CAN'T FIND HIM ANY-WHERE.
WHAT'S THE UPROAR?
STEP
OH.
LIEU-TENANT GENERAL BARIK!
WE CAN'T FIND GEN-ERAL RIVAN.
IT AP-PEARS THAT HE'S AWAY FROM HEAD-QUAR-TERS...
!
AGAIN!
I JUST HOPE HE'S NOT CAUSING TROUBLE.

Story 7: The Legend Lives

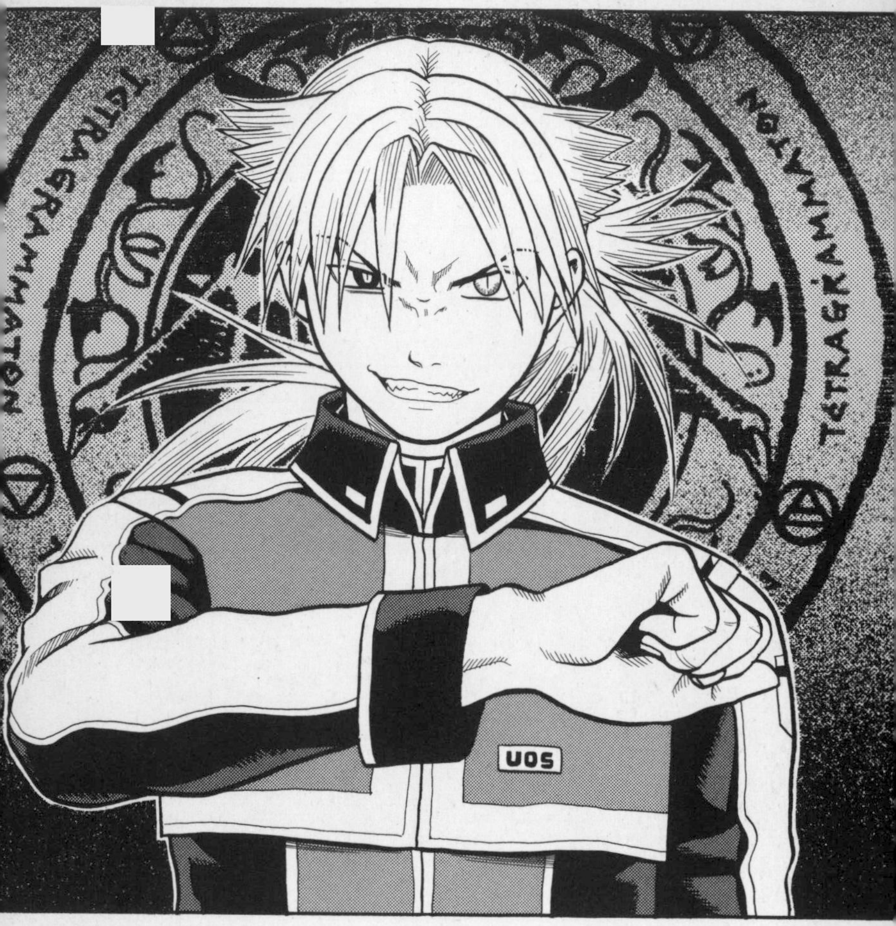
TETRAGRAMMATON
TETRAGRAMMATON
UOS

READ THIS WAY

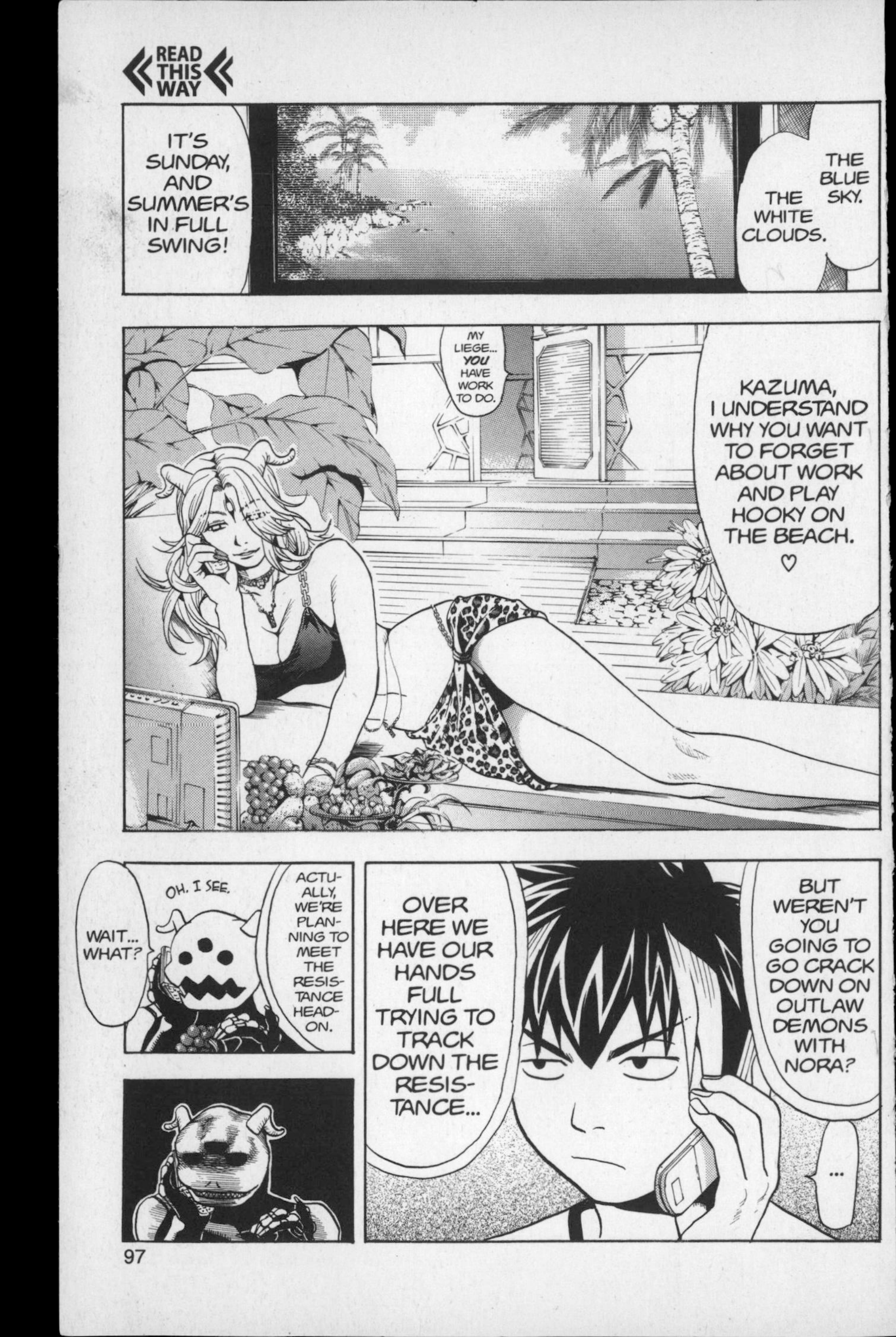
THE BLUE SKY. THE WHITE CLOUDS.
IT'S SUNDAY, AND SUMMER'S IN FULL SWING!
KAZUMA, I UNDERSTAND WHY YOU WANT TO FORGET ABOUT WORK AND PLAY HOOKY ON THE BEACH. ♡
MY LIEGE... YOU HAVE WORK TO DO.
BUT WEREN'T YOU GOING TO GO CRACK DOWN ON OUTLAW DEMONS WITH NORA?
OVER HERE WE HAVE OUR HANDS FULL TRYING TO TRACK DOWN THE RESISTANCE...
...
ACTUALLY, WE'RE PLANNING TO MEET THE RESISTANCE HEAD-ON.
OH. I SEE.
WAIT... WHAT?

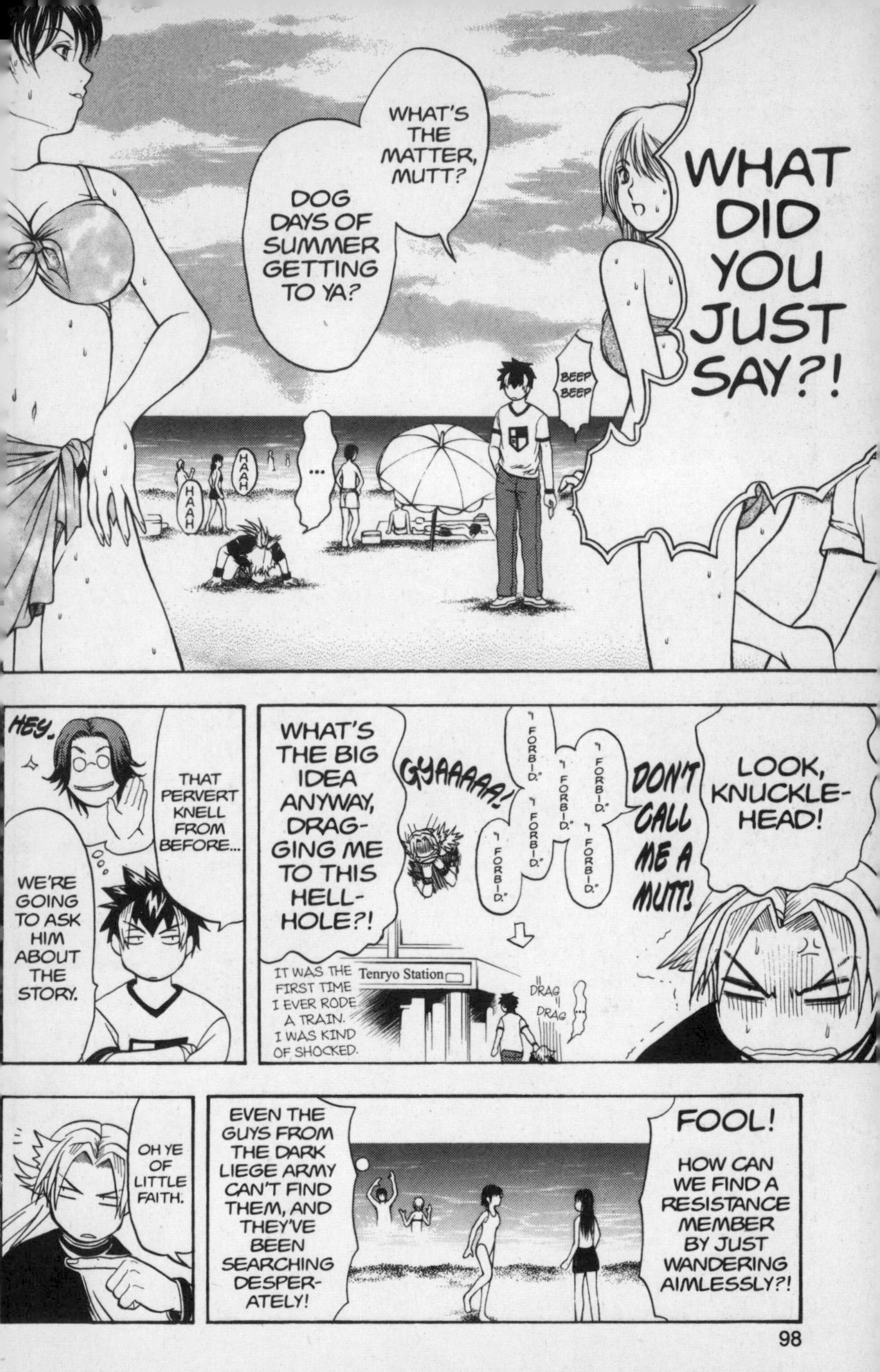

WHAT'S THE MATTER, MUTT?
DOG DAYS OF SUMMER GETTING TO YA?
WHAT DID YOU JUST SAY?!
BEEP BEEP
...
HAAH HAAH
LOOK, KNUCKLEHEAD!
DON'T CALL ME A MUTT!
"I FORBID." "I FORBID." "I FORBID." "I FORBID." "I FORBID."
GYAAAAAA!
WHAT'S THE BIG IDEA ANYWAY, DRAGGING ME TO THIS HELLHOLE?!
Tenryo Station
IT WAS THE FIRST TIME I EVER RODE A TRAIN. I WAS KIND OF SHOCKED.
DRAG DRAG
...
HEY.
THAT PERVERT KNELL FROM BEFORE...
WE'RE GOING TO ASK HIM ABOUT THE STORY.
FOOL!
HOW CAN WE FIND A RESISTANCE MEMBER BY JUST WANDERING AIMLESSLY?!
EVEN THE GUYS FROM THE DARK LIEGE ARMY CAN'T FIND THEM, AND THEY'VE BEEN SEARCHING DESPERATELY!
OH YE OF LITTLE FAITH.

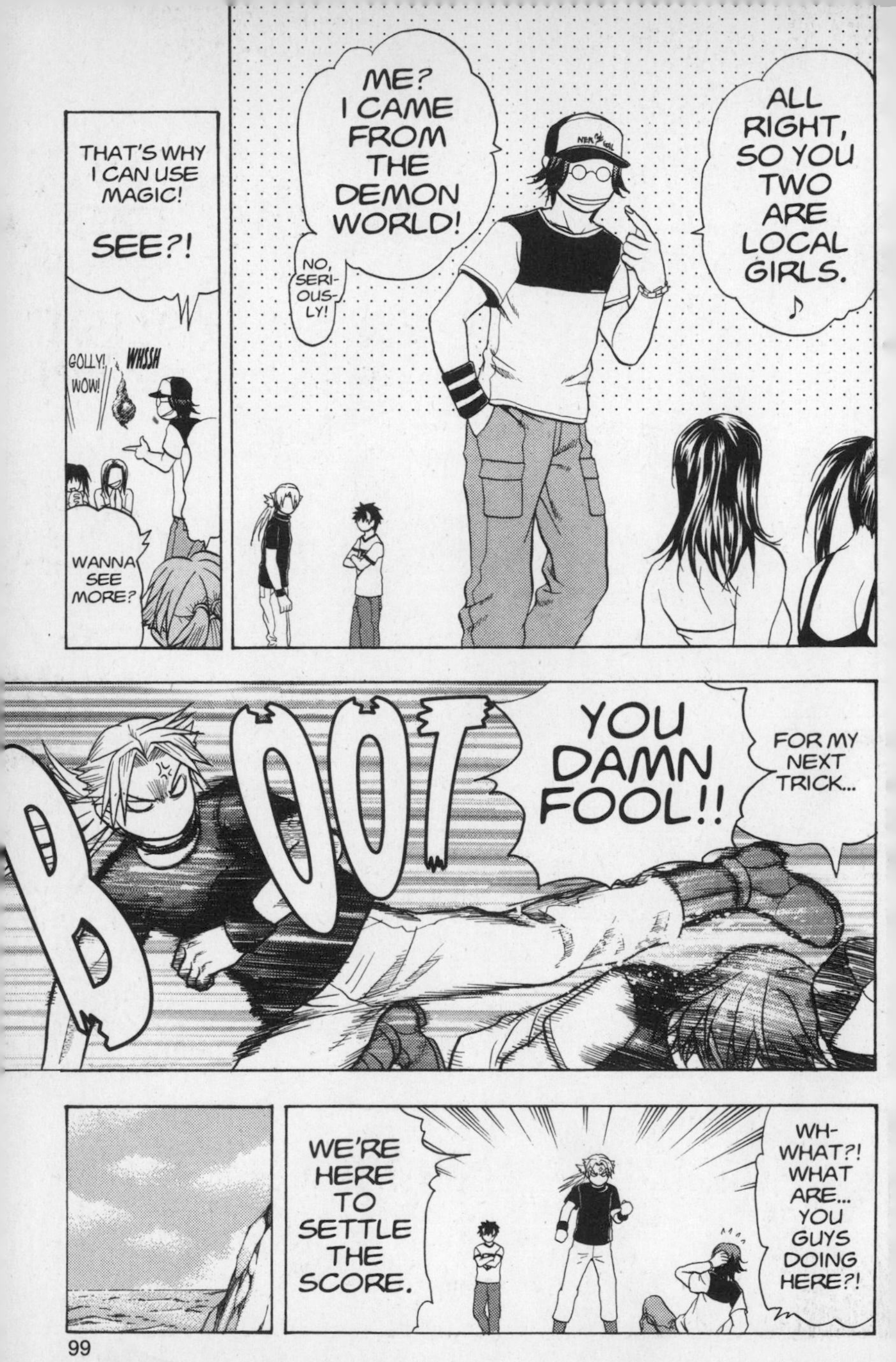
ALL RIGHT, SO YOU TWO ARE LOCAL GIRLS. ♪
ME? I CAME FROM THE DEMON WORLD!
NO, SERIOUSLY!
THAT'S WHY I CAN USE MAGIC! SEE?!
WHSSH
GOLLY! WOW!
WANNA SEE MORE?
FOR MY NEXT TRICK...
YOU DAMN FOOL!!
BOOT
WH-WHAT?! WHAT ARE... YOU GUYS DOING HERE?!
WE'RE HERE TO SETTLE THE SCORE.

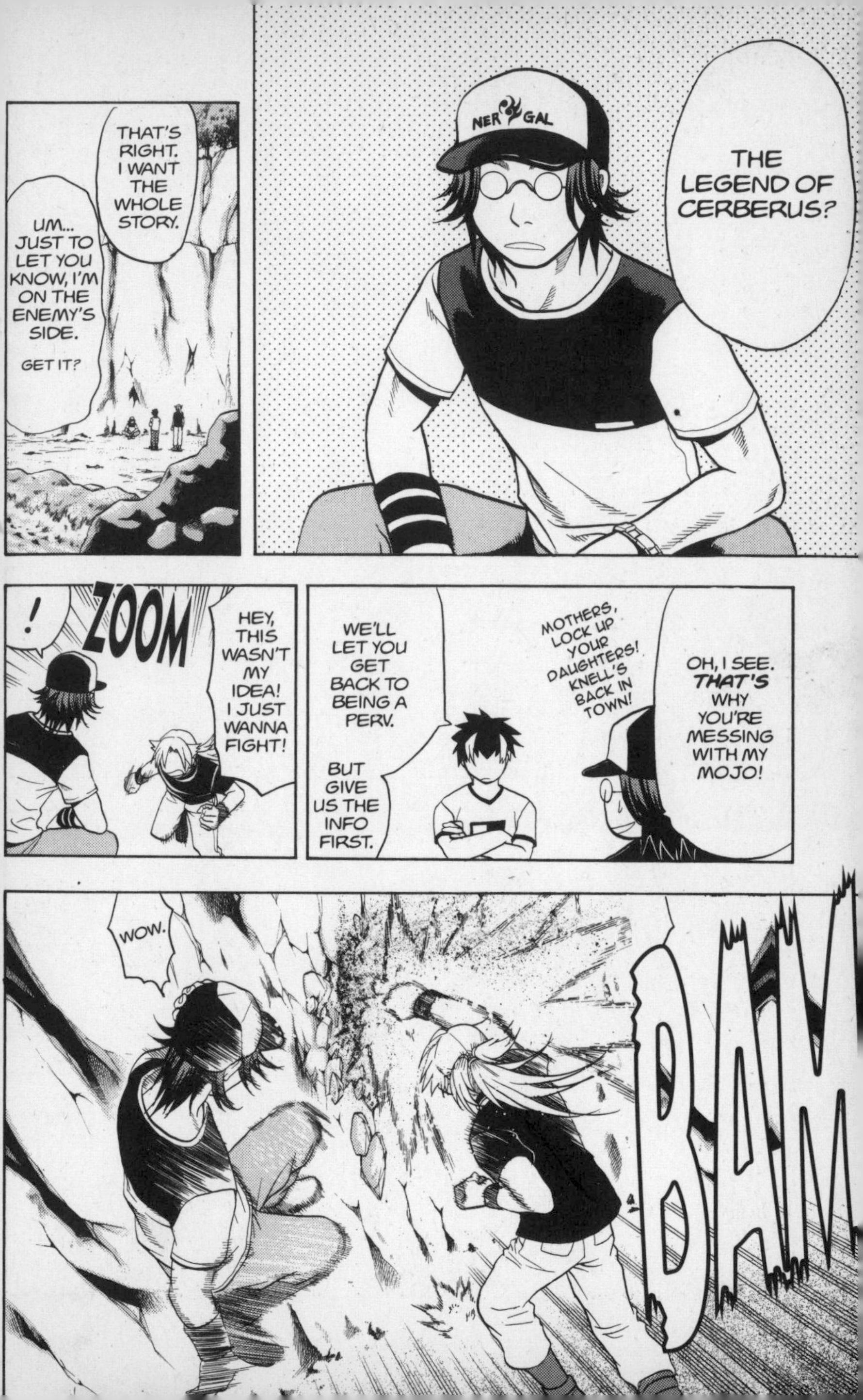
THE LEGEND OF CERBERUS?
THAT'S RIGHT. I WANT THE WHOLE STORY.
UM... JUST TO LET YOU KNOW, I'M ON THE ENEMY'S SIDE.
GET IT?
OH, I SEE. ***THAT'S*** WHY YOU'RE MESSING WITH MY MOJO!
MOTHERS, LOCK UP YOUR DAUGHTERS! KNELL'S BACK IN TOWN!
WE'LL LET YOU GET BACK TO BEING A PERV.
BUT GIVE US THE INFO FIRST.
HEY, THIS WASN'T MY IDEA! I JUST WANNA FIGHT!
ZOOM
!
BAM
WOW.

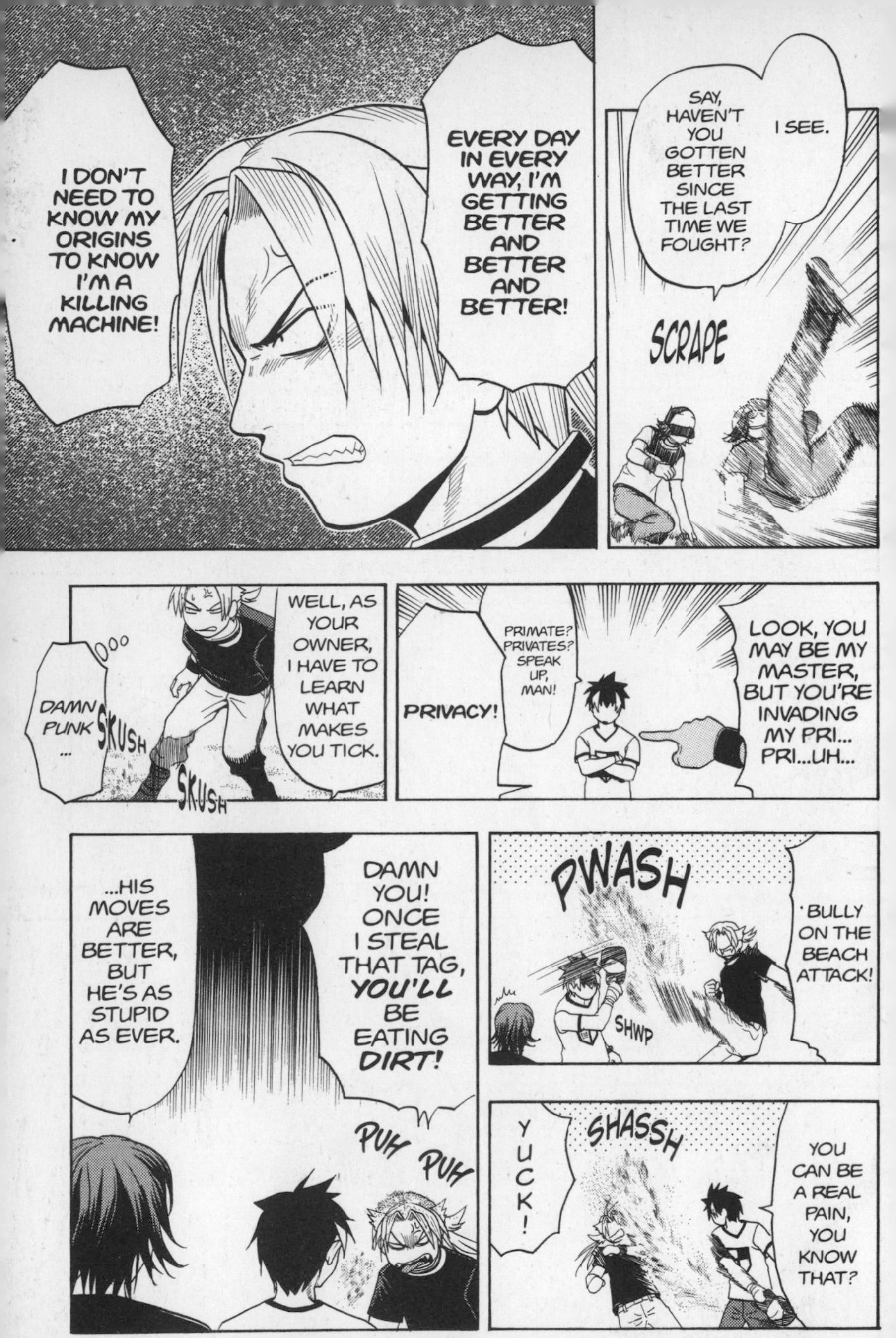
I SEE.
SAY, HAVEN'T YOU GOTTEN BETTER SINCE THE LAST TIME WE FOUGHT?
SCRAPE
EVERY DAY IN EVERY WAY, I'M GETTING BETTER AND BETTER AND BETTER!
I DON'T NEED TO KNOW MY ORIGINS TO KNOW I'M A KILLING MACHINE!
LOOK, YOU MAY BE MY MASTER, BUT YOU'RE INVADING MY PRI... PRI...UH...
PRIMATE? PRIVATES? SPEAK UP, MAN!
PRIVACY!
WELL, AS YOUR OWNER, I HAVE TO LEARN WHAT MAKES YOU TICK.
OOO
DAMN PUNK...
SKUSH
SKUSH
BULLY ON THE BEACH ATTACK!
PWASH
SHWP
YOU CAN BE A REAL PAIN, YOU KNOW THAT?
SHASSH
YUCK!
DAMN YOU! ONCE I STEAL THAT TAG, *YOU'LL* BE EATING *DIRT!*
...HIS MOVES ARE BETTER, BUT HE'S AS STUPID AS EVER.
PUK PUK

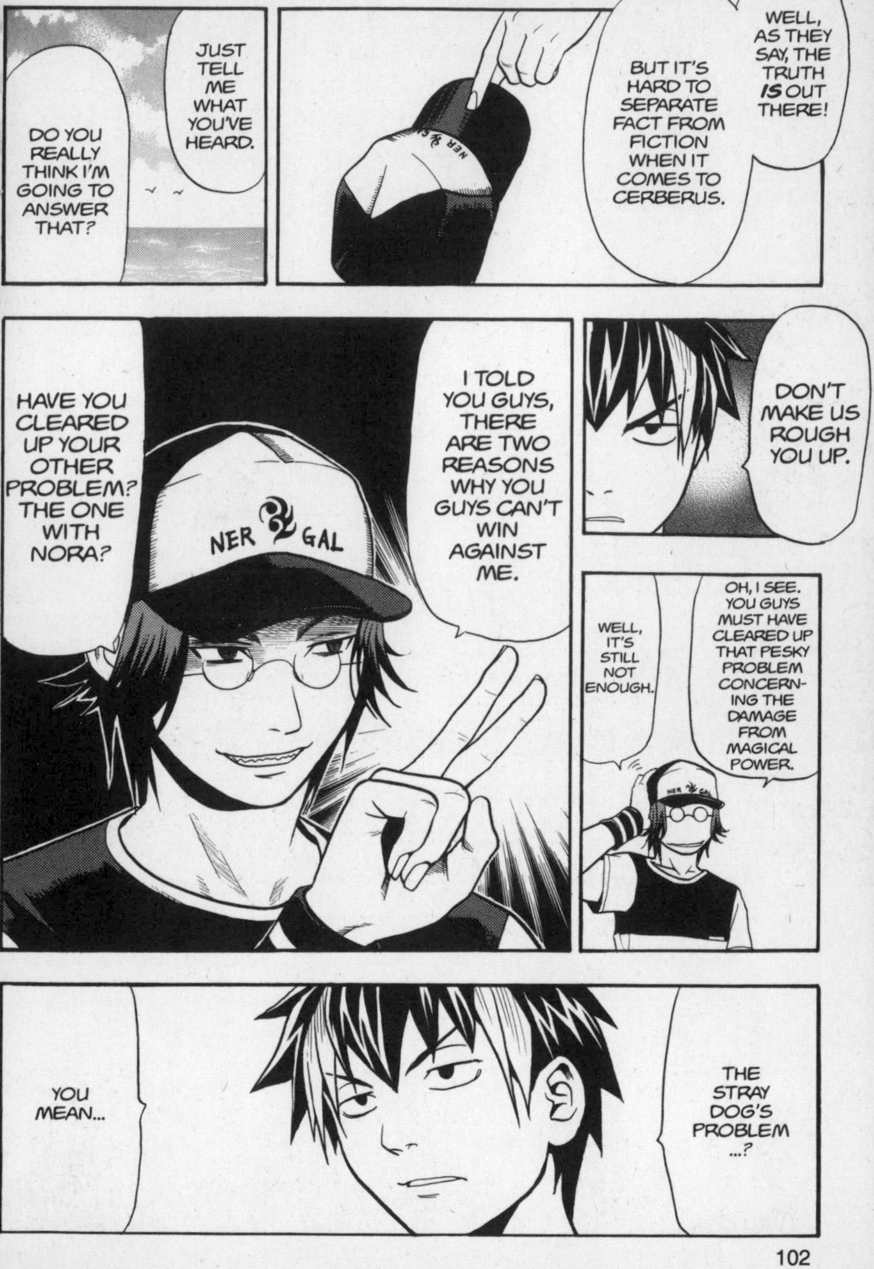
WELL, AS THEY SAY, THE TRUTH *IS* OUT THERE!
BUT IT'S HARD TO SEPARATE FACT FROM FICTION WHEN IT COMES TO CERBERUS.
JUST TELL ME WHAT YOU'VE HEARD.
DO YOU REALLY THINK I'M GOING TO ANSWER THAT?
DON'T MAKE US ROUGH YOU UP.
OH, I SEE. YOU GUYS MUST HAVE CLEARED UP THAT PESKY PROBLEM CONCERNING THE DAMAGE FROM MAGICAL POWER.
WELL, IT'S STILL NOT ENOUGH.
I TOLD YOU GUYS, THERE ARE TWO REASONS WHY YOU GUYS CAN'T WIN AGAINST ME.
NER GAL
HAVE YOU CLEARED UP YOUR OTHER PROBLEM? THE ONE WITH NORA?
THE STRAY DOG'S PROBLEM ...?
YOU MEAN...

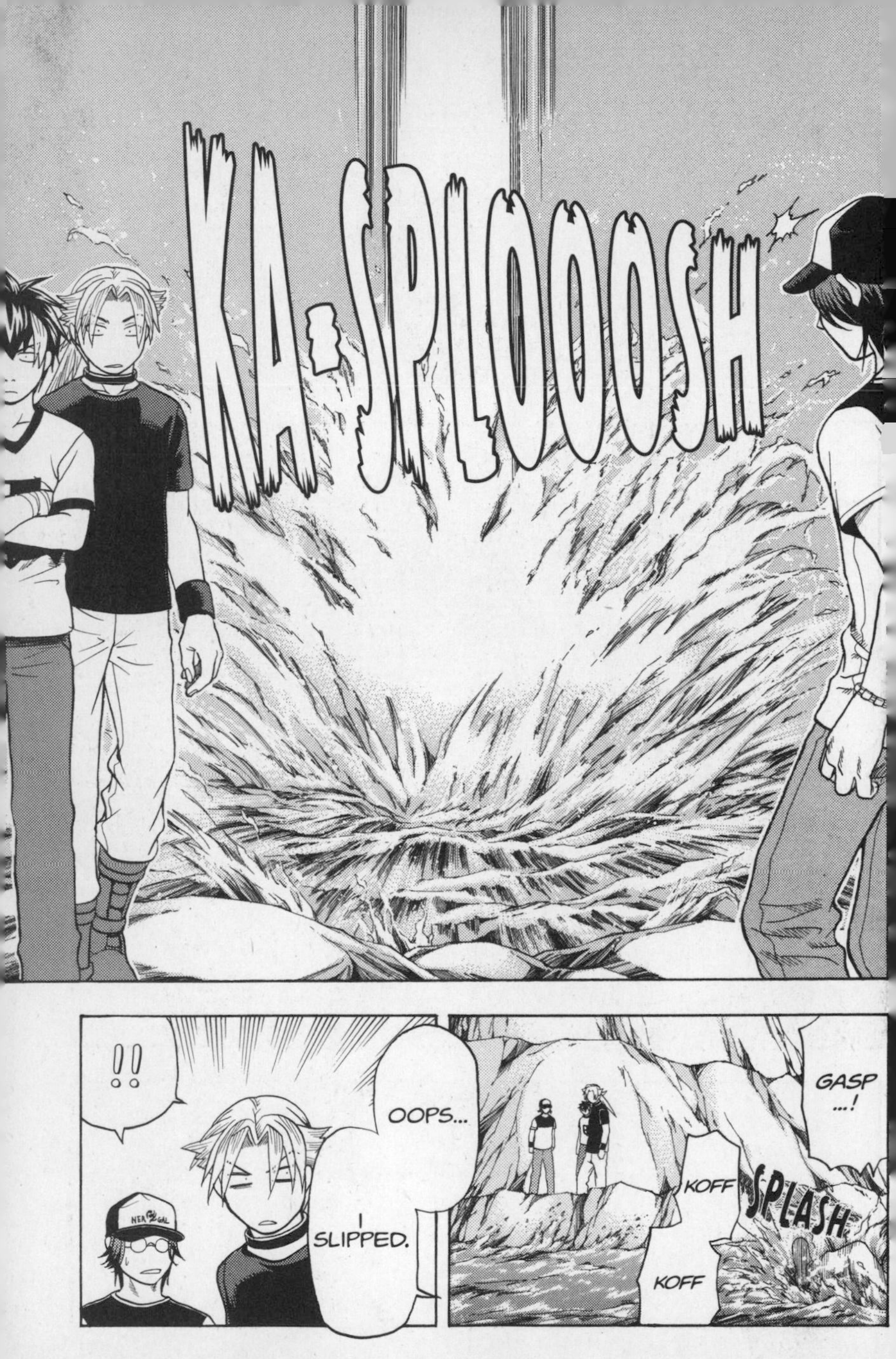
KA-SPLOOOSH
GASP ...!
KOFF
SPLASH
KOFF
!!
OOPS...
I SLIPPED.

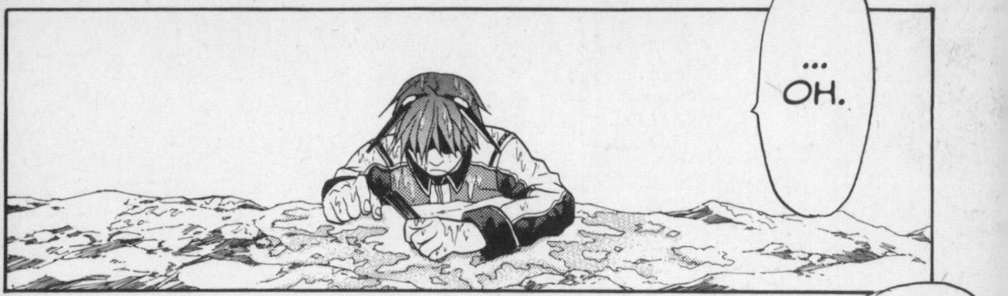
...OH.
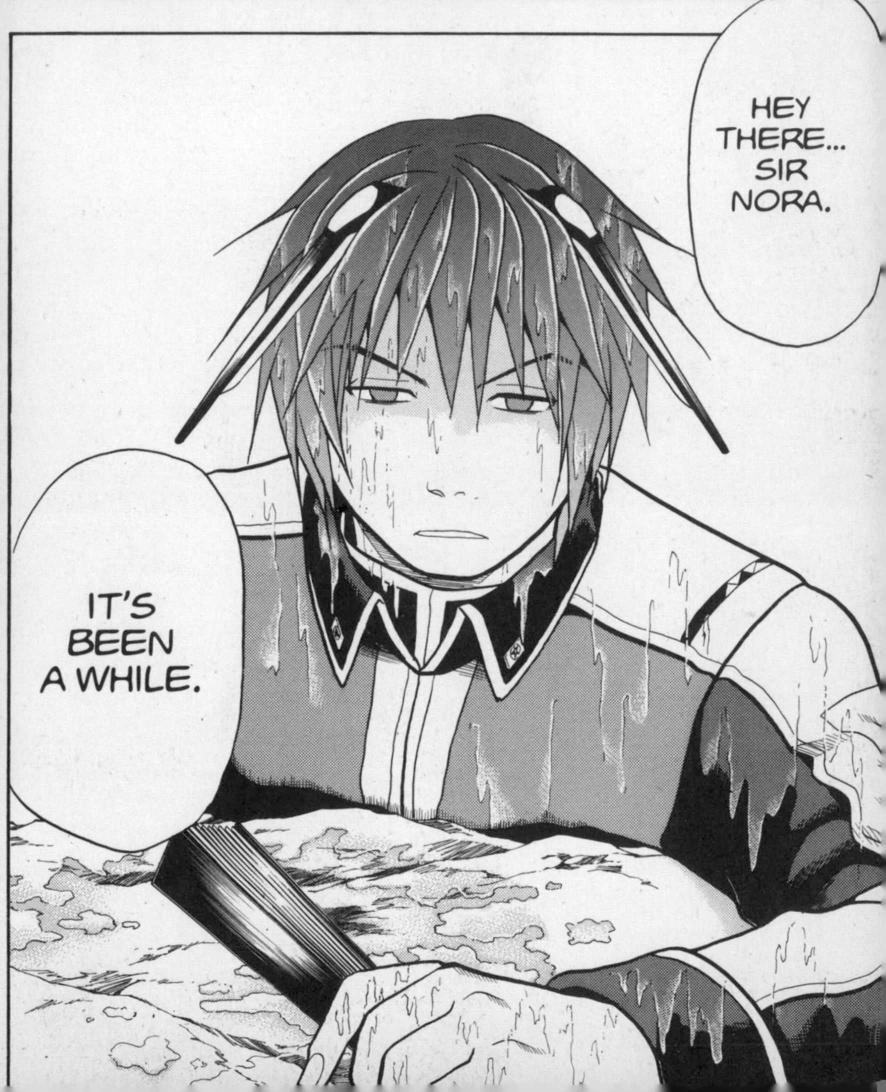
HEY THERE... SIR NORA.
IT'S BEEN A WHILE.

READ THIS WAY

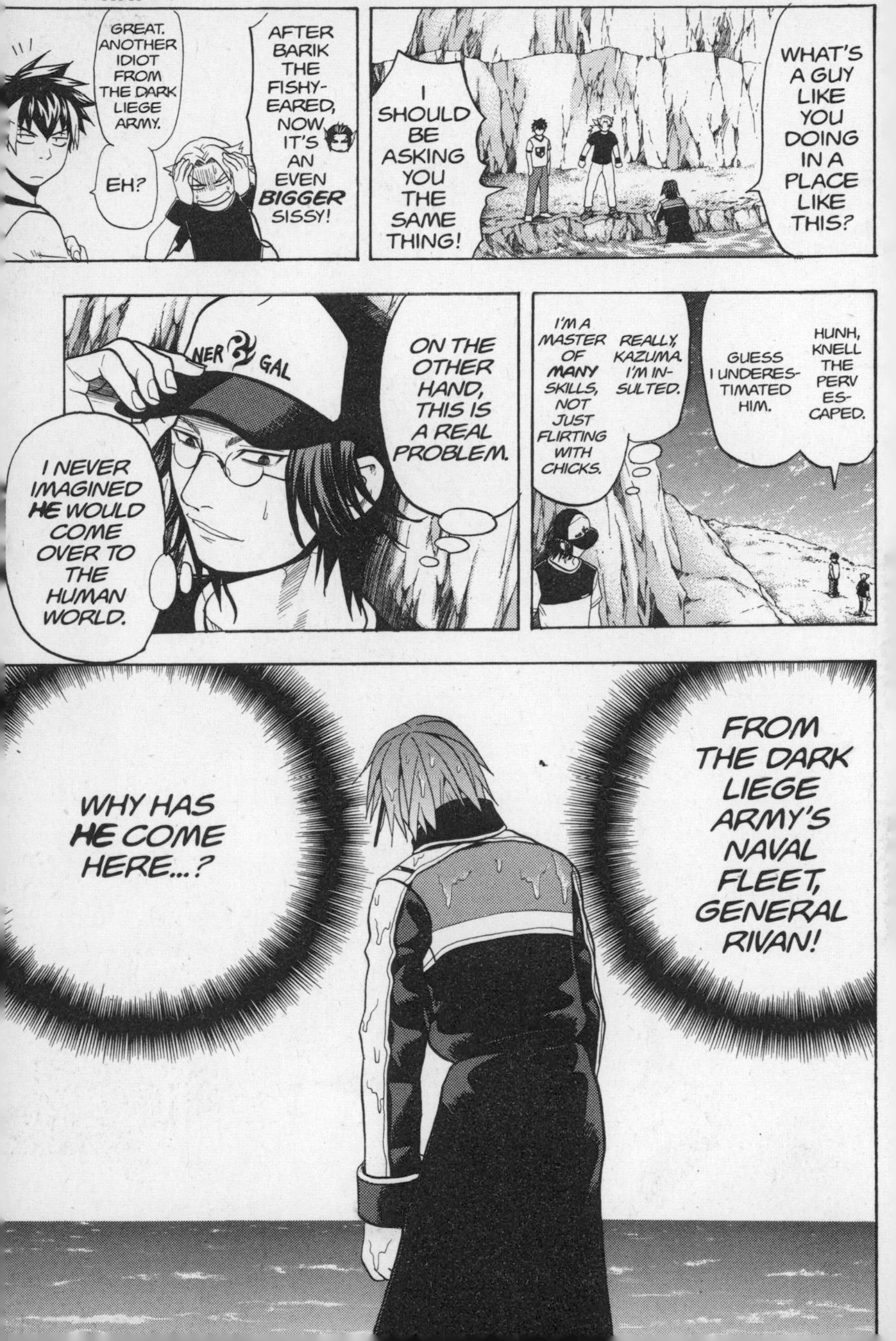
WHAT'S A GUY LIKE YOU DOING IN A PLACE LIKE THIS?
I SHOULD BE ASKING YOU THE SAME THING!
AFTER BARIK THE FISHY-EARED, NOW, IT'S AN EVEN BIGGER SISSY!
GREAT. ANOTHER IDIOT FROM THE DARK LIEGE ARMY.
EH?
HUNH, KNELL THE PERV ESCAPED.
GUESS I UNDERESTIMATED HIM.
REALLY, KAZUMA. I'M INSULTED.
I'M A MASTER OF MANY SKILLS, NOT JUST FLIRTING WITH CHICKS.
ON THE OTHER HAND, THIS IS A REAL PROBLEM.
NER GAL
I NEVER IMAGINED HE WOULD COME OVER TO THE HUMAN WORLD.
FROM THE DARK LIEGE ARMY'S NAVAL FLEET, GENERAL RIVAN!
WHY HAS HE COME HERE...?

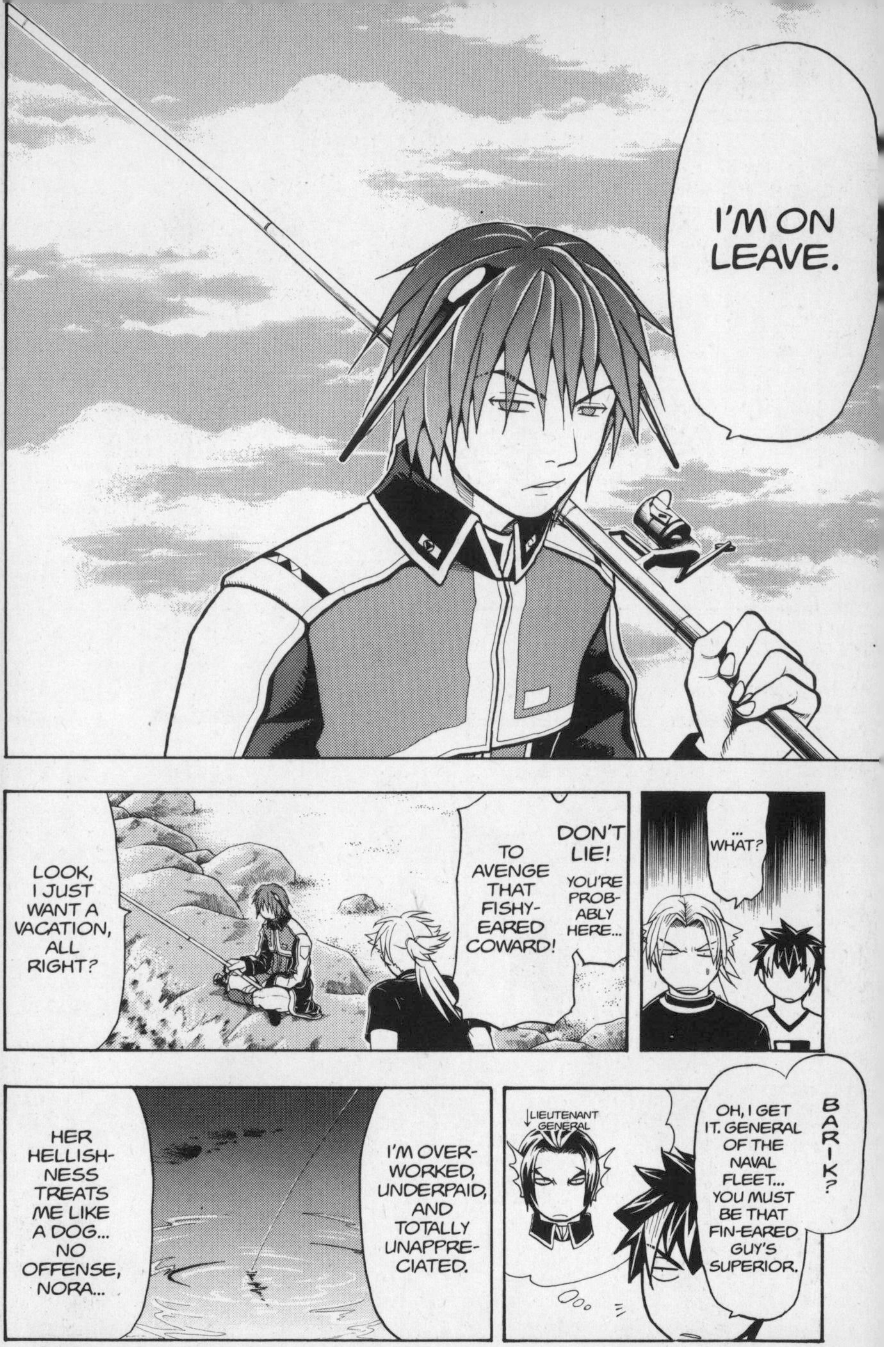
I'M ON LEAVE.
... WHAT?
DON'T LIE!
YOU'RE PROBABLY HERE...
TO AVENGE THAT FISHY-EARED COWARD!
LOOK, I JUST WANT A VACATION, ALL RIGHT?
BARIK?
OH, I GET IT. GENERAL OF THE NAVAL FLEET... YOU MUST BE THAT FIN-EARED GUY'S SUPERIOR.
↓LIEUTENANT GENERAL
I'M OVERWORKED, UNDERPAID, AND TOTALLY UNAPPRECIATED.
HER HELLISHNESS TREATS ME LIKE A DOG... NO OFFENSE, NORA...

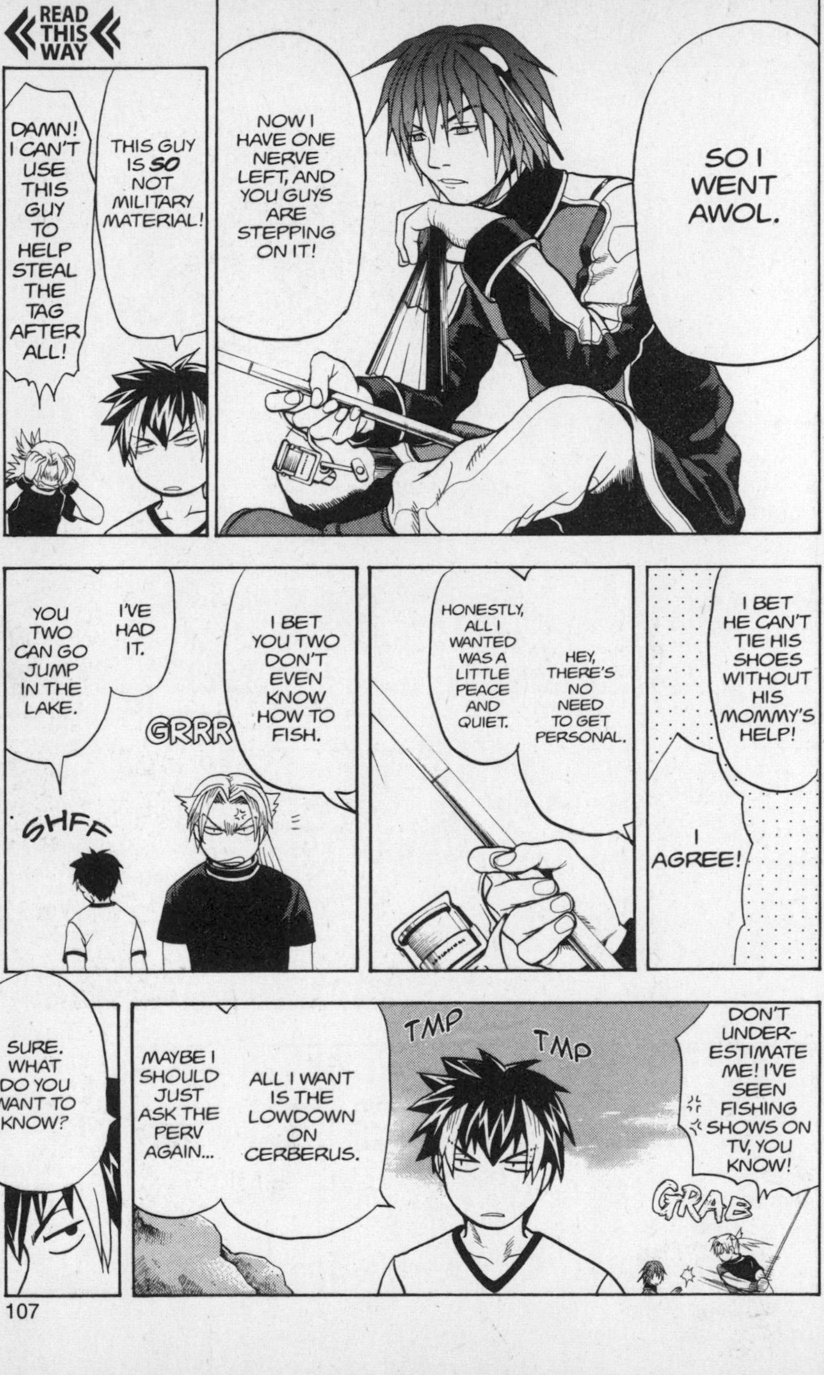
READ THIS WAY
SO I WENT AWOL.
NOW I HAVE ONE NERVE LEFT, AND YOU GUYS ARE STEPPING ON IT!
THIS GUY IS *SO* NOT MILITARY MATERIAL!
DAMN! I CAN'T USE THIS GUY TO HELP STEAL THE TAG AFTER ALL!
I BET HE CAN'T TIE HIS SHOES WITHOUT HIS MOMMY'S HELP!
I AGREE!
HEY, THERE'S NO NEED TO GET PERSONAL.
HONESTLY, ALL I WANTED WAS A LITTLE PEACE AND QUIET.
I BET YOU TWO DON'T EVEN KNOW HOW TO FISH.
GRRR
I'VE HAD IT.
YOU TWO CAN GO JUMP IN THE LAKE.
SHFF
DON'T UNDER-ESTIMATE ME! I'VE SEEN FISHING SHOWS ON TV, YOU KNOW!
GRAB
TMP
TMP
ALL I WANT IS THE LOWDOWN ON CERBERUS.
MAYBE I SHOULD JUST ASK THE PERV AGAIN...
SURE. WHAT DO YOU WANT TO KNOW?

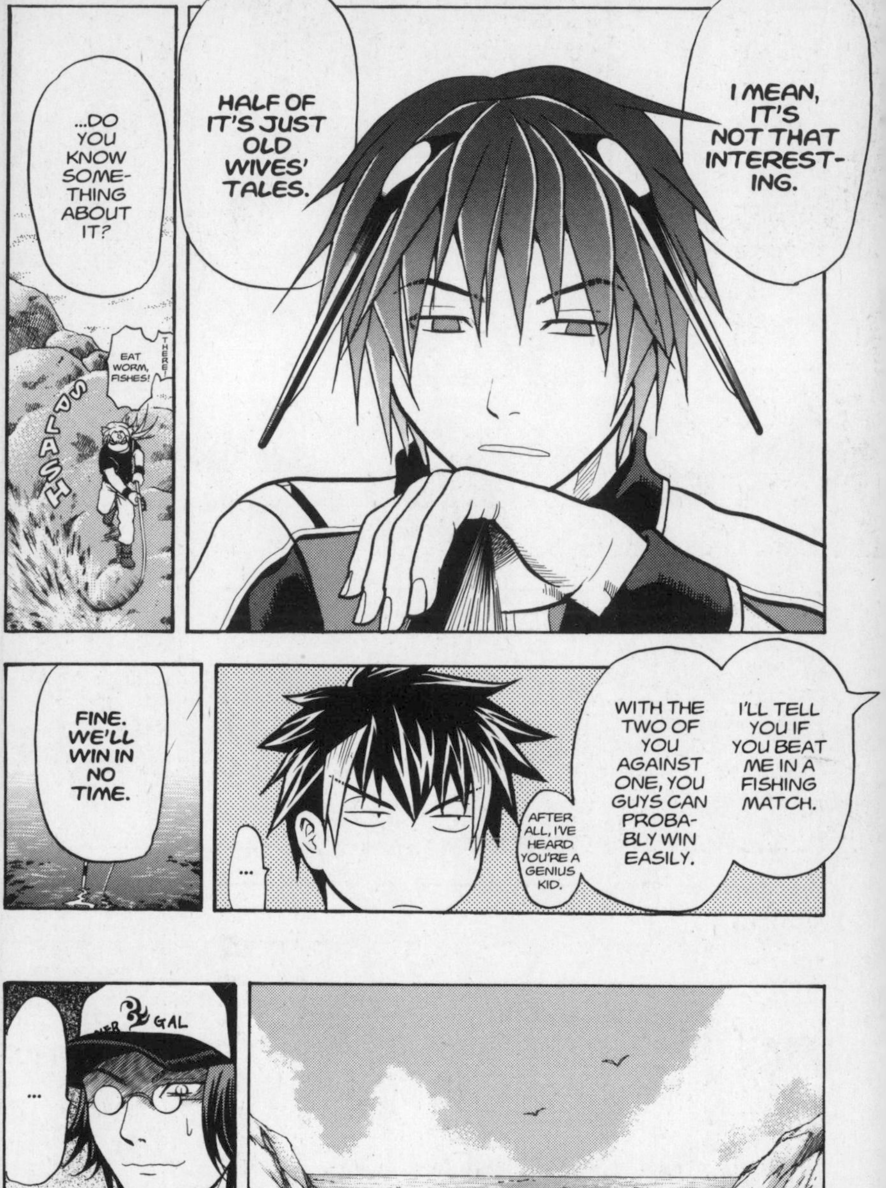
I MEAN, IT'S NOT THAT INTERESTING.
HALF OF IT'S JUST OLD WIVES' TALES.
...DO YOU KNOW SOMETHING ABOUT IT?
THERE!
EAT WORM, FISHES!
SPLASH
I'LL TELL YOU IF YOU BEAT ME IN A FISHING MATCH.
WITH THE TWO OF YOU AGAINST ONE, YOU GUYS CAN PROBABLY WIN EASILY.
AFTER ALL, I'VE HEARD YOU'RE A GENIUS KID.
...
FINE. WE'LL WIN IN NO TIME.
...

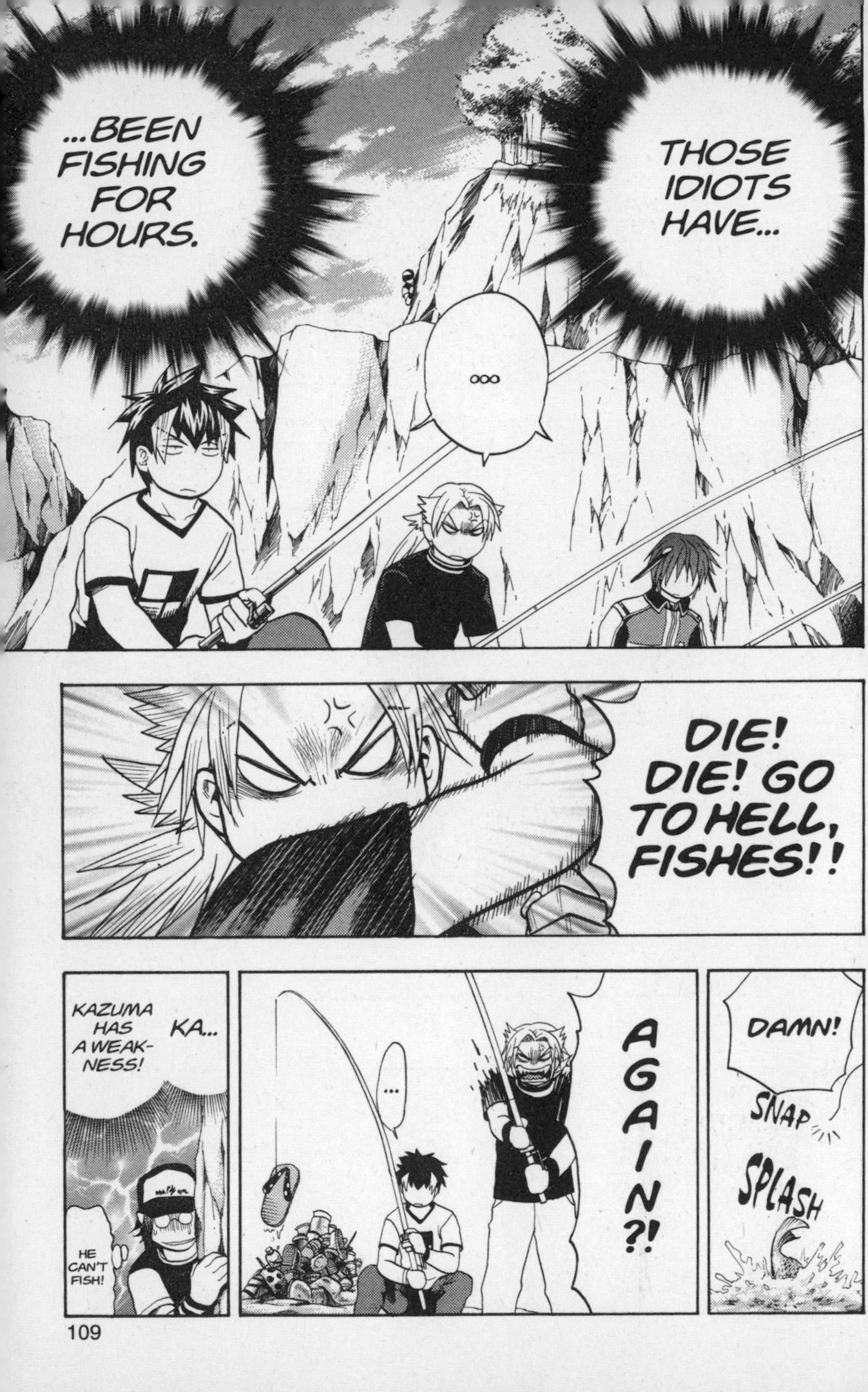
THOSE IDIOTS HAVE...
...BEEN FISHING FOR HOURS.
...
DIE! DIE! GO TO HELL, FISHES!!
DAMN!
SNAP
SPLASH
AGAIN?!
...
KA...
KAZUMA HAS A WEAK-NESS!
HE CAN'T FISH!

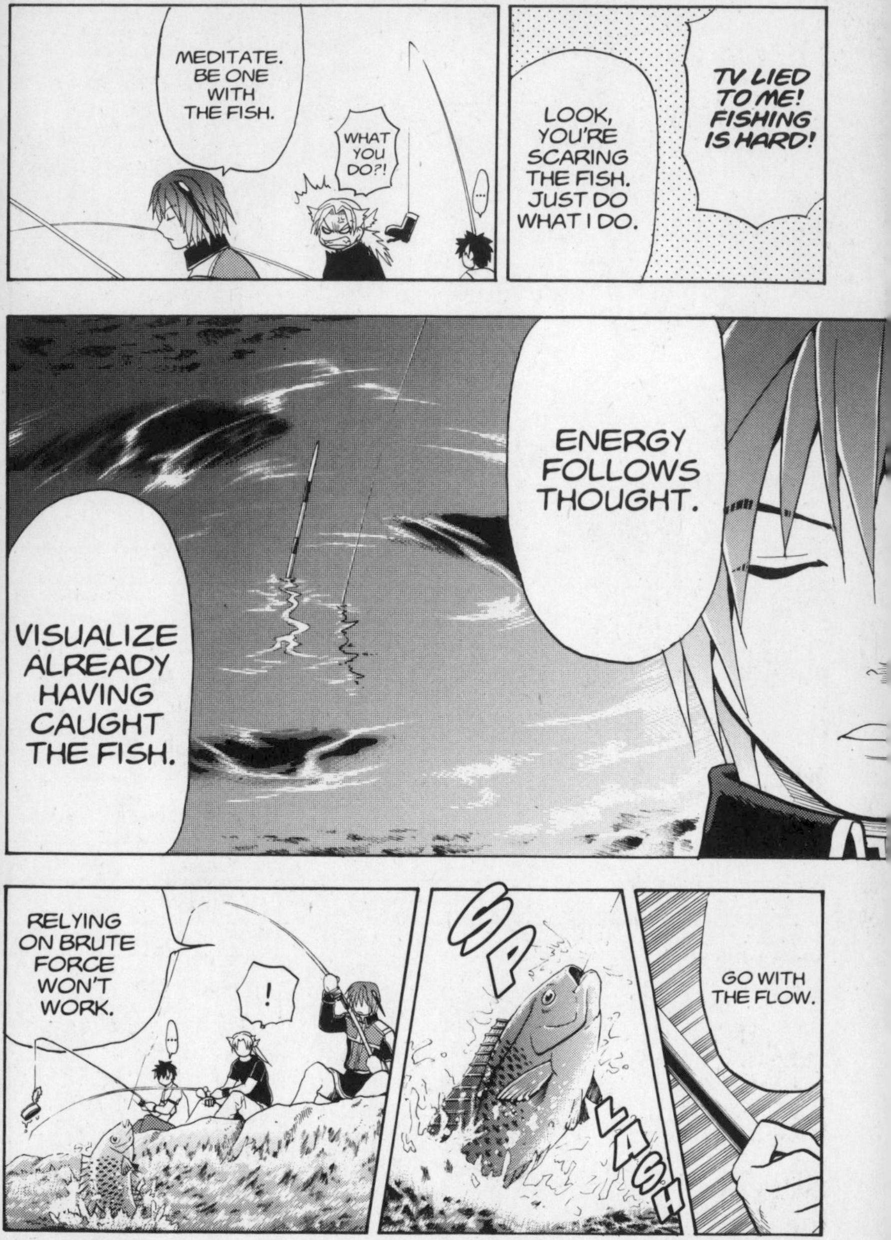
TV LIED TO ME! FISHING IS HARD!
LOOK, YOU'RE SCARING THE FISH. JUST DO WHAT I DO.
MEDITATE. BE ONE WITH THE FISH.
WHAT YOU DO?!
...
ENERGY FOLLOWS THOUGHT.
VISUALIZE ALREADY HAVING CAUGHT THE FISH.
GO WITH THE FLOW.
SPLASH
RELYING ON BRUTE FORCE WON'T WORK.
!
...

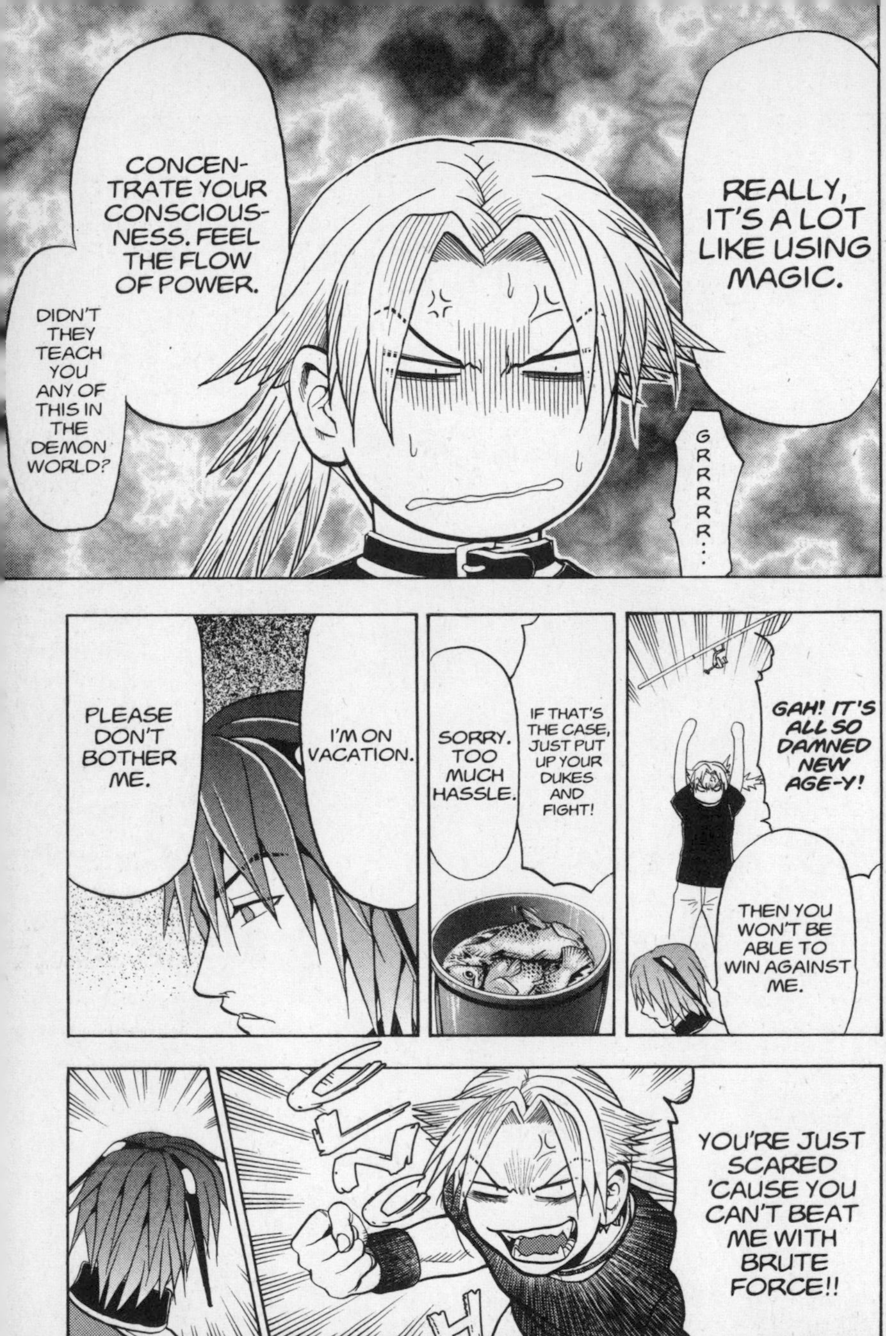
REALLY, IT'S A LOT LIKE USING MAGIC.
GRRRRR...
CONCEN-TRATE YOUR CONSCIOUS-NESS. FEEL THE FLOW OF POWER.
DIDN'T THEY TEACH YOU ANY OF THIS IN THE DEMON WORLD?
GAH! IT'S ALL SO DAMNED NEW AGE-Y!
THEN YOU WON'T BE ABLE TO WIN AGAINST ME.
IF THAT'S THE CASE, JUST PUT UP YOUR DUKES AND FIGHT!
SORRY. TOO MUCH HASSLE.
I'M ON VACATION.
PLEASE DON'T BOTHER ME.
YOU'RE JUST SCARED 'CAUSE YOU CAN'T BEAT ME WITH BRUTE FORCE!!

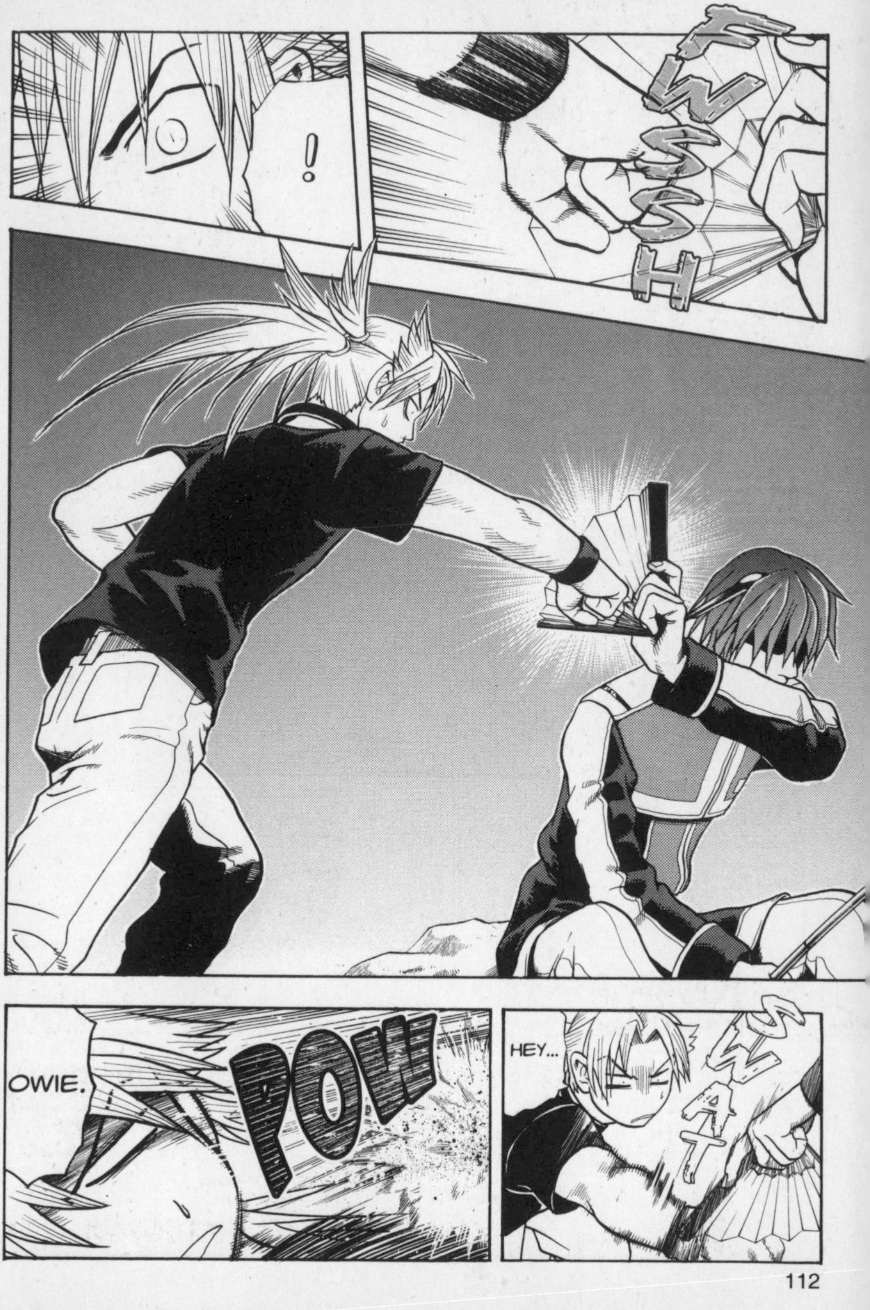
FWSSH
!
HEY...
SWAT
POW
OWIE.

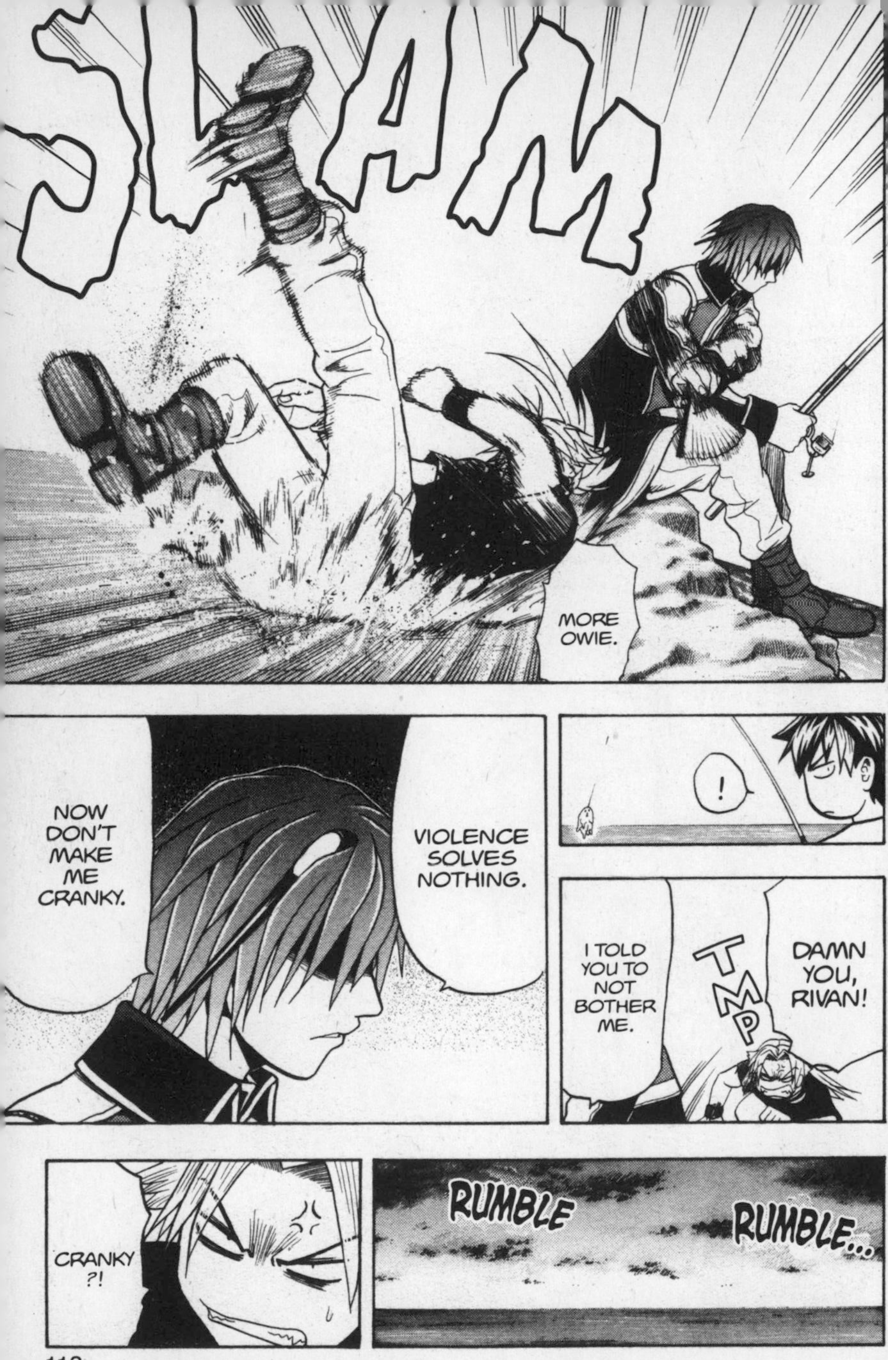
SLAM
MORE OWIE.
!
DAMN YOU, RIVAN!
TMP
I TOLD YOU TO NOT BOTHER ME.
VIOLENCE SOLVES NOTHING.
NOW DON'T MAKE ME CRANKY.
RUMBLE
RUMBLE...
CRANKY ?!

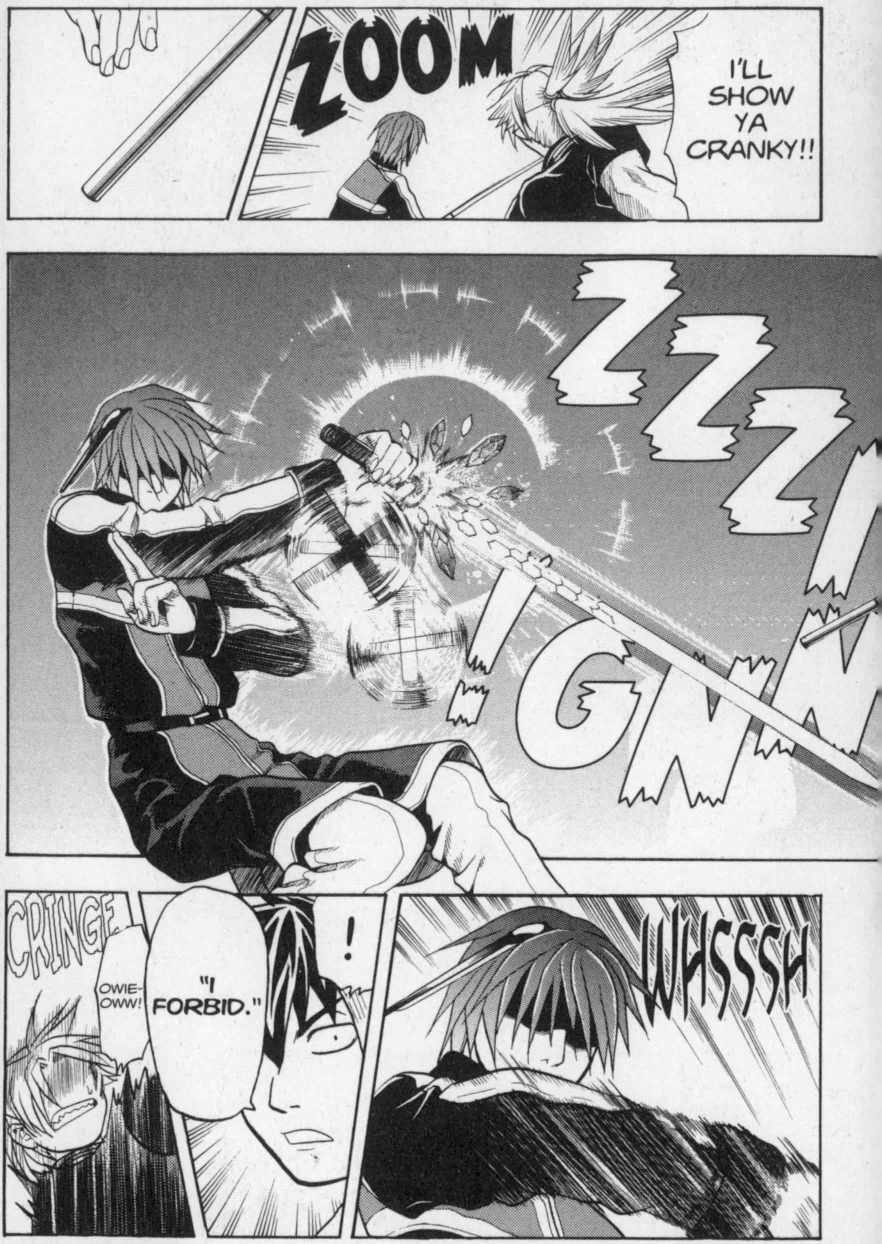
I'LL SHOW YA CRANKY!!
ZOOM
ZZZING!
WHSSSH
!
"I FORBID."
OWIE-OWW!
CRINGE

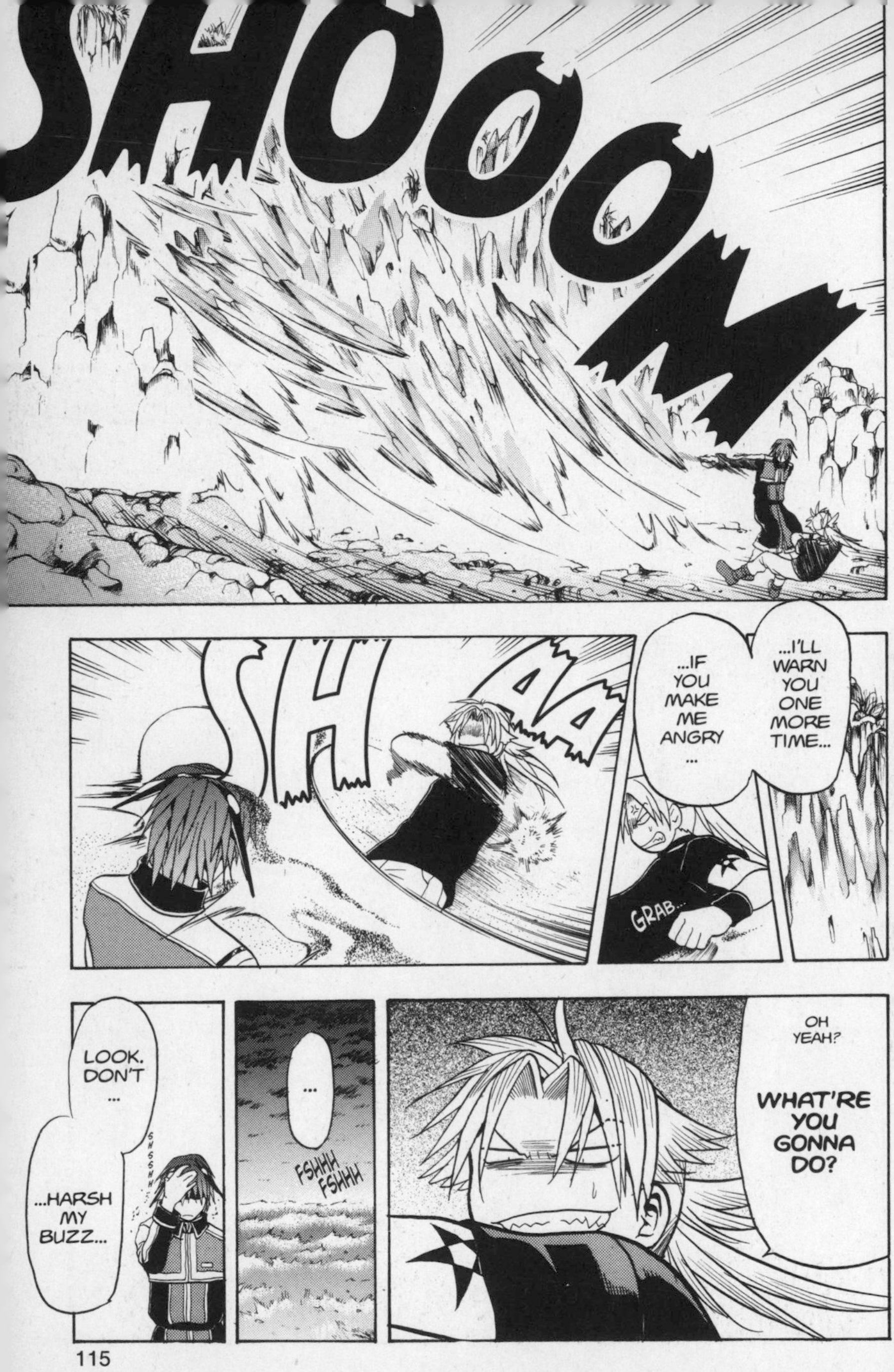
SHOOOM
...I'LL WARN YOU ONE MORE TIME...
...IF YOU MAKE ME ANGRY ...
GRAB...
SHAA
OH YEAH?
WHAT'RE YOU GONNA DO?
...
FSHHH FSHHH
LOOK. DON'T ...
...HARSH MY BUZZ...

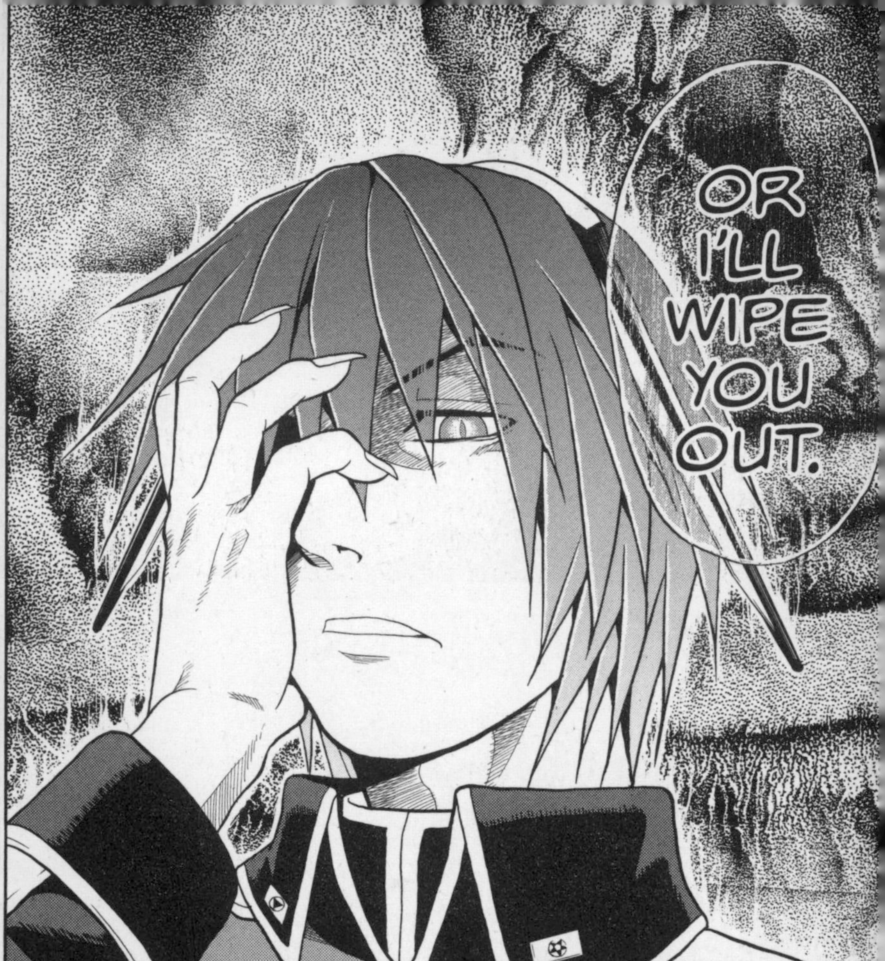
OR I'LL WIPE YOU OUT.
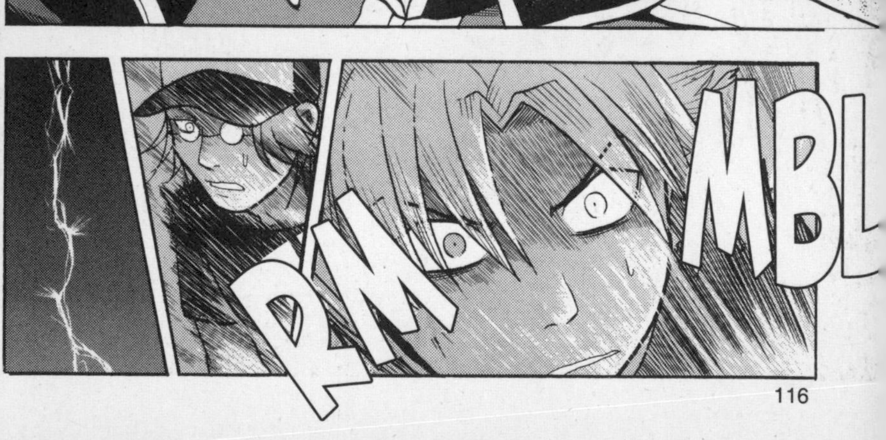
RMMBL

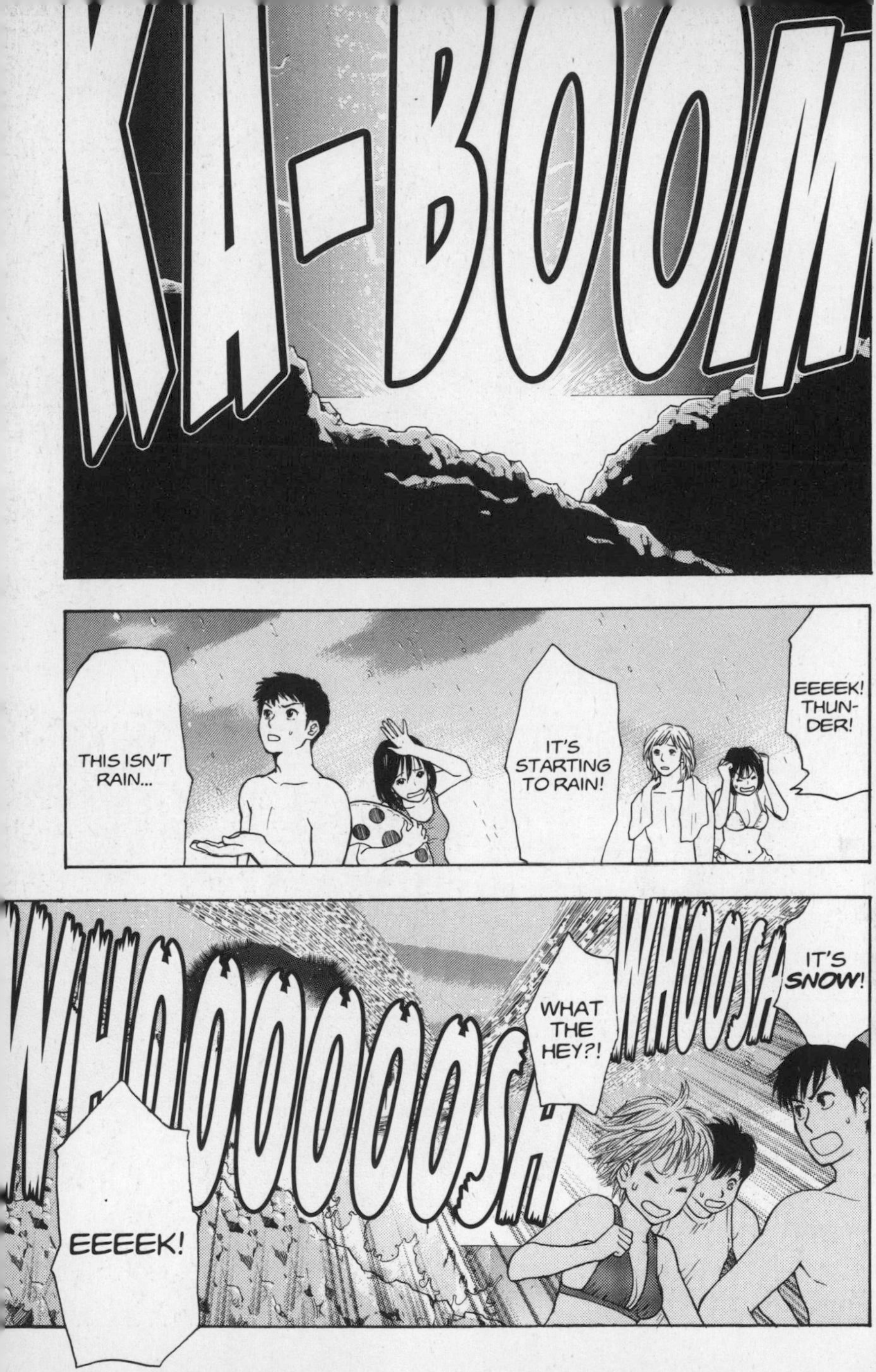
KA-BOOM
EEEEK! THUNDER!
IT'S STARTING TO RAIN!
THIS ISN'T RAIN...
IT'S SNOW!
WHOOSH
WHAT THE HEY?!
WHOOOOOOSH
EEEEK!

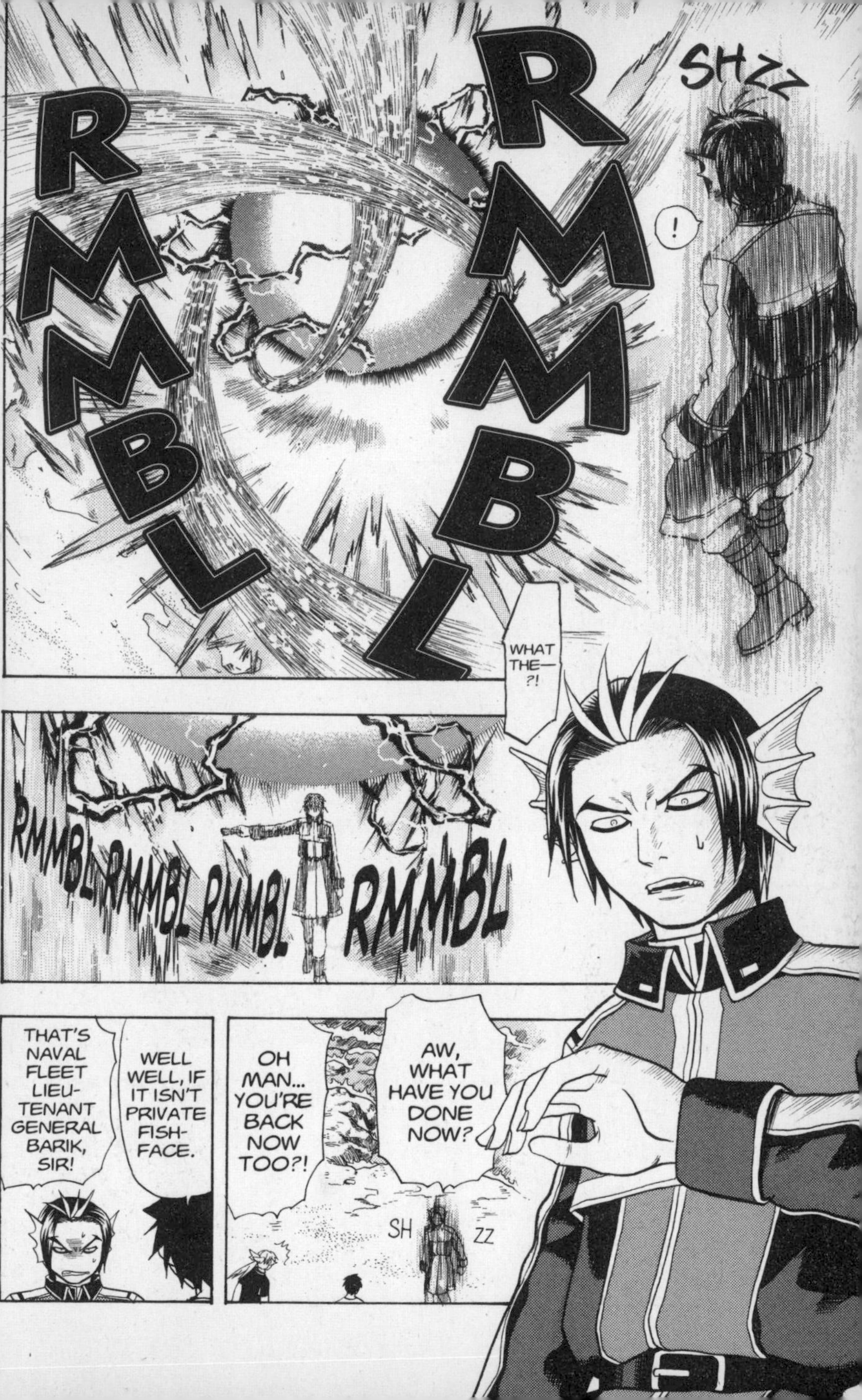
SHZZ
!
RMMBL
RMMBL
WHAT THE—?!
RMMBL RMMBL RMMBL RMMBL
AW, WHAT HAVE YOU DONE NOW?
OH MAN... YOU'RE BACK NOW TOO?!
SH ZZ
WELL WELL, IF IT ISN'T PRIVATE FISH-FACE.
THAT'S NAVAL FLEET LIEU-TENANT GENERAL BARIK, SIR!

READ THIS WAY

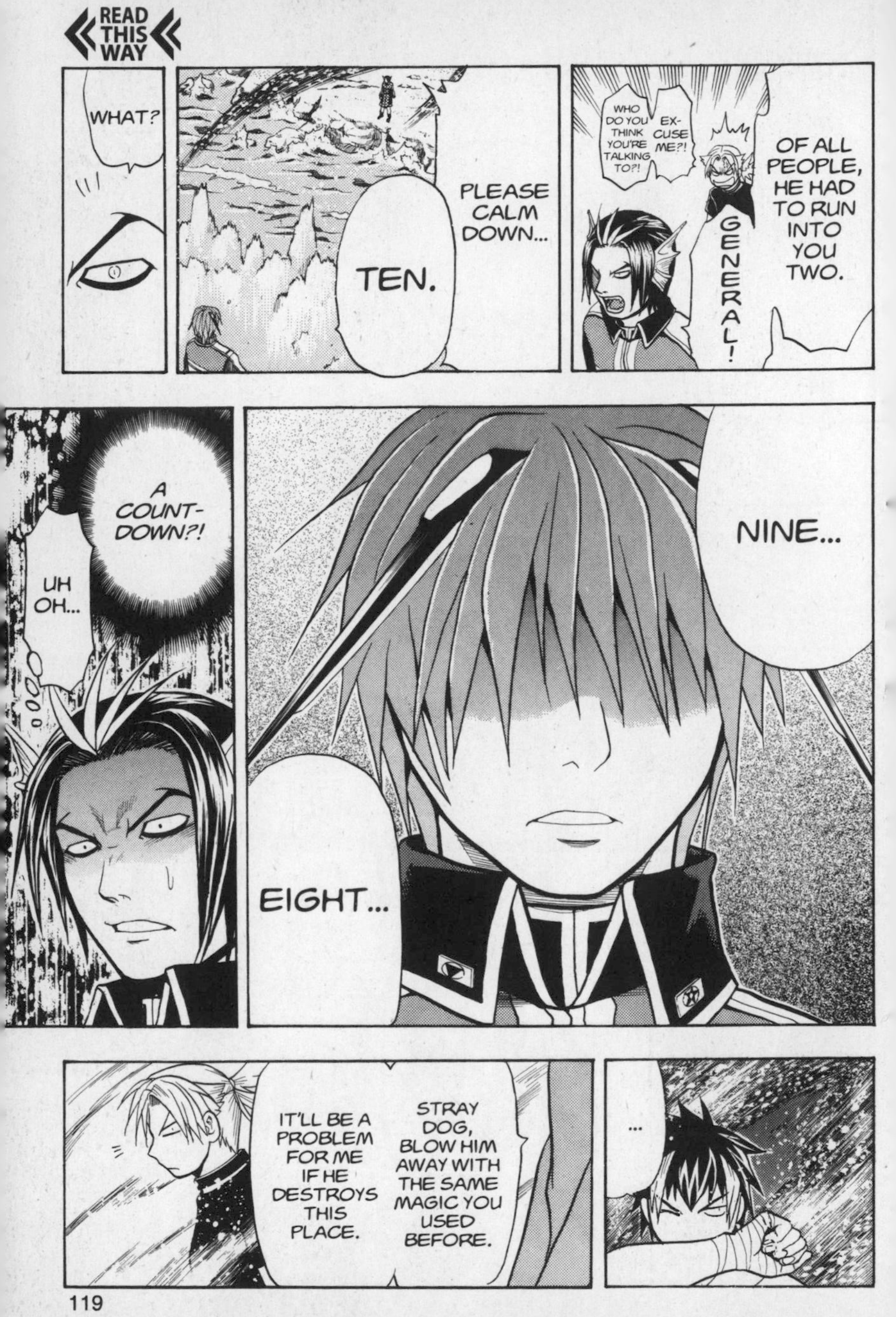
OF ALL PEOPLE, HE HAD TO RUN INTO YOU TWO.
GENERAL!
EXCUSE ME?!
WHO DO YOU THINK YOU'RE TALKING TO?!
PLEASE CALM DOWN...
TEN.
WHAT?
NINE...
EIGHT...
A COUNT-DOWN?!
UH OH...
...
STRAY DOG, BLOW HIM AWAY WITH THE SAME MAGIC YOU USED BEFORE.
IT'LL BE A PROBLEM FOR ME IF HE DESTROYS THIS PLACE.

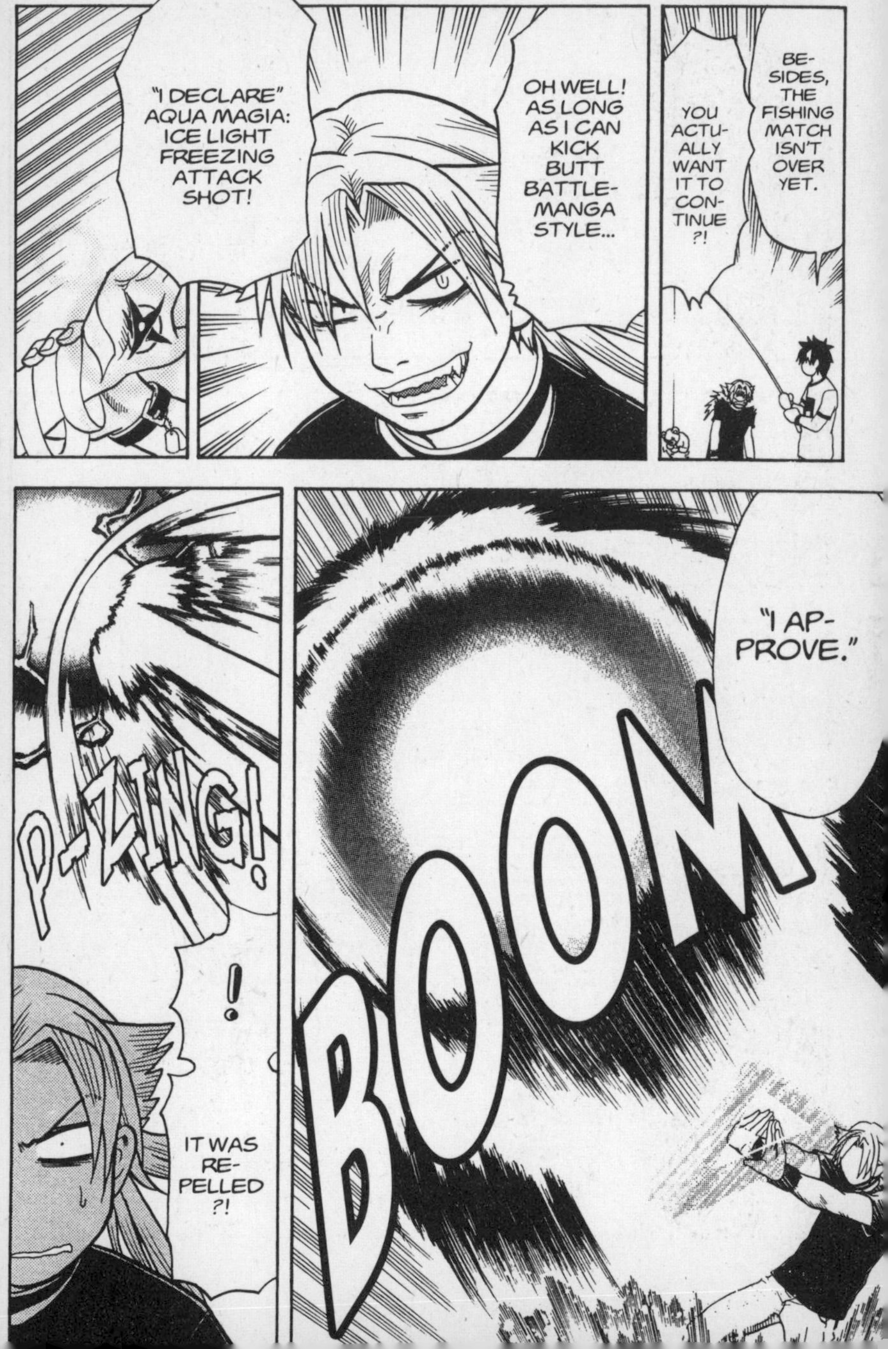
BESIDES, THE FISHING MATCH ISN'T OVER YET.
YOU ACTUALLY WANT IT TO CONTINUE?!
OH WELL! AS LONG AS I CAN KICK BUTT BATTLE-MANGA STYLE...
"I DECLARE" AQUA MAGIA: ICE LIGHT FREEZING ATTACK SHOT!
"I APPROVE."
BOOM
P-ZING!
!
IT WAS REPELLED?!

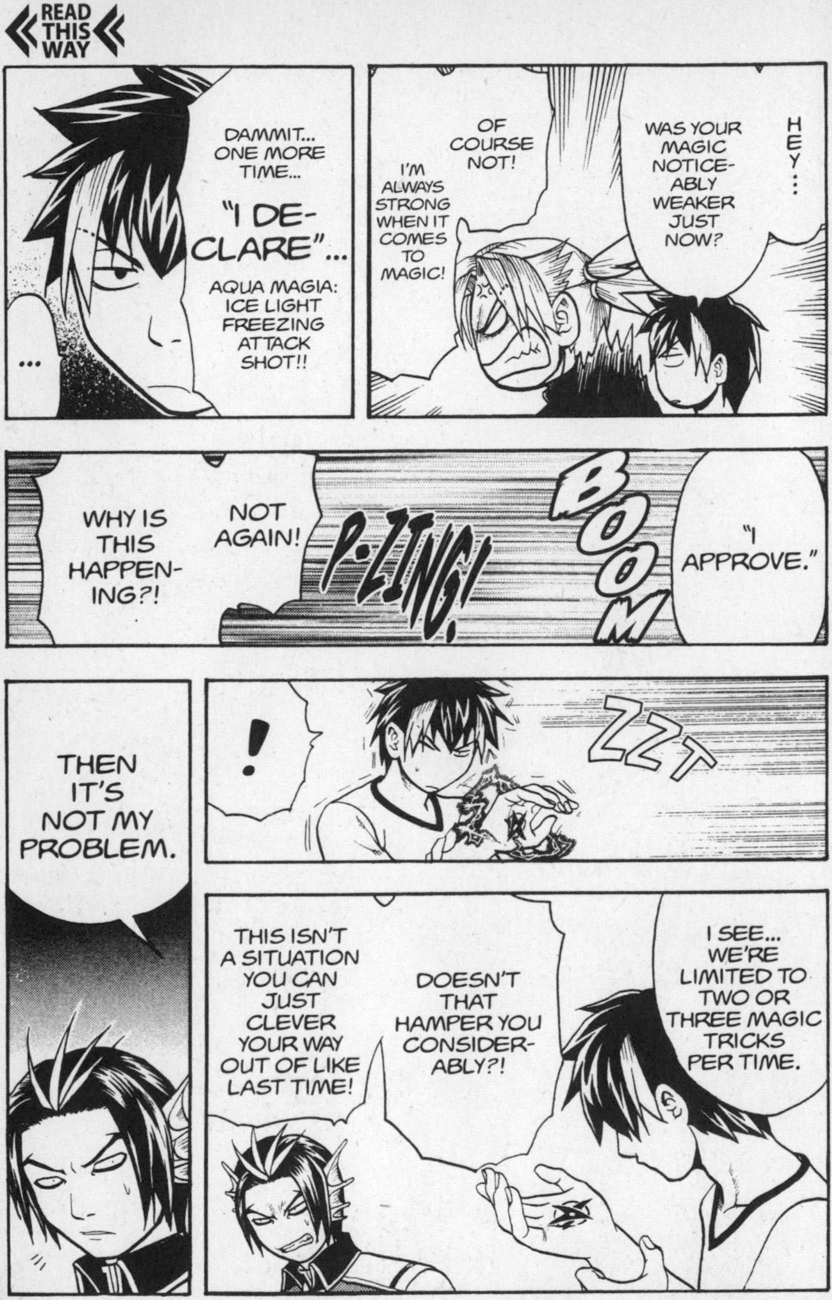
READ THIS WAY
HEY...
WAS YOUR MAGIC NOTICE-ABLY WEAKER JUST NOW?
OF COURSE NOT!
I'M ALWAYS STRONG WHEN IT COMES TO MAGIC!
DAMMIT... ONE MORE TIME...
"I DE-CLARE"...
AQUA MAGIA: ICE LIGHT FREEZING ATTACK SHOT!!
...
"I APPROVE."
BOOM
P-LING!
NOT AGAIN!
WHY IS THIS HAPPEN-ING?!
ZZT
!
THEN IT'S NOT MY PROBLEM.
I SEE... WE'RE LIMITED TO TWO OR THREE MAGIC TRICKS PER TIME.
DOESN'T THAT HAMPER YOU CONSIDER-ABLY?!
THIS ISN'T A SITUATION YOU CAN JUST CLEVER YOUR WAY OUT OF LIKE LAST TIME!

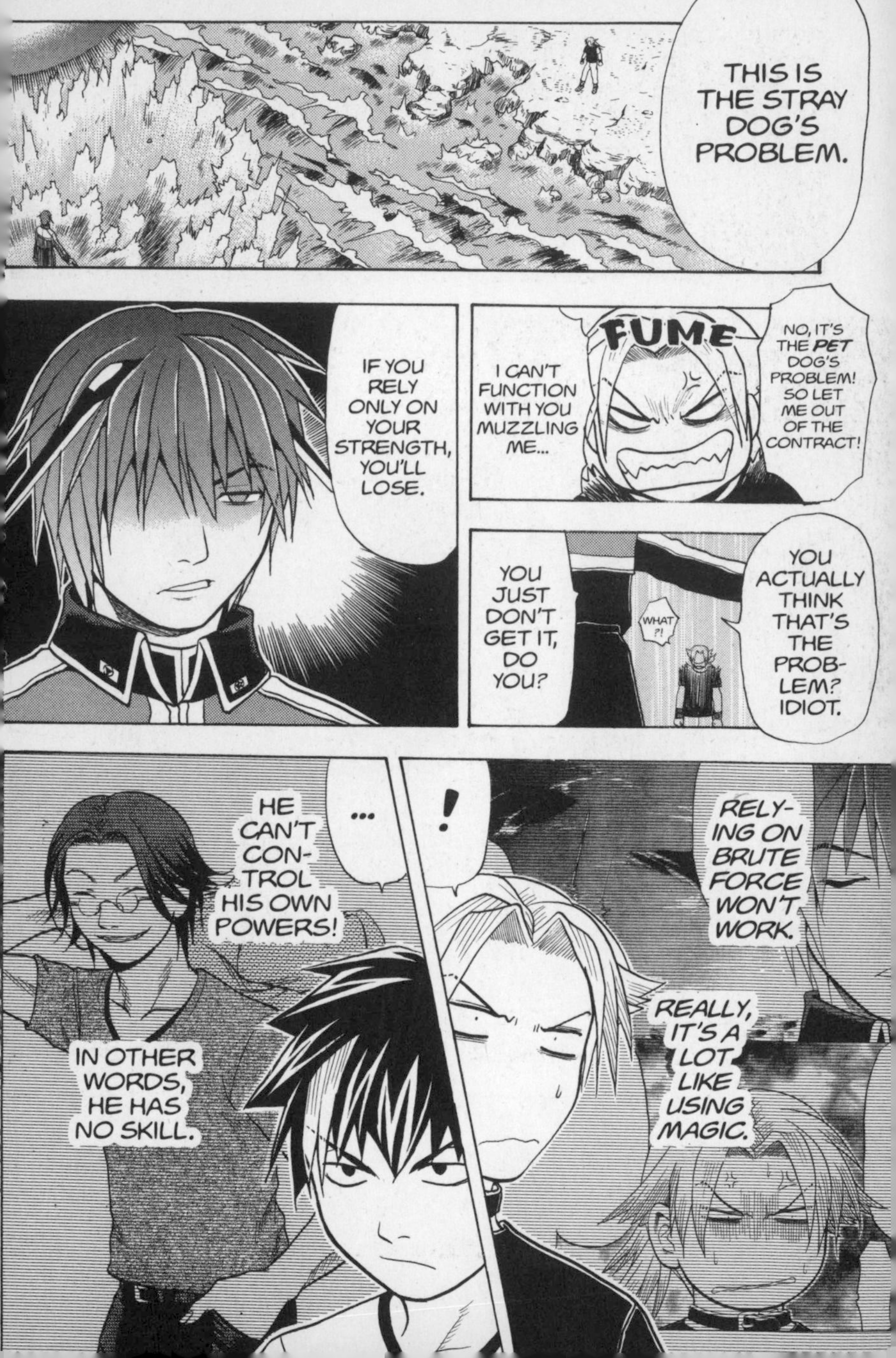
THIS IS THE STRAY DOG'S PROBLEM.
NO, IT'S THE PET DOG'S PROBLEM! SO LET ME OUT OF THE CONTRACT!
FUME
I CAN'T FUNCTION WITH YOU MUZZLING ME...
YOU ACTUALLY THINK THAT'S THE PROB-LEM? IDIOT.
WHAT?!
YOU JUST DON'T GET IT, DO YOU?
IF YOU RELY ONLY ON YOUR STRENGTH, YOU'LL LOSE.
RELY-ING ON BRUTE FORCE WON'T WORK.
!
...
HE CAN'T CON-TROL HIS OWN POWERS!
REALLY, IT'S A LOT LIKE USING MAGIC.
IN OTHER WORDS, HE HAS NO SKILL.

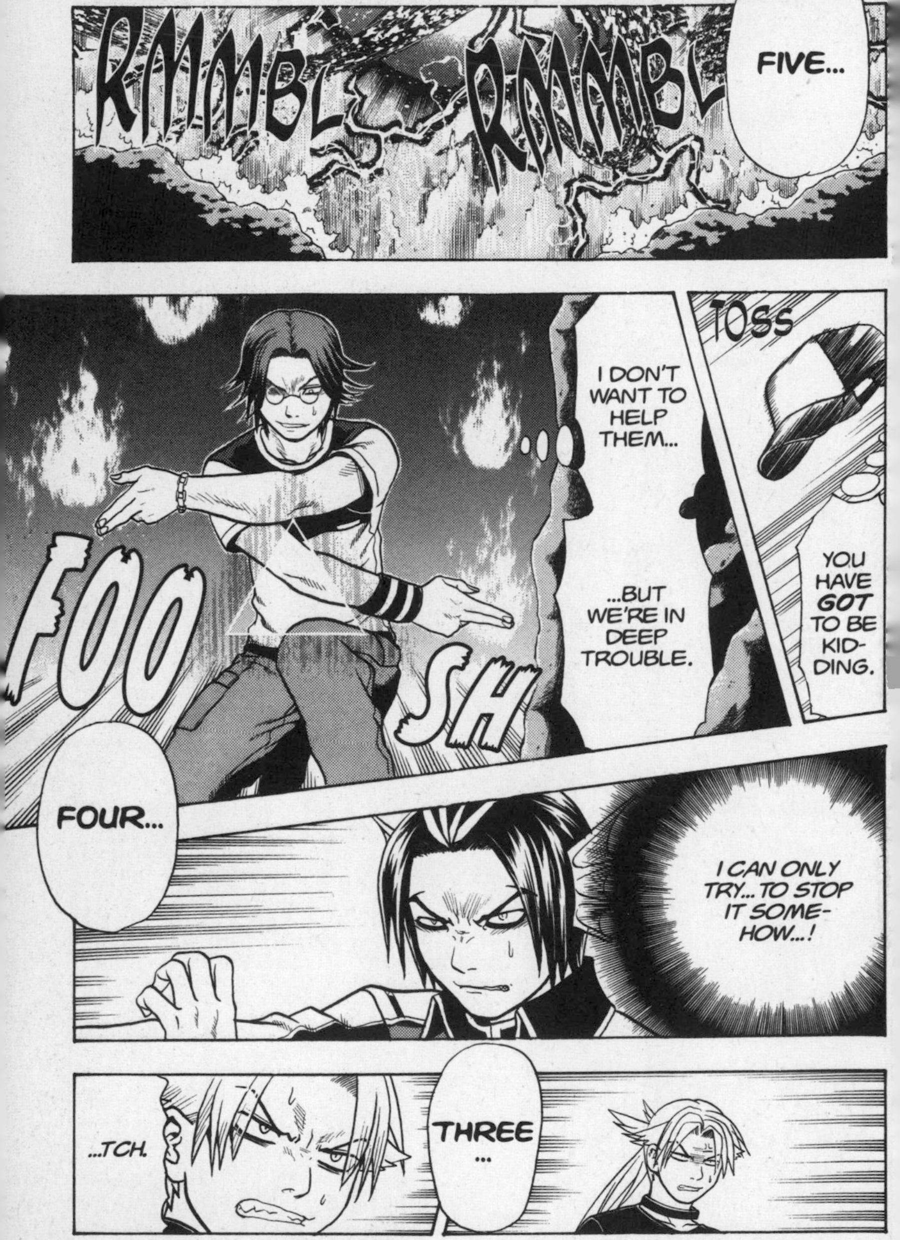
FIVE...
RMMBL RMMBL
TOSS
YOU HAVE GOT TO BE KID-DING.
I DON'T WANT TO HELP THEM...
...BUT WE'RE IN DEEP TROUBLE.
FOOSH
I CAN ONLY TRY... TO STOP IT SOME-HOW...!
FOUR...
THREE ...
...TCH.

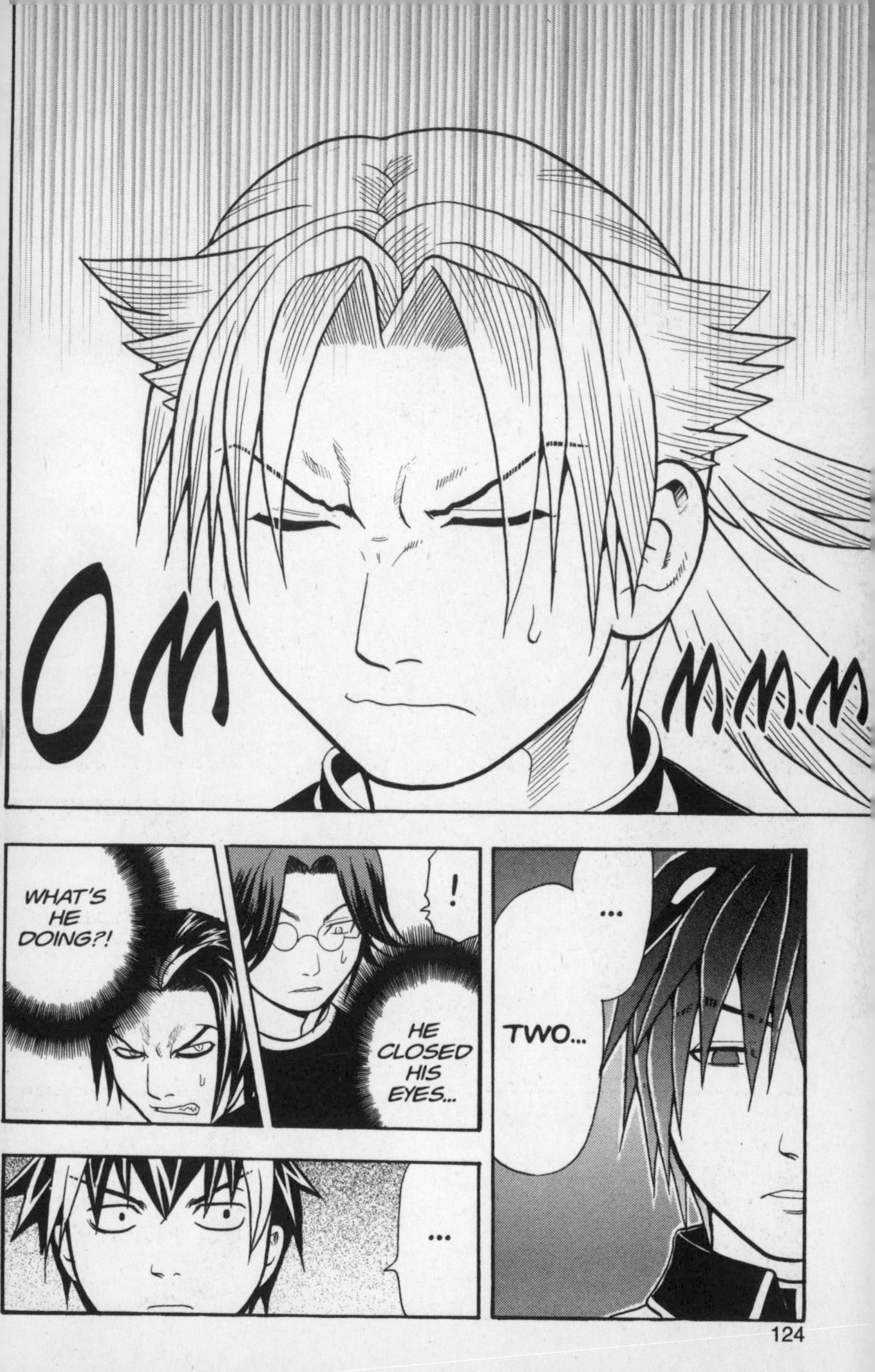
OM
MMM
...
TWO...
!
HE CLOSED HIS EYES...
WHAT'S HE DOING?!
...

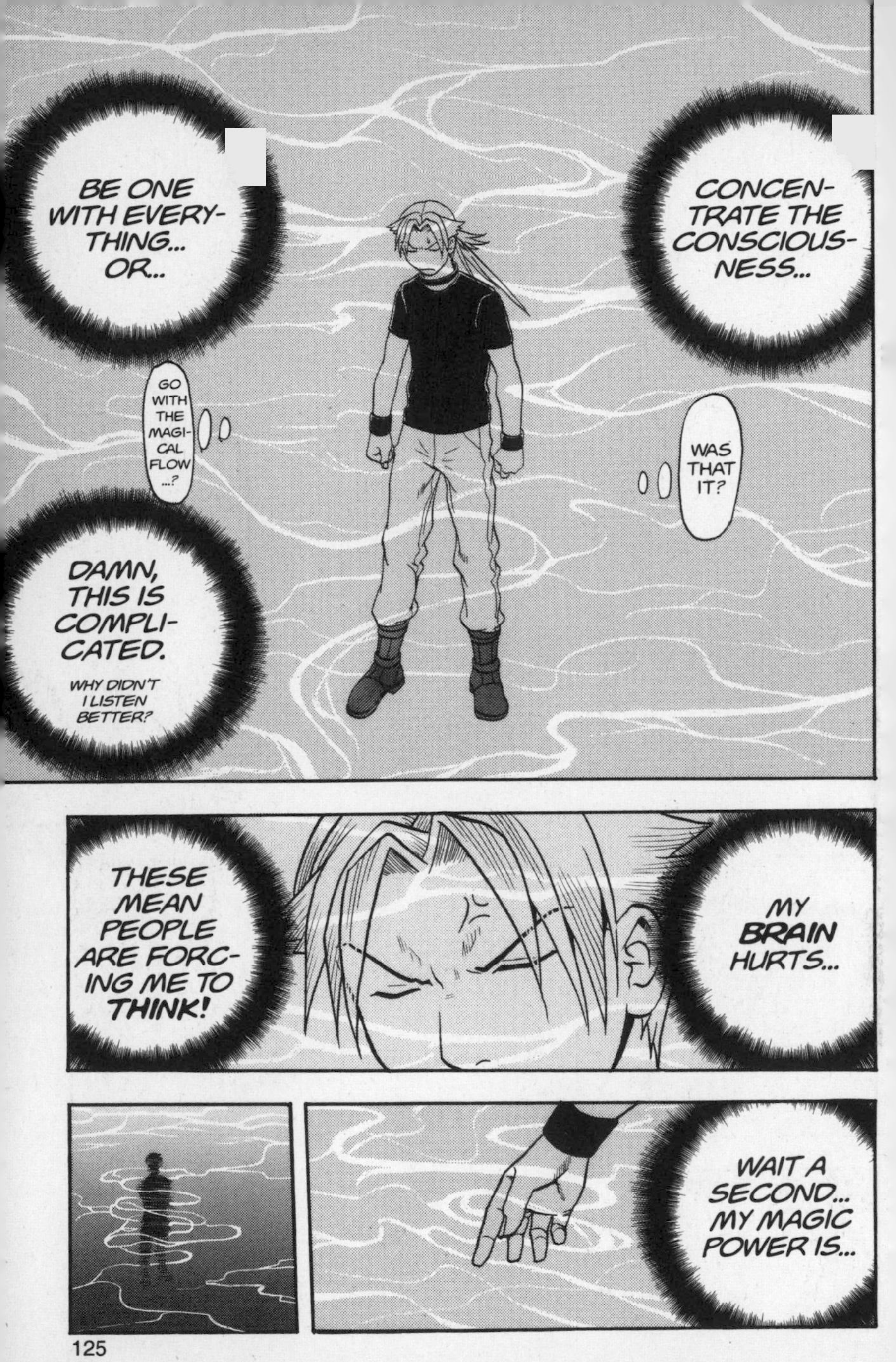
CONCENTRATE THE CONSCIOUSNESS...
WAS THAT IT?
BE ONE WITH EVERYTHING... OR...
GO WITH THE MAGICAL FLOW...?
DAMN, THIS IS COMPLICATED.
WHY DIDN'T I LISTEN BETTER?
MY BRAIN HURTS...
THESE MEAN PEOPLE ARE FORCING ME TO THINK!
WAIT A SECOND... MY MAGIC POWER IS...

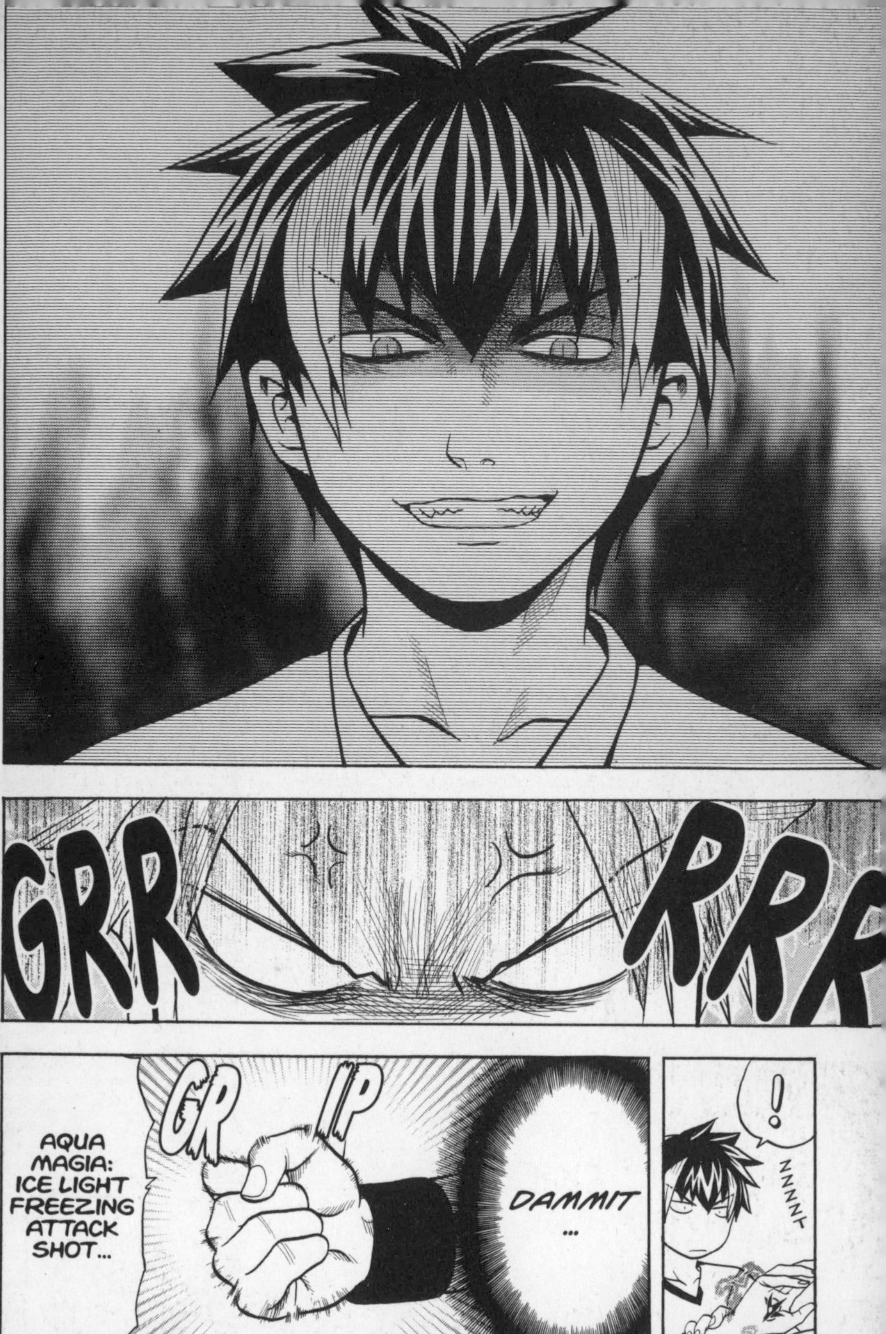
GRR
RRR
!
ZZZZT
GRIP
DAMMIT ...
AQUA MAGIA: ICE LIGHT FREEZING ATTACK SHOT...

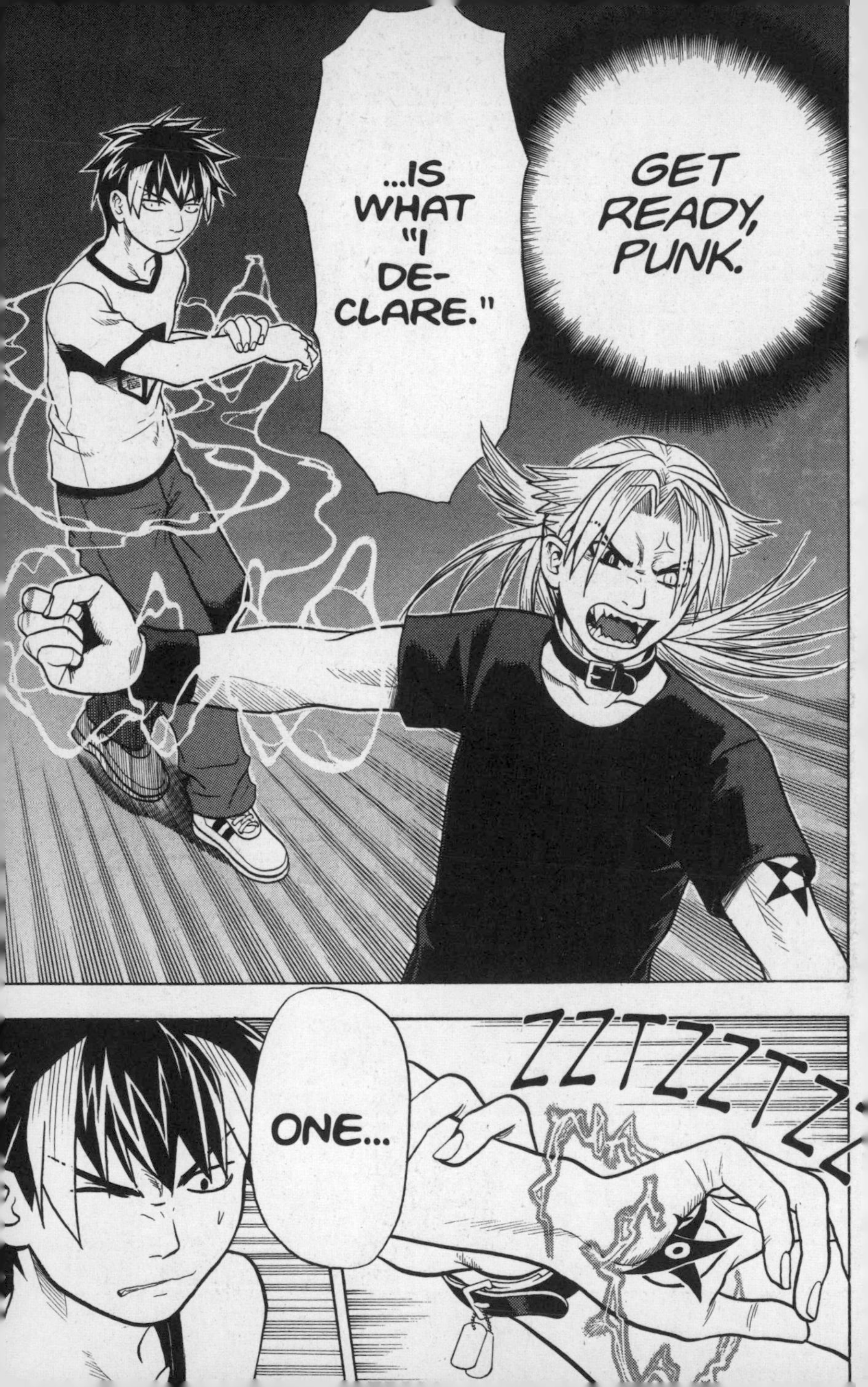
GET READY, PUNK.
...IS WHAT "I DE-CLARE."
ZZTZZTZZ
ONE...

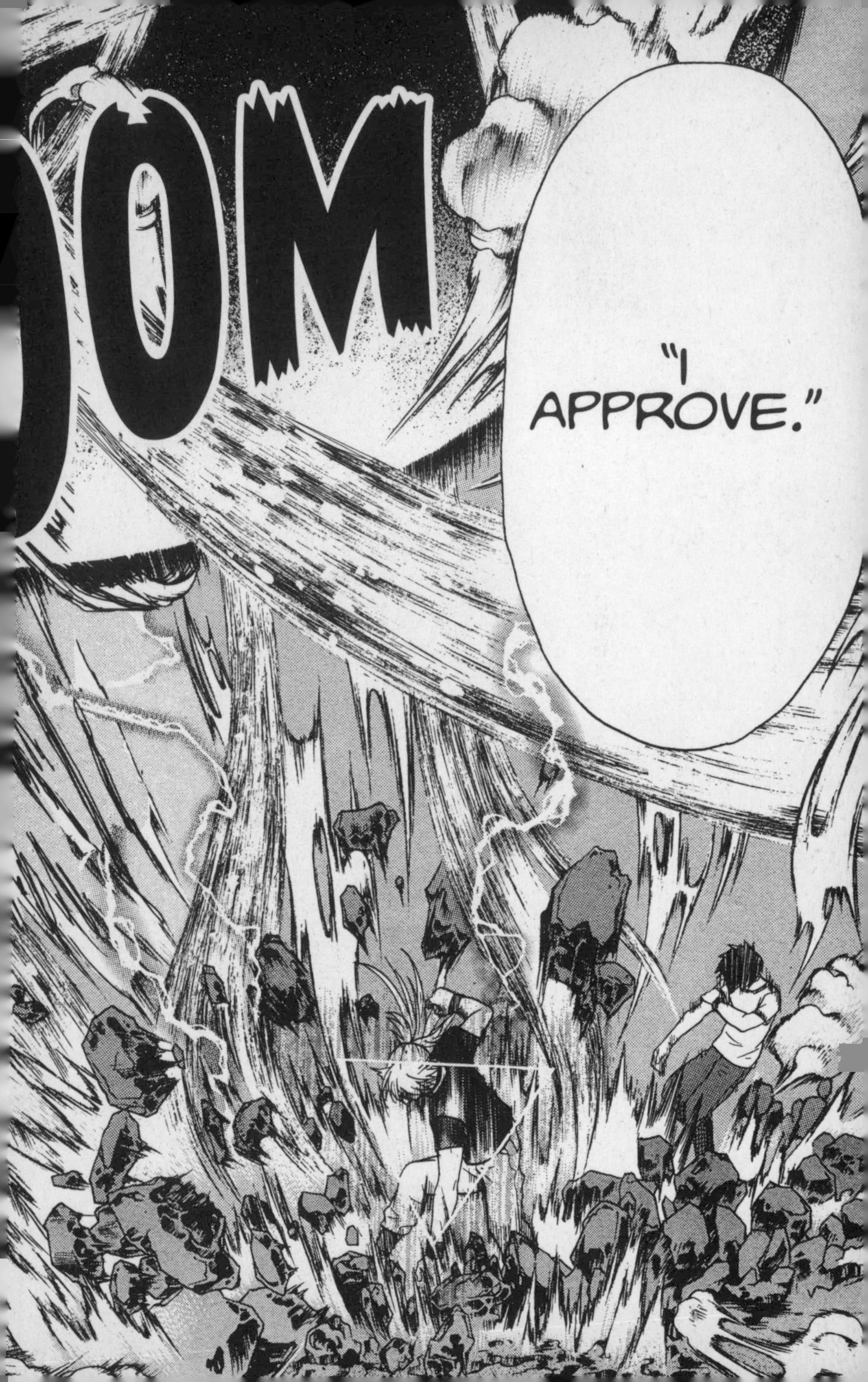
"I APPROVE."
OOM

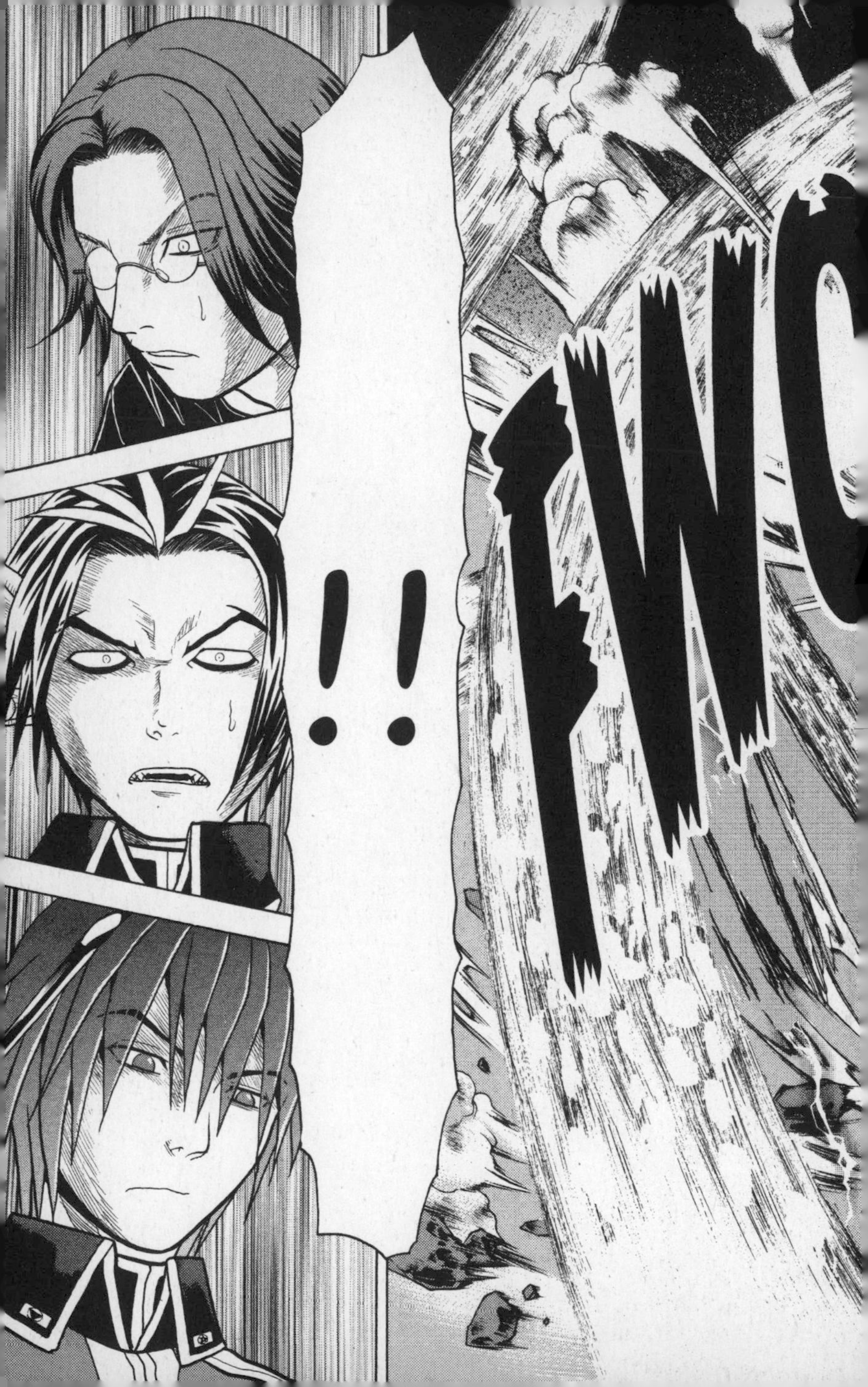
!!

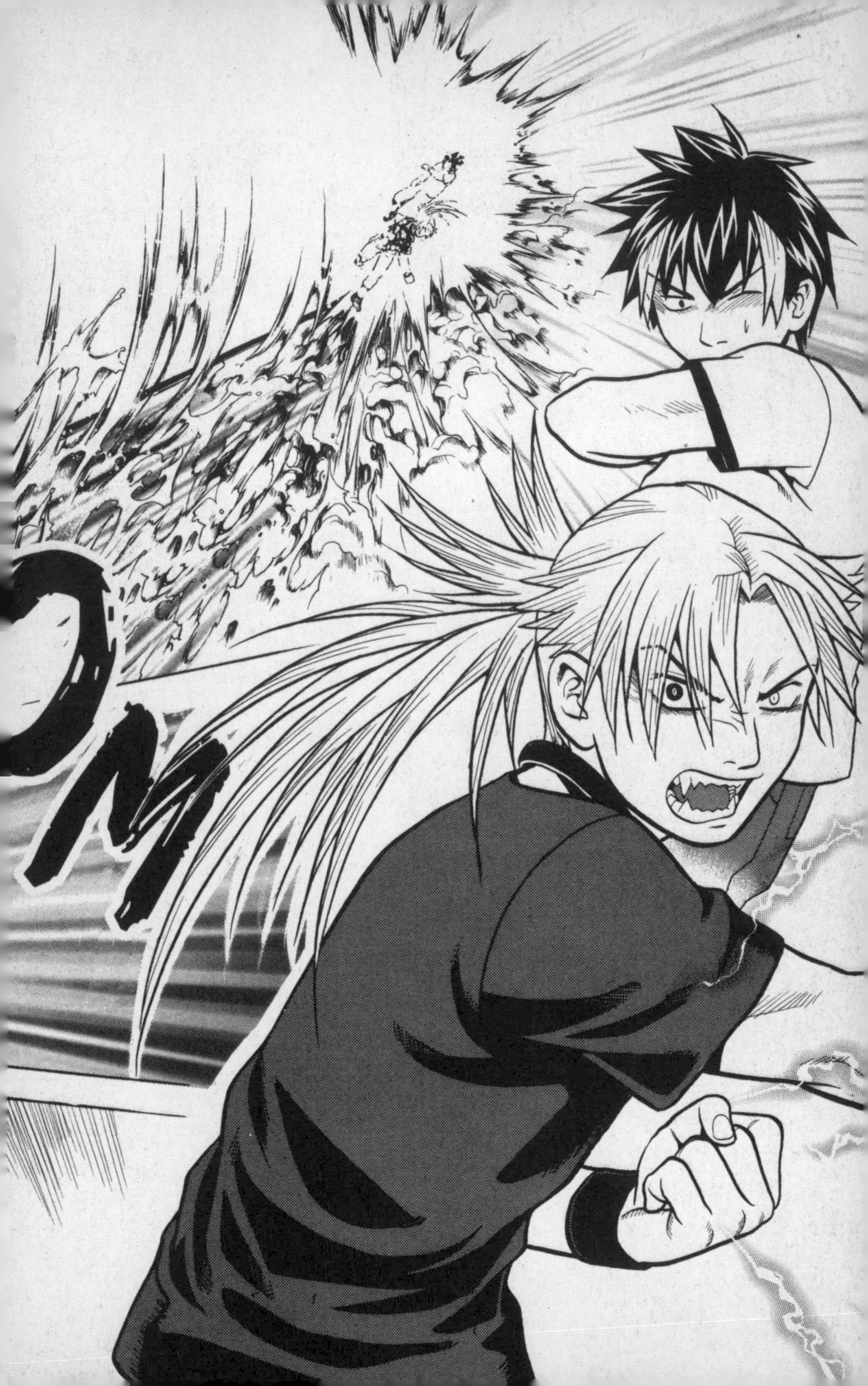

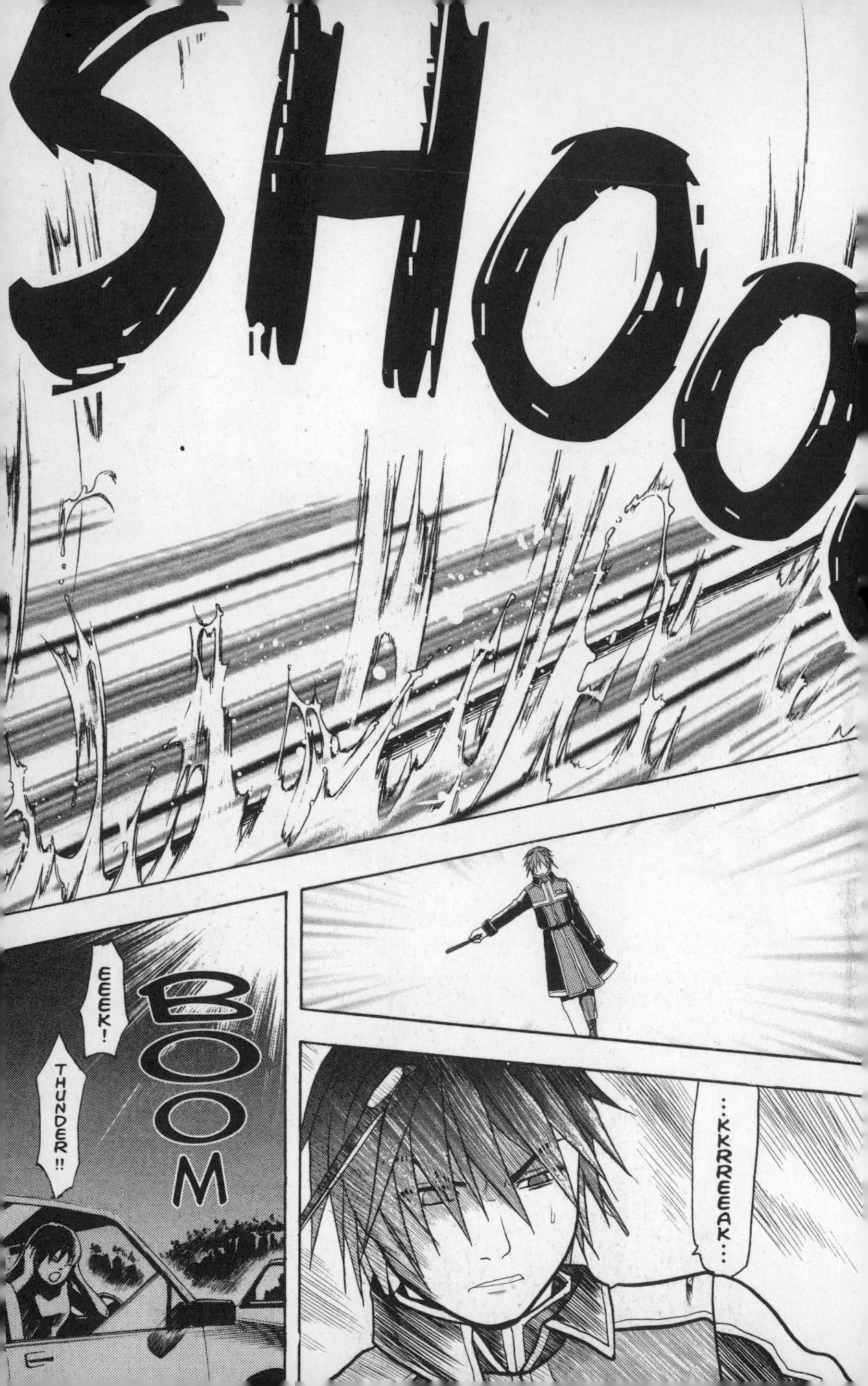
SHOO
...KKRREEAK...
EEEK!
THUNDER!!
BOOM

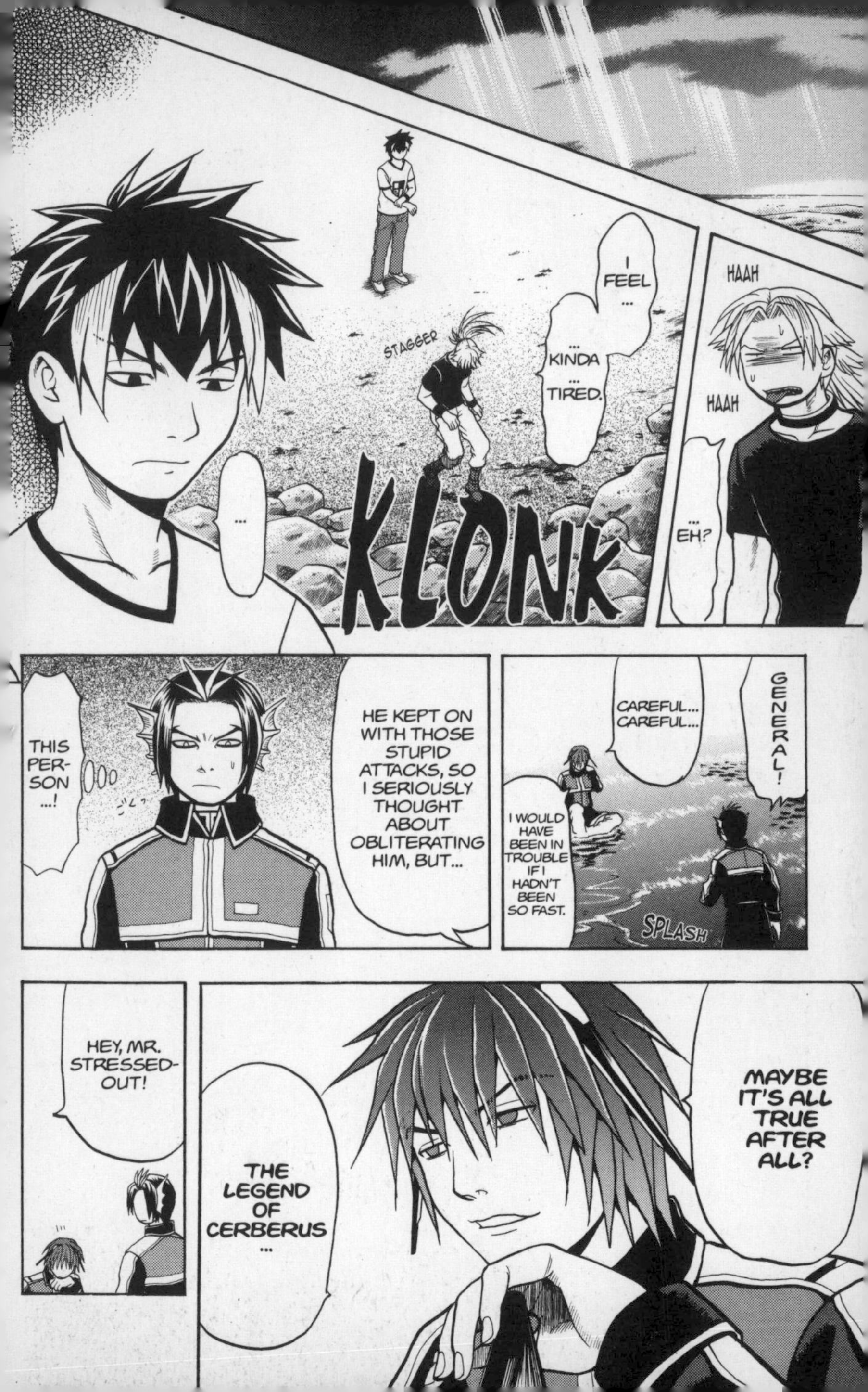
HAAH
HAAH
...EH?
I FEEL ...
... KINDA ... TIRED.
STAGGER
KLONK
...
GENERAL!
CAREFUL... CAREFUL...
I WOULD HAVE BEEN IN TROUBLE IF I HADN'T BEEN SO FAST.
SPLASH
HE KEPT ON WITH THOSE STUPID ATTACKS, SO I SERIOUSLY THOUGHT ABOUT OBLITERATING HIM, BUT...
THIS PER-SON ...!
MAYBE IT'S ALL TRUE AFTER ALL?
THE LEGEND OF CERBERUS ...
HEY, MR. STRESSED-OUT!

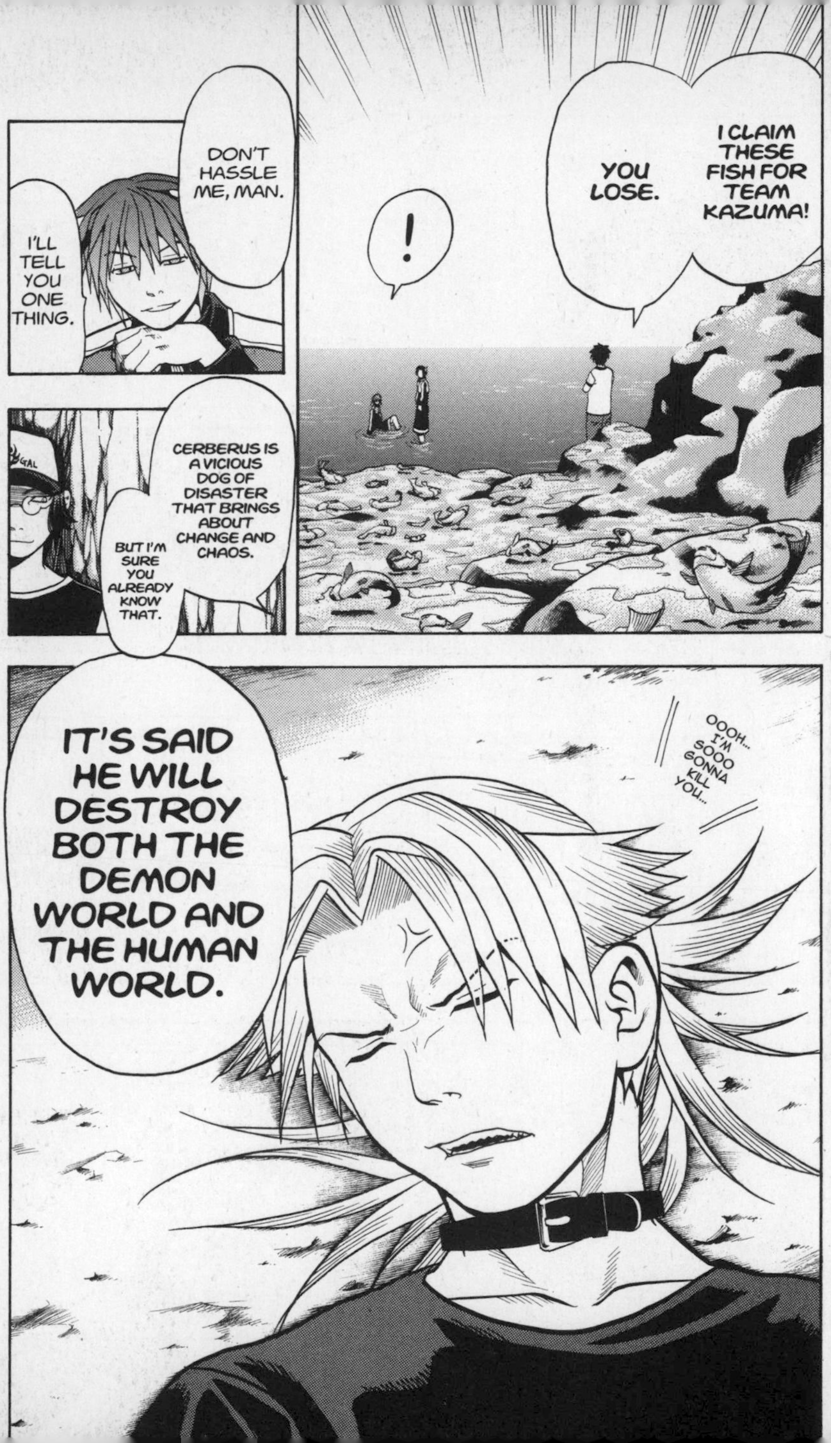
YOU LOSE. I CLAIM THESE FISH FOR TEAM KAZUMA!
!
DON'T HASSLE ME, MAN.
I'LL TELL YOU ONE THING.
CERBERUS IS A VICIOUS DOG OF DISASTER THAT BRINGS ABOUT CHANGE AND CHAOS.
BUT I'M SURE YOU ALREADY KNOW THAT.
OOOH... I'M SOOO GONNA KILL YOU...
IT'S SAID HE WILL DESTROY BOTH THE DEMON WORLD AND THE HUMAN WORLD.

MANGA-KA REPORT 1: NORA'S STRANGE HAIRSTYLE

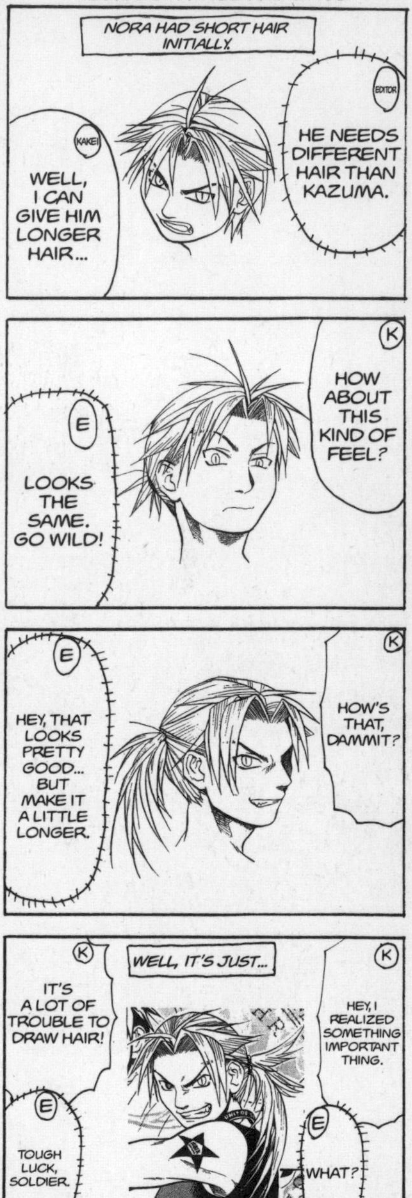
NORA HAD SHORT HAIR INITIALLY.
EDITOR
HE NEEDS DIFFERENT HAIR THAN KAZUMA.
KAKEI
WELL, I CAN GIVE HIM LONGER HAIR...
K
HOW ABOUT THIS KIND OF FEEL?
E
LOOKS THE SAME. GO WILD!
K
HOW'S THAT, DAMMIT?
E
HEY, THAT LOOKS PRETTY GOOD... BUT MAKE IT A LITTLE LONGER.
K
HEY, I REALIZED SOMETHING IMPORTANT THING.
WELL, IT'S JUST...
K
IT'S A LOT OF TROUBLE TO DRAW HAIR!
E
WHAT?
E
TOUGH LUCK, SOLDIER.

MANGA-KA REPORT 2: CONFESSIONS OF A ROOKIE ARTIST

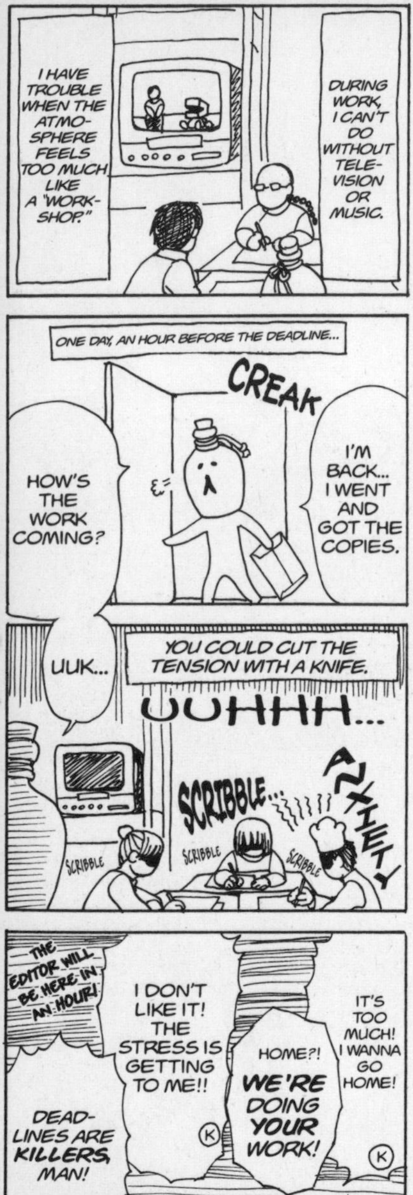
DURING WORK, I CAN'T DO WITHOUT TELEVISION OR MUSIC.
I HAVE TROUBLE WHEN THE ATMOSPHERE FEELS TOO MUCH LIKE A "WORKSHOP."
ONE DAY, AN HOUR BEFORE THE DEADLINE...
CREAK
I'M BACK... I WENT AND GOT THE COPIES.
HOW'S THE WORK COMING?
YOU COULD CUT THE TENSION WITH A KNIFE.
UUK...
UUHHH...
ANXIETY
SCRIBBLE...
SCRIBBLE
SCRIBBLE
SCRIBBLE
IT'S TOO MUCH! I WANNA GO HOME!
K
HOME?! WE'RE DOING YOUR WORK!
K
I DON'T LIKE IT! THE STRESS IS GETTING TO ME!!
THE EDITOR WILL BE HERE IN AN HOUR!
DEADLINES ARE KILLERS, MAN!

Story 8: The Rage Ignites

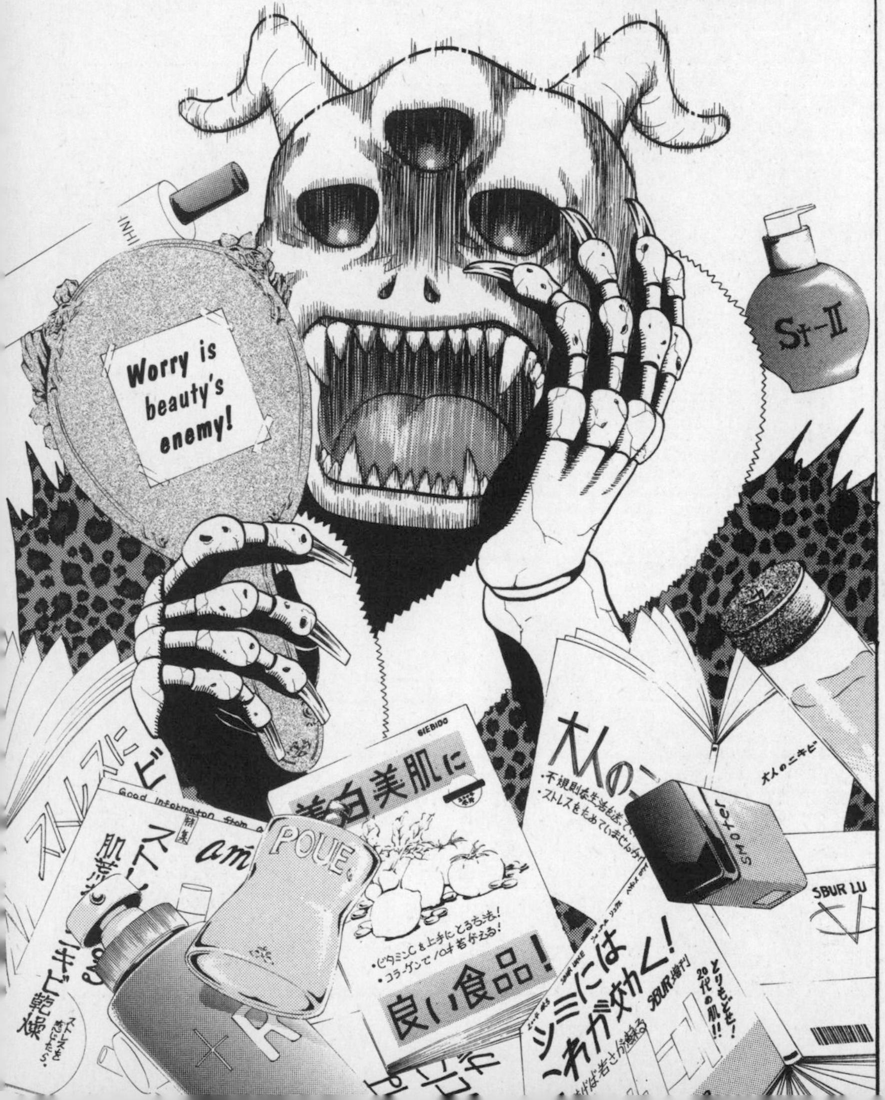
Worry is beauty's enemy!
大人のニキビ
良い食品!
シミにはこれが効く!
St-II

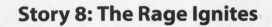

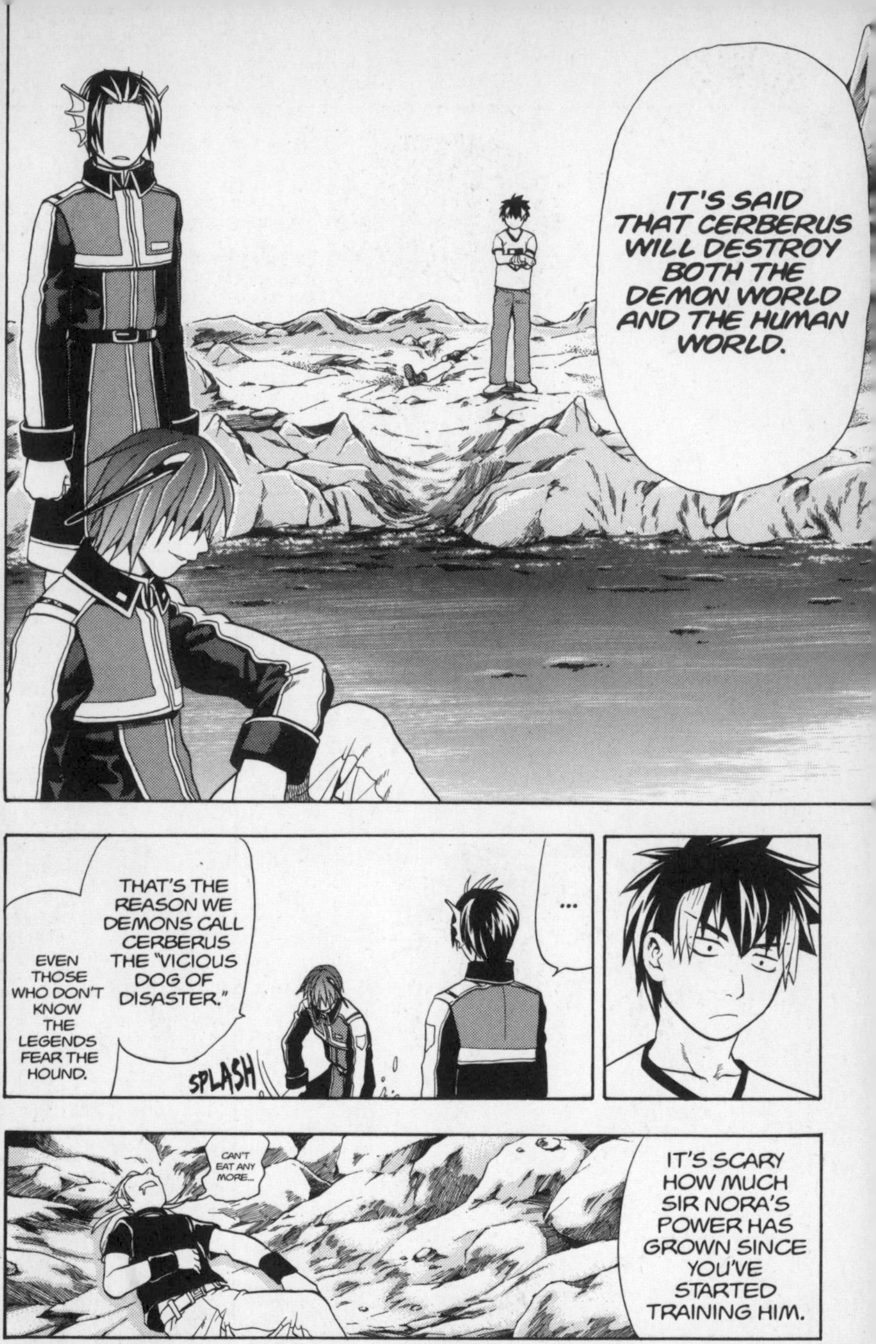
IT'S SAID THAT CERBERUS WILL DESTROY BOTH THE DEMON WORLD AND THE HUMAN WORLD.
...
THAT'S THE REASON WE DEMONS CALL CERBERUS THE "VICIOUS DOG OF DISASTER."
EVEN THOSE WHO DON'T KNOW THE LEGENDS FEAR THE HOUND.
SPLASH
IT'S SCARY HOW MUCH SIR NORA'S POWER HAS GROWN SINCE YOU'VE STARTED TRAINING HIM.
CAN'T EAT ANY MORE...

READ THIS WAY

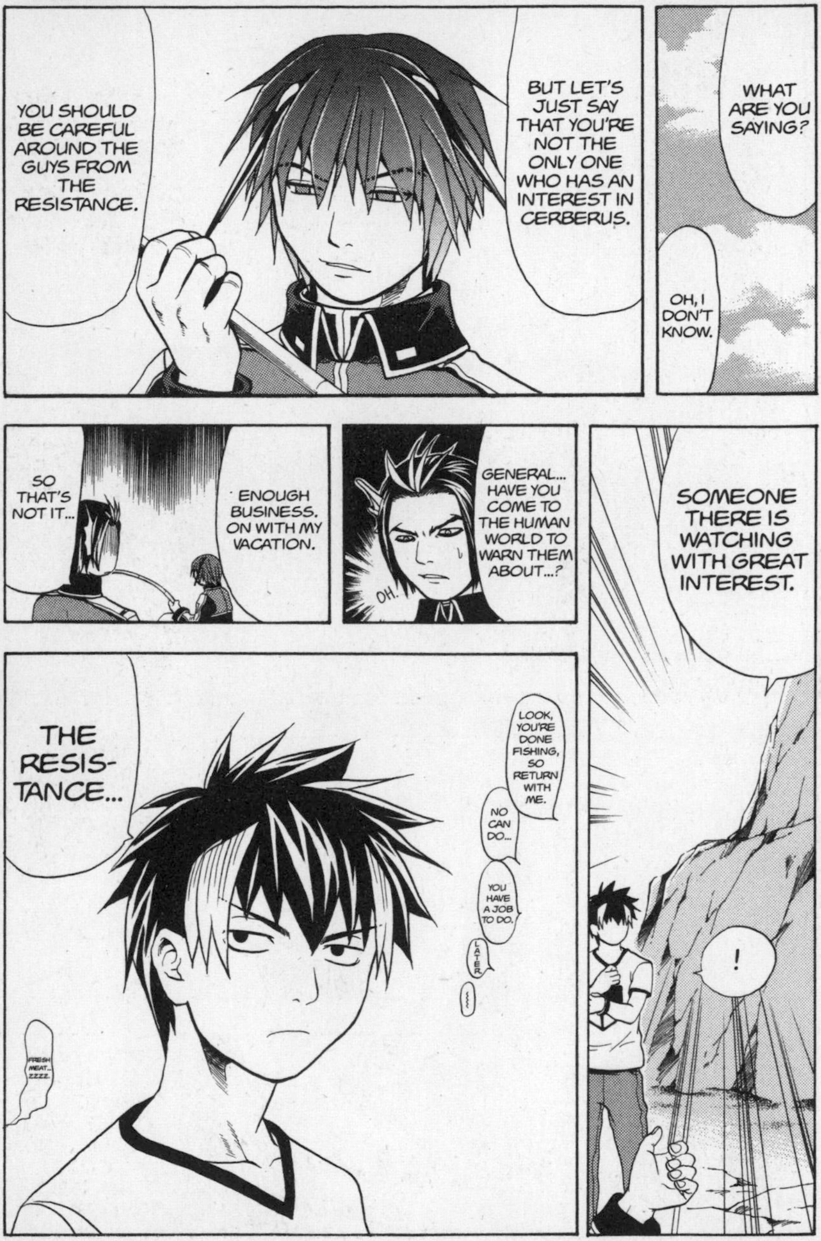
WHAT ARE YOU SAYING?
OH, I DON'T KNOW.
BUT LET'S JUST SAY THAT YOU'RE NOT THE ONLY ONE WHO HAS AN INTEREST IN CERBERUS.
YOU SHOULD BE CAREFUL AROUND THE GUYS FROM THE RESISTANCE.
GENERAL... HAVE YOU COME TO THE HUMAN WORLD TO WARN THEM ABOUT...?
OH.
SOMEONE THERE IS WATCHING WITH GREAT INTEREST.
ENOUGH BUSINESS. ON WITH MY VACATION.
SO THAT'S NOT IT...
!
LOOK, YOU'RE DONE FISHING, SO RETURN WITH ME.
NO CAN DO...
YOU HAVE A JOB TO DO.
LATER
THE RESIS- TANCE...
FRESH MEAT... ZZZZ.

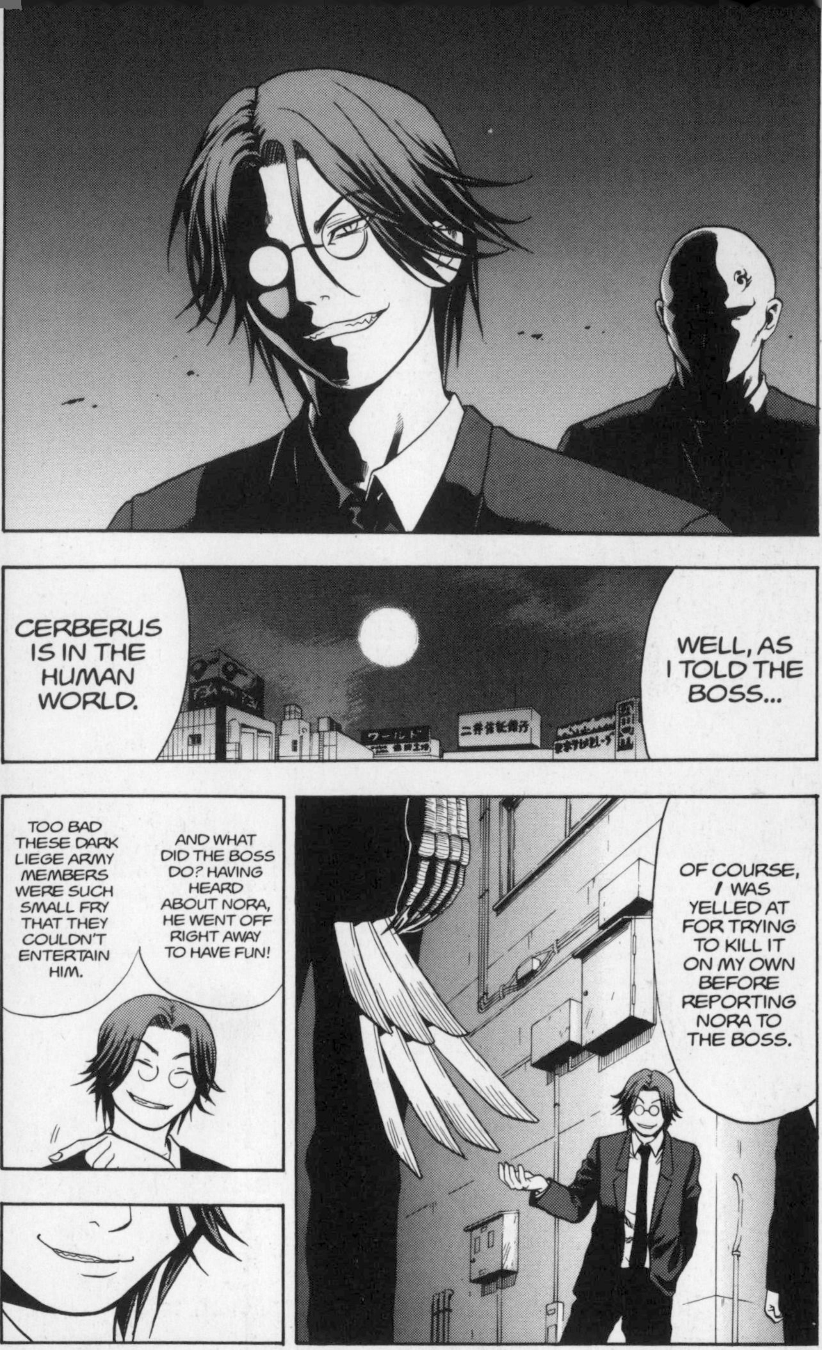
WELL, AS I TOLD THE BOSS...
CERBERUS IS IN THE HUMAN WORLD.
OF COURSE, I WAS YELLED AT FOR TRYING TO KILL IT ON MY OWN BEFORE REPORTING NORA TO THE BOSS.
AND WHAT DID THE BOSS DO? HAVING HEARD ABOUT NORA, HE WENT OFF RIGHT AWAY TO HAVE FUN!
TOO BAD THESE DARK LIEGE ARMY MEMBERS WERE SUCH SMALL FRY THAT THEY COULDN'T ENTERTAIN HIM.

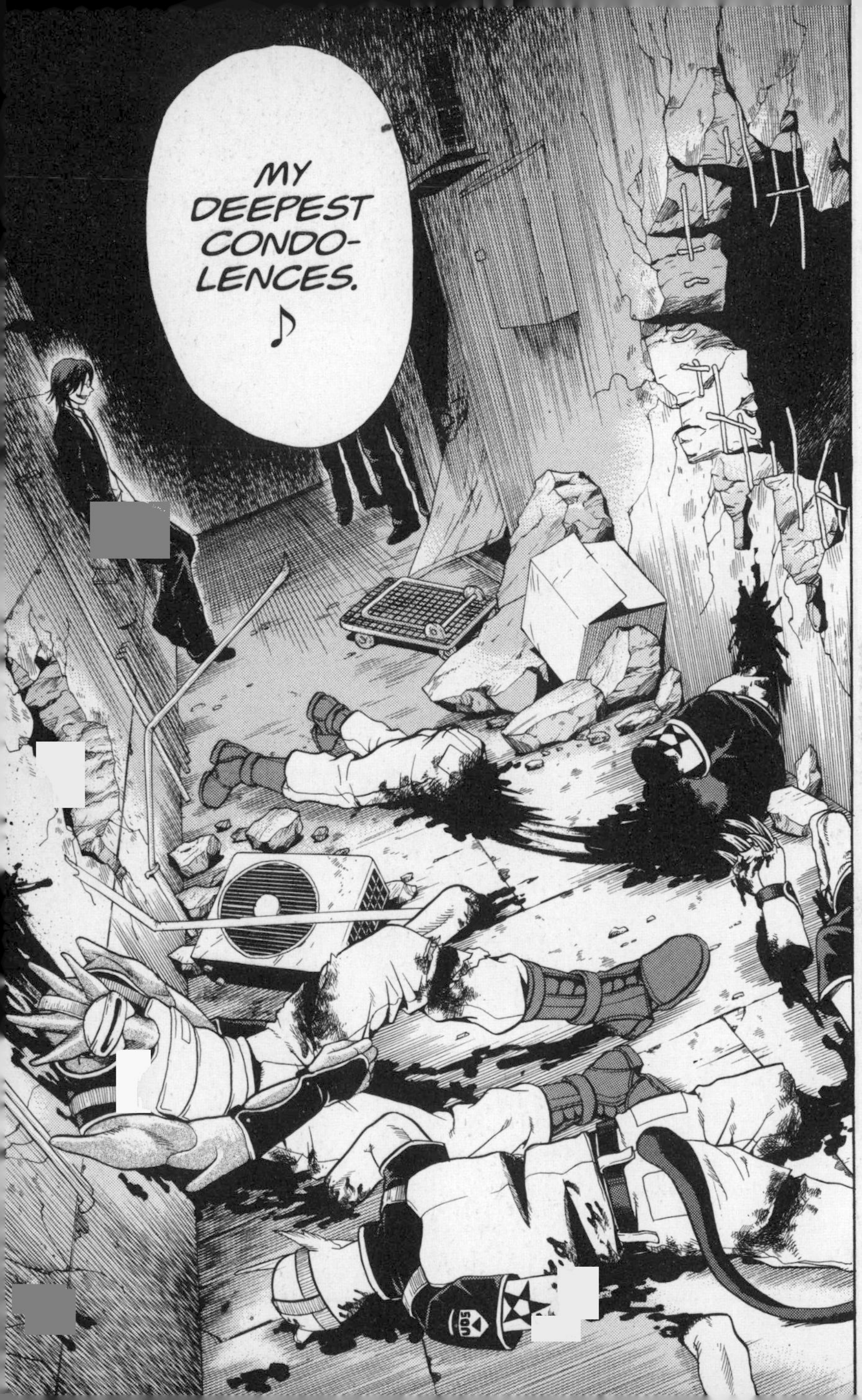
MY DEEPEST CONDO-LENCES. ♪

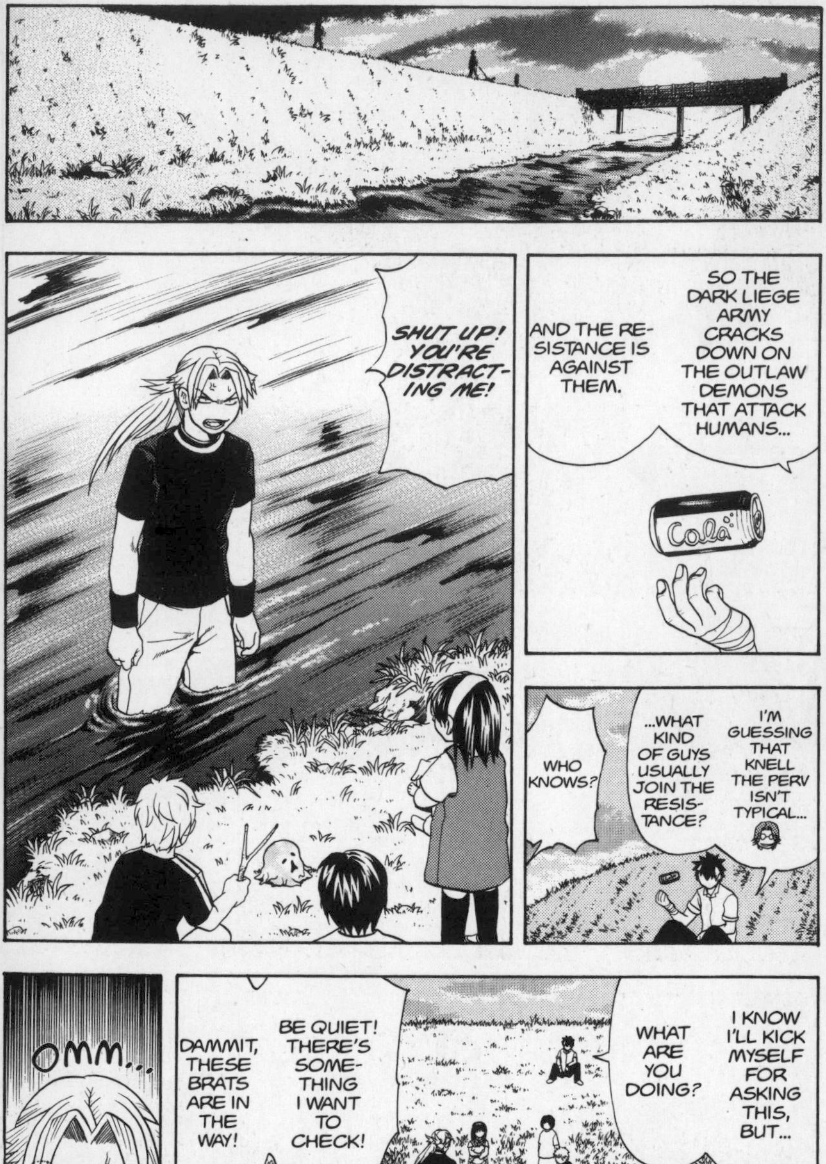
SO THE DARK LIEGE ARMY CRACKS DOWN ON THE OUTLAW DEMONS THAT ATTACK HUMANS...
AND THE RESISTANCE IS AGAINST THEM.
Cola
I'M GUESSING THAT KNELL THE PERV ISN'T TYPICAL...
...WHAT KIND OF GUYS USUALLY JOIN THE RESISTANCE?
WHO KNOWS?
SHUT UP! YOU'RE DISTRACTING ME!
I KNOW I'LL KICK MYSELF FOR ASKING THIS, BUT...
WHAT ARE YOU DOING?
BE QUIET! THERE'S SOMETHING I WANT TO CHECK!
DAMMIT, THESE BRATS ARE IN THE WAY!
SCRAM!
OMM...

READ THIS WAY

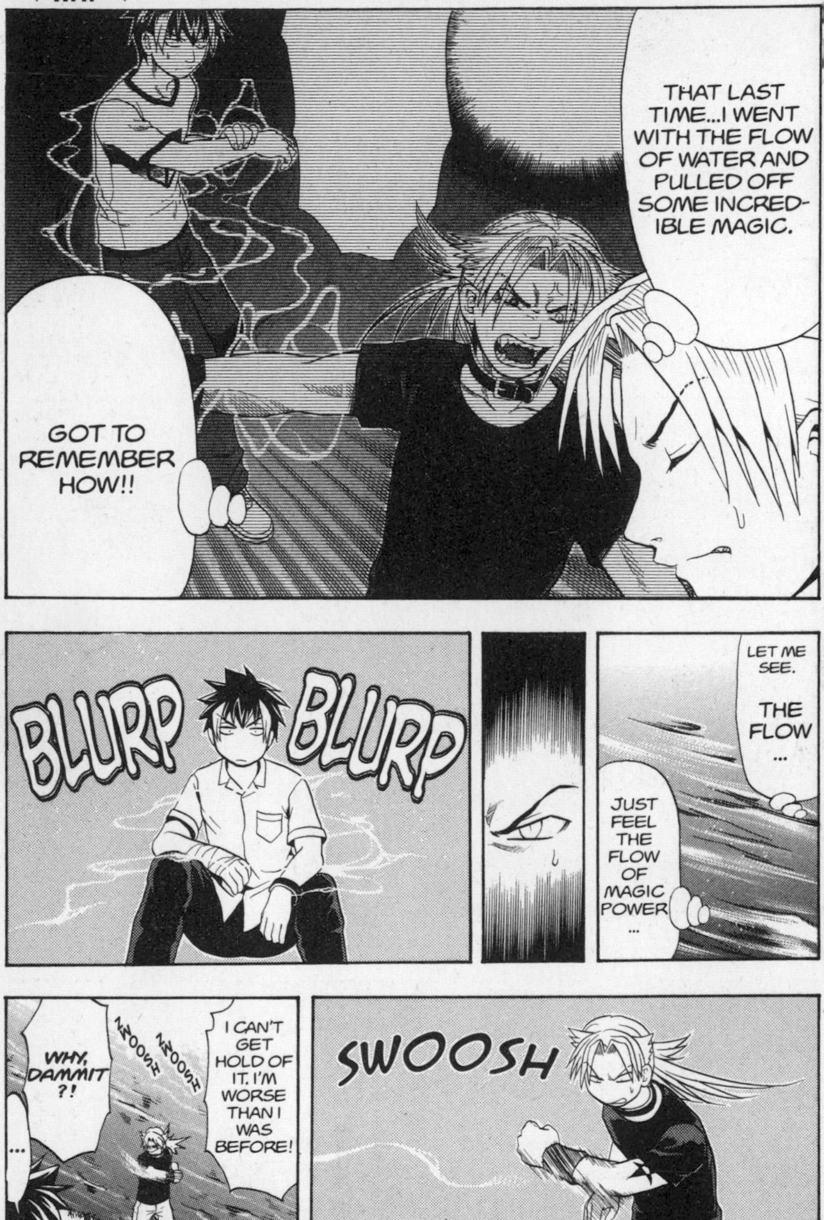
THAT LAST TIME...I WENT WITH THE FLOW OF WATER AND PULLED OFF SOME INCREDIBLE MAGIC.
GOT TO REMEMBER HOW!!
LET ME SEE. THE FLOW ...
JUST FEEL THE FLOW OF MAGIC POWER ...
BLURP
BLURP
SWOOSH
I CAN'T GET HOLD OF IT. I'M WORSE THAN I WAS BEFORE!
WOOSH
WOOSH
WHY, DAMMIT ?!
...

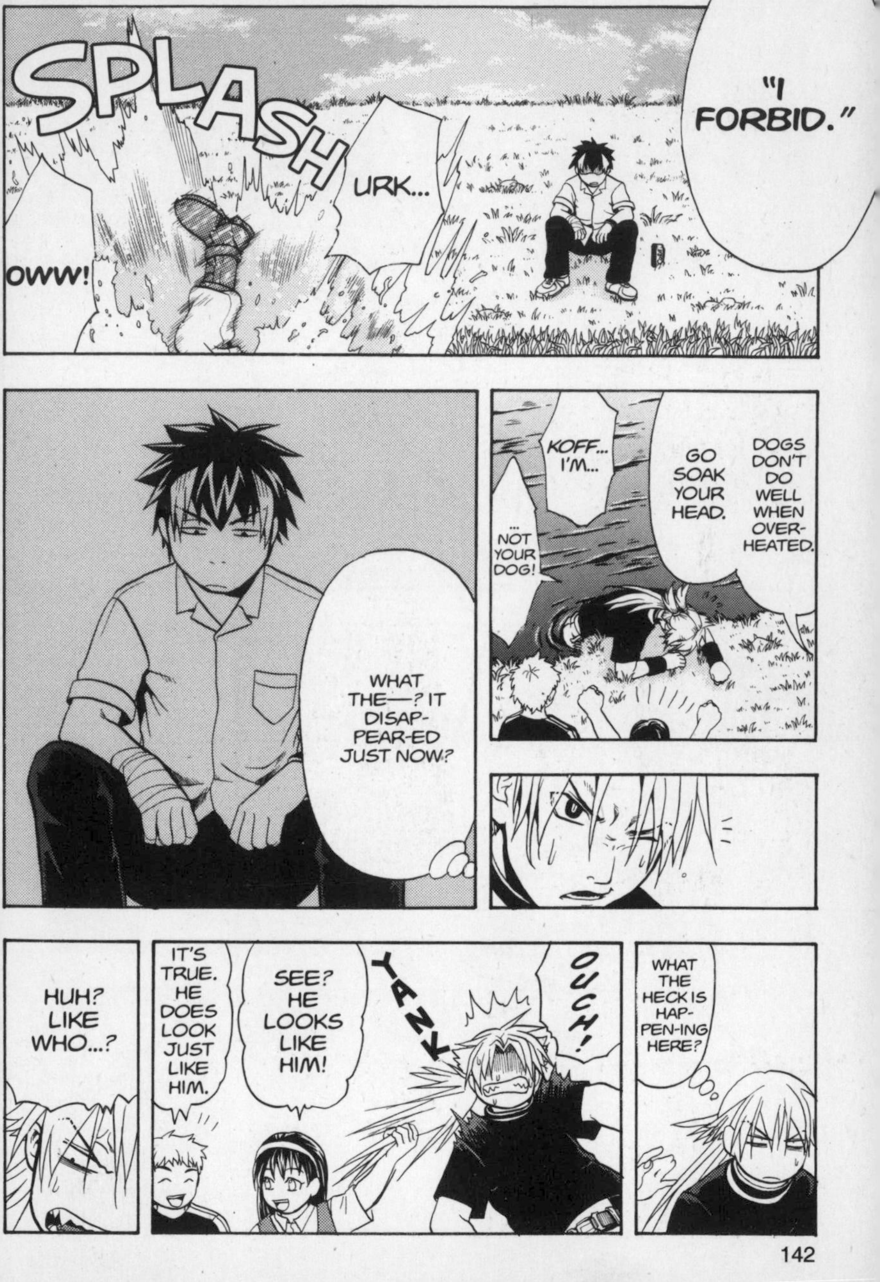
"I FORBID."
SPLASH
URK...
OWW!
DOGS DON'T DO WELL WHEN OVER-HEATED.
GO SOAK YOUR HEAD.
KOFF... I'M...
...NOT YOUR DOG!
WHAT THE—? IT DISAP-PEAR-ED JUST NOW?
WHAT THE HECK IS HAP-PEN-ING HERE?
OUCH!
YANK
SEE? HE LOOKS LIKE HIM!
IT'S TRUE. HE DOES LOOK JUST LIKE HIM.
HUH? LIKE WHO...?

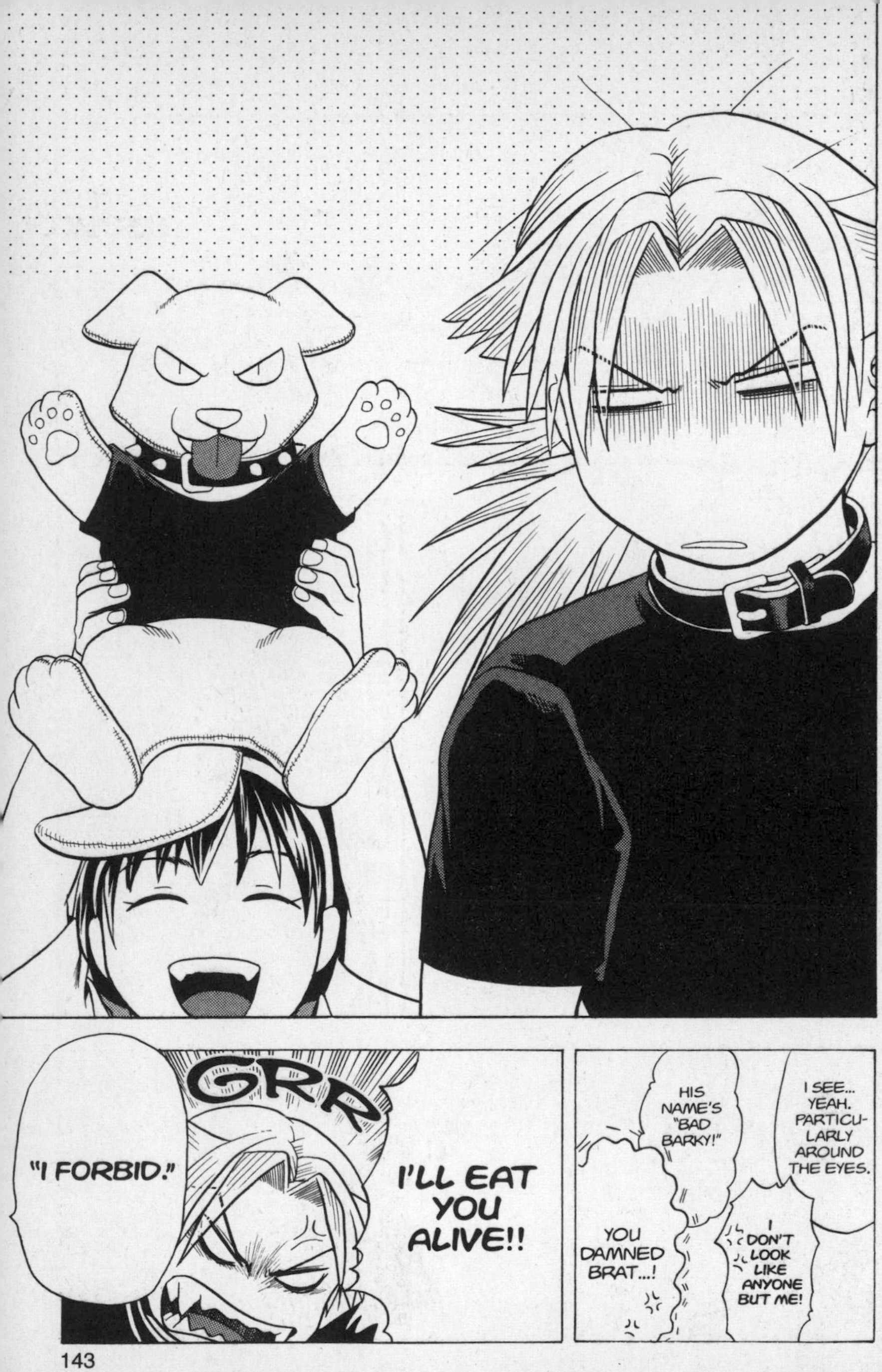
I SEE... YEAH. PARTICU-LARLY AROUND THE EYES.
HIS NAME'S "BAD BARKY!"
I DON'T LOOK LIKE ANYONE BUT ME!
YOU DAMNED BRAT...!
GRR
I'LL EAT YOU ALIVE!!
"I FORBID."

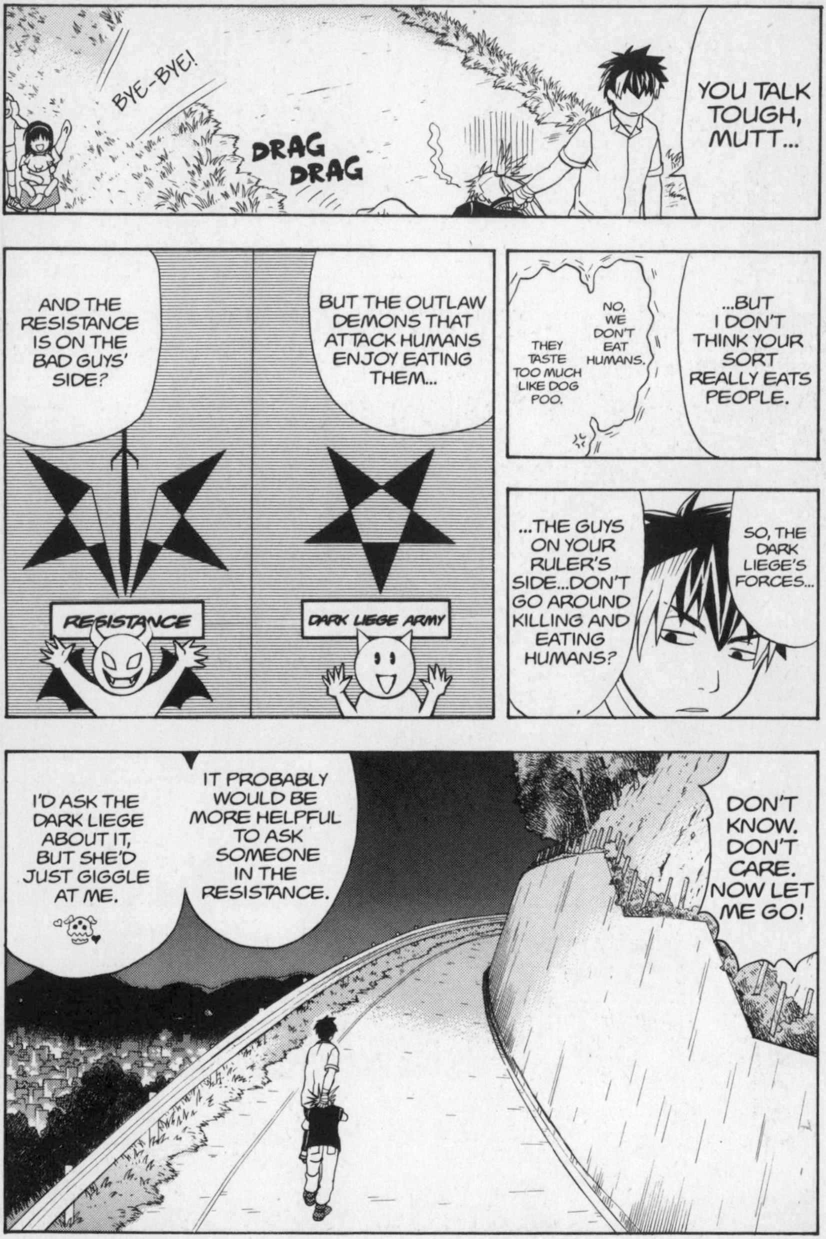
YOU TALK TOUGH, MUTT...
DRAG DRAG
BYE-BYE!
...BUT I DON'T THINK YOUR SORT REALLY EATS PEOPLE.
NO, WE DON'T EAT HUMANS.
THEY TASTE TOO MUCH LIKE DOG POO.
SO, THE DARK LIEGE'S FORCES...
...THE GUYS ON YOUR RULER'S SIDE...DON'T GO AROUND KILLING AND EATING HUMANS?
BUT THE OUTLAW DEMONS THAT ATTACK HUMANS ENJOY EATING THEM...
DARK LIEGE ARMY
AND THE RESISTANCE IS ON THE BAD GUYS' SIDE?
RESISTANCE
DON'T KNOW. DON'T CARE. NOW LET ME GO!
IT PROBABLY WOULD BE MORE HELPFUL TO ASK SOMEONE IN THE RESISTANCE.
I'D ASK THE DARK LIEGE ABOUT IT, BUT SHE'D JUST GIGGLE AT ME.

READ THIS WAY

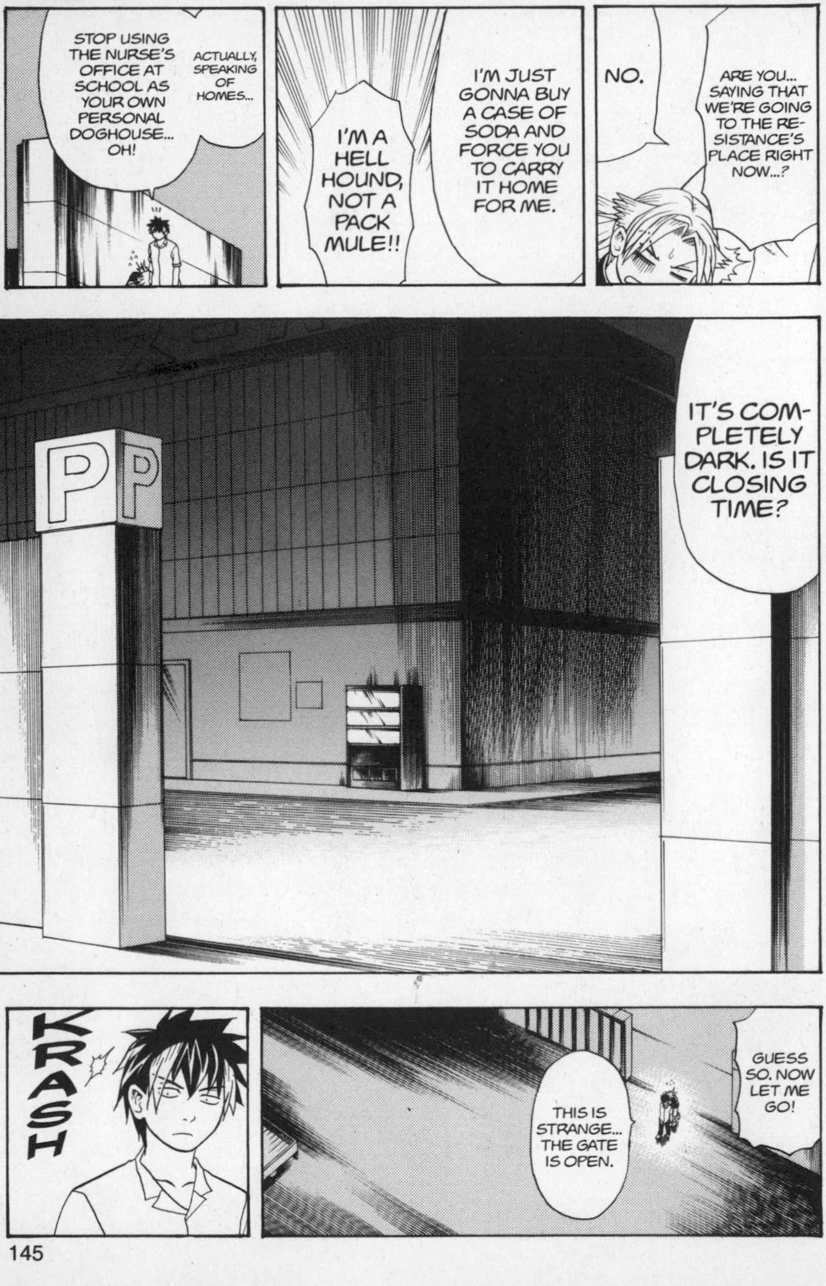

ARE YOU... SAYING THAT WE'RE GOING TO THE RE-SISTANCE'S PLACE RIGHT NOW...?
NO.
I'M JUST GONNA BUY A CASE OF SODA AND FORCE YOU TO CARRY IT HOME FOR ME.
I'M A HELL HOUND, NOT A PACK MULE!!
ACTUALLY, SPEAKING OF HOMES...
STOP USING THE NURSE'S OFFICE AT SCHOOL AS YOUR OWN PERSONAL DOGHOUSE... OH!
IT'S COM-PLETELY DARK. IS IT CLOSING TIME?
GUESS SO. NOW LET ME GO!
THIS IS STRANGE... THE GATE IS OPEN.
KRASH

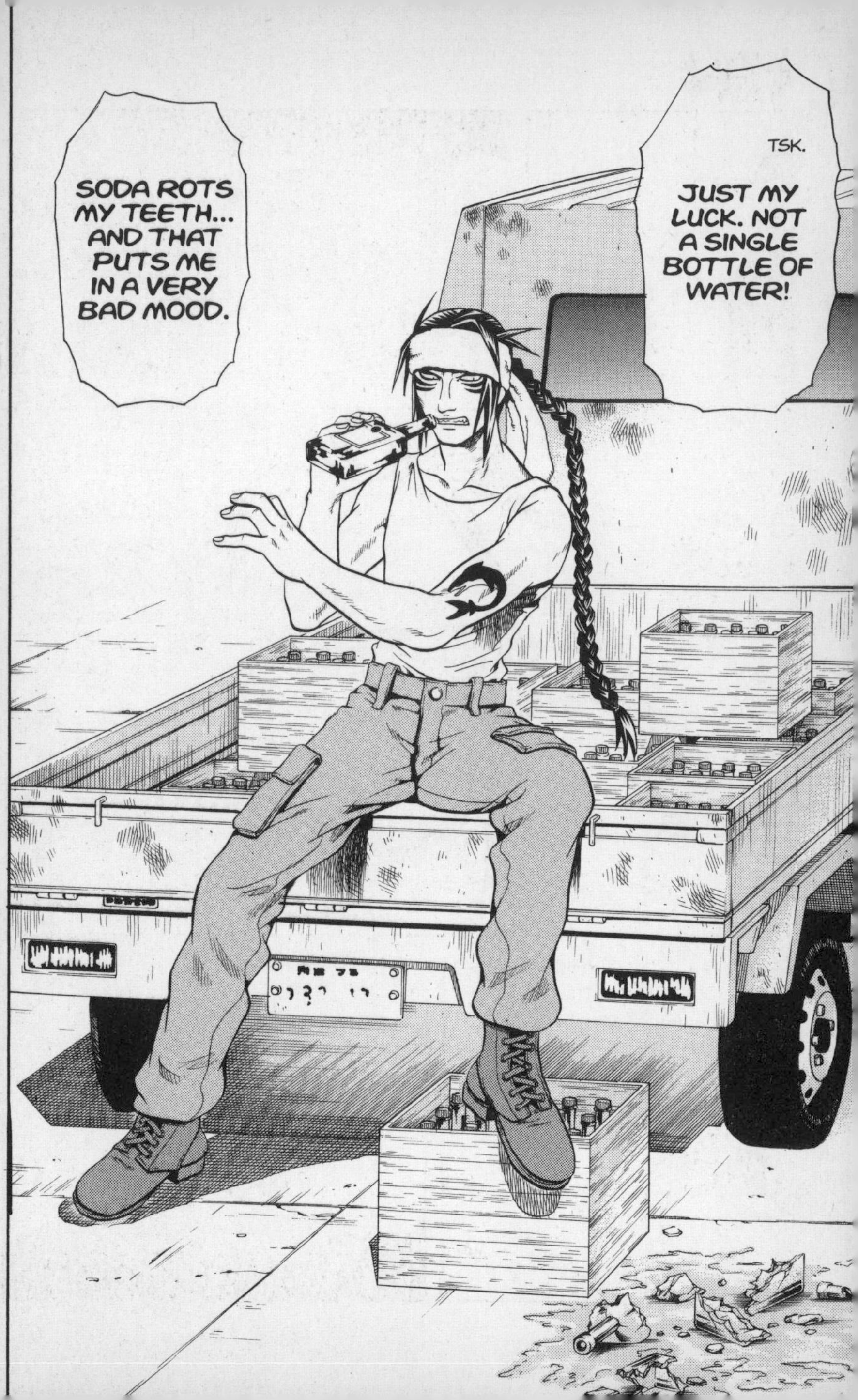
TSK.
JUST MY LUCK. NOT A SINGLE BOTTLE OF WATER!
SODA ROTS MY TEETH... AND THAT PUTS ME IN A VERY BAD MOOD.

READ THIS WAY

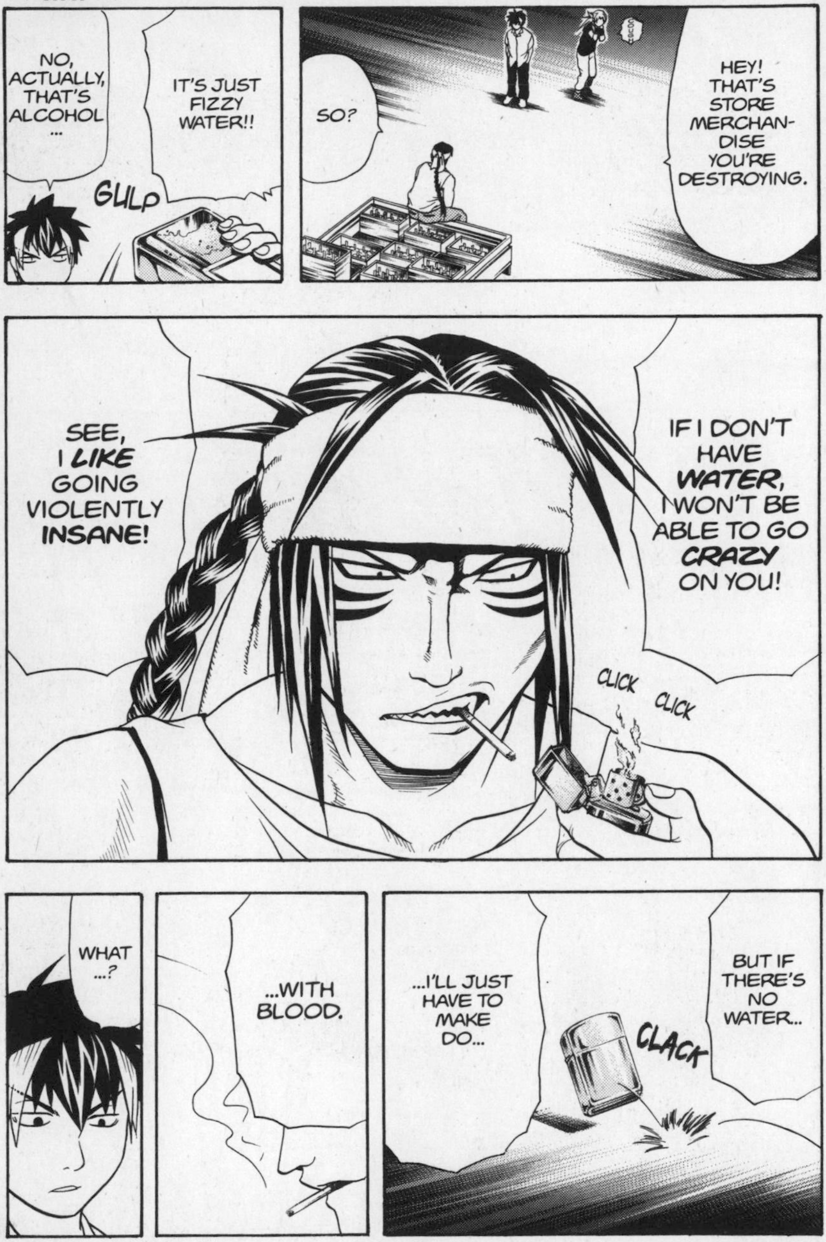
HEY! THAT'S STORE MERCHANDISE YOU'RE DESTROYING.
SO?
IT'S JUST FIZZY WATER!!
NO, ACTUALLY, THAT'S ALCOHOL ...
GULP
IF I DON'T HAVE WATER, I WON'T BE ABLE TO GO CRAZY ON YOU!
SEE, I LIKE GOING VIOLENTLY INSANE!
CLICK CLICK
BUT IF THERE'S NO WATER...
...I'LL JUST HAVE TO MAKE DO...
CLACK
...WITH BLOOD.
WHAT ...?

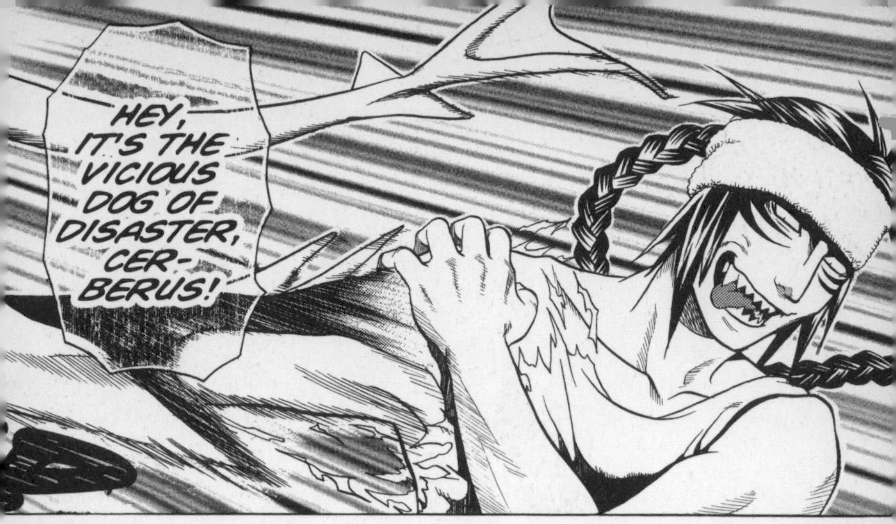
HEY, IT'S THE VICIOUS DOG OF DISASTER, CER-BERUS!
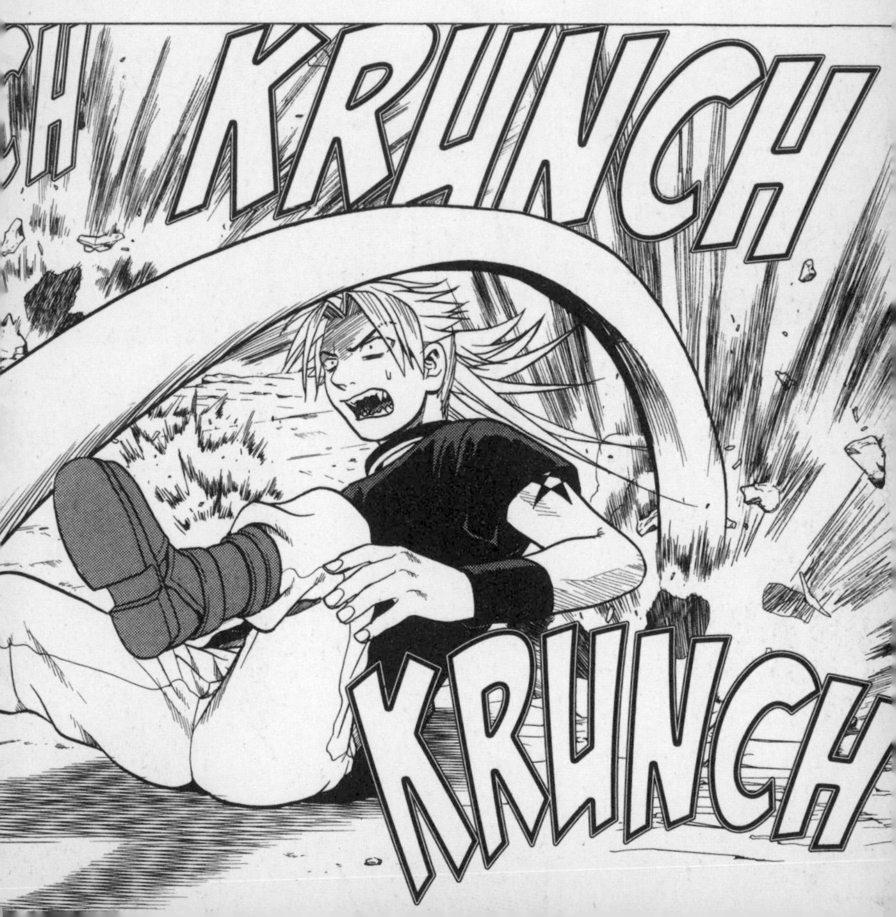
KRUNCH
KRUNCH

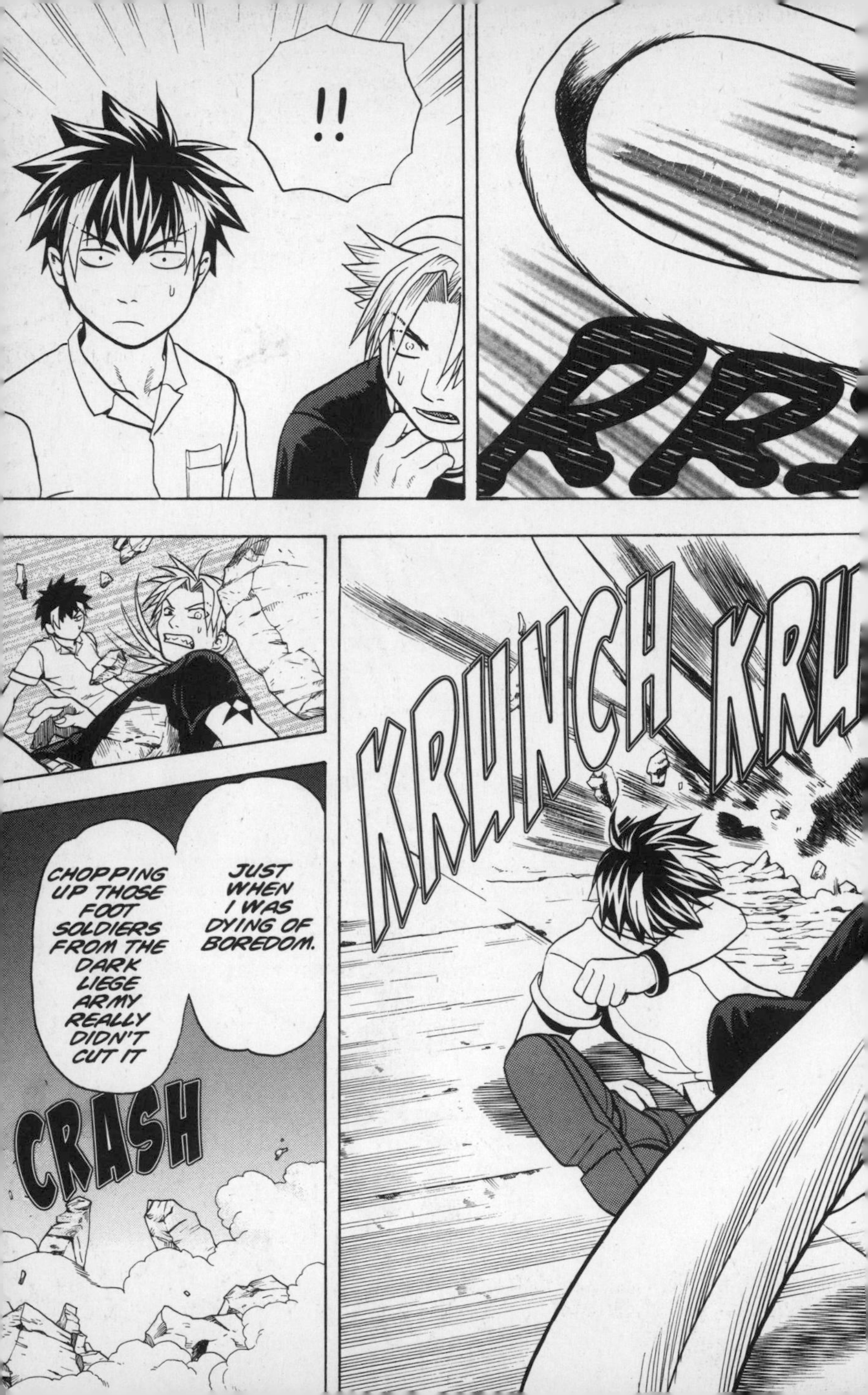
RR
!!
KRUNCH KRU
JUST WHEN I WAS DYING OF BOREDOM.
CHOPPING UP THOSE FOOT SOLDIERS FROM THE DARK LIEGE ARMY REALLY DIDN'T CUT IT
CRASH

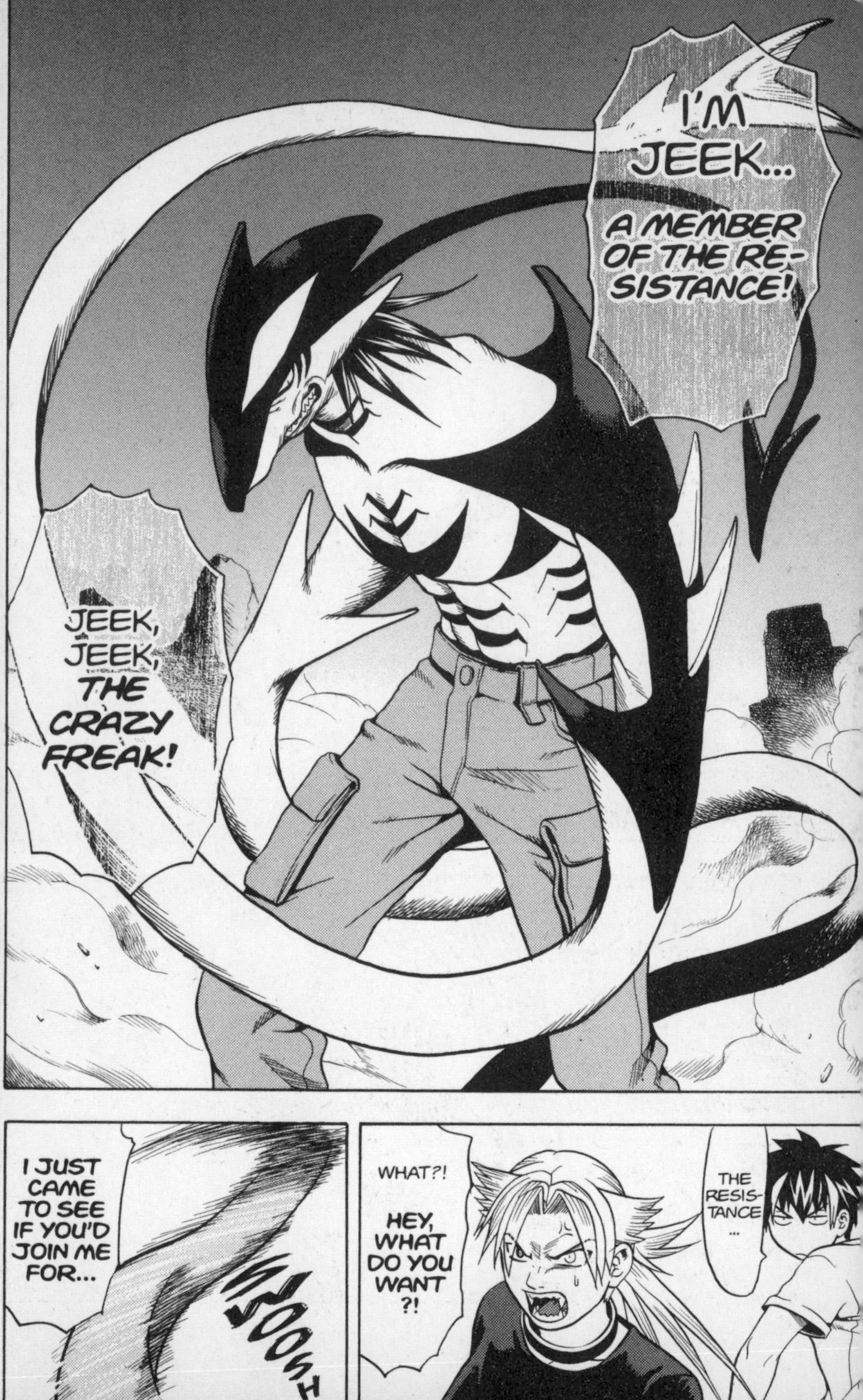
I'M JEEK... A MEMBER OF THE RE-SISTANCE!
JEEK, JEEK, THE CRAZY FREAK!
THE RESIS-TANCE ...
WHAT?!
HEY, WHAT DO YOU WANT ?!
I JUST CAME TO SEE IF YOU'D JOIN ME FOR...
WOOSH

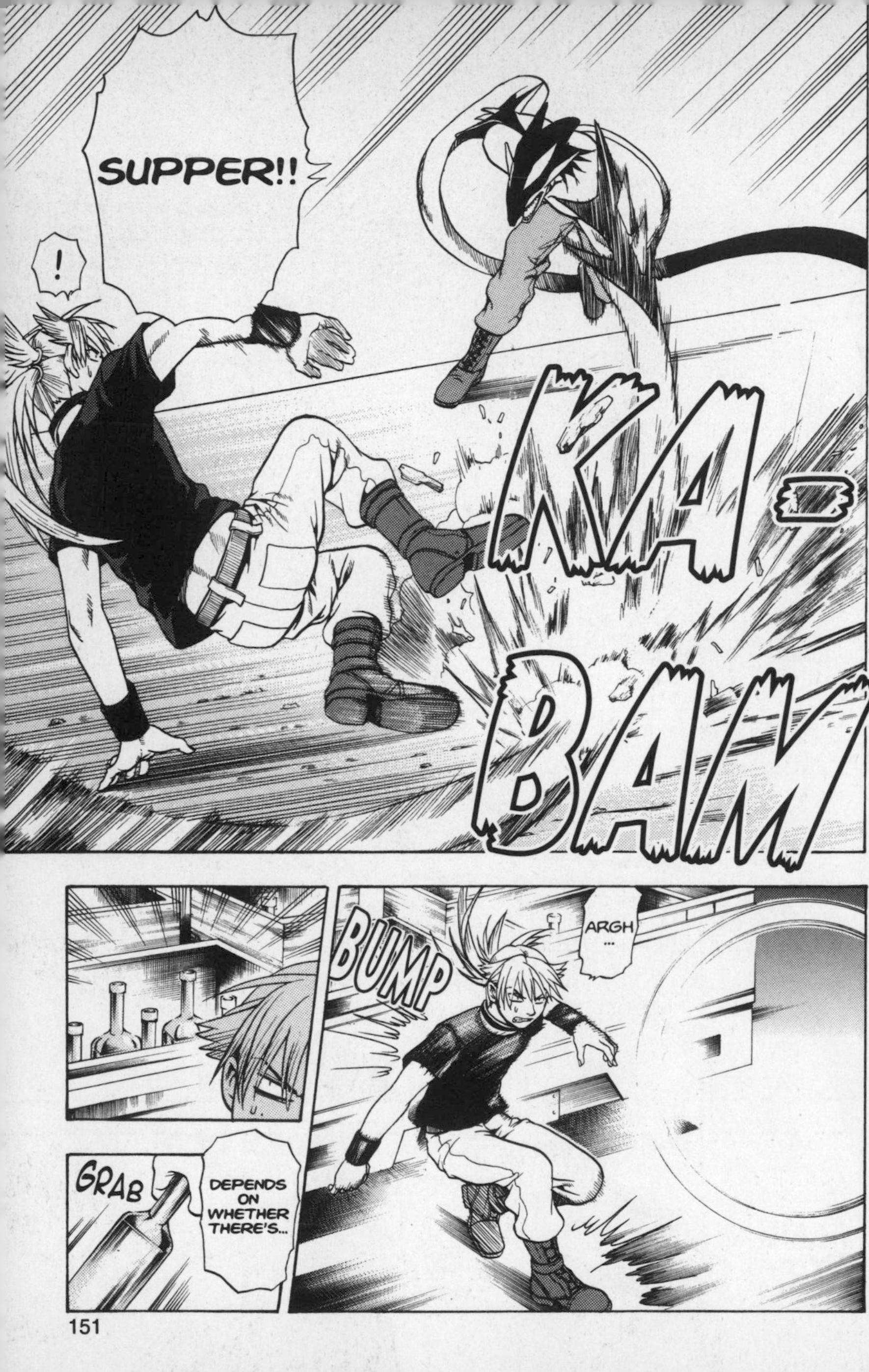
SUPPER!!
!
KA-BAM
BUMP
ARGH ...
GRAB
DEPENDS ON WHETHER THERE'S...

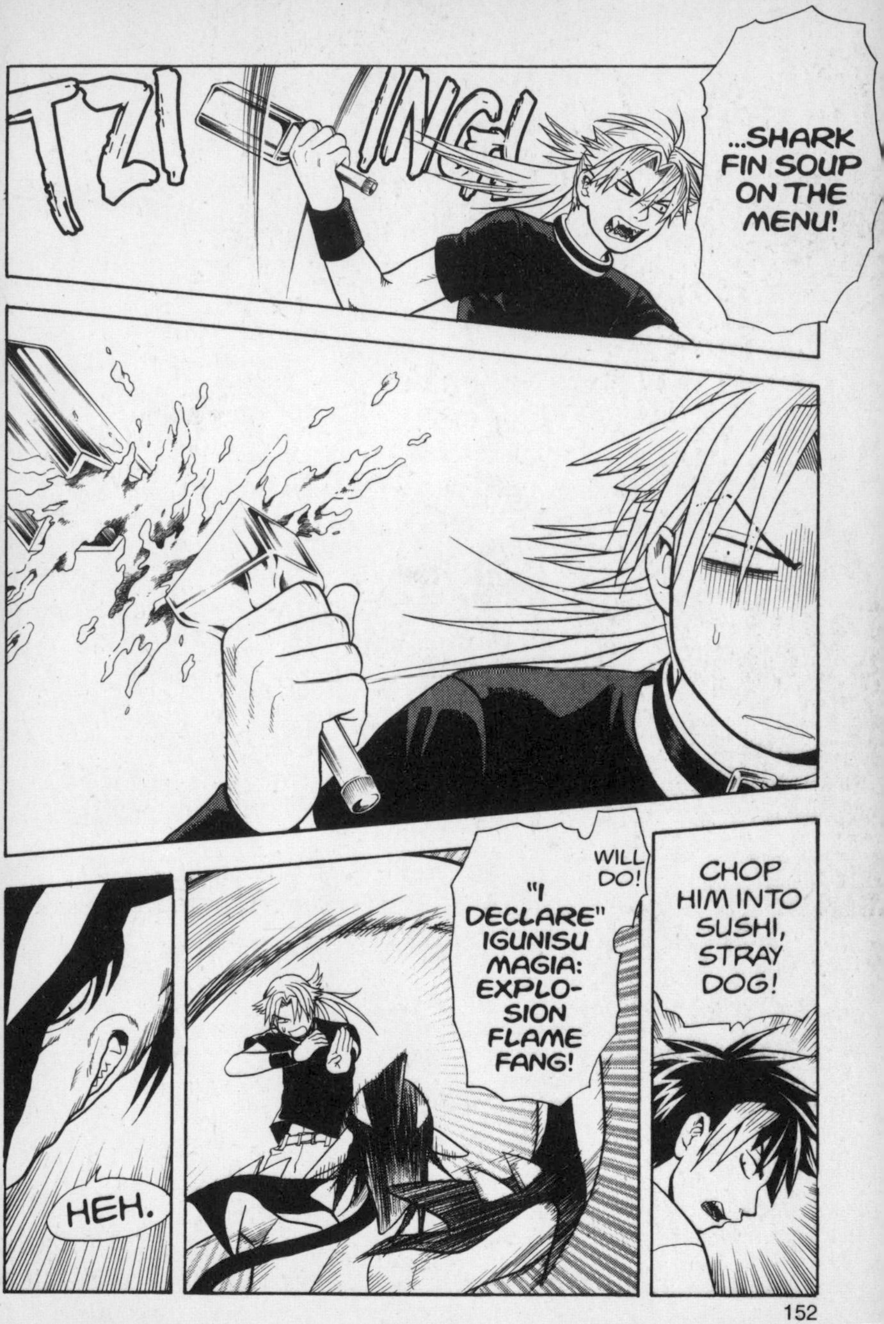
...SHARK FIN SOUP ON THE MENU!
TZI ING!
CHOP HIM INTO SUSHI, STRAY DOG!
WILL DO!
"I DECLARE" IGUNISU MAGIA: EXPLOSION FLAME FANG!
HEH.

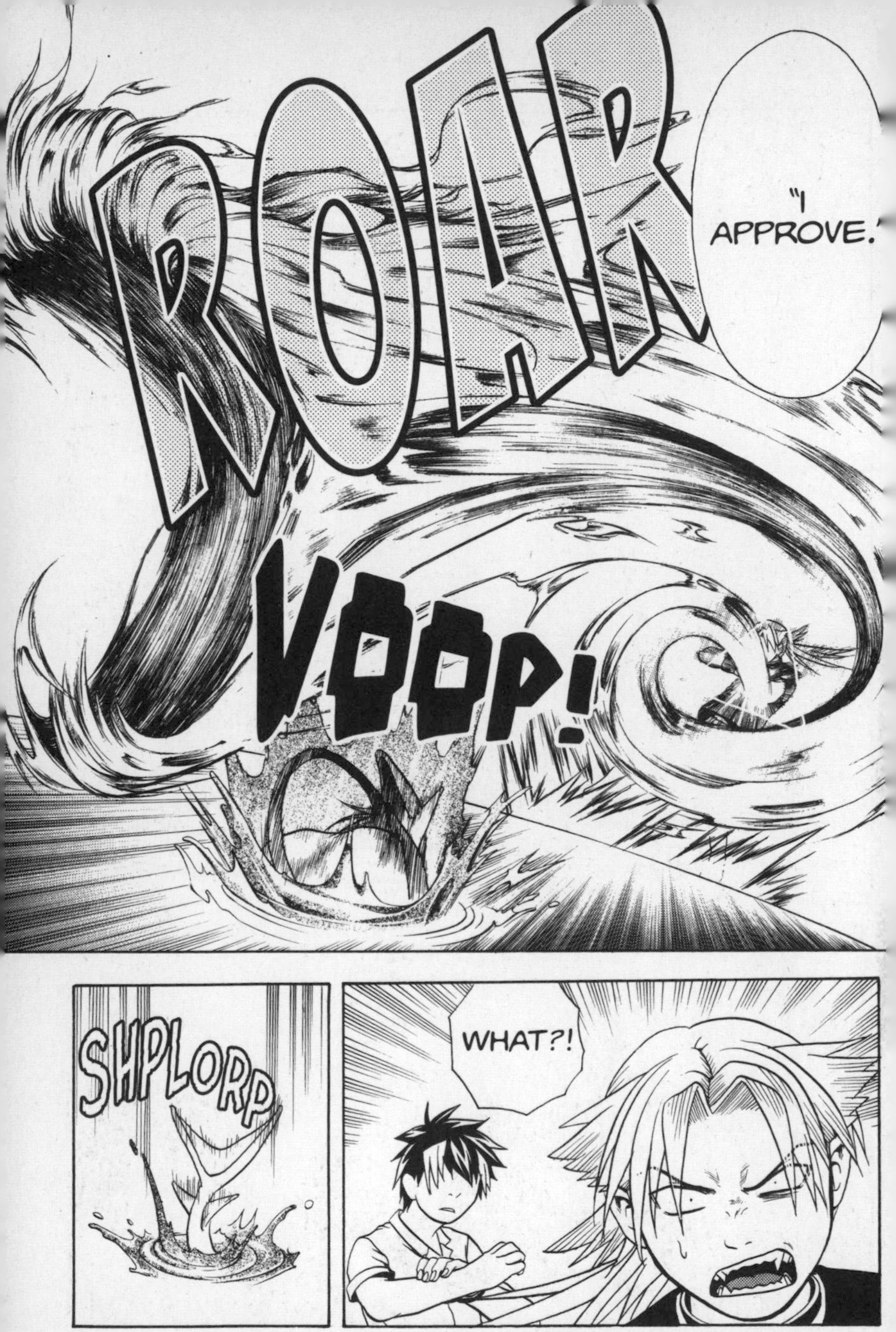
"I APPROVE."
ROAR
VOOP!
WHAT?!
SHPLORP

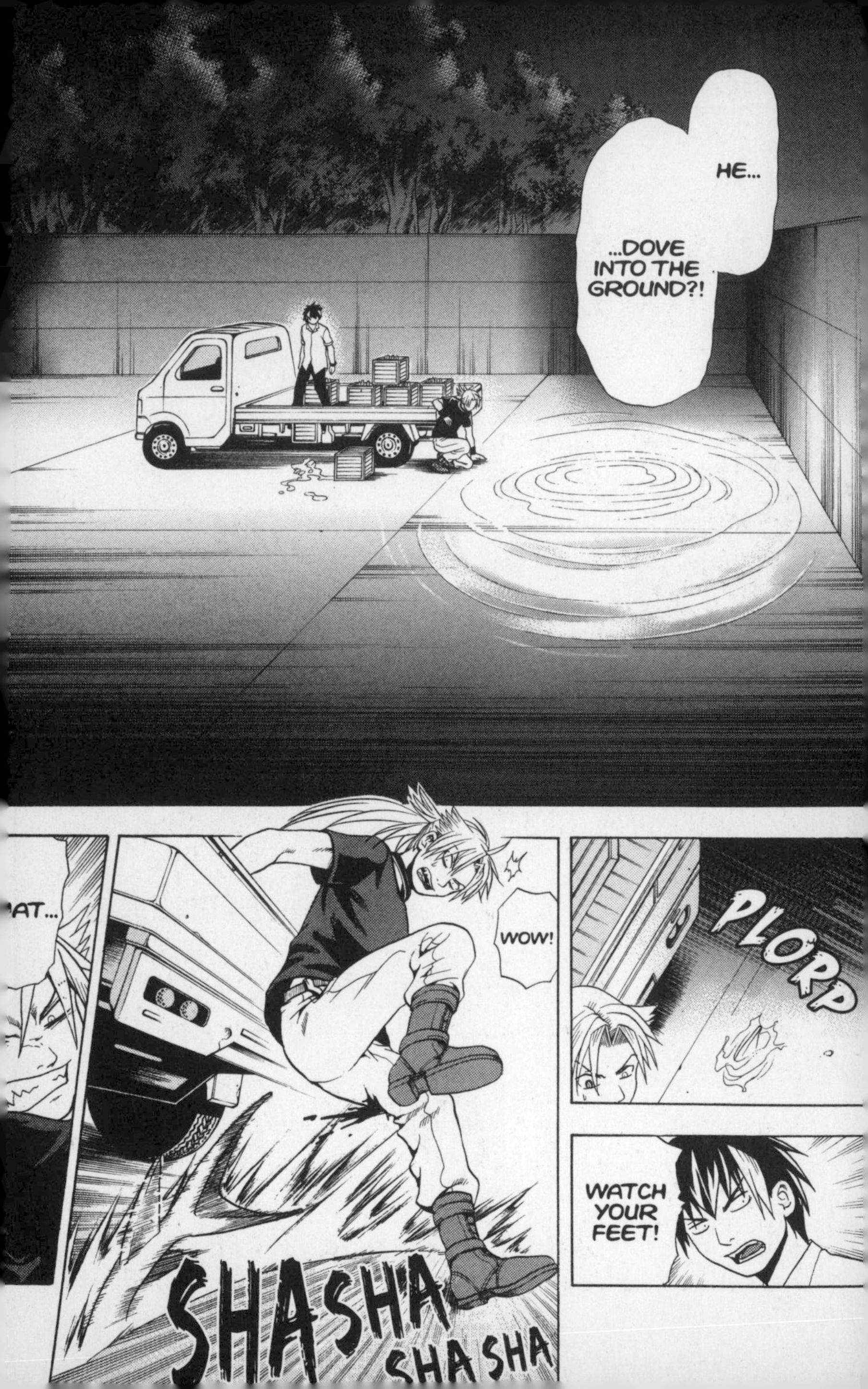
HE...
...DOVE INTO THE GROUND?!
PLORP
WATCH YOUR FEET!
WOW!
SHASHA
SHASHA

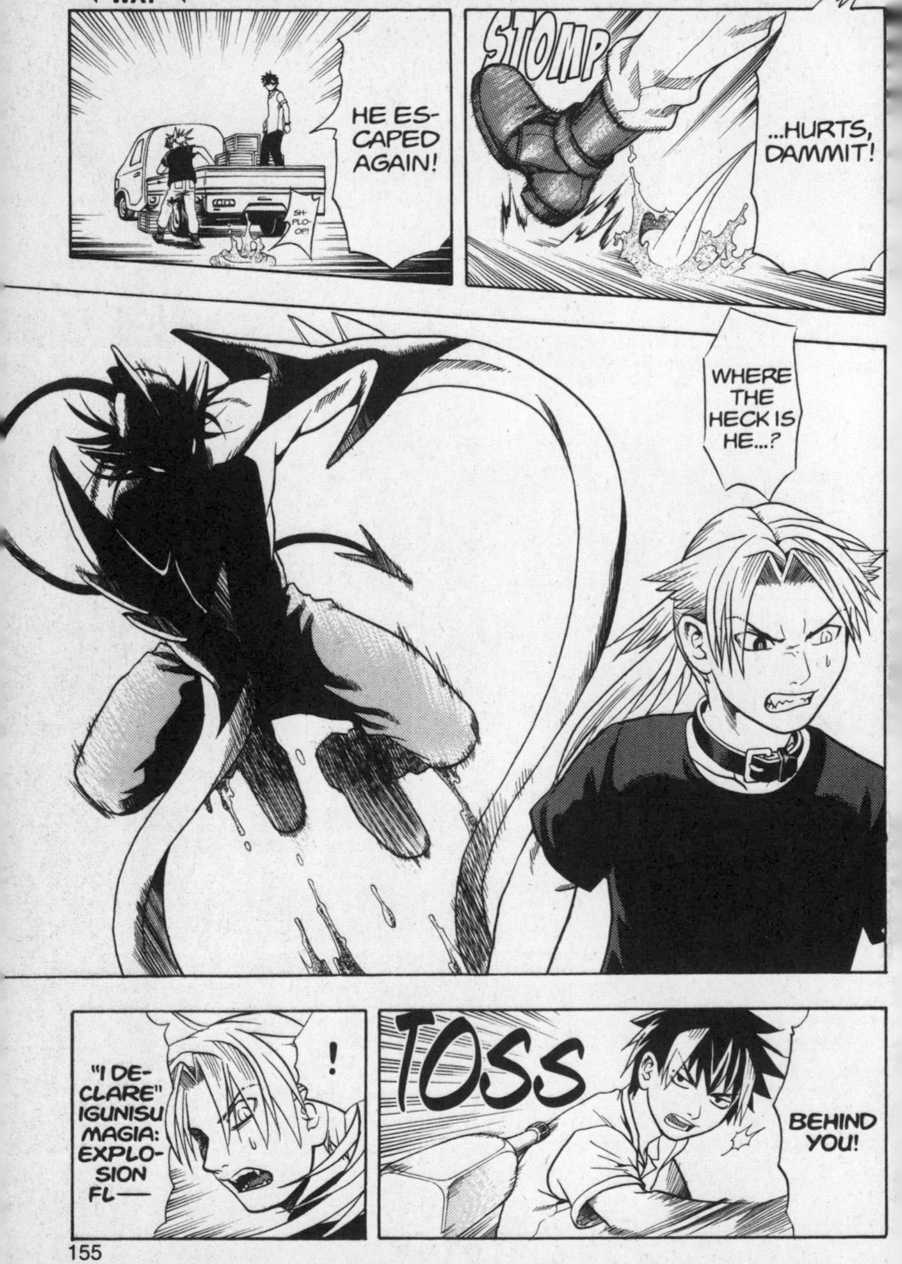
STOMP
...HURTS, DAMMIT!
HE ES-CAPED AGAIN!
SH-PLO-OP!
WHERE THE HECK IS HE...?
TOSS
BEHIND YOU!
!
"I DE-CLARE" IGUNISU MAGIA: EXPLO-SION FL—

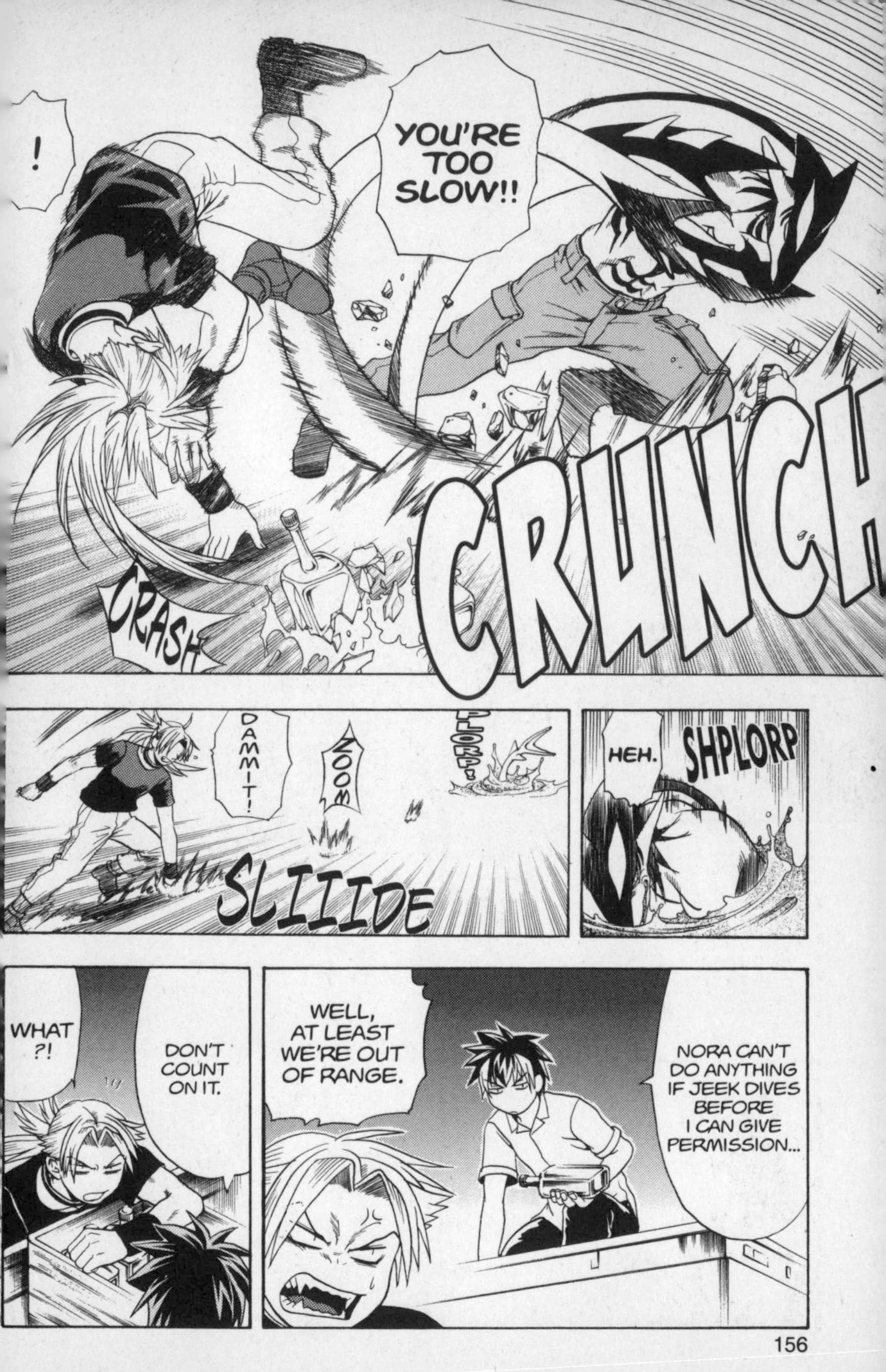
YOU'RE TOO SLOW!!
!
CRUNCH
CRASH
SHPLORP
HEH.
PLORP!
ZOOM
DAMMIT!
SLIIIDE
NORA CAN'T DO ANYTHING IF JEEK DIVES BEFORE I CAN GIVE PERMISSION...
WELL, AT LEAST WE'RE OUT OF RANGE.
DON'T COUNT ON IT.
WHAT?!

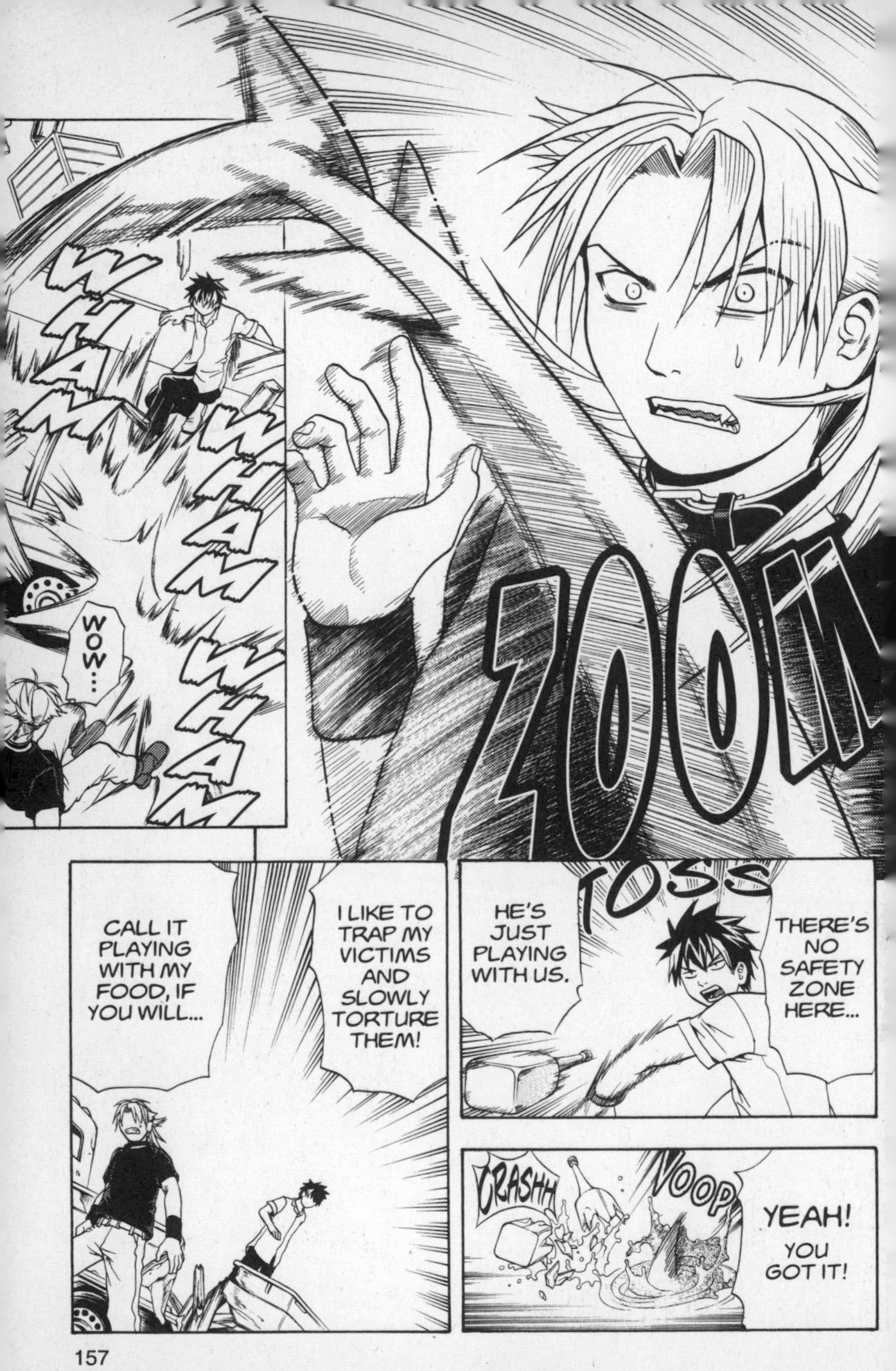
ZOOM
WHAM
WHAM
WHAM
WOW...
TOSS
THERE'S NO SAFETY ZONE HERE...
HE'S JUST PLAYING WITH US.
CRASHH
VOOP
YEAH!
YOU GOT IT!
I LIKE TO TRAP MY VICTIMS AND SLOWLY TORTURE THEM!
CALL IT PLAYING WITH MY FOOD, IF YOU WILL...

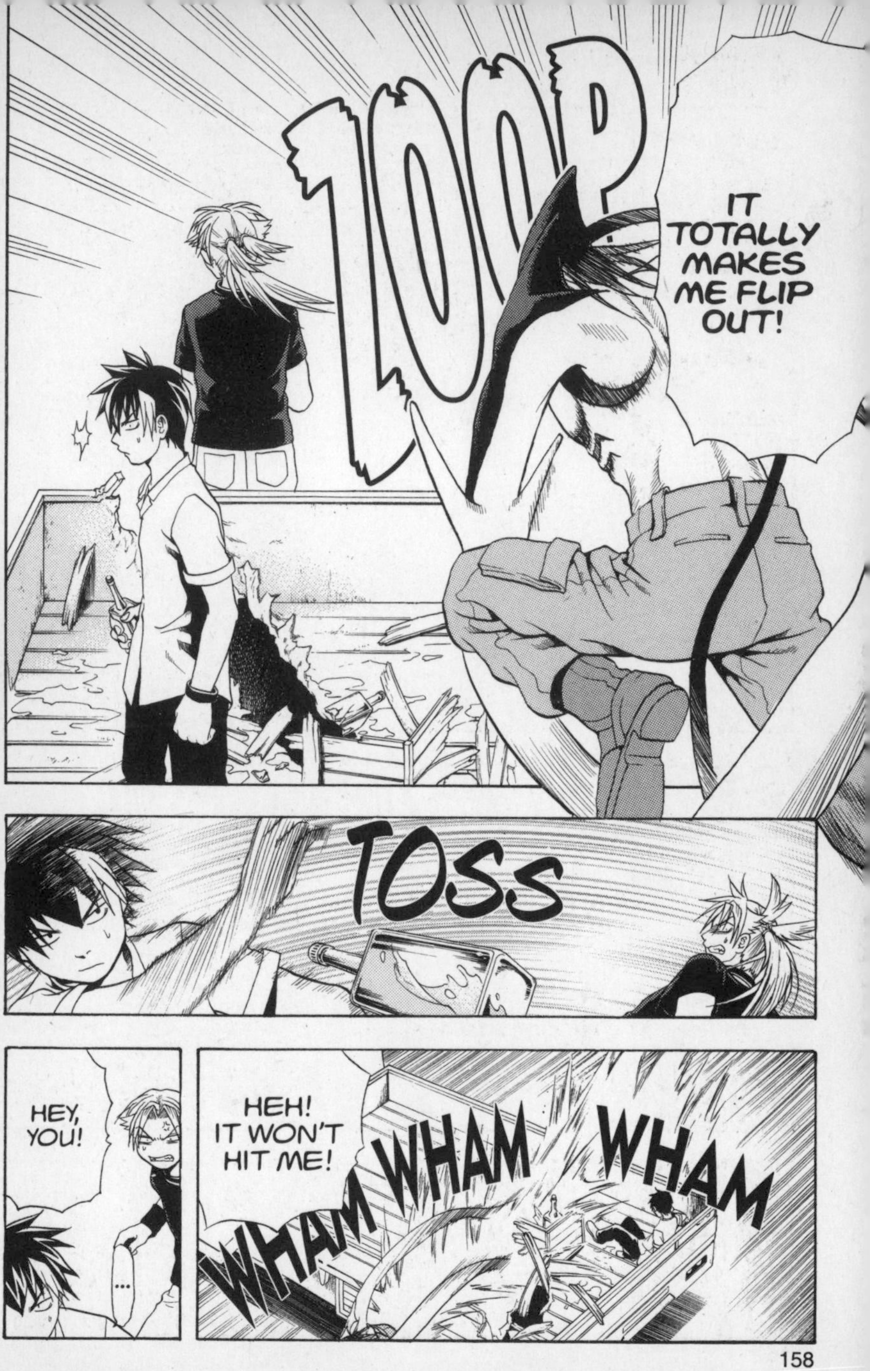
IT TOTALLY MAKES ME FLIP OUT!
TOOP
TOSS
HEH! IT WON'T HIT ME!
WHAM WHAM WHAM WHAM
HEY, YOU!
...

READ THIS WAY

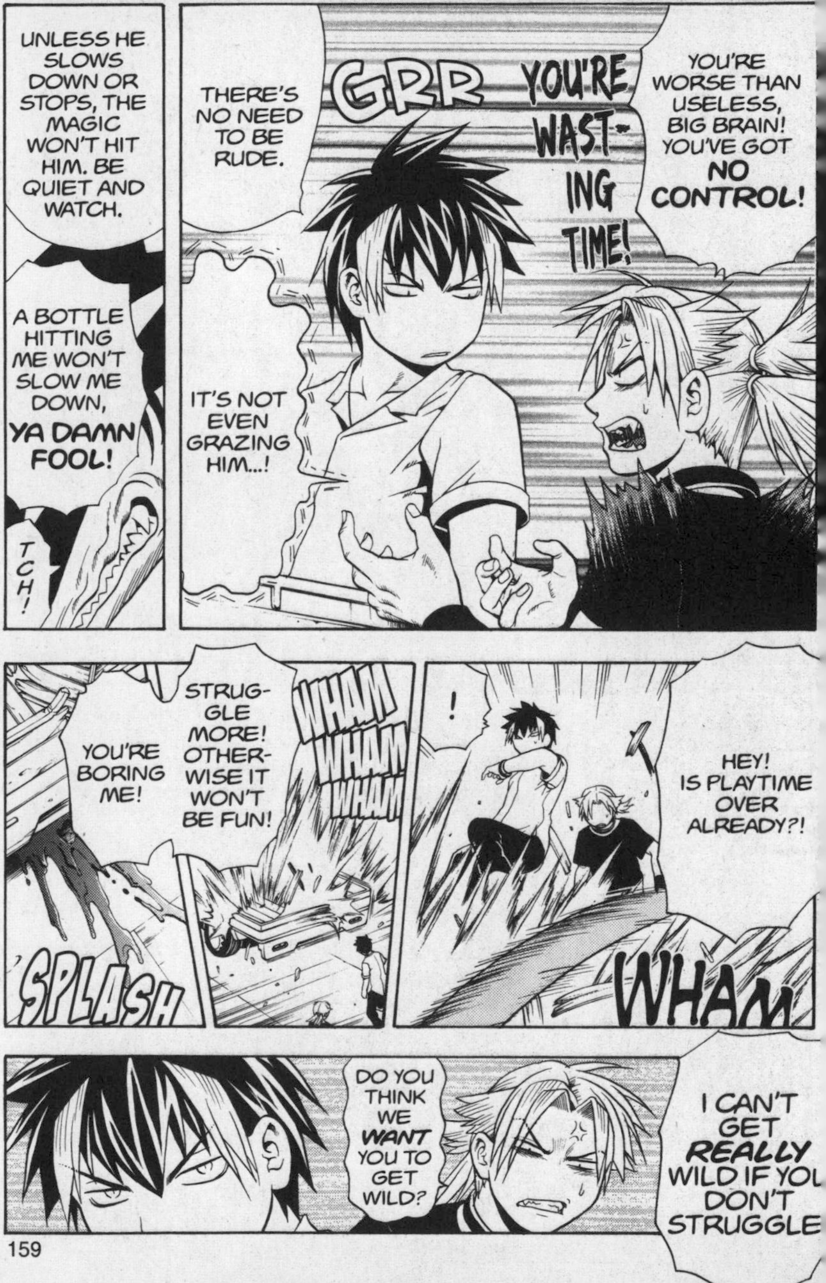
YOU'RE WORSE THAN USELESS, BIG BRAIN! YOU'VE GOT NO CONTROL!
YOU'RE WASTING TIME!
GRR
THERE'S NO NEED TO BE RUDE.
IT'S NOT EVEN GRAZING HIM...!
UNLESS HE SLOWS DOWN OR STOPS, THE MAGIC WON'T HIT HIM. BE QUIET AND WATCH.
A BOTTLE HITTING ME WON'T SLOW ME DOWN, YA DAMN FOOL!
TCH!
HEY! IS PLAYTIME OVER ALREADY?!
!
WHAM
WHAM WHAM WHAM
STRUGGLE MORE! OTHERWISE IT WON'T BE FUN!
YOU'RE BORING ME!
SPLASH
I CAN'T GET REALLY WILD IF YO DON'T STRUGGLE
DO YOU THINK WE WANT YOU TO GET WILD?

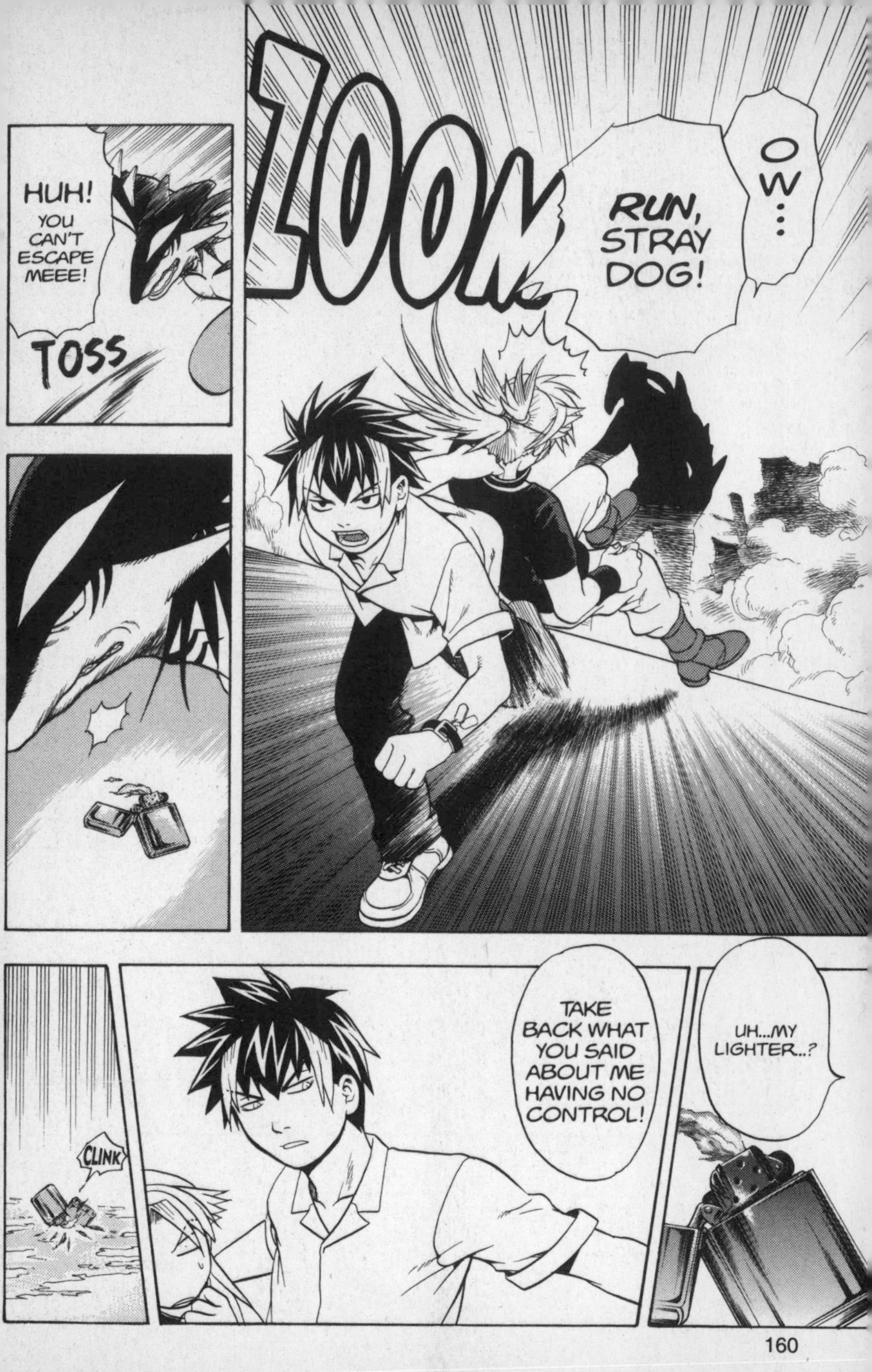
OW...
RUN, STRAY DOG!
ZOOM
HUH! YOU CAN'T ESCAPE MEEE!
TOSS
UH...MY LIGHTER...?
TAKE BACK WHAT YOU SAID ABOUT ME HAVING NO CONTROL!
CLINK

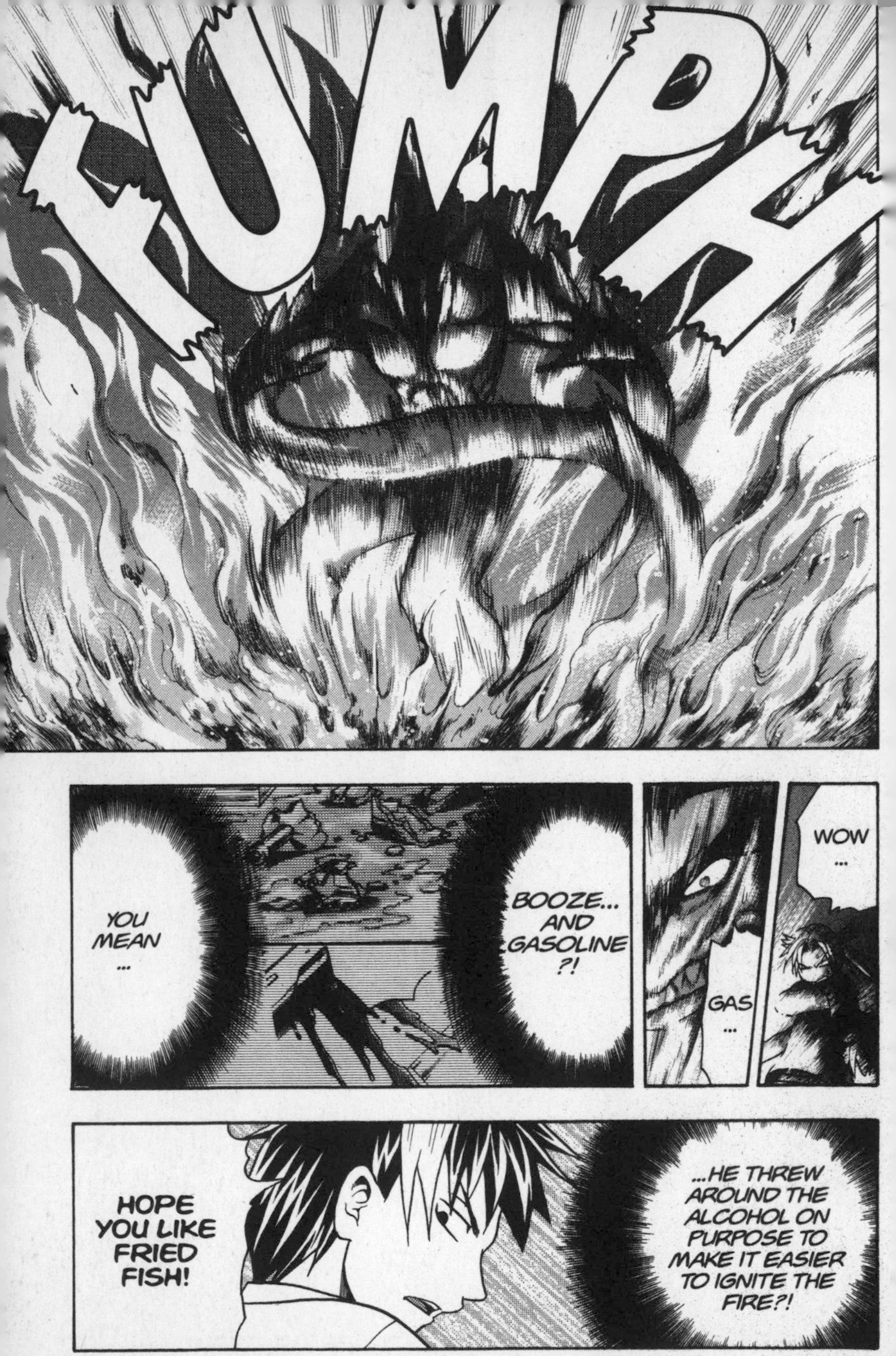
FUMP!
WOW ...
GAS ...
BOOZE... AND GASOLINE ?!
YOU MEAN ...
...HE THREW AROUND THE ALCOHOL ON PURPOSE TO MAKE IT EASIER TO IGNITE THE FIRE?!
HOPE YOU LIKE FRIED FISH!

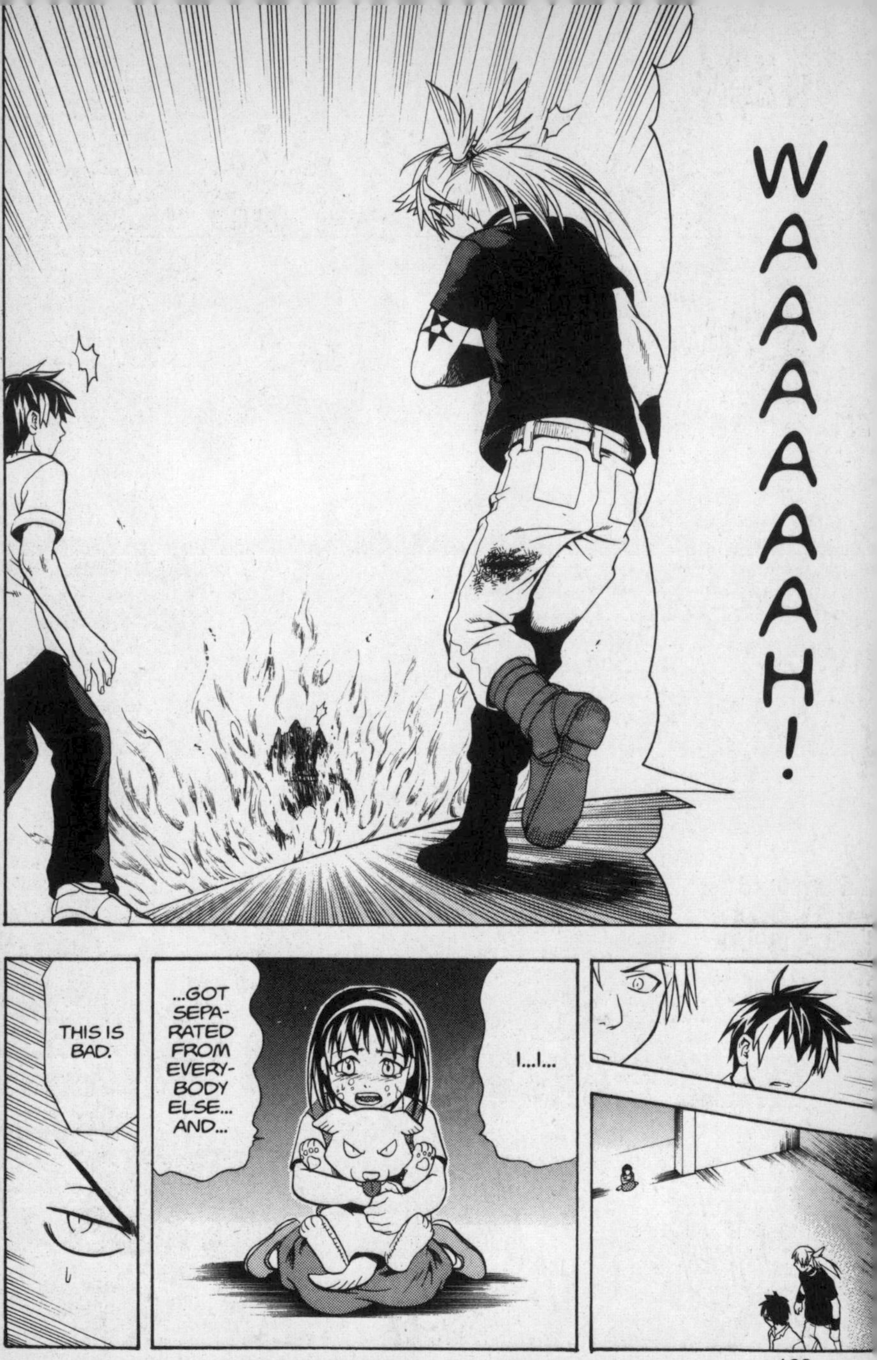
WAAAAAAH!
I...I...
...GOT SEPARATED FROM EVERYBODY ELSE... AND...
THIS IS BAD.

READ THIS WAY

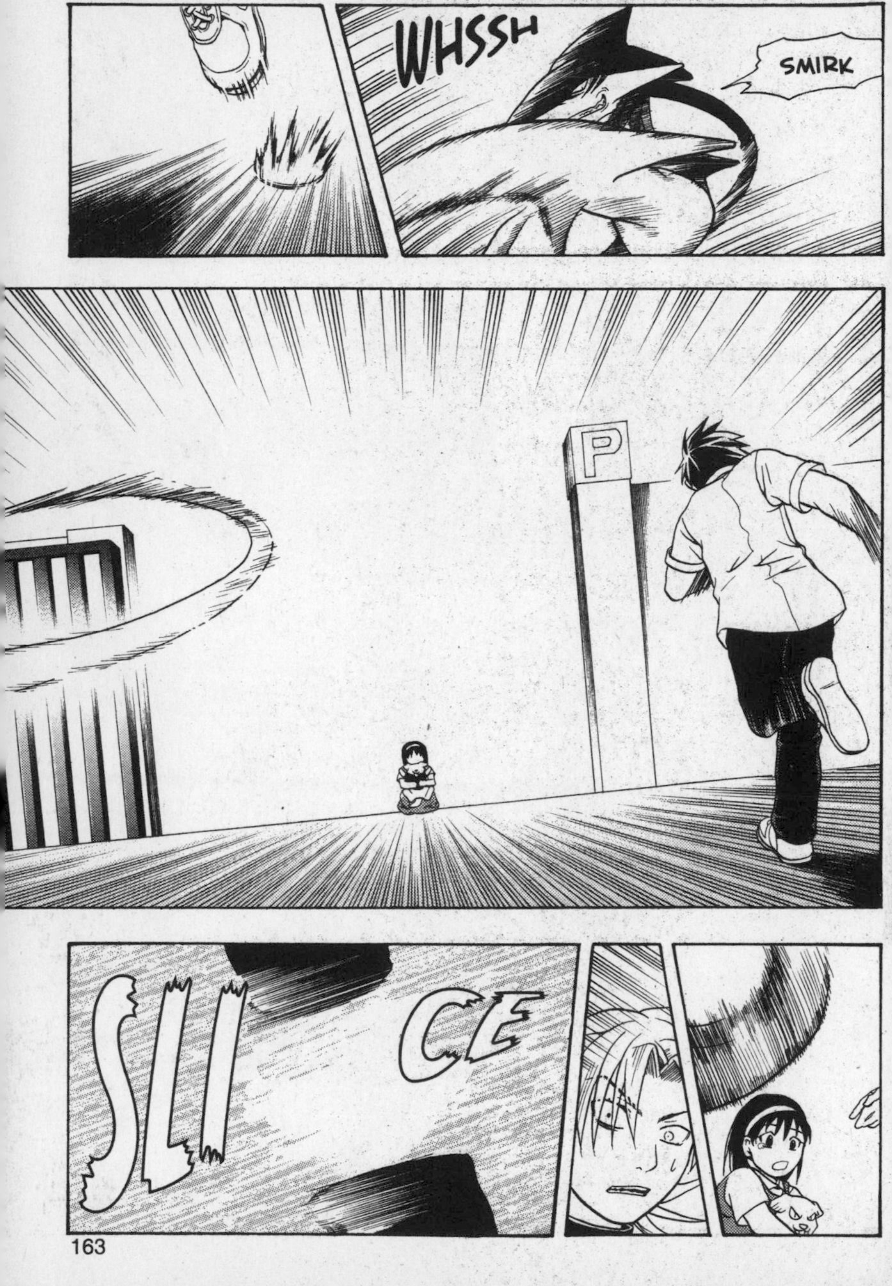
WHSSH
SMIRK
SLI CE

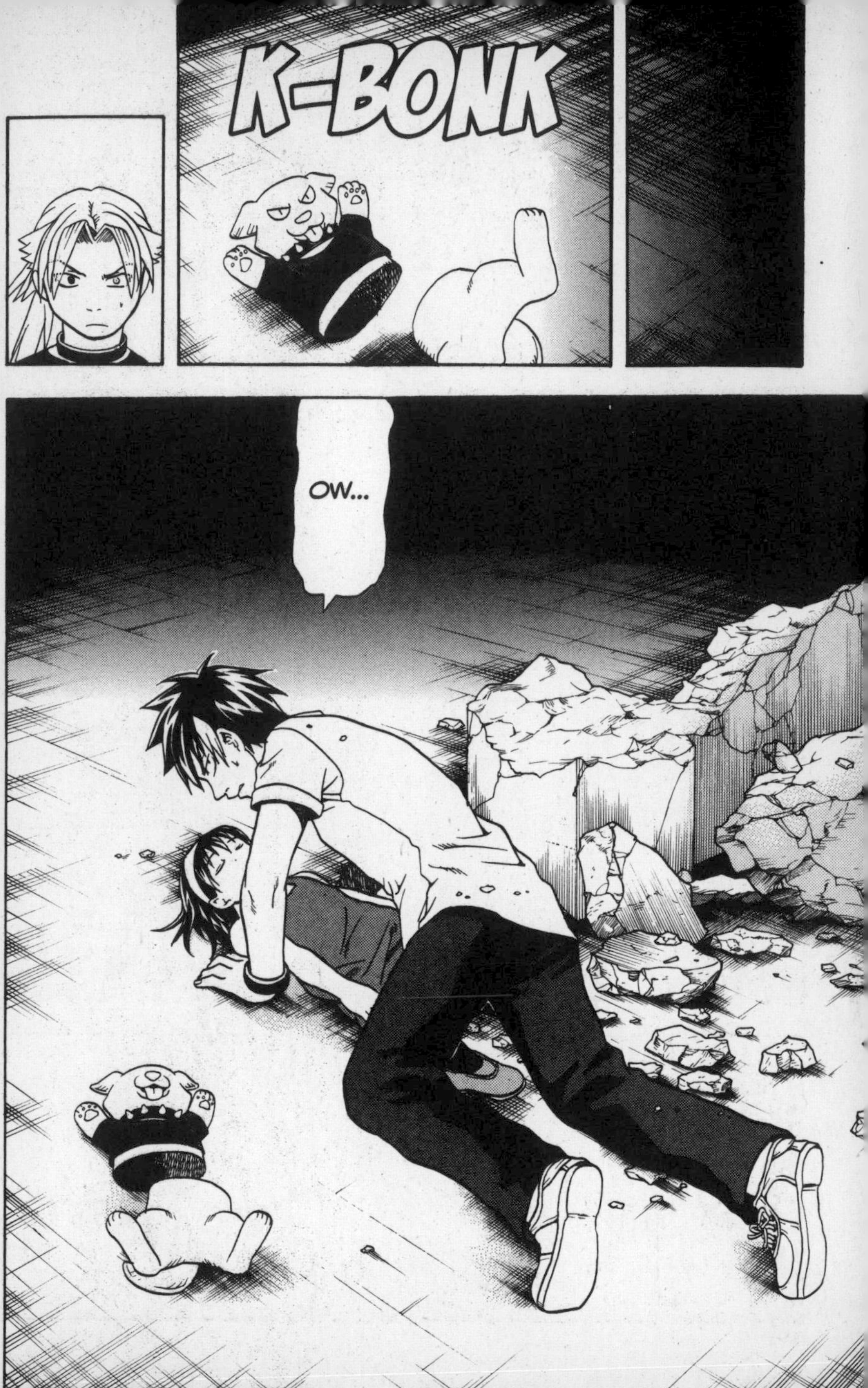
K-BONK
OW...

READ THIS WAY

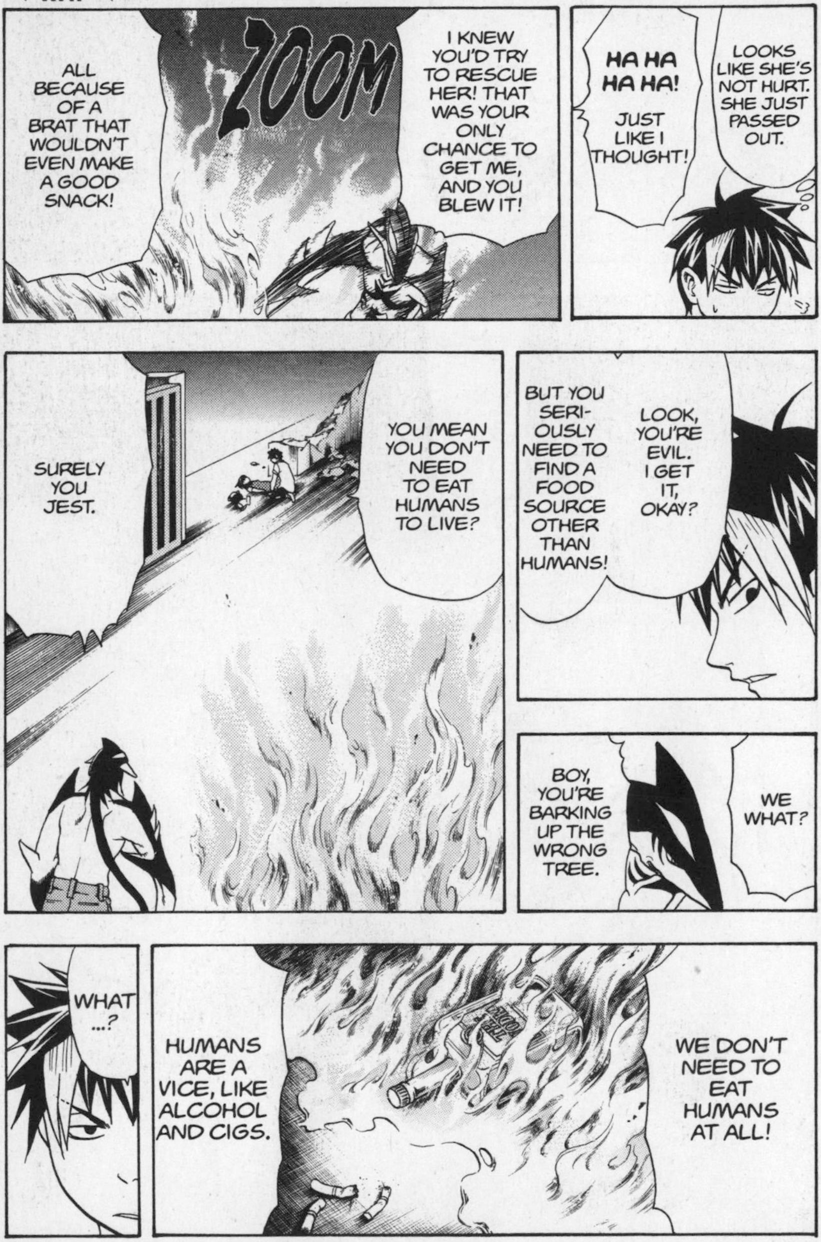
LOOKS LIKE SHE'S NOT HURT. SHE JUST PASSED OUT.
HA HA HA HA! JUST LIKE I THOUGHT!
I KNEW YOU'D TRY TO RESCUE HER! THAT WAS YOUR ONLY CHANCE TO GET ME, AND YOU BLEW IT!
ZOOM
ALL BECAUSE OF A BRAT THAT WOULDN'T EVEN MAKE A GOOD SNACK!
LOOK, YOU'RE EVIL. I GET IT, OKAY?
BUT YOU SERI-OUSLY NEED TO FIND A FOOD SOURCE OTHER THAN HUMANS!
WE WHAT?
BOY, YOU'RE BARKING UP THE WRONG TREE.
YOU MEAN YOU DON'T NEED TO EAT HUMANS TO LIVE?
SURELY YOU JEST.
WE DON'T NEED TO EAT HUMANS AT ALL!
HUMANS ARE A VICE, LIKE ALCOHOL AND CIGS.
WHAT ...?

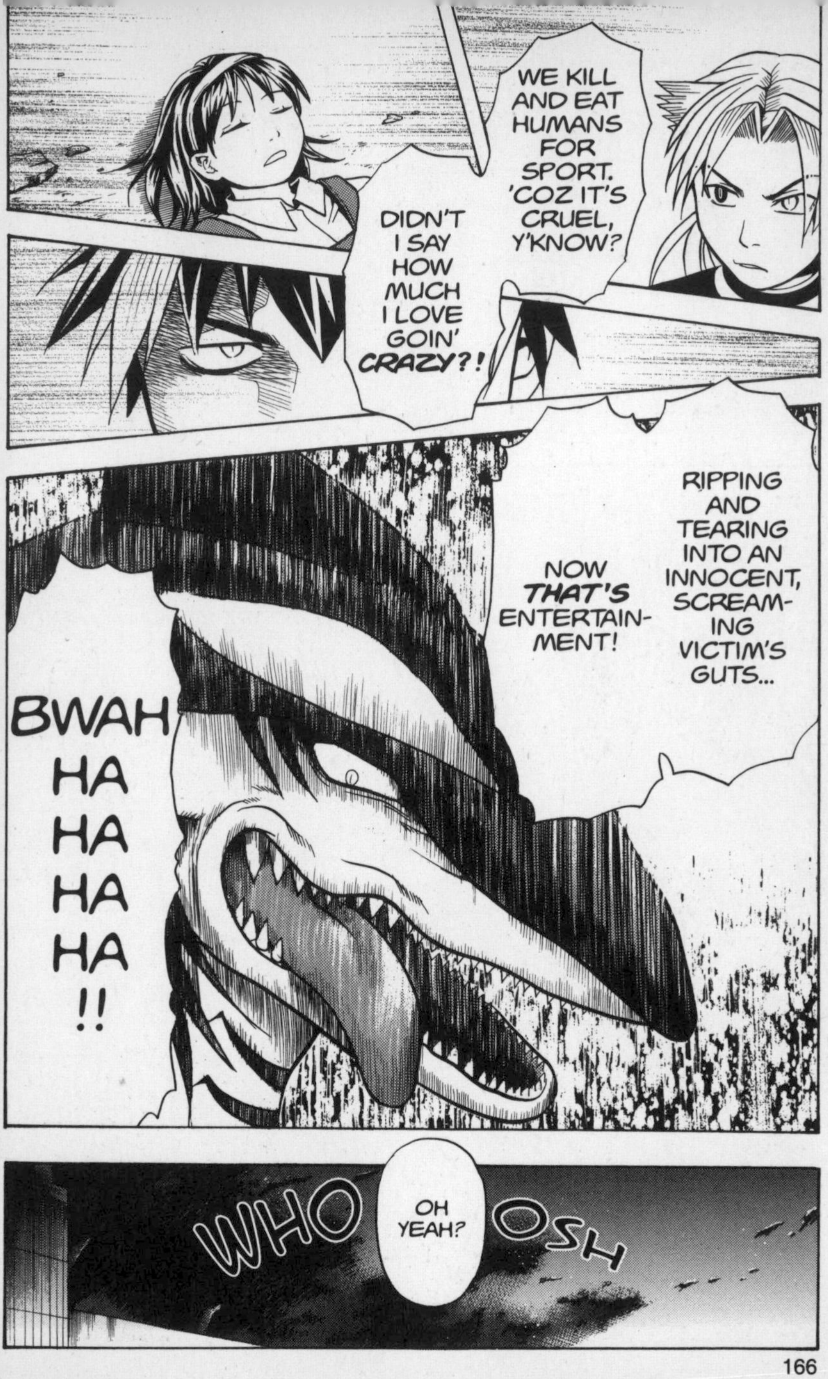
WE KILL AND EAT HUMANS FOR SPORT. 'COZ IT'S CRUEL, Y'KNOW?
DIDN'T I SAY HOW MUCH I LOVE GOIN' ***CRAZY***?!
RIPPING AND TEARING INTO AN INNOCENT, SCREAMING VICTIM'S GUTS...
NOW ***THAT'S*** ENTERTAINMENT!
BWAH HA HA HA HA!!
WHOOSH
OH YEAH?

READ THIS WAY

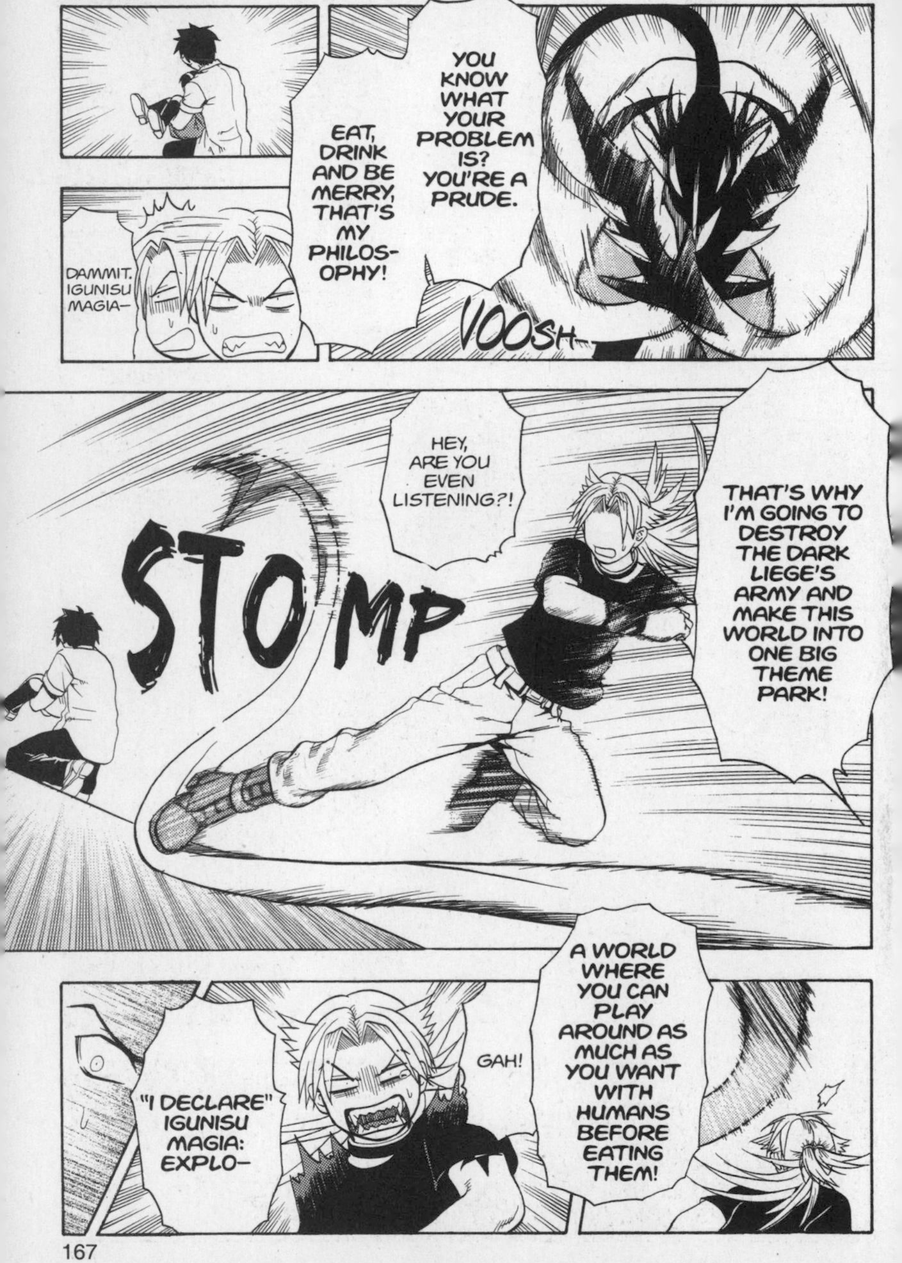
YOU KNOW WHAT YOUR PROBLEM IS? YOU'RE A PRUDE.
EAT, DRINK AND BE MERRY, THAT'S MY PHILOSOPHY!
VOOSH
DAMMIT. IGUNISU MAGIA—
THAT'S WHY I'M GOING TO DESTROY THE DARK LIEGE'S ARMY AND MAKE THIS WORLD INTO ONE BIG THEME PARK!
HEY, ARE YOU EVEN LISTENING?!
STOMP
A WORLD WHERE YOU CAN PLAY AROUND AS MUCH AS YOU WANT WITH HUMANS BEFORE EATING THEM!
GAH!
"I DECLARE" IGUNISU MAGIA: EXPLO—

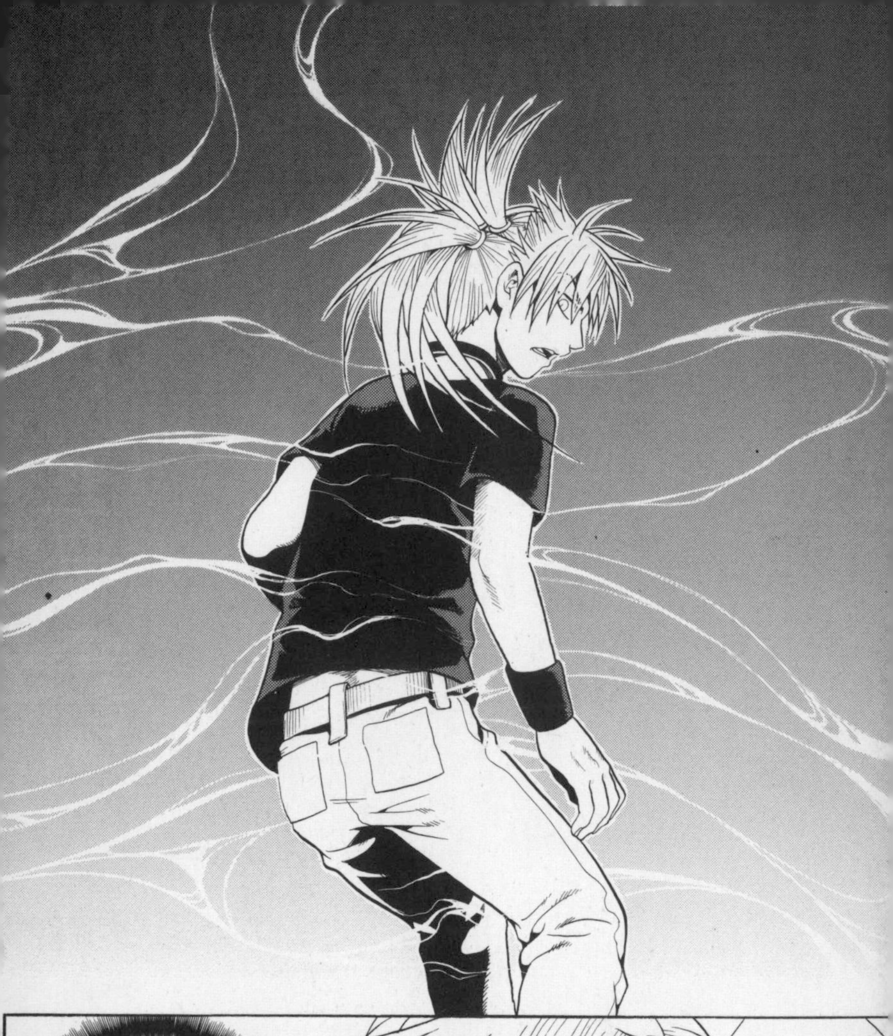
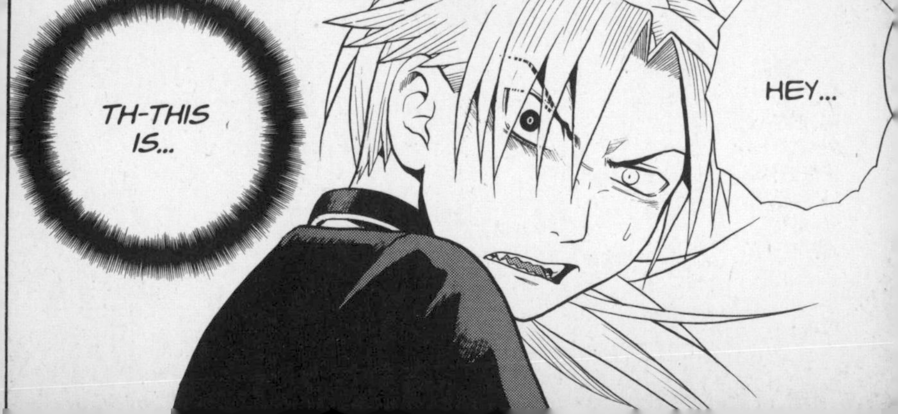
HEY...
TH-THIS IS...

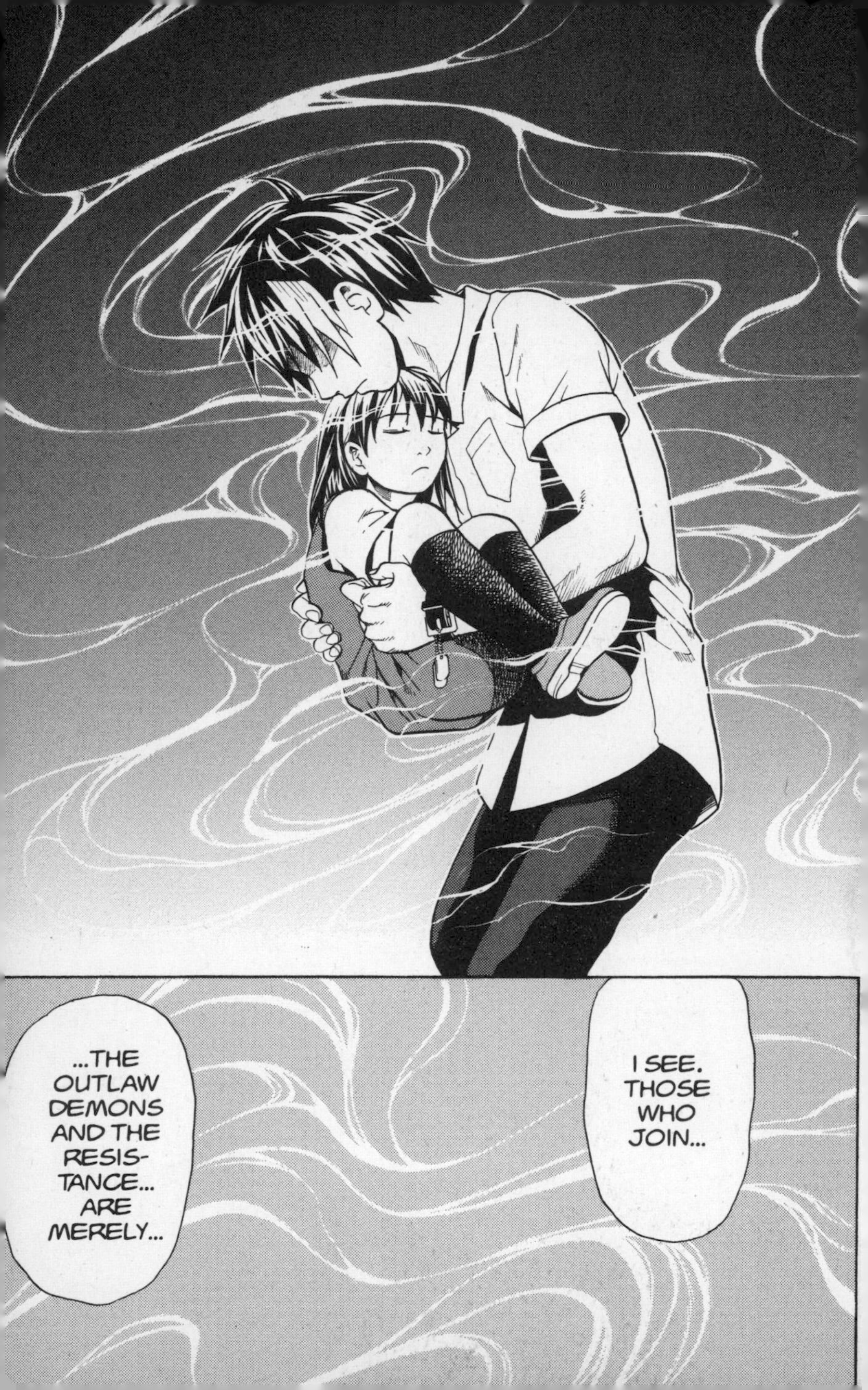
I SEE. THOSE WHO JOIN...
...THE OUTLAW DEMONS AND THE RESISTANCE... ARE MERELY...

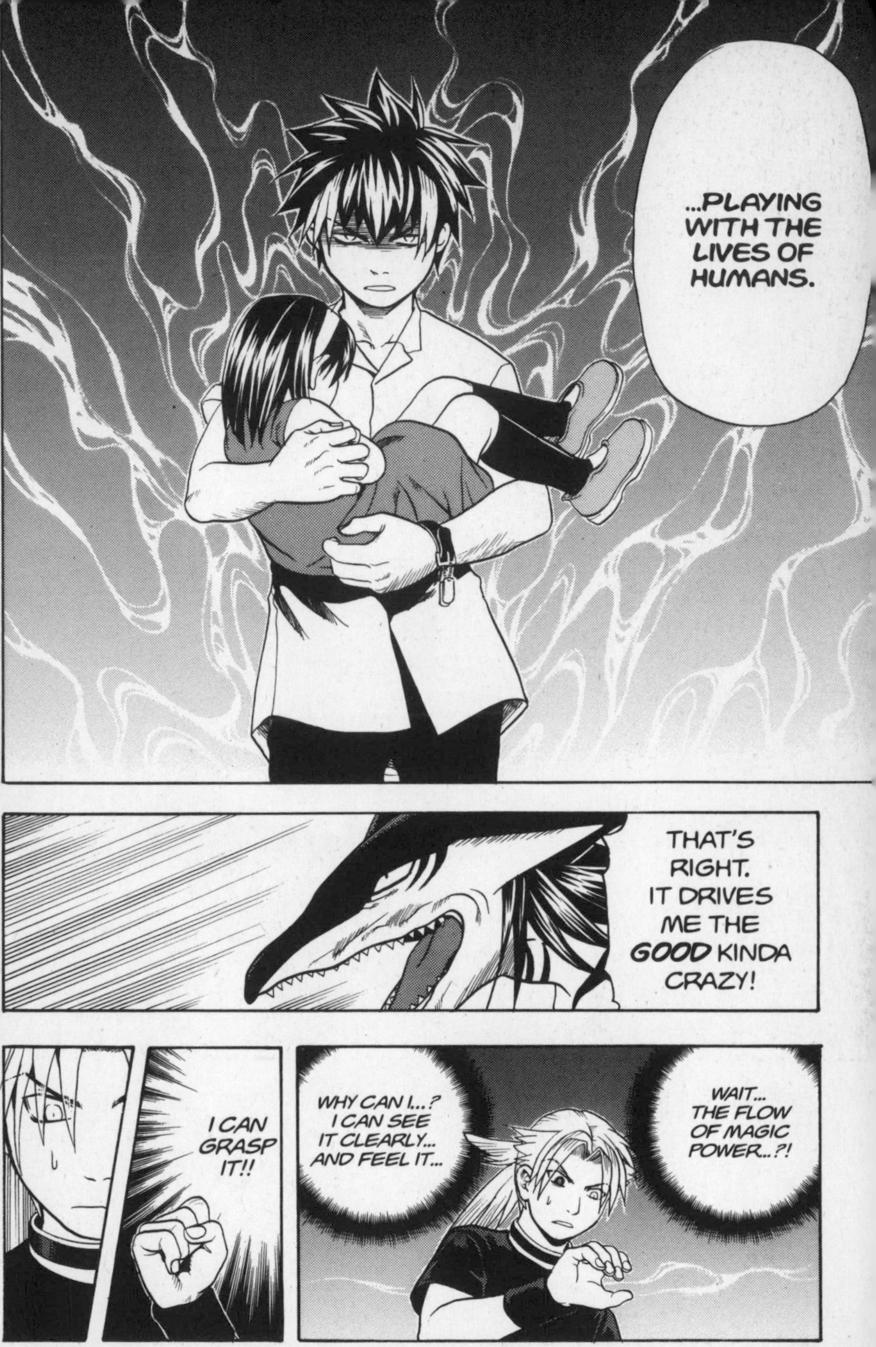
...PLAYING WITH THE LIVES OF HUMANS.
THAT'S RIGHT. IT DRIVES ME THE GOOD KINDA CRAZY!
WAIT... THE FLOW OF MAGIC POWER...?!
WHY CAN I...? I CAN SEE IT CLEARLY... AND FEEL IT...
I CAN GRASP IT!!

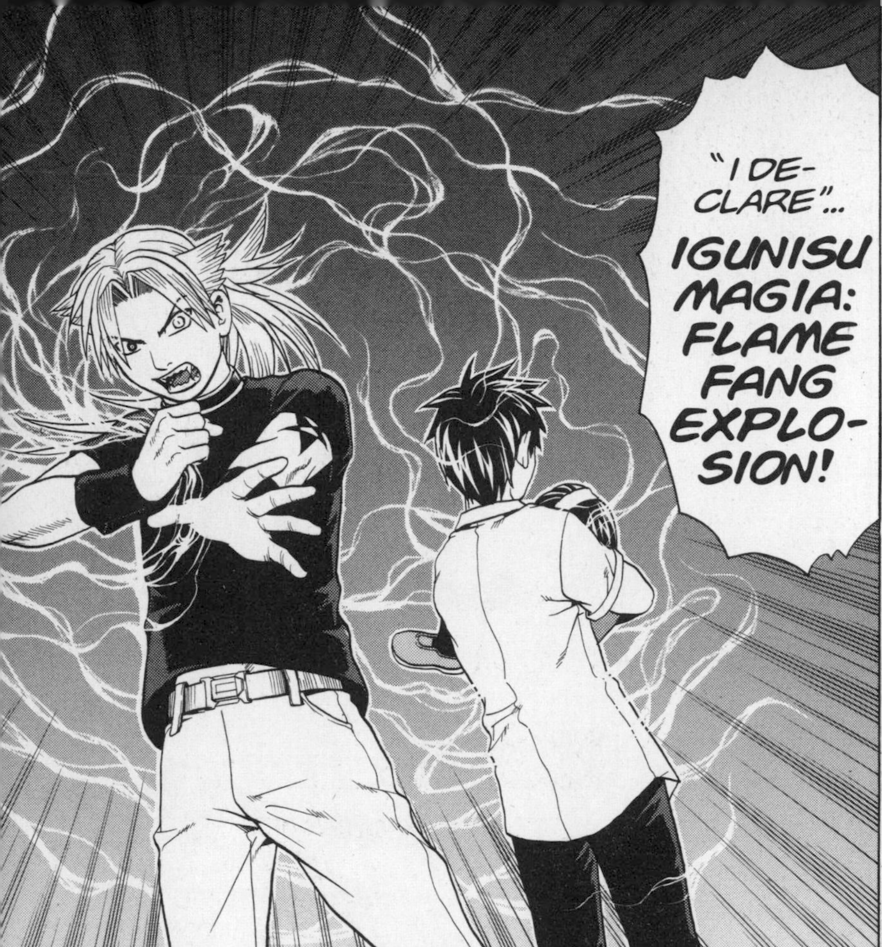
"I DE-
CLARE"...
IGUNISU MAGIA: FLAME FANG EXPLOSION!

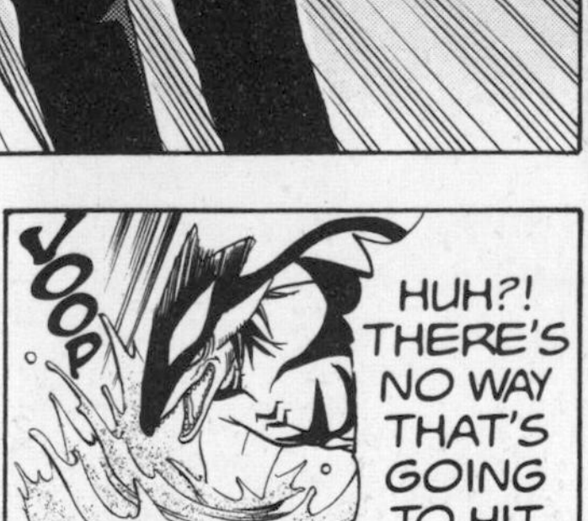
JOOP
HUH?! THERE'S NO WAY THAT'S GOING TO HIT ME!

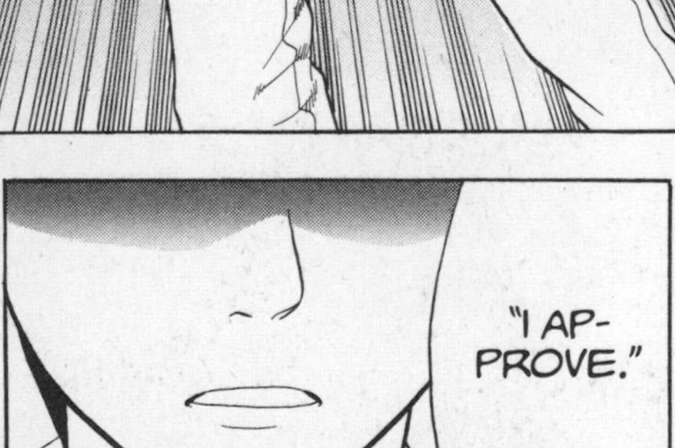
"I AP-
PROVE."

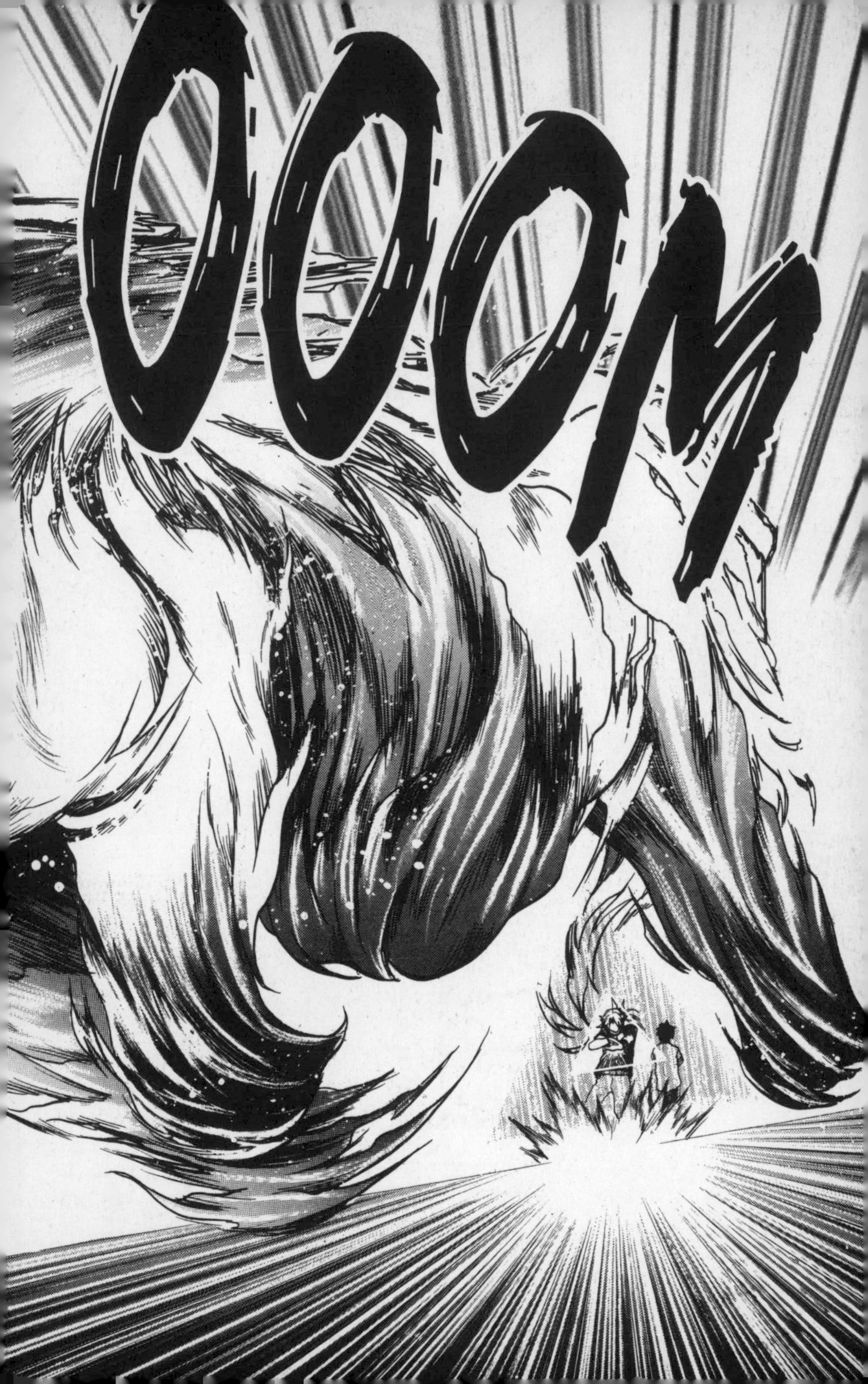
OOOM

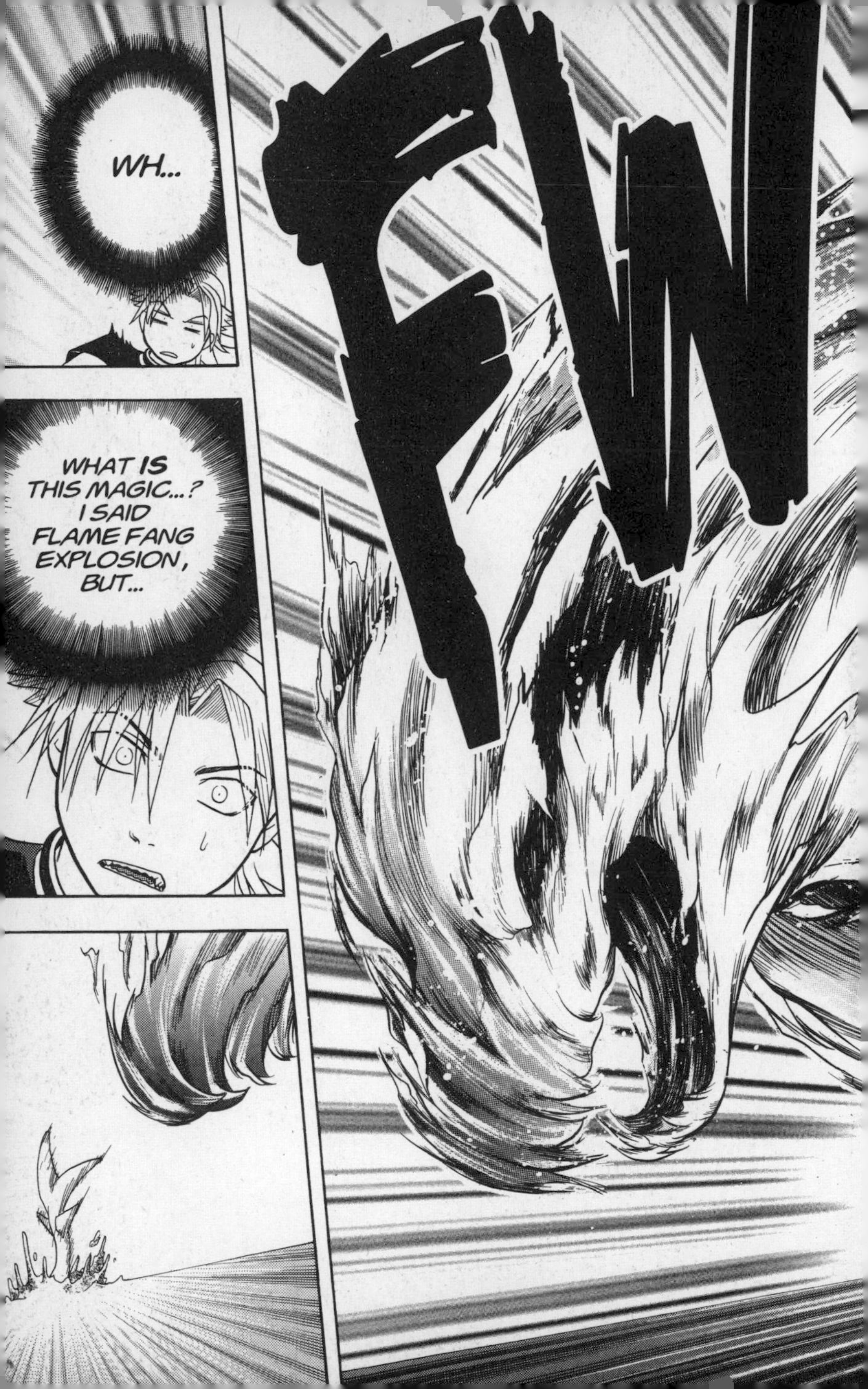
FWN
WH...
WHAT IS THIS MAGIC...? I SAID FLAME FANG EXPLOSION, BUT...

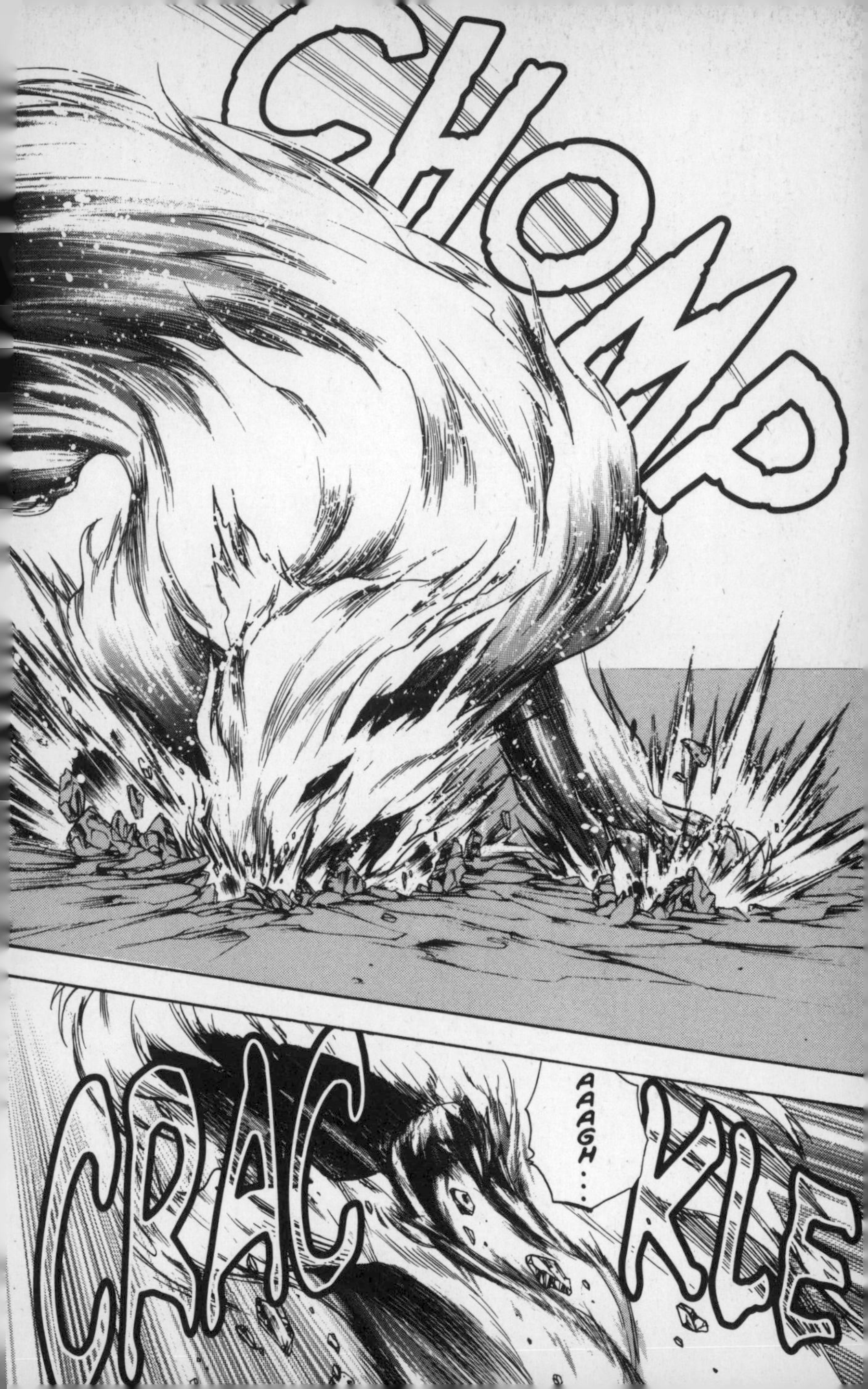
CHOMP
CRAC
AAAGH...
KLE

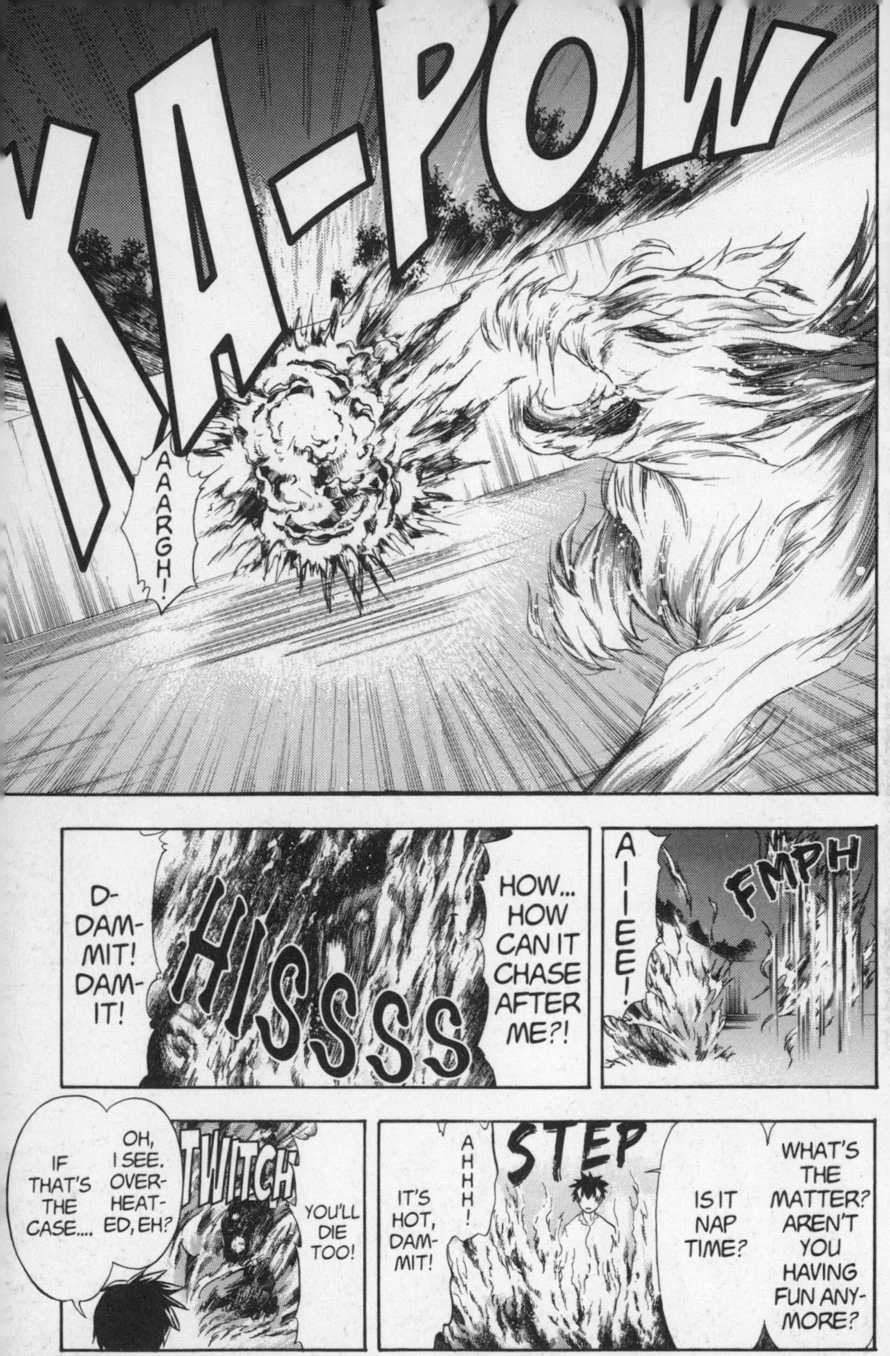
KA-POW
AAAARGH!
FMPH
AIIEE!
HOW... HOW CAN IT CHASE AFTER ME?!
HISSSS
D-DAMMIT! DAMMIT!
WHAT'S THE MATTER? AREN'T YOU HAVING FUN ANYMORE?
IS IT NAP TIME?
STEP
AHHHH!
IT'S HOT, DAMMIT!
YOU'LL DIE TOO!
TWITCH
OH, I SEE. OVERHEATED, EH?
IF THAT'S THE CASE....

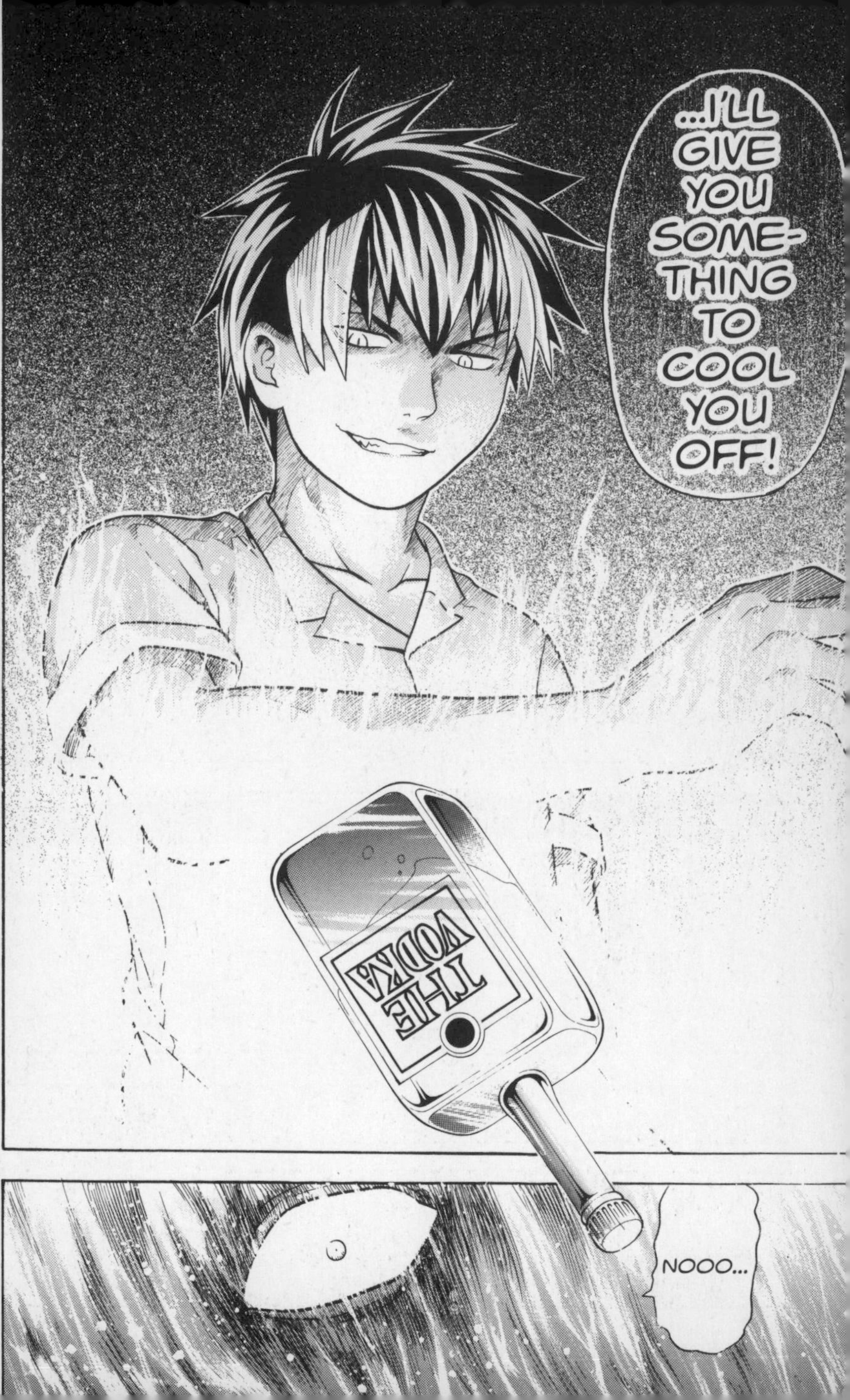
...I'LL GIVE YOU SOME-THING TO COOL YOU OFF!
THE VODKA
NOOO...

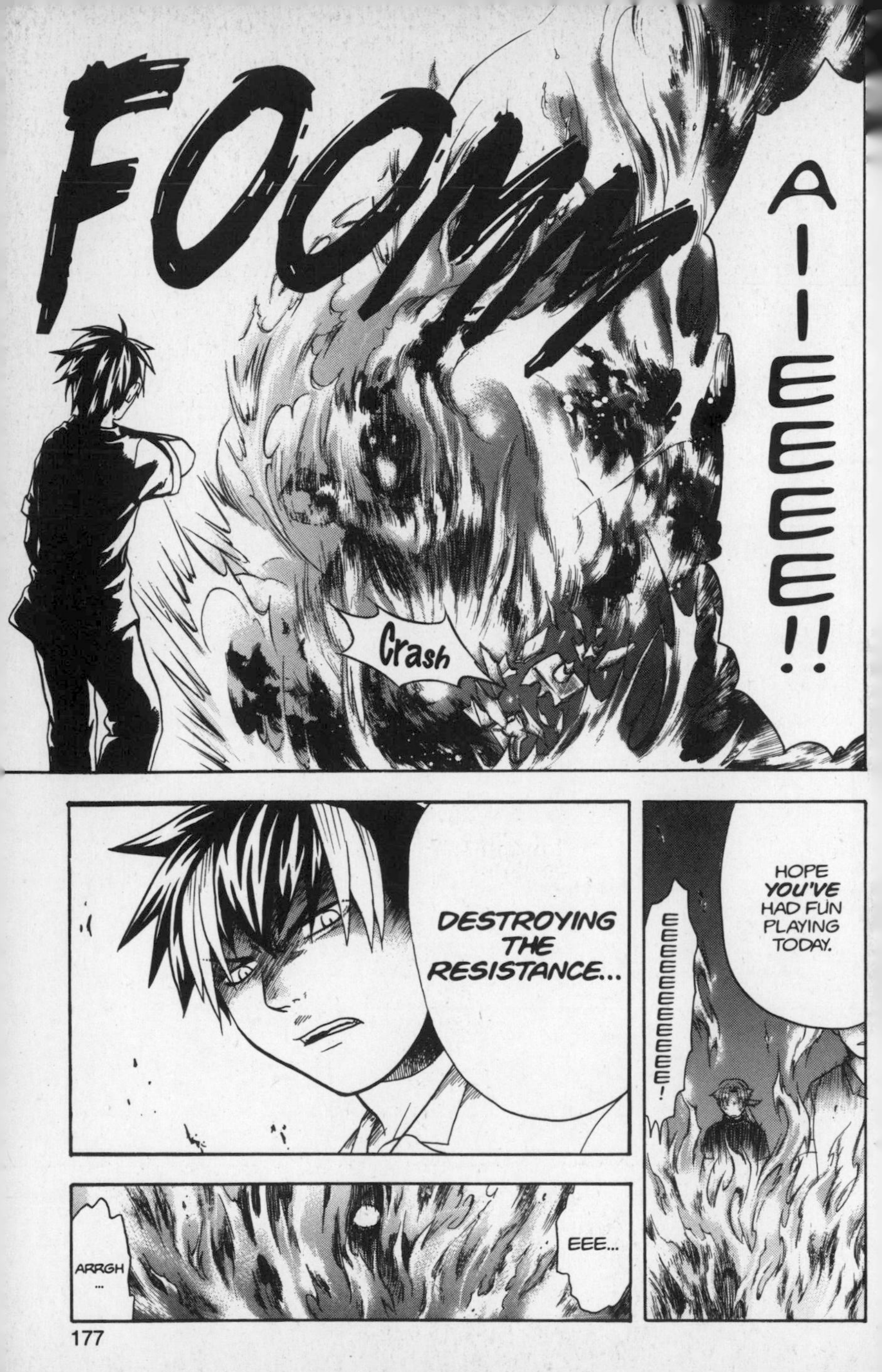
FOOM
AIIEEEE!!
Crash
HOPE YOU'VE HAD FUN PLAYING TODAY.
EEEEEEEEEEEEE!
DESTROYING THE RESISTANCE...
EEE...
ARRGH ...

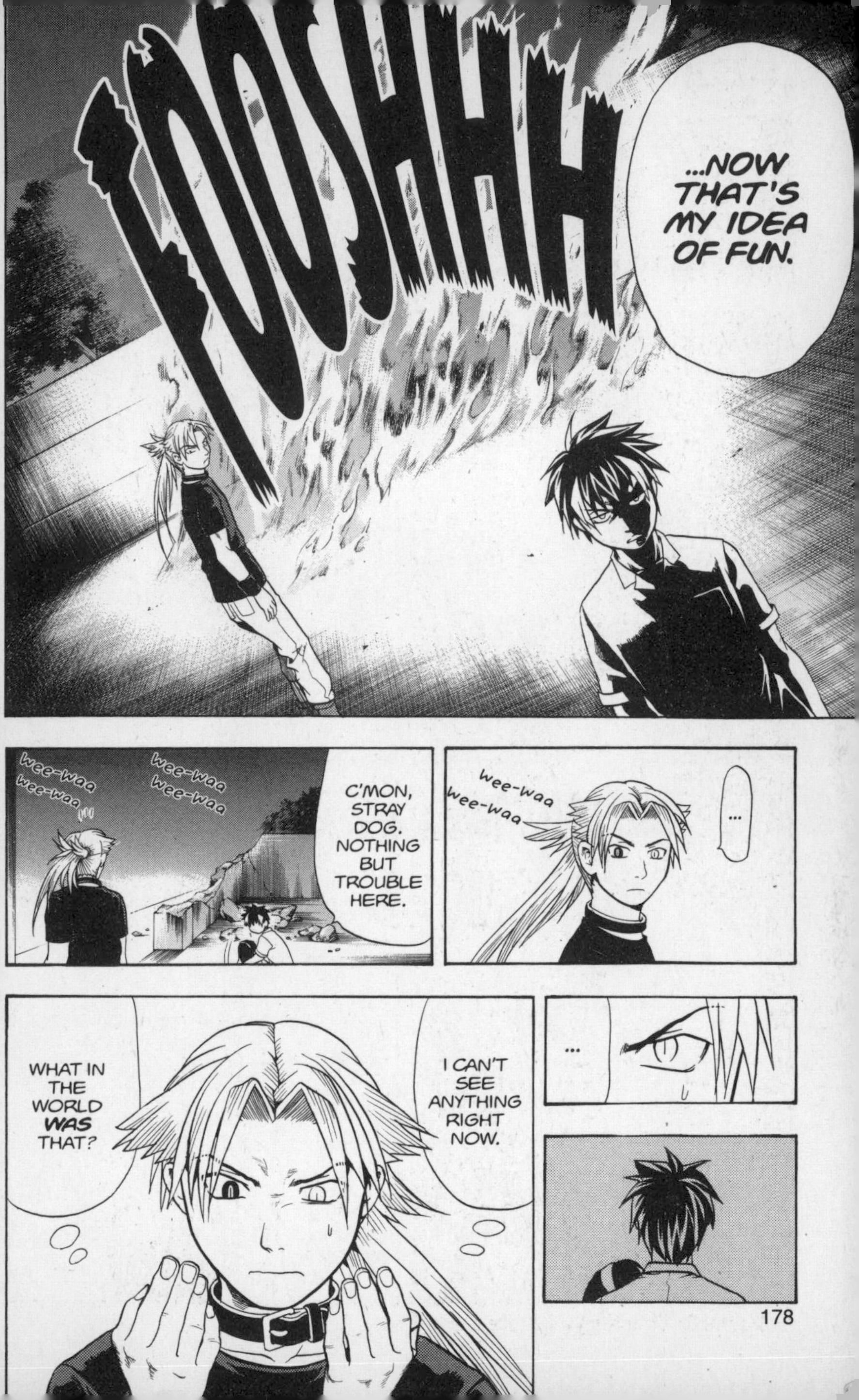
FOOSHHH
...NOW THAT'S MY IDEA OF FUN.
wee-waa wee-waa
...
wee-waa wee-waa
wee-waa wee-waa
C'MON, STRAY DOG. NOTHING BUT TROUBLE HERE.
...
I CAN'T SEE ANYTHING RIGHT NOW.
WHAT IN THE WORLD **WAS** THAT?

READ THIS WAY

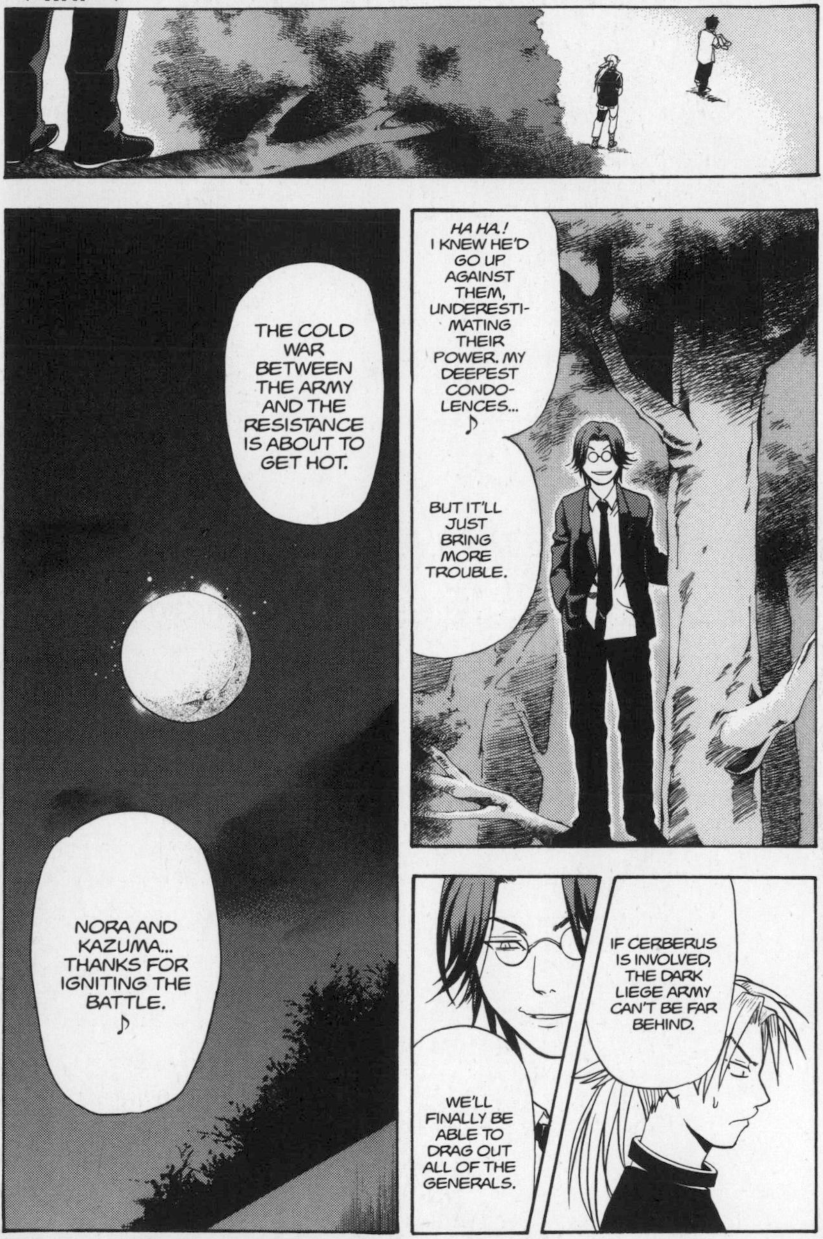

HA HA! I KNEW HE'D GO UP AGAINST THEM, UNDERESTI-MATING THEIR POWER. MY DEEPEST CONDO-LENCES... ♪
BUT IT'LL JUST BRING MORE TROUBLE.
IF CERBERUS IS INVOLVED, THE DARK LIEGE ARMY CAN'T BE FAR BEHIND.
WE'LL FINALLY BE ABLE TO DRAG OUT ALL OF THE GENERALS.
THE COLD WAR BETWEEN THE ARMY AND THE RESISTANCE IS ABOUT TO GET HOT.
NORA AND KAZUMA... THANKS FOR IGNITING THE BATTLE. ♪

Volume 2: The Rage Ignites–End

KNELL

HEIGHT : 177 CM
FAVORITE FOOD : BLUEBERRY TARTS
LEAST FAVORITE FOOD : ICE CREAM OR ANY OTHER FROZEN SNACK
INTERESTS AND SPECIAL TALENTS : OGLING AND FLIRTING
NOTES : A HIGH-RANKING DEMON WHO SEEMS TO BE PLAYING BOTH SIDES AGAINST EACH OTHER IN THE WAR BETWEEN THE DARK LIEGE ARMY AND THE RESISTANCE. OR MAYBE IT'S ALL JUST AN ELABORATE SCHEME TO HIT ON GIRLS.

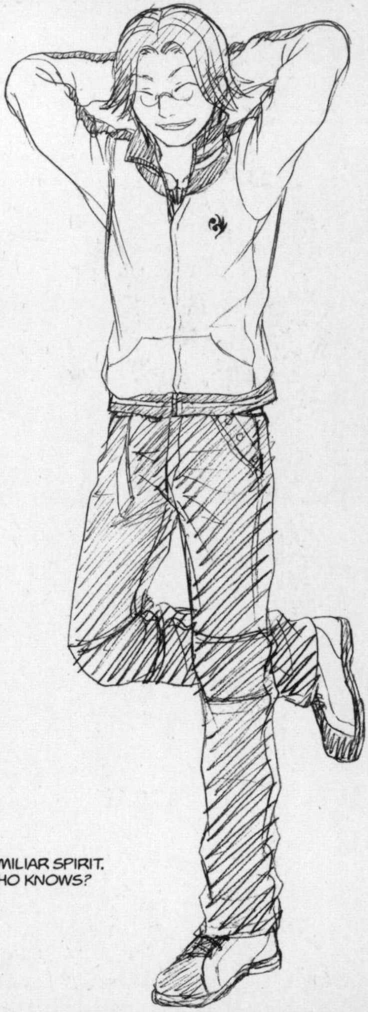

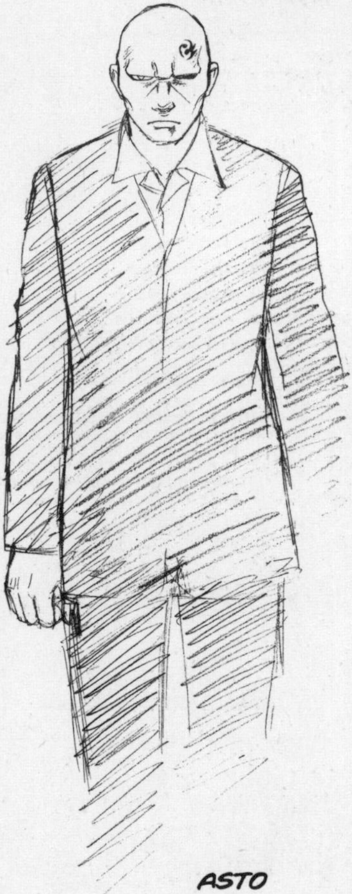

ASTO

HEIGHT : 199 CM
FAVORITE FOOD : ?
LEAST FAVORITE FOOD : ?
INTERESTS AND SPECIAL TALENTS : ?
NOTES : HE'S KNELL'S FAMILIAR SPIRIT. BEYOND THAT, WHO KNOWS?

CHARACTER DATA

BARIK

HEIGHT : 174 CM
FAVORITE FOOD : RECIPES USING EGGS
LEAST FAVORITE FOOD : SALTY-SPICY SQUID (HE WON'T EVEN TRY A BITE!)
INTERESTS AND SPECIAL TALENTS : TRAINING HIMSELF
NOTES : A CLUMSY, FIN-EARED LIEUTENANT GENERAL THAT NORA (IF YOU LISTEN TO NORA) FEELS IS NOTHING MORE THAN A SURLY PUTDOWN ARTIST. HE RESPECTS HIS SUPERIORS, BUT HE'S AMBITIOUS-SO WATCH OUT!

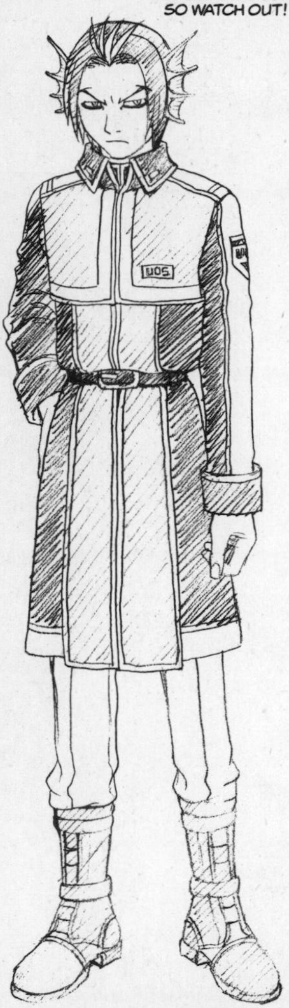

RIVAN

HEIGHT : 185 CM
FAVORITE FOOD : BEAN-JAM CAKE
LEAST FAVORITE FOOD : FISH, BELIEVE IT OR NOT
INTERESTS AND SPECIAL TALENTS : FISHING, VACATIONS
NOTES : AN UNDISCIPLINED NO-GOODNIK (ACCORDING TO KAZUMA, ANYWAY) WHOS LAID-BACK PHILOSOPHY IS AT ODDS WITH HIS TEMPERAMENT. RUMOR HAS IT HE'S FROM AN IMPORTANT FAMILY LINEAGE, B NO ONE WHO'S ASKED HIM ABOUT IT HAS LIVED TO TELL THE TALE!

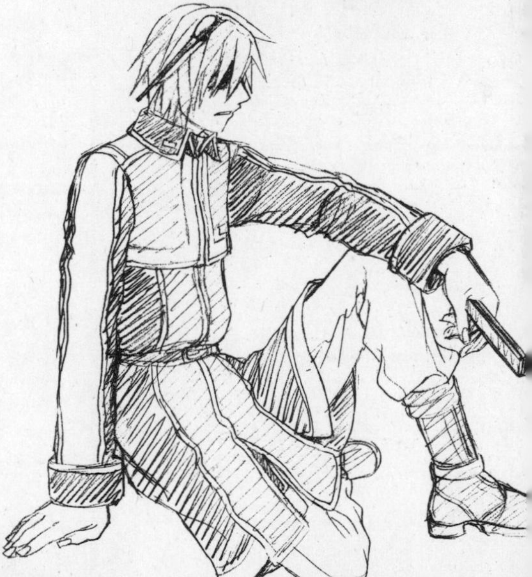

STAFF INTRODUCTION

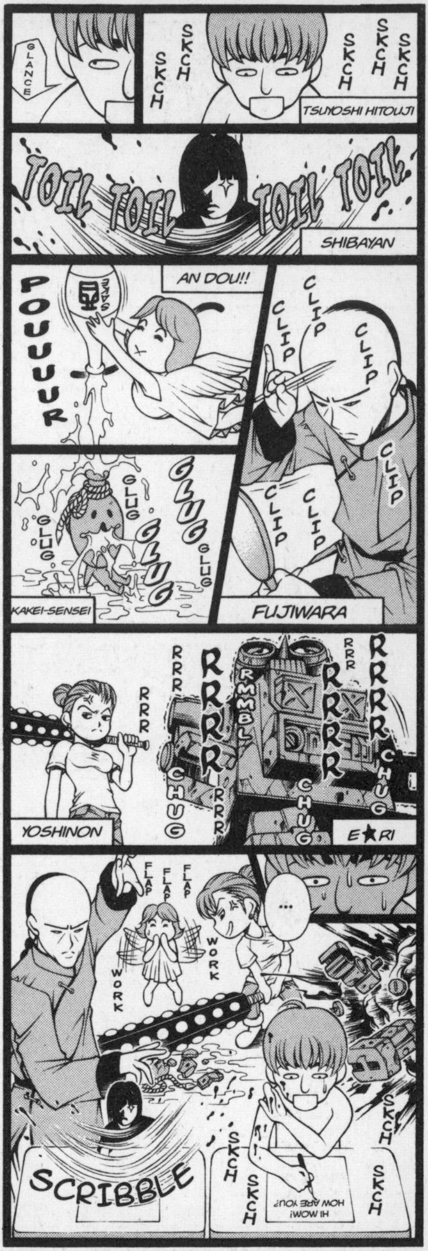

SKCH SKCH SKCH SKCH
GLANCE
TSUYOSHI HITOUJI
TOIL TOIL TOIL TOIL
SHIBAYAN
CLIP CLIP CLIP
AN DOU!!
POUUUUR
CLIP CLIP CLIP
FUJIWARA
GLUG GLUG GLUG GLUG
KAKEI-SENSEI
RRR RRRR RRRR
CHUG CHUG
E★RI
RMMBL
RRR RRRR RRR
CHUG
YOSHINON
...
FLAP FLAP FLAP
WORK WORK
SKCH SKCH
SKCH SKCH
HI MOM! HOW ARE YOU?
SCRIBBLE

DRAWN BY: MR. HITOUJI, WHO ASKED "WHO I WOULD BE USING" IN MY WORK. HE WAS SHOCKED AT THE REPLY: "THE COOK AT TROJAN HORSE."

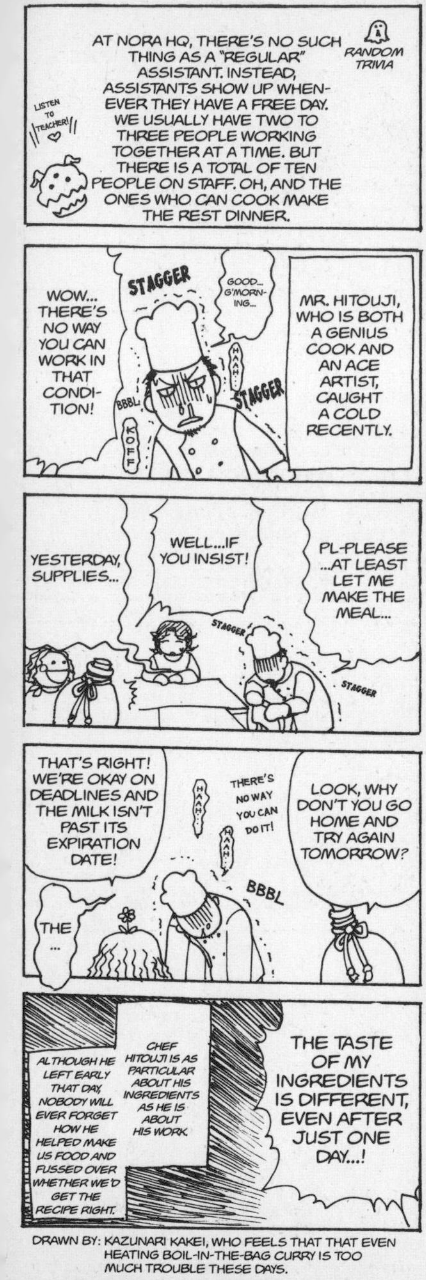

RANDOM TRIVIA
AT NORA HQ, THERE'S NO SUCH THING AS A "REGULAR" ASSISTANT. INSTEAD, ASSISTANTS SHOW UP WHENEVER THEY HAVE A FREE DAY. WE USUALLY HAVE TWO TO THREE PEOPLE WORKING TOGETHER AT A TIME. BUT THERE IS A TOTAL OF TEN PEOPLE ON STAFF. OH, AND THE ONES WHO CAN COOK MAKE THE REST DINNER.
LISTEN TO TEACHER!
MR. HITOUJI, WHO IS BOTH A GENIUS COOK AND AN ACE ARTIST, CAUGHT A COLD RECENTLY.
GOOD... G'MORNING...
STAGGER
HAAH...
STAGGER
WOW... THERE'S NO WAY YOU CAN WORK IN THAT CONDITION!
BBBL
KOFF
PL-PLEASE ...AT LEAST LET ME MAKE THE MEAL...
WELL...IF YOU INSIST!
YESTERDAY, SUPPLIES...
STAGGER
STAGGER
LOOK, WHY DON'T YOU GO HOME AND TRY AGAIN TOMORROW?
THERE'S NO WAY YOU CAN DO IT!
HAAH...
HAAH...
THAT'S RIGHT! WE'RE OKAY ON DEADLINES AND THE MILK ISN'T PAST ITS EXPIRATION DATE!
BBBL
THE ...
THE TASTE OF MY INGREDIENTS IS DIFFERENT, EVEN AFTER JUST ONE DAY...!
CHEF HITOUJI IS AS PARTICULAR ABOUT HIS INGREDIENTS AS HE IS ABOUT HIS WORK.
ALTHOUGH HE LEFT EARLY THAT DAY, NOBODY WILL EVER FORGET HOW HE HELPED MAKE US FOOD AND FUSSED OVER WHETHER WE'D GET THE RECIPE RIGHT.

DRAWN BY: KAZUNARI KAKEI, WHO FEELS THAT THAT EVEN HEATING BOIL-IN-THE-BAG CURRY IS TOO MUCH TROUBLE THESE DAYS.

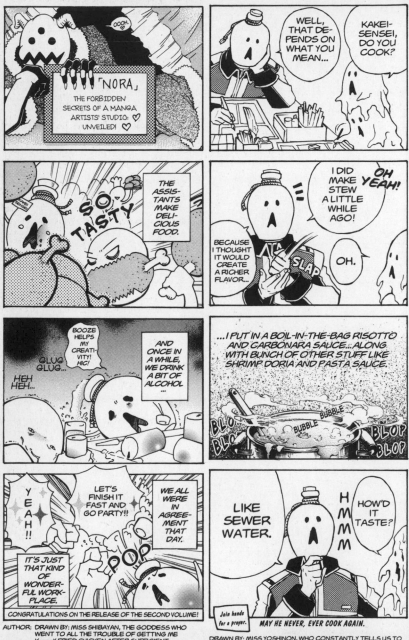

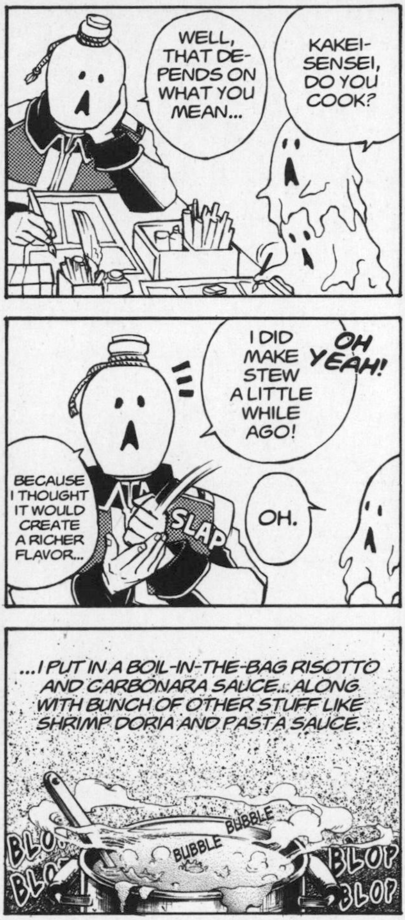
KAKEI-SENSEI, DO YOU COOK?
WELL, THAT DEPENDS ON WHAT YOU MEAN...
OH YEAH!
I DID MAKE STEW A LITTLE WHILE AGO!
OH.
BECAUSE I THOUGHT IT WOULD CREATE A RICHER FLAVOR...
SLAP
...I PUT IN A BOIL-IN-THE-BAG RISOTTO AND CARBONARA SAUCE... ALONG WITH BUNCH OF OTHER STUFF LIKE SHRIMP DORIA AND PASTA SAUCE.
BUBBLE
BUBBLE
BLOP BLOP
HOW'D IT TASTE?
HMMMM
LIKE SEWER WATER.
Join hands for a prayer.
MAY HE NEVER, EVER COOK AGAIN.

DRAWN BY: MISS YOSHINON, WHO CONSTANTLY TELLS US TO GROW UP, SHUT UP, AND GET BACK TO WORK.

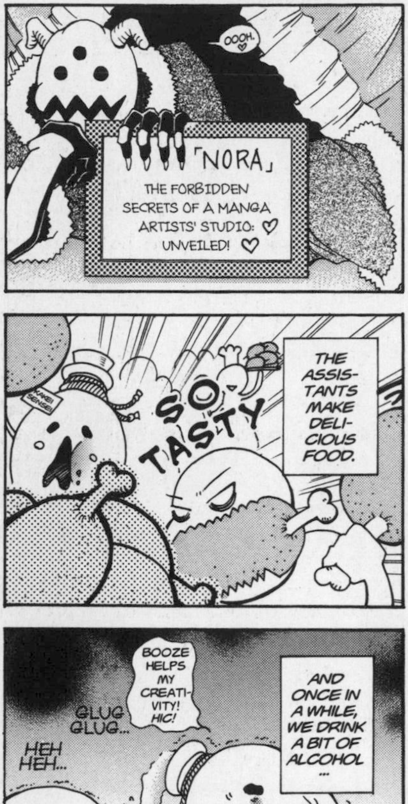
OOOH.
「NORA」
THE FORBIDDEN SECRETS OF A MANGA ARTISTS' STUDIO: UNVEILED!
THE ASSISTANTS MAKE DELICIOUS FOOD.
SO TASTY
KAKEI SENSEI
AND ONCE IN A WHILE, WE DRINK A BIT OF ALCOHOL...
BOOZE HELPS MY CREATIVITY! HIC!
GLUG GLUG...
HEH HEH...
WE ALL WERE IN AGREEMENT THAT DAY.
LET'S FINISH IT FAST AND GO PARTY!!
YEAH!!
POP
IT'S JUST THAT KIND OF WONDERFUL WORKPLACE.
CONGRATULATIONS ON THE RELEASE OF THE SECOND VOLUME!

AUTHOR: DRAWN BY: MISS SHIBAYAN, THE GODDESS WHO WENT TO ALL THE TROUBLE OF GETTING ME K------Y FRIED CHICKEN AFTER SUFFICIENT NAGGING FROM ME.

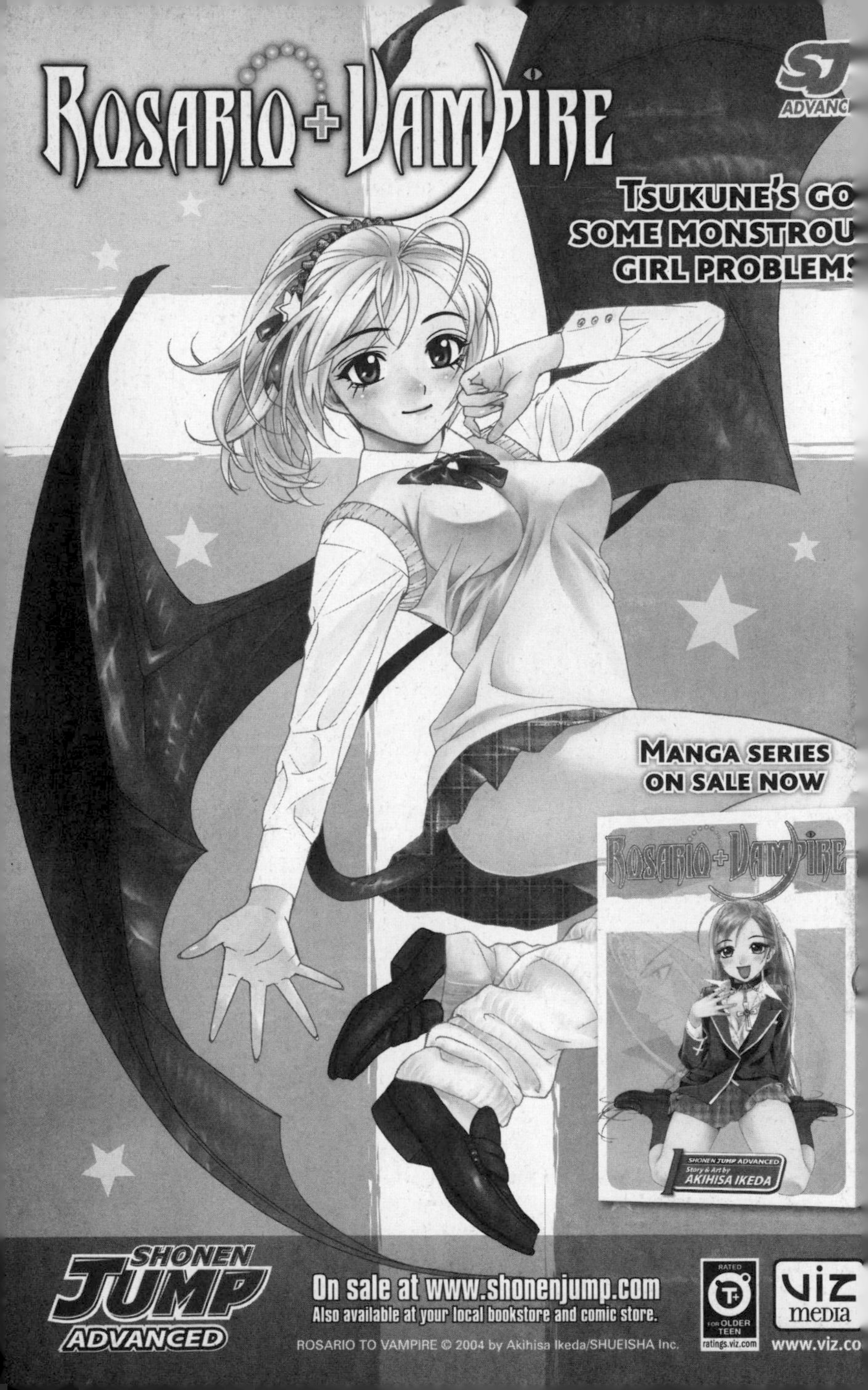
ROSARIO+VAMPIRE
SJ ADVANC
TSUKUNE'S GO
SOME MONSTROU
GIRL PROBLEMS
MANGA SERIES
ON SALE NOW
ROSARIO+VAMPIRE
SHONEN JUMP ADVANCED
Story & Art by
AKIHISA IKEDA
SHONEN JUMP ADVANCED
On sale at www.shonenjump.com
Also available at your local bookstore and comic store.
ROSARIO TO VAMPIRE © 2004 by Akihisa Ikeda/SHUEISHA Inc.
RATED
T+
FOR OLDER TEEN
ratings.viz.com
VIZ media
www.viz.co

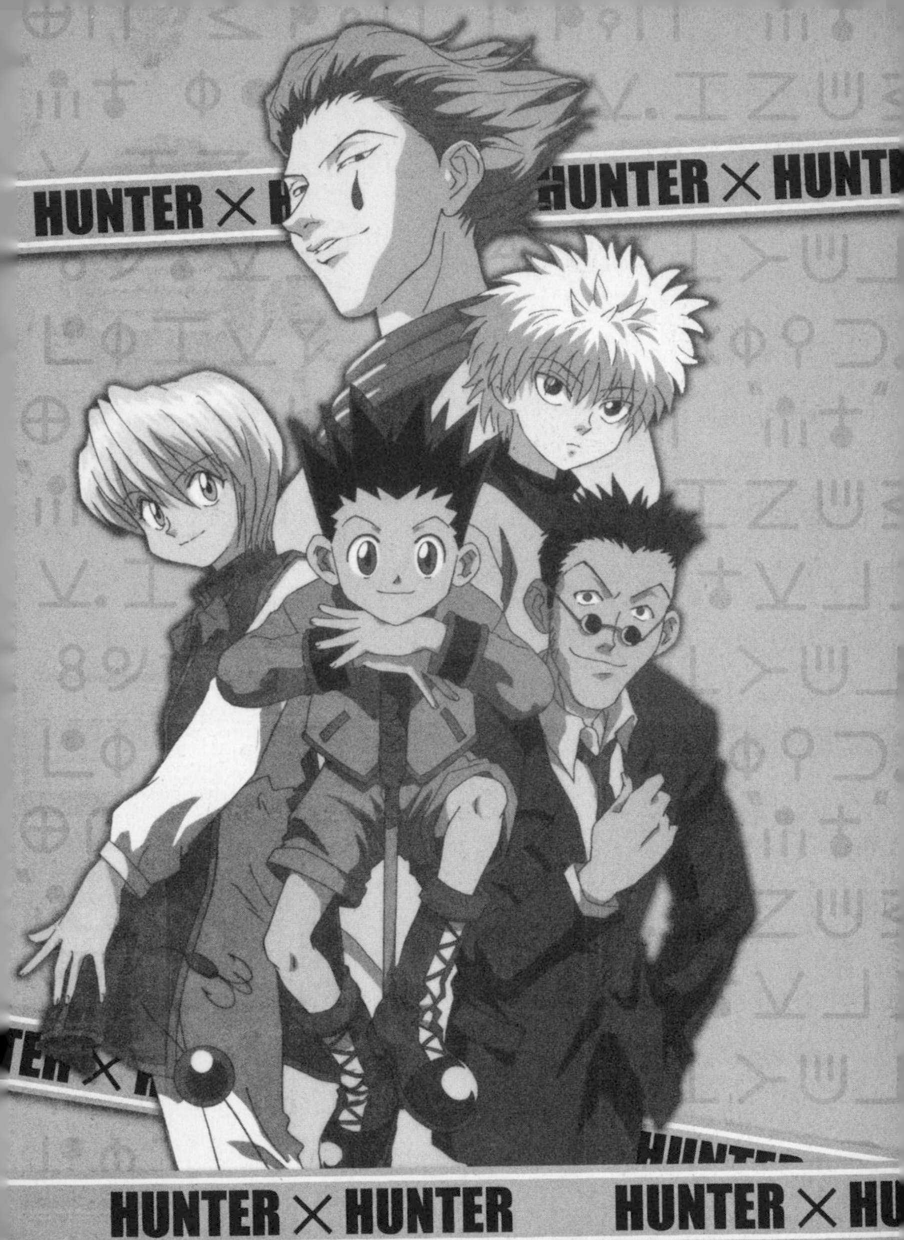

HUNTER × HUNTER

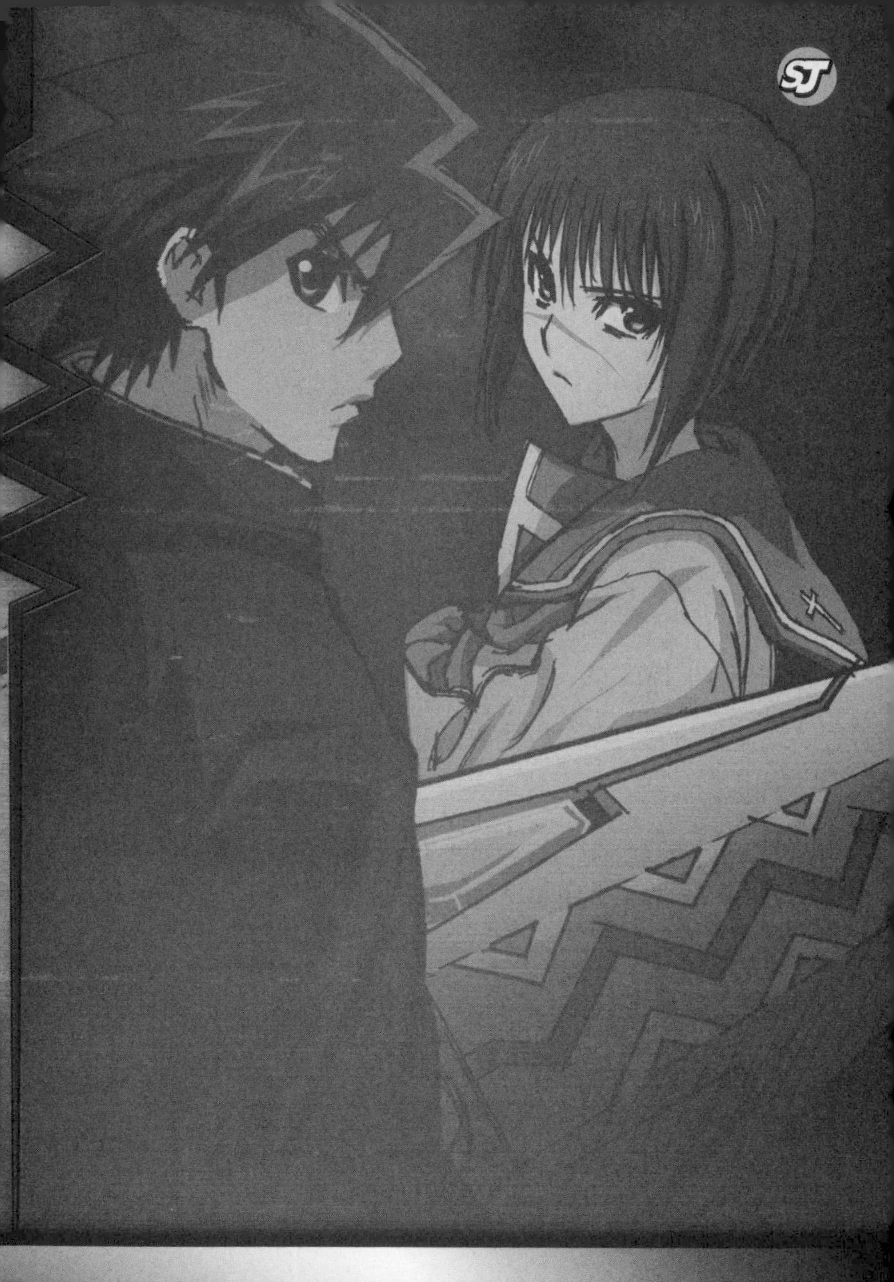

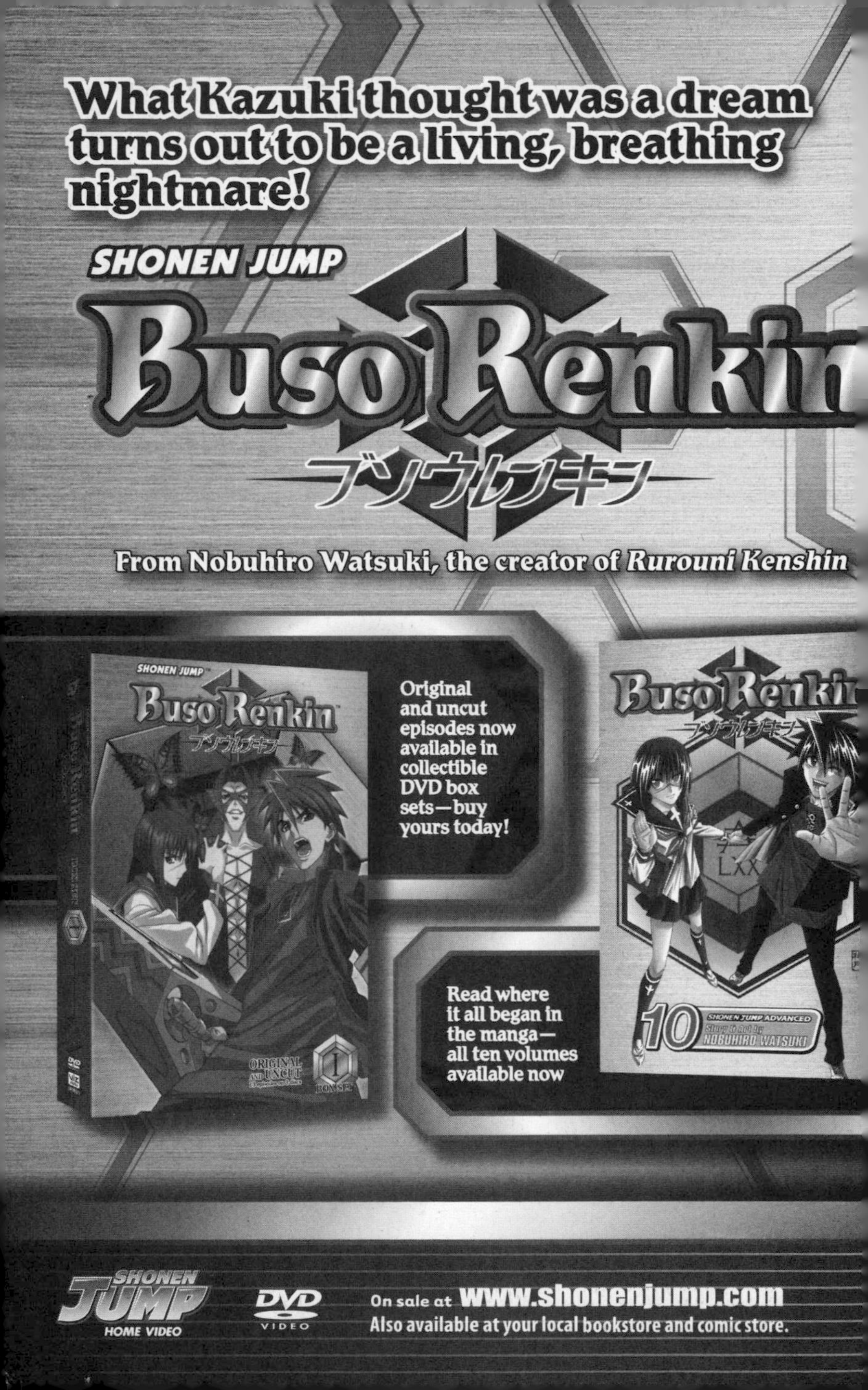
What Kazuki thought was a dream turns out to be a living, breathing nightmare!
SHONEN JUMP
Buso Renkin
ブソウレンキン
From Nobuhiro Watsuki, the creator of *Rurouni Kenshin*
SHONEN JUMP
Buso Renkin
ブソウレンキン
ORIGINAL AND UNCUT
BOX SET
Original and uncut episodes now available in collectible DVD box sets—buy yours today!
Buso Renkin
ブソウレンキン
10
SHONEN JUMP ADVANCED
NOBUHIRO WATSUKI
Read where it all began in the manga—all ten volumes available now
SHONEN JUMP HOME VIDEO
DVD VIDEO
On sale at www.shonenjump.com
Also available at your local bookstore and comic store.

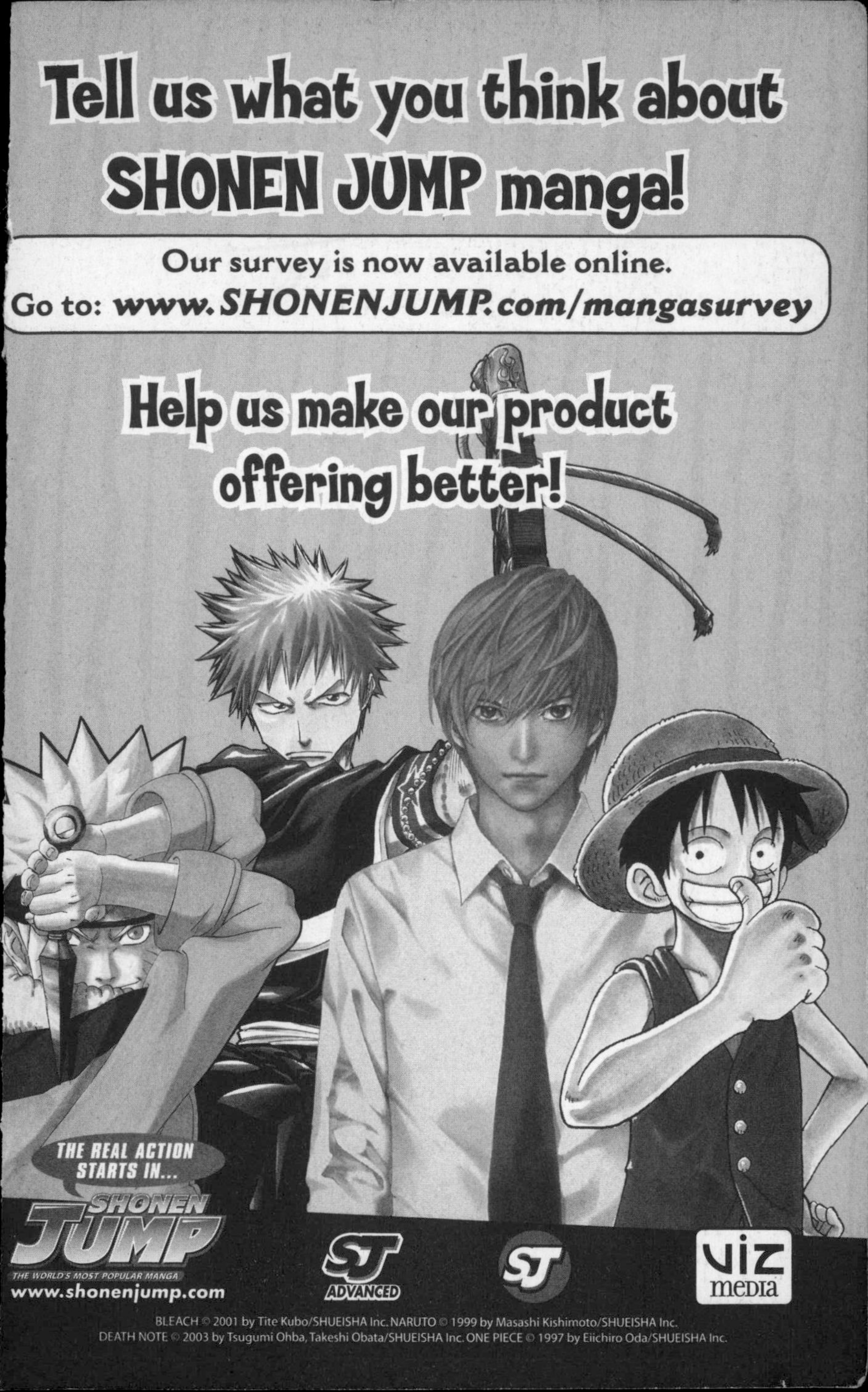

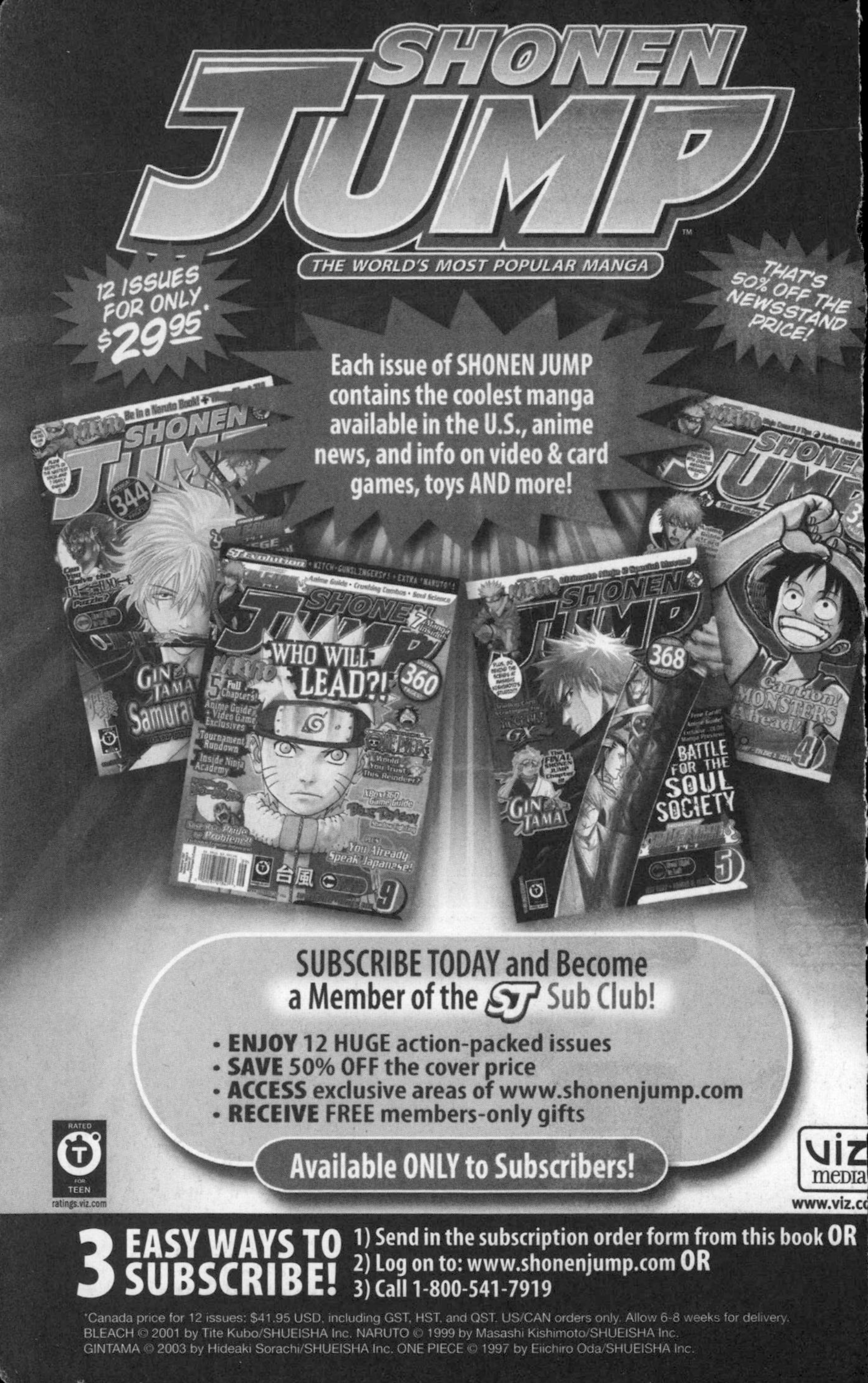
SHONEN JUMP™
THE WORLD'S MOST POPULAR MANGA
12 ISSUES FOR ONLY $29.95*
THAT'S 50% OFF THE NEWSSTAND PRICE!
Each issue of SHONEN JUMP contains the coolest manga available in the U.S., anime news, and info on video & card games, toys AND more!
SUBSCRIBE TODAY and Become a Member of the SJ Sub Club!
• ENJOY 12 HUGE action-packed issues
• SAVE 50% OFF the cover price
• ACCESS exclusive areas of www.shonenjump.com
• RECEIVE FREE members-only gifts
Available ONLY to Subscribers!
RATED T FOR TEEN
ratings.viz.com
viz media
www.viz.com
3 EASY WAYS TO SUBSCRIBE!
1) Send in the subscription order form from this book OR
2) Log on to: www.shonenjump.com OR
3) Call 1-800-541-7919
*Canada price for 12 issues: $41.95 USD, including GST, HST, and QST. US/CAN orders only. Allow 6-8 weeks for delivery.
BLEACH © 2001 by Tite Kubo/SHUEISHA Inc. NARUTO © 1999 by Masashi Kishimoto/SHUEISHA Inc.
GINTAMA © 2003 by Hideaki Sorachi/SHUEISHA Inc. ONE PIECE © 1997 by Eiichiro Oda/SHUEISHA Inc.

Save 5 • ‖‖‖‖‖‖‖‖‖ over price!

Over 300 pages per issue!

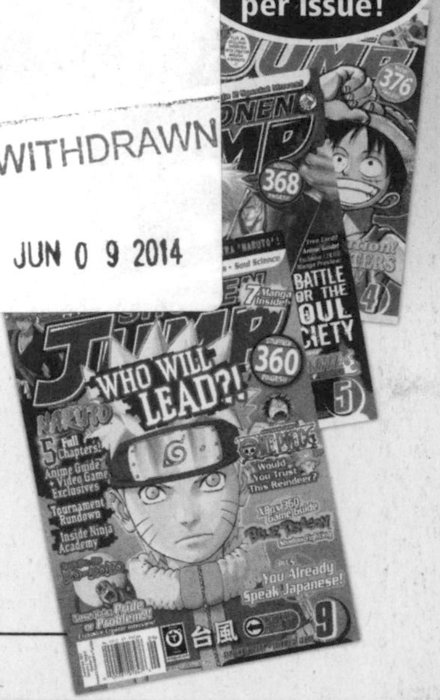

Each ____
conta ____
avail ____
**news, and info on video &
card games, toys AND more!**

☑ **YES!** Please enter my one-year
subscription (12 HUGE issues)
to **SHONEN JUMP** at the LOW
SUBSCRIPTION RATE of **$29.95!**

NAME _____

ADDRESS _____

CITY _____ **STATE** ___ **ZIP** ___

E-MAIL ADDRESS _____ P7GNC1

☐ **MY CHECK IS ENCLOSED** (PAYABLE TO SHONEN JUMP) ☐ **BILL ME LATER**

CREDIT CARD: ☐ **VISA** ☐ **MASTERCARD**

ACCOUNT # _____ **EXP. DATE** _____

SIGNATURE _____

CLIP AND MAIL TO ➡

SHONEN JUMP
Subscriptions Service Dept.
P.O. Box 515
Mount Morris, IL 61054-0515